Piotr Steinkeller
History, Texts and Art in Early Babylonia

Studies in Ancient Near Eastern Records

General Editor:
Gonzalo Rubio

Editors:
Nicole Brisch, Petra Goedegebuure, Markus Hilgert,
Amélie Kuhrt, Peter Machinist, Piotr Michalowski,
Cécile Michel, Beate Pongratz-Leisten, D. T. Potts,
Kim Ryholt

Volume 15

Piotr Steinkeller

History, Texts and Art in Early Babylonia

Three Essays

DE GRUYTER

ISBN 978-1-5015-1906-2
e-ISBN (PDF) 978-1-5015-0477-8
e-ISBN (EPUB) 978-1-5015-0475-4
ISSN 2161-4415

Library of Congress Cataloging-in-Publication Data
A CIP catalog record for this book has been applied for at the Library of Congress.

Bibliographic information published by the Deutsche Nationalbibliothek
The Deutsche Nationalbibliothek lists this publication in the Deutsche Nationalbibliografie;
detailed bibliographic data are available in the Internet at http://dnb.dnb.de.

© 2019 Walter de Gruyter Inc., Boston/Berlin
This volume is text- and page-identical with the hardback published in 2017.
Printing: Hubert & Co. GmbH & Co. KG, Göttingen
♾ Printed on acid-free paper
Printed in Germany

www.degruyter.com

To Jenai, who made it possible

Contents

Essay 2

Essay 3

Preface

This volume presents three essays, which are expanded versions of unpublished papers I gave, in various forms and on different occasions, over the last fifteen years.[1] Since these papers are thematically related, and since they represent what is, in many respects, a summation of decades worth of thinking and writing about the shape and dynamics of the history of third millennium Babylonia and the ways in which that history is reflected in ancient written sources and art, it occurred to me that it might be useful to publish them together. That is how this book came about.

Among the leitmotifs that weave their way through these three essays, the following two are especially prominent. The first of them is the proposition that, as I have repeatedly strived to demonstrate in my work, the course of the third millennium history of Babylonia was to a large extent shaped by the differences that originally distinguished the society and culture of southern Babylonia from those existing in Babylonia's northern half. Such differences can be discerned in the political, social, and economic organization of both regions and, even more clearly, in the areas of language and religion. In my view, the process underlying the early history of Babylonia is best described as a creative conversion, through which two, originally quite distinctive societies and cultures, gradually assimilated to one another, in the end becoming a completely new entity. As far as we can tell, this process of conversion was generally peaceful and friction free. It certainly was not enforced in any way or fashion. In the same way that there came into being, by the end of the third millennium, a single Sumero-Akkadian language and a single Sumero-Akkadian religion, the political and social institutions of Babylonia too were of a hybrid nature. That process of mutual assimilation had begun extremely early, probably already in Late

---

1 The original version of Essay 1 was presented, under the title "Writing, Kingship and Political Discourse in Early Babylonia," at the conference "Writing Civilization: Literacy and Social Transformation in Early Mesopotamia," The Raymond and Beverly Sackler Art and Archaeology Lecture Series, University of Connecticut, School of Fine Arts, Storrs, April 16, 2004. The forerunner of Essay 2 was my keynote address (same title) at the summer program "Ideology, Power and Religious Change in Antiquity, 3000 BC – AD 600," Graduiertenschule für Geisteswissenschaften Göttingen, Georg-August Göttingen Universität, July 20–24, 2015. Essay 3 goes back to "Mythical Realities of the Early Babylonian History: Thoughts about the Modern Study of Ancient Mesopotamian History," read at the 4th International Melammu Congress, "Schools of Oriental Studies and the Development of Modern Historiography," Ravenna, October 13–17, 2001.

DOI 10.1515/9781501504778-001

Uruk times.[2] In all likelihood, its course was far from being simple and straight-forward. However, due to the near-complete absence of written data from the early phases of the Early Dynastic period, one may only guess about the specifics of this development.

The other central theme of the essays presented here is my contention that the kingship of early southern Babylonia had a very peculiar form, and that it differed significantly from that existing at the time in northern Babylonia. The characteristics of the southern kingship and its evolution over the course of the third millennium (and going back into the Late Uruk period, see especially Appendix 1), especially as it concerns its interaction with the kingship and cultural institutions of northern Babylonia, are studied in detail, especially in Essays 1 and 2. In Essay 2 I also argue that the concept of divine king, which was introduced by Naram-Suen, was an instrument of that ruler's unificatory policies, whose purpose was to transcend the limitations imposed by the tenets of the southern ideology of kingship. It is further suggested that the divination of Šulgi and his successors was motivated by similar political aims.

My understanding of the nature of the southern kingship leads me develop a number of secondary points. One of them is the proposition that the peculiarity of the southern ideology of kingship finds a direct reflection in the historical writings and art. I base this idea mainly on the fact that the other literary civilizations of the ancient world with which such a comparison may be made (Egypt, Mesoamerica, and China) do indeed demonstrate the existence of such a nexus. I then proceed to define (primarily in Essay 1) the nature of the historical sources surviving from the third-millennium South and contrast them with those that may be attributed to the northern historical tradition. In conclusion, I argue that, as a consequence of the special character of the southern ideology of rulership – in particular, the absence in it of a developed dynastic tradition – the society of early southern Babylonia showed a remarkable lack of interest in things historical. Hence the pronounced absence there of historical narratives, dynastic histories, and chronographic sources (such as king-lists and a developed system of dating methods). As I argue, this situation contrasts sharply with what one encounters later under the Sargonic kings and their successors, the kings of Ur, when different attitudes toward history and, consequently, different forms of history writing and different royal imagery had come into being.

---

2 The earliest certain evidence of Sumero-Semitic contact in Babylonia is provided by the occurrences of the Semitic loanword maš-gan$_2$ (Akk. *maškanu*), "settlement," in the sources of Late Uruk date (Steinkeller 1995b: 695; Monaco 2016: 10 and notes 62 and 68).

The causes of this – obviously very puzzling – disinterest in history are then explored in greater depth. Here I hypothesize that another factor that may have contributed to this phenomenon was the influence of a powerful social group (identified by me as the "Managerial Class") that was a characteristic element of the social and political landscape of southern Babylonia since Late Uruk times. As a distinctive and solidly entrenched social group, the Managerial Class of Babylonia had its own political agenda, which probably often remained at odds with the politics of the king. In particular, it appears that this group opposed the concept of strong dynastic rule. Because of this, going as far back as the Late Uruk period, the lexical, scholarly, and literary sources (whose authors were none other than the members of the Managerial Class) assume a characteristically ahistorical stance, completely ignoring the "history of facts." The attitudes and political agendas of the Managerial Class may also have contributed to the virtual absence of genuine historical and chronographic sources. Such sources were introduced only under the Sargonic kings, a tradition that was subsequently continued by the kings of Ur. Beginning in the Isin period, the members of the Managerial Class began to create their own version of history, which sought to legitimize and to fortify their traditional status vis-à-vis the ruling circles. Toward that goal they invented texts that presented them as the original source of political power in Babylonia, as well as the masters of statecraft, thereby making themselves indispensable (or at least hoping to be perceived as such) to the kings. Propagandistic sources of this type continued to be composed down to the Seleucid period.

Finally, in Essay 3 I address the question of how the modern historian is to approach the early Babylonian "historical" sources, both the ones that are believed to be properly "historical," and those that are conflations of historical facts and their literary embellishments (the so-called "historical-literary" texts). Here I submit, in essence, that there is no substantial difference between these two types of materials – as well as the ones usually referred to as "literary" texts *sensu stricto*. In my view, all of these texts are about "mythical history," and not the "history of facts." In conclusion, I suggest that this native historical construct may productively be explored and used as an alternative to the standard historical analysis.

It needs to be emphasized that what the reader is going to find in these essays is a very personal view of the third millennium history, offered by one student of this subject. Due to the extremely fragmentary nature of the surviving data (both as concerns written sources and archaeological evidence), any understanding of the facts and the broader significance of that phase of Babylonia's history must to a large extent be hypothetical, and, because of this, open to question and allowing alternative interpretations. By no means do I claim that this history of mine is the definitive one. Nevertheless, I believe that this personal "vision" deserves consideration, since it offers a connected and internally consistent picture of the evolution of the Babylonian kingship, historical writing, and art from Late Uruk into Old Babylonian times. Moreover, this picture results from the thorough consideration of a very extensive (if not complete) body of extant data, be they textual, archaeological, or art historical. While my "vision" might not provide all the answers, it should, I hope, inspire new ideas and suggest directions for future research.

The scholarly literature dealing with the third millennium is huge, and so it was impossible, especially in the essay format I have adopted for this book, to refer to everything significant that has been written on this subject. Thus my choice of references and citations is necessarily selective; omissions do not imply disregard (or disrespect). In general, I have followed the policy Henri Frankfort used in his *Kingship and the Gods*: "We have quoted when we felt that acknowledgment was due or that a useful purpose would be served by explicitly refuting an opinion ... In other cases disagreement could be implied by silence and this book spared the burden of controversy" (1948: ix). Some controversy could not be avoided nonetheless. If I offended anyone, he or she may rest assured that none of it was personally meant. Such is the nature of the scholar's business – *if* one is to conduct it conscientiously, and *if* some real progress (particularly in this difficult and controversial area of research) is to be made.

Last but not least I wish to offer my warm thanks to Gonzalo Rubio for accepting these essays for publication in the SANER series, and to Christopher Woods and Ryan Winters, both of whom read the original manuscript and offered numerous comments and suggestions for improvement. My further thanks go to two anonymous reviewers for their respective critical assessments, to Florian Ruppenstein for his expert and patient editorial assistance, as well to Trey Nation and Andrew Pottorf, who carefully checked the whole manuscript for style and technical errors. Needless to say, the final responsibility for this book's content and form rests with me alone.

Essay 1

Writing, Kingship and Political Discourse in Early Babylonia: Reflections on the Nature and Function of Third Millennium Historical Sources

> In real history there are no new chapters and no new beginnings.
> Ernst Gombrich

1 Preface

This essay aims to study the inter-relationship between the ideology of kingship and the historical and chronographic sources that a given culture produces. More specifically, I will attempt to investigate how the ideas about kingship influence and shape attitudes toward history, both past and present, and how those attitudes then impact the character and the types of historical materials. My premise is that there is a direct connection between the two.

The case study I will be using to test this hypothesis is ancient Mesopotamia during the third millennium BC, more exactly the last four centuries of it, roughly the period between 2400 and 2000 BC. On occasion, though, I will be venturing back into Mesopotamia's last prehistoric phase, which is named the Uruk period after the extremely important city of Uruk in southern Iraq. Uruk was undeniably the source of Mesopotamian urbanism, and the place where Sumerian culture as we know it, and all the later Sumerian institutions, were born. It was also in Uruk that cuneiform writing in all likelihood was invented.

The specific geographical area I will be concerned with is Babylonia, roughly the region extending from Baghdad in central modern Iraq all the way down to the Persian Gulf. Within Babylonia, one further distinguishes between "southern Babylonia," which was the home of the Sumerians, and which therefore is commonly referred to as "Sumer"; and "northern Babylonia," which was largely inhabited by the Semitic Akkadians. The latter area is called "Akkade" or "Akkad," after a city in that region that gave rise, around 2300 BC, to a powerful dynasty – and subsequently, to an empire – of the very same name. The border between the southern and northern portions of Babylonia ran roughly north of the city of Nippur, the religious and cultural capital of the Sumerians. In this essay, the terms "southern Babylonia" and "Sumer" will be used interchangeably.

DOI 10.1515/9781501504778-002

2 Early Historical Sources of Southern Babylonia

The early inhabitants of southern Babylonia left to us a relatively limited corpus of cuneiform inscriptions, written on clay and on stone, which are of a dedicatory character, and which involve royal figures. For reasons of convenience – if nothing else, cuneiform scholars have traditionally classified these materials as "royal" or "historical." The designation "royal" is technically correct, and therefore acceptable, though it may not be a particularly apt description, since it says little about the nature and purpose of these materials. The label "historical" is much more problematic. This is because, with a few notable exceptions, the materials in question are exclusively dedications of public buildings (usually temples) or objects to deities, which, apart from identifying the donor and specifying his patronymic and titles, do not usually dwell on his peronal accomplishments other than building activities. If any historical information is included, it is usually brief and always incidental to the main purpose of the inscription, which is dedication.[3] In my opinion, therefore, the name "historical" should properly by reserved for the texts that were written with a specific purpose of recording historical information, of making this information public in some form, and of preserving it for posterity.

All of these inscriptions — and I stress again that I am referring only to the earliest sources of this type stemming from southern Babylonia – show essentially the same basic pattern: "to deity so-and-so, the ruler named so-and-so erected temple X or presented object Y." With the passage of time, the custom of adding or inserting into this pattern some historical information developed.[4] Quite often this historical part takes the form of a temporal clause, as in the following example: "when (king Šu-Suen) built the Amorite wall (called) 'The one that keeps Tidnum at a distance,' and so he turned the Amorite's foot back to his land, he then erected for god Šara his beloved temple" (RIME 3/2 327–328 Šu-Suen 17).[5] This section grew progressively more extensive, becoming eventually the longest (and sometimes the most important) element of the inscription. Even

---

3 As cogently argued by Govert Van Driel (1973a; 1973b), the vast majority of the Mesopotamian "royal" or "historical" inscriptions are best characterized as "dedicatory," irrespective of whether they deal with the consecration of buildings or objects. This renders unnecessary the common practice of sub-categorizing these sources further into "building" and "votive" inscriptions.
4 The earliest notable example of this pattern is found in one of the inscriptions of Ur-Nanše of Lagaš (RIME 1 89–93 Ur-Nanše 6b). This source begins with a description of Ur-Nanše's building activities, offering then a substantial narrative of his conflict with Umma and Ur.
5 Examples of this formulation appear already in the ED inscriptions from Lagaš. See RIME 1 180–182 En-anatum I 9 ii 13 – iv 9.

in such cases, however, the inscription nearly always has a dedicatory character, often beginning with the invocation of a deity. This pattern can still be discerned in the first millennium royal inscriptions from Babylonia and Assyria – though in most other respects the latter documents differ quite dramatically from the early Sumerian inscriptions I am concerned with presently.

What is markedly absent among all the early Sumerian records of this kind are true historical inscriptions, the ones whose *primary* function was to glorify a particular royal figure and his lineage or to commemorate specific historical events (other than temple-building). Or, to put it differently, sources that are primarily concerned with dynastic history. As we will see later, such texts, which may best be characterized as "elite display" inscriptions,[6] appeared for the first time under the Sargonic kings, becoming one of the hallmarks of that period.

Here I need to offer the following caveat. Among the corpus of early Sumerian royal inscriptions one finds a few texts that do contain a good deal of historical information.[7] This is particularly true of one of the inscriptions of En-metena of Lagaš (ca. 2350 BC), which is concerned with a border conflict between Lagaš and its neighbor Umma (RIME 1 194–199 En-metena 1).[8] Another notable example of such a source is the famous "Stele of the Vultures" (ca. 2400 BC), which too comes from Lagaš and deals with the same border dispute (RIME 1 126–140 E-anatum 1). The Stele additionally is provided with rich iconography, which, at least from that perspective, makes it a truly monumental artifact. However, while these inscriptions name historical facts,[9] the primary function of both of them is

---

6 Noting the fact that the Sargonic and Ur III inscriptions of this kind are generally phrased as dedications, Van Driel 1973a: 102 argued against the use of the term "triumphal" in reference to them, consequently including such sources under the category of "dedicatory" sources. In spite of this characteristic, however, the markedly different patterns and phraseology of these texts, as well as the fact that many of them were intended for public display, are sufficient grounds to classify them as "elite display" inscriptions (or "triumphal" inscriptions, if one prefers to use Van Driel's term).

7 Averbeck 2002: 100 writes that "many of the Presargonic royal inscriptions contain or consist almost entirely of historical narratives." This conclusion is not supported by the actual data. As I show in the following, sources to which such characteristics may be ascribed are exceedingly few.

8 For a reconstruction and detailed discussion of this conflict, see Cooper 1981a.

9 Such information is considerably less extensive in the inscription recorded on the Stele, which, as one may judge from what survives of it, is mainly concerned with the sworn promises of the defeated ruler of Umma not to encroach on Lagaš' fields in the future.

that of legal documents, since they serve to confirm Lagaš' title to the contested territories. Because of this, also in these two cases historical information is of *secondary* importance to the main purpose of these sources, which is the demonstration of ownership rights to a particular strip of land. Therefore, even though these two texts (especially the En-metena piece) are replete with historical information, I would be reluctant to lend such clusters of historical facts the designation of "historical narrative," reserving this term for sources whose express purpose was to record historical events.[10]

In my view, the case of the En-metena inscription and the "Stele of the Vultures" is broadly analogous to that of the Middle Babylonian and early Neo-Babylonian *kudurrū* or symbolic boundary stones, which date to the second half of the second millennium BC and later times. Made of stone and often provided with elaborate iconography, these objects likewise establish title to landed property. Like the former inscriptions, some of the *kudurrū* too involve royal figures and contain extensive historical narratives.[11] As a matter of fact, these particular records are more informative in this respect than any of the proper "historical" sources that have come down to us from the period in question. In spite of this, however, it would be a mistake to classify them as historical sources *sensu stricto*.

However, there exist two early Sumerian royal inscriptions for which the label "historical" might be appropriate. The first of them is the inscription of Lugal-zagesi, a late Early Dynastic ruler of Uruk and a rival of Sargon of Akkade, which survives on several stone bowls presented by this ruler to the god Enlil at Nippur (RIME 1 433–437 Lugal-zagesi 1). Although this inscription adheres to a dedicatory pattern,[12] its main section (i 36 – iii 2) may be classified as a "historical" text in its own right, in that it deals exclusively with Lugal-zagesi's personal accomplishments. This is even though it does not name *any specific historical events* – beyond a poetic description of the extent of Lugal-zagesi's political influence. For this conclusion, the highly elevated style of this section of the inscription is significant as well: "when Enlil, master of all countries, gave to Lugal-zagesi the kingship of the Land, directed all the eyes of the Land toward him, put all the countries under his foot, and, from the east to the west, subjected them to him, etc." This kind of rhetoric, which focuses on the figure of the king, represents a complete *novum* among the early Sumerian materials. When

---

10 When treated in isolation from other early Sumerian royal inscriptions, the En-metena text could indeed be seen as a genuine historical narrative. See, e. g., Averbeck 2002: 102: "It is hard for me to understand why the Enmetena inscription should not be called 'history writing.'"
11 See Paulus 2014: 296–304 KḪ I 1, 402–415 MŠ 4, 503–510 NKU I 2, 693–703 MAI II 1.
12 "For Enlil etc." in i 1–35, followed then by a dedication in iii 3–40.

viewed from this perspective, the Lugal-zagesi text clearly anticipates the voice of the Sargonic royal inscriptions.

The other inscription I have in mind is that of Utu-hegal of Uruk, the unifier of southern Babylonia following the so-called Gutian *interregnum* (at ca. 2100 BC) (RIME 2 283–293 Utu-hegal 4). Here the label "historical" is even more appropriate, since this text consists practically entirely of historical narrative. Moreover, there is no clear evidence that it recorded any sort of dedication.[13] These facts make the Utu-hegal inscription completely unique, not only among the third millennium materials, but equally among later Mesopotamian sources of broadly historical content. However, the evaluation of this inscription is complicated by the fact that it survives only in later, Old Babylonian copies. This opens up a possibility that, despite its seemingly genuine late third millennium characteristics, as pertains to its orthography and grammar, the Utu-hegal inscription may actually be a literary text, which was composed subsequent to Utu-hegal's own time.

The data presented thus far establish quite conclusively that the corpus of early Sumerian royal inscriptions contains precious little that may be described as properly "historical" by any stretch of imagination. In this connection, it is equally significant that virtually none of these materials were meant for public consumption. This we can tell based on what the physical destinations of these records are known to have been: either the foundations of temples or, in the case of votive objects, sacred areas that remained inaccessible to the public at large. It becomes evident, therefore, that the intended audience of these records was not human but divine.[14] As such, these dedicatory inscriptions – together with the pictorial imagery that they may have accompanied – were strictly part of a discourse between the rulers and the divine realm.[15]

---

13 The only possible hint of this is the isolated mention of Enlil in line 1, which could indicate the presence of a dedication at the end of the original text (if such indeed had existed).

14 That audience included future rulers, who might chance upon these inscriptions in the course of their rebuilding activities.

15 For similar conclusions, see Tadmor 1997. In reference to the Neo-Assyrian royal inscriptions, Tadmor wrote specifically as follows: "Indeed, it could justifiably be argued that the gods were viewed as the primary audience of all the dedicatory-commemorative texts, especially those which begin with an invocation to the major gods of Assyria ... the gods were the immediate and the most obvious audience, even before the princely reader of the future who is addressed in the epilogues" (ibid. 331); "The unseen audience of the ARI was the ever-present gods and the future priestly reader. Their content also presumably had a natural and interested audience in the state elite, non-literate as well as literate" (ibid. 334). Because of this, these materials were not unlike the Neo-Assyrian letters to gods, in which a ruler would report about his performance to a particular deity (Tadmor 1997: 331–332). Differently Liverani: "The existence of

As we shall see later, this situation changed very significantly during the Sargonic period (2350–2100 BC), when, for the first time, we encounter records that are primarily concerned with the glorification of kings and their exploits. This is fully reflected both in written messages and the images associated with them. It is also from Sargonic times that we have clear evidence of public display of such records (for example, at the city of Nippur, which functioned as the religious capital of Sumer). As a matter of fact, the Sargonic period witnessed profound transformations and changes in almost every area of culture and ideology. These transformations affected not only the character of historical sources, but also, and even more profoundly, the attitudes toward history – both past and present.

Undoubtedly connected with the absence of elite display records – and even more symptomatic of this whole phenomenon – is the lack in early southern Babylonia of chronographic sources – such as year-names and the lists of rulers, to name only the two most typical types of such records.

Although the Sumerians were consummate accountants and administrators – a tradition that went back to Uruk times – even in that area they made little effort to keep track of chronology. The only method of dating used in administrative records was to identify the sequential year of a particular reign, but usually even without specifying the ruler's name (as practiced in ED IIIb Lagaš and Umma). Such information apparently was deemed redundant, as it could be gleaned from the relative location of a given document within the archival sequence.[16]

It is probably significant that, outside of Egypt, the earliest list of rulers known from the ancient Near East comes not from Babylonia but from Ebla in northern Syria, ca. 2350 BC (Archi 2001; Bonechi 2001).

Also from Ebla we have the earliest examples of year-names,[17] that is, the practice of naming each year after a specific event. This dating method is a uni-

---

[popular] propaganda is demonstrated by the existence of celebrative inscriptions and monuments, exhibited in the major sanctuaries of the country" (2002: 153). But, as I just pointed out, the overwhelming majority of such materials were not "exhibited" in temples in any manner. Therefore, Liverani's statement is applicable only to the true display monuments such as those of the Sargonic rulers, which indeed were exhibited in the sacred and other locales. See the discussion below.

16 It appears that the tablets belonging to a particular reign would be placed in a single container or a group of containers. These containers would then be provided with labels identifying the ruler in question. Possible examples of such labels are the clay bullae DP 11–22 (ED IIIb Lagaš). These are uninscribed, though sealed with cylinder seals belonging to the rulers and other high officials of Lagaš.

17 See, e.g., *in* DIŠ mu Ma-ri$_2$^{ki} GIN$_2$.ŠE$_3$ *aš$_2$-ti* 'À-ti-NI^{ki}, "the year when Mari fought with AtiNI" (ARET 7 115 v 1–6); DIŠ mu TIL Ma-ri$_2$^{ki}, "the year when Mari was defeated/finished" (ARET 1 34

versal phenomenon, which is documented both in ancient and modern times. It was used in Egypt already during the First Dynasty (see below pp. 16–17). The Chinese of the archaic Anyang period too identified individual years in this way (Bagley 2004: 223). In more recent times, the Sioux elders selected one principal event each year for the tribe historian to memorize; such dating formulae were called "winter counts."

In Babylonia, the earliest examples of year-names appear at the very beginning of the Sargonic period. They belong to the reign of Sargon of Akkade, as well as to those of En-šakušana and Lugal-zagesi of Uruk (A. Westenholz 1975: 115). Since the latter two rulers were Sargon's contemporaries (Sallaberger and Schrakamp 2015: 93), and since both of them campaigned in northern Babylonia, it appears highly probable that this dating method had been known in northern Babylonia at that time, and that its usage by the two kings in question represents a borrowing. This in turn suggests that year-names had been used in northern Babylonia (particularly at Kiš) even before Sargon, a corroboration of which may be sought in the presence of this dating method in Ebla. However, this point cannot be verified at present, since the ED III economic documentation from northern Babylonia is practically non-existent. Be that as it may, year-names gained popularity in Babylonia only during the Sargonic period. But even then their use was very sporadic.[18] It was not until Ur III times that year-names became a standard and even indispensable element of economic and legal documents. Year-names continued to be regularly used under the successive dynasties until the end of the Old Babylonian period.

There are also reasons to think that the earliest attempt to compile a king-list in Babylonia likewise occurred during the Sargonic period. I address this question in greater detail below pp. 37, 40.

But, in spite of these chronographic innovations, namely, the use of year-formulae and the existence of a king-list (the so-called "Sumerian King List," henceforth SKL), it is doubtful that, even as late as the beginning of the second millennium and probably even much later, the Babylonians possessed any permanent system to keep a continuous track of their rulers, such as existed, for example, in Egypt already in the Early Dynastic period. Examples here are the Pa-

---

iii 1–3). These formulae are usually placed at the end of the tablet. However, their use is quite infrequent. For other examples of Ebla year-names and discussion, see Archi 1996: 11–13.

18 In fact, only some forty year-names of the Sargonic kings are known. See Gelb and Kienast 1990: 50–58. The number of tablets bearing these formulae is about the same. The year-names of Sargon and Rimuš are introduced by mu, "year." However, starting with the reign of Naram-Suen, the introductory formula is *in* DIŠ MU, which resembles the formulae used earlier at Ebla (see the preceding note). This suggests a possible connection between the two.

lermo Stone and similar listings of Egyptian kings, which I discuss below p. 17. By this system I mean a centrally kept list of kings and their reigns, usually inscribed on stone and accessible to the public to at least some degree, which was periodically updated by designated officials.[19] That no such system existed in Babylonia is strongly indicated by the SKL, whose history we can now much better understand thanks to a new manuscript, dating to the Ur III period (Steinkeller 2003). The many discrepancies between this manuscript and its later version(s) demonstrate that there were no independent chronographic sources in existence that one could consult to verify chronological problems. Particularly telling here is the case of the Sargonic kings of Rimuš and Maništušu. While the later versions of the SKL make Maništušu the successor of Rimuš, in the Ur III ms these two rulers are listed in the opposite order. If the Ur III text is correct on that score, one would need to conclude that the erroneous sequence had crept into the list sometime after the Ur III period, due, apparently, to some accident in scribal transmission, and, in the absence of any way to verify the information, it eventually acquired canonic status.[20]

Another characteristic feature of early southern Babylonian culture, which, in my opinion, is closely connected with the Sumerian attitudes toward history writing, is the absence (or at least great scarcity) of display or monumental art that focuses on the figure of the ruler and his achievements. Although there are sporadic examples of such images in the archaic age (and I will discuss them later), it is only in Sargonic times that they appear in force.

---

19 Or, alternatively, some institution or office expressly concerned with recording and maintaining this type of information.

20 Even if the sequence Rimuš – Maništušu should prove to be the correct one, this case would still be indicative of the absence of any permanent storage of chronographic data at that point of Babylonian history. As for Rimuš and Miništušu, the only evidence that might indicate Rimuš' chronological priority is the fact that both the inscriptions of Sargon and Rimuš mention a general of Marhaši named Šidga'u (RIME 2 22–24 Sargon 8 Caption 16, 55–57 Rimuš 7:10–11). Although not being conclusive, this evidence favors the assumption that Rimuš was the direct successor of Sargon.

3 Historical Sources of Egypt, Mesoamerica, and Ancient China

3.1 Introductory Remarks

The question thus arises: why did the early Babylonians show so little interest in recording historical facts, and why is their art virtually devoid of what may be classified as elite display, i.e., images that glorify the feats of specific rulers? This is a valid question, since in many other early civilizations that knew writing the situation was just the opposite.

To illustrate this point, I will use the examples of the early Egyptian, Mesoamerican, and Chinese cultures. Even a cursory examination of the writing systems of those three civilizations reveals the presence of common features among them. Of those features, the most significant one is the practical application of these writings, since all three of them were used primarily as a tool of official or elite display. To put it more broadly, one could say that the main function of these writings was commemoration. Or, if one opts for a narrower definition, then it is possible to conclude that the essential purpose of these scripts was to recognize or to glorify a particular individual and his lineage. Thus, most of the inscriptions that survive from archaic Egypt, Mesoamerica, and early China are what may be described as historical records, in that they deal with prominent personages and specific historical events. Equally characteristic of these inscriptions is their pervasive concern with chronology. This concern is sometimes so central that, in such instances, records need be classified as chronographic or calendrical.

That the Egyptian, Mesoamerican, and Chinese writings differed fundamentally from the cuneiform one as regards their function is generally recognized by scholarship. To cite Joyce Marcus:

> As in the case of early Mesoamerican hieroglyphic inscriptions (and in striking contrast to economic texts recorded by the early Sumerians), the functions of early Egyptian writing were to commemorate the deeds of rulers and legitimize their divine right to rule ... The content of early [Egyptian] texts on stone was 'history,' the association of a ruler with an important event (such as taking office, or the taking of captives), the acquisition of titles, and the linking of a ruler to a divine origin or to earlier rulers (real or fictional). These texts accompanied and complemented pictorial scenes that portrayed the ruler, a pattern analogous to the way the Zapotec and Maya used texts to accompany depictions of their rulers. Some early Egyptian texts feature king lists that attempt to establish an unbroken genealogy back to fictional rulers. These king lists supply a divine origin for the reigning ruler, by linking him to the first few kings, some of whom where actually gods. Such divine prologues and the use of remote ancestors to establish the right to rule were also used by all Mesoamerican groups. (Marcus 1992: 20–23)

One of the characteristic features shared by the Egyptian, Mesoamerican, and Chinese writings is the fact that, as was repeatedly observed by various writers, the invention of these scripts coincided with the beginning of dynastic history, that is, the founding of royal dynasties and the emergence of discrete political entities, be it territorial states (as in the case of Egypt) or city-states (as in the case in Mesoamerica and China). Thus, referring to archaic Egypt, Richard B. Parkinson writes that "the origins of Egyptian writing seem bound up with this creation of the centralized state" (1999: 73). Similar conclusions were reached by Nicolai Grube about the early history of the Maya: "The Maya record of the founding of royal dynasties goes along with the beginning of writing ... Writing and the beginning of dynastic history are closely connected phenomena in Ancient Egypt and China" (1995: 2).

This brings us, finally, to the controversial question of the ultimate purpose of the invention of these three writing systems. While most scholars tend to think that in Egypt, Mesoamerica and China the original cause of the invention of writing was public display, there have also been some dissenting voices, which claim that, at least in Egypt and China, the writing was invented for administrative purposes.[21] It is necessary, therefore, to review, however briefly, the earliest inscribed materials that have come down from Egypt, Mesoamerica, and China.

3.2 Egypt

In Egypt, the earliest surviving inscriptions are of a display character. The most representative examples of these materials, which are documented since Dynasty 0 or the final phase of the Naqada III period, are the celebrated palette and the macehead of king Narmer (Wengrow 2006: 41–44; O'Connor 2011). A similar macehead, excavated in Hierakonpolis, names a ruler who has conventionally been identified as King Scorpion II (Wengrow 2006: 213–214). This ruler likewise is commonly assigned to Dynasty 0. Significantly, there also exists at least one rock inscription of an indisputably display nature dating to Dynasty 0. Located at Wadi el-Qash in the Eastern Desert, this record is an abbreviated version of Narmer's name (MacArthur 2010: 116–117 and fig. 5.3). For another possible example of such an early rock inscription, found in the Western Desert, see below.

From the time of Dynasty 0 and the First Dynasty, there additionally survives a large body of year-names associated with various rulers, among them Narmer

---

21 This position has been articulated most extensively and assertively by Nicholas Postgate, Tao Wang, and Toby Wilkinson 1995; Postgate 2005. For similar views, see also Haicheng Wang 2014.

and several kings of the First Dynasty (Kaplony 1963; Wengrow 2006: 128–129, 204–205). These appear on small tags made of ivory or wood. Such labels are usually pierced, which indicates that they were originally attached to various objects or commodities. The label with Narmer's name is of particular interest here, since it concerns the same event as the Narmer palette, suggesting the dependence of such year-names on display inscriptions.

It appears certain that it was on the basis of such year-names that king lists (or "annals," as they are called by Egyptologists) were compiled. The earliest example of a fully-fledged Egyptian king list is the Palermo Stone and its associated fragments, which probably dates to the mid Fifth Dynasty (Wilkinson 2000; Hsu 2010). The Palermo Stone begins with a listing of pre-dynastic rulers (Dynasty 0), continuing then with the dynastic kings into the middle of the Fifth Dynasty.

Already during the First Dynasty, however, one finds prototypes of these sources, which may be characterized as emergent or "mini" king-lists. Appearing on two cylinder seals, of which now only clay impressions survive (Dreyer 1986; Dreyer et al. 1996; Wengrow 2006: 131–132 and fig. 6.3), these are sequential listings of royal figures. One of these seals records, in a reverse order, the Horus names of all the rulers of the First Dynasty. The other seal names the first five kings of the First Dynasty and queen Merneith. A number of similar listings of royal names are found also on stone vessels and a statue, which name the rulers of the First and the Second Dynasties (Cervelló-Autouri 2003: 170 and n. 4). A similar vessel, now in the Egyptian Museum in Cairo, bears the names of several kings of the Third Dynasty (Tiradritti 1999: 32 figure below, JE 88345).

Apart from the display inscriptions and the chronographic records I just enumerated, there exists yet another group of early Egyptian written records that needs to be discussed here. These are inscribed bone tags or labels from the "proto-royal" Tomb U-j in the Umm el-Qa'ab cemetery near Abydos (Baines 2004: 154–165; Stauder 2010: 138–142; Dreyer 2011: 134–135). Dating probably to shortly before Dynasty 0, these tags, which number ca. 160 individual pieces, fall into two distinctive groups. The tags of the first type are inscribed only with numerals. It is safe to assume that these numerals specified the quantities of goods with which the tags had originally been associated. The tags of the second type bear one to four hieroglyphic signs. It has been suggested that these signs identify the places that supplied the goods or commodities in question.

Of these two kinds of written messages, only the hieroglyphic ones qualify to be described as a form (however incipient) of writing. But these brief inscriptions are merely identification or ownership marks, in the manner of the slightly later *serekhs* (royal names), which one finds inscribed or painted on pottery vessels.[22] As such, they differ substantially from the *bona fide* use of writing in administration, such as that one encounters in Babylonia during the Late Uruk period.[23] Neither do these identification marks necessarily suggest that the Egyptian writing was *invented* for utilitarian purposes, since these graphs could easily have been adopted from display inscriptions.

As a matter of fact, there survives a display inscription that may be contemporaneous with the Tomb U-j tags. The record in question forms part of a rock tableau from Gebel Tjauti in the Western Desert, which was discovered and published by John C. Darnell (2002: 10–19 Gebel Tjauti Rock Inscription 1). Included in this tableau is a falcon atop of a scorpion, which may plausibly be interpreted as a royal name. As suggested by Darnell (2002: 14), this ruler could be the same person as the presumed owner of Tomb U-j, who has been identified by some scholars as King Scorpion I.[24] The latter hypothesis rests on the fact that Tomb U-j yielded a number of pottery vessels inscribed in ink with the figure of a scorpion, which plausibly represents the name of the tomb's owner (Wengrow 2006: 201 fig. 9.12; Dreyer 2011: 134).

To summarize these facts, public display appears to have been the most probable cause of the origin of the Egyptian script. For this view, see Baines 1988: 194–200; 1989; 2004; Wengrow 2006: 203–217; Stauder 2010. As indicated by the tags of Tomb U-j, already at its very inception the Egyptian script had administrative applications as well. But such uses appear to have been very limited and of secondary nature. One may conjecture that, had there existed an extensive administrative documentation in archaic Egypt, it would likely have taken the form of ostraca, which are as durable as cuneiform tablets. But such early sources are completely absent in the surviving record.

3.3 Mesoamerica

Moving on to Mesoamerica, the Mayan inscriptions – and the same is true of the Aztec and other Mesoamerican written records – deal almost exclusively with

---

22 In terms of their function, these marks are roughly analogous to the impressions of uninscribed cylinder seals in early Babylonia.

23 Examples of similar labels, which probably date to the Uruk IV period, are also known from Babylonia. See Woods, Teeter, and Emberling 2010: 71–72 nos. 41–43; MSVO 1 238 and 239; MSVO 4 75–77.

24 This ruler, who is believed to have belonged to the beginning of Dynasty 0, is different from King Scorpion II of the Hierakonpolis macehead.

historical and ritual events. These sources usually record life histories and achievements of a single ruler, most commonly focusing on one or more events central to the ruler's life and reign, such as "birth, accession to power, marriage, the birth of offspring, the presentation of an heir apparent, warfare, the taking of distinguished captives (and their sacrifice), as well as the celebration of calendrically ordained rituals and anniversary rites connected with previous events (often associated with the ceremonial shedding of one's own blood), and death" (Coe and Kerr 1998: 56).

Some of these monuments functioned as king lists and dynastic chronicles. A good example here is Altar Q at Copán, Honduras, which depicts sixteen successive rulers. Beginning with the founder of the dynasty, named K'inich Yax K'uk' Mo', whose reign began at 426 AD, this document records some 400 years of uninterrupted history (Martin and Grube 2008: 192–193; Sharer 2012: 30). An even more extensive source of this type is the Hieroglyphic Stairway at Copán, which has been described as the "ancient world's most massive inscription" (Stewart 2015). Inscribed with some 2,200 glyphs, it offers a detailed history of K'inich Yax K'uk' Mo's dynasty (Fash 2002; Sharer and Taxler 2006: 339–343).

Although some scholars have argued that the Mesoamerican writings were extensively used in administration, and that they even may have been invented for that purpose (e. g., Postgate, Wang, and Wilkinson 1995: 471–472), there is no evidence of either of these. This is not only because we lack any physical examples of the use of any of those scripts for purely administrative purposes, but also because there are no references to such uses in the surviving narrative sources, both the native ones and the early colonial records written in Spanish. Had such administrative records existed but were lost, due to their being written on some perishable material, it is certain that some mention of them would have survived, particularly in the post-conquest accounts. It is simply inconceivable that the Spanish chroniclers would have omitted to mention the existence of such documentation, if only as a curiosity. In fact, colonial records contain extensive descriptions of the writing systems and their practical applications. For example, in a *relación* from 1588 Antonio de Ciudad Real writes as follows: "in their antiquity they had characters and letters, with which they used to write their stories and ceremonies and methods of sacrifices to their idols, and their calendar, in books made of a certain tree and they were very long strips of a *cuarta* or *tercia* in width that were folded and gathered in such a way that they looked more or less like a book bound in quarto" (Coe and Kerr 1998: 169). Similar descriptions are found in Bishop Diego de Landa's *Relación de las cosas de Yucatán*. In this connection, it should be noted parenthetically that samples of the perishable *khipu* writing of the Incas did survive, as did the copious descriptions of it and its applications in colonial records.

It is well known that the Maya and other Mesoamerican peoples produced books or codices, primarily because a few specimens of such books have survived (Sharer and Taxler 2006: 127–129). These were made of bark paper coated with burnished white gesso, and were usually bound in jaguar-skin covers. Such codices are frequently depicted in Maya art, as are the scribes themselves, who are easily identifiable because of their characteristic garb. For such representations, see Coe and Kerr 1998: 89–110, 169–171. The Maya scribes are shown in a variety of situations; we find them writing or handling books, overseeing the delivery of tribute, and participating in ritual feasts and other official events. Significantly, books are the only type of records represented in such scenes.

We also know with certainty that the Mesoamerican codices were used to keep records of tribute. As a matter of fact, an example of such a record has come down to us. It is the second section of the Aztec "Mendoza Codex," which lists taxes that the vassal kingdoms were required to pay to the king of Tenochtitlan (Longhena 2000: 171).

Moreover, the recording of tribute is depicted in at least one Maya image. The scene in question comes from the celebrated Fenton Vase, which, according to Schele and Miller, "shows one lord who seems to deliver, or account for, a great pile of bundled textiles topped by a full basket set in front of the enthroned ruler. A smaller lord seated behind the royal cushion may reach for a codex and his accounting tools" (1986: 144 and 170–171 pls. 54 and 54a).

However, the inclusion of such information in Mesoamerican codices and the depictions of codices in art in no way bespeak the widespread use of other (one might call them "lesser") administrative records. On the contrary, they forcefully argue against the very existence of such documentation.[25]

---

25 Perhaps inevitably, some scholars have speculated that a large output of Mayan writing may have been in perishable form, such as palm leaves and wooden objects. See, e. g., Houston 2000: 148–149; 2004: 300. A support for this contention has been sought in isolated images that appear to show deities and animals writing on palm leaves or bark. Notwithstanding that such representations are few and questionable at that, it would not at all be surprising if such materials had in fact been used in some situations and for specific purposes. But it is a far cry from supposing that they were employed extensively in administration. This point could only be demonstrated by the actual finds of such materials or a large body of images depicting them – and such evidence is lacking at this time. This kind of idle speculation, which echoes similar claims about the existence of perishable writing materials in early China (see below) and the Harappan civilization, is not only futile but also methodologically suspect. An unfortunate example of the extreme use of such "methodology" is a recent book by Haicheng Wang 2014, who, in his zeal to demonstrate the presence and primacy of administrative records in early China and everywhere else in the ancient world, exploits such tenuous or inconclusive or simply non-existent data *ad absurdum*. By this logic, one could make a claim for any ancient civilization devoid of

Hence there is little reason to think that the Mesoamerican writing systems arose from administrative needs. This, in fact, is the opinion held by the majority Mesoamerican specialists, who are in agreement that the Mayan and other Mesoamerican scripts were invented for the purposes of elite display – however broadly one wants to define it, whether to glorify rulers and their lineages or to mark the ownership of valuable artifacts (the so-called "name-tags") belonging to the members of political elite.

3.4 China

As for ancient China, the earliest surviving inscriptions date to the late Shang period (ca. 1200 BC). Excavated at the site of Anyang in northern China, these materials fall essentially into two groups: a very large corpus of oracle texts inscribed on bones and turtle shells and a much smaller body of inscriptions on bronze vessels (Bagley 2004: 191–216). The same site also yielded sporadic inscriptions on stone and pottery, as well as a few records on bone and shell that are not concerned with divination.

Similar examples of inscribed bronze vessels were found in a number of other northern China sites, which date to the early Western Zhou period (ca. 1050 BC), and are associated with the Yan dynasty. Particularly important among them are the ones coming from Liulihe, the capital city of the Yan (Sun 2003). The practice of inscribing bronze vessels continued during the later phases of the Zhou period, which yielded the longest and most informative records of this type.

The Anyang oracle texts are of ritual character and come from what assuredly was a royal milieu. As such, they may best be classified as royal texts. Certain aspects of these materials suggest that they were displayed in some fashion (Bagley 2004: 199–200). As considered by various scholars, the most likely context to which these artifacts are to be assigned is ancestor worship.

The inscriptions on bronze vessels are usually classified into identification or ownership marks and statements (Chang 1980: 21–23, 169; von Falkenhausen 2011). The identification marks consist of one or more signs that represent clan or family emblems, a kinship term or title, and one of the ten celestial stems or daysigns. The statements usually describe the circumstance of the vessel's preparation. Additionally, they may include various information of a historical nature,

---

writing that it actually had a script, though it has not survived due the perishable nature of the writing medium used.

such as military campaigns, royal visits, gifts, agricultural and ancestral rites, feasts, marriages, etc. Some of these data are closely comparable to the Egyptian year-names I have discussed earlier.

It is generally agreed by Chinese scholars that these types of inscribed bronze vessels were emblems of royal power and that they were objects of elite display. Like the oracle texts, these artifacts too probably played a role in the ancestral cult (as suggested by their common inclusion among burial materials).

No records of overtly administrative or economic character survive from any of these early sites. It has been speculated, however, that apart from the materials mentioned earlier, the Anyang scribes also used narrow strips of bamboo or wood as a writing surface.[26] Such bamboo books are known to have existed later, the earliest documented examples here being those found in the tomb of Marquis Yi, who died in 433 BC. As for the evidence implicating the existence of such books at Anyang, various scholars cited particular characteristics of the Anyang script (such as the fact that the writing is arranged in narrow vertical columns, possibly therefore mirroring its use on bamboo strips) and the presence in this script of a sign that probably depicts a book of this type. While hypothetical, these data argue plausibly that these kinds of writing materials may indeed have been known at Anyang. It is an entirely different matter, however, how extensive the use of such bamboo or wooden books may have been and what specific purposes they might have served. The evidence in hand offers no clues in either respect.

This particular issue was treated extensively by Robert W. Bagley 2004: 220–226, and these views need to be addressed in some detail. To begin with, Bagley takes it for granted that "significant amounts of Anyang writing have been lost" (ibid. 222). This is not an unreasonable assumption, though a more cautious scholar would perhaps say "some amount" to gauge the volume of those "lost" materials. More problematic is what Bagley does next. Trying to get a sense of what those hypothetical Anyang records may have been, he uses the early Babylonian economic records as possible clues. By this kind of extrapolation, he comes up with a list of possible candidates.[27] In my view, this approach

---

26 For this opinion, see most recently Bagley 2004: 216, who asserts that such materials "must have been the everyday writing surface at Anyang." See also Shaughnessy 2010: 216.

27 Particularly questionable here is Bagley's conclusion that "the Anyan writing system could not have functioned without lexical lists" (2004: 222). As shown by the many literate ancient civilizations that never used lexical lists (Egyptian, Mayan, Minoan/Mycenaean – as well as the early Chinese, in my view), this assertion is patently false. See my discussion below p. 51, where I emphasize the fact that Mesopotamia is the only documented case of an ancient civili-

is not only unproductive – since such speculations cannot be proved (or disproved) in any way, but also methodologically dubious. This is because, as I would argue, the Babylonian materials in question constitute a very special case, consequently not being applicable to the Anyang situation as comparative evidence. As I discuss it later in this essay, the Uruk script and the records written in that script were a comparatively late outgrowth of the highly sophisticated para-writing administrative system that existed for many generations earlier. Even more fundamentally, that particular administrative system had arisen from – and indeed had been predicated on the presence of – a historically unique socio-economic institution: a characteristically egalitarian community that centered around the temple-household and its manifold economic resources, in the form of agricultural lands, orchards, animal herds, fisheries, etc., and which had a peculiar form of political leadership. As far as one can determine at this time, neither this kind of administrative system nor any elements of the socio-economic and political organization within which this system operated are in evidence at Anyang. Therefore, until such (or at least comparable) data are produced, any recourse to the Babylonian data as a way of inferring about the possible uses of writing at Anyang is completely pointless – and probably also detrimental to the proper assessment of this phenomenon. As a matter of fact, Bagley recognizes this point partly himself, since he concludes his article by suggesting that "we should be looking for functional precursors of writing, including perhaps systems of numeration like the token systems of the Near East" (ibid. 236). In my view, this would be a much more productive approach to this issue.

Similar conclusions about the inapplicabilty of the Babylonian situation as a comparative model for the uses of other early scripts were reached by Andreás Stauder 2010: 143. Although Stauder addresses primarily the question of the Egyptian writing, his observations are fully relevant for the Mesoamerican and Chinese scripts as well. Therefore, they deserve to be quoted in full:

> Due to the lack of direct evidence in the late fourth millennium, a general argument sometimes is made that the emergent Egyptian state must have needed writing for administrative control. This however need not have been the case. The classical image of the Egyptian bureaucratic state is based on material from considerably later times ... Furthermore, the sit-

---

zation that used such sources extensively. For a more restrained (and, in my opinion, much more realistic) view of the scribal training at Anyang, see Smith 2011. Note especially this conclusion: "The minimal hypothesis accounts well for the evidence of scribal training reviewed here and could comfortably accommodate the available evidence for writing on wood and bamboo as the product of activities by a handful of literate specialists supporting the ritual activities of the Shang king and his immediate family" (ibid. 205).

uation as found in late fourth-millennium southern Mesopotamia cannot be generalized uncritically to the vastly differing Egyptian society, economy, and early state. Other parallels, such as in Mesoamerica (e. g., Inca quipus) or in fifth- and early fourth-millennium Greater Mesopotamia (e. g., Arslantepe in southern Turkey ...), illustrate how societies developing toward early state structures may well manage the level of administrative control they need by non-linguistically oriented record-keeping techniques of various sorts. Writing becomes a requisite only at a later stage. (2010: 143)[28]

3.5 Summary

In summary of this review, we will be justified in concluding that the most likely cause of the invention of writing in Egypt, Mesoamerica, and China were the needs of elite display. We have also seen that, at least in the beginning, these scripts, together with the iconography that often accompanied them, were employed primarily to record what may broadly be described as "dynastic history," with the figure of the ruler and his lineage being their main focus. Yet another characteristic shared by these three corpora is the presence among them of sources of a distinctively chronographic nature, such as year-names, king lists, and dynastic histories.

At the same time, it is clear that, since very early on, both the Egyptians and the Chinese used their respective scripts also for accounting and administrative purposes. The case of the Mesoamerican writings appears to have been significantly different in this respect, since, judging from the data presently available, their use in administration was marginal at best.

4 Archaic Cuneiform Script and the History of Late Uruk Times

Now, although much still remains unclear about the origins of cuneiform, one fact is absolutely certain: the cuneiform writing system was invented with an express objective of recording administrative information — as contrasted with the purpose of elite display.

This event took place in southern Babylonia, almost certainly at the city of Uruk, toward the end of the fourth millennium BC or, in archaeological terms, the Uruk IV–III periods. When viewed from the perspective of its later history, the invention of cuneiform looms as a development of monumental proportions.

---

28 For the highly circumscribed role of writing in the early Babylonian administrative praxis, see Steinkeller 2004a and below pp. 24–25, 52–55.

However, the actual contribution of that first, incipient form of script to the economy as it existed at that time was very modest indeed.[29] During that early phase of Babylonian history economic institutions were already highly developed, their operations being facilitated by a very sophisticated and efficient administrative system, which employed various types of para-writing devices and methods. See in detail below pp. 52–55. Therefore, this earliest script played no perceptible role in the processes that had brought about the Uruk society and economy. Its real contribution rather was to provide the Uruk administrators with an extensive database for budgeting and economic prognostication (Woods 2015).

Addressing the positions of P. Wheatley and C. Lévi-Strauss, both of whom considered writing to have been a prime mover in the development of complex societies, and with Lévi-Strauss additionally viewing writing as a technology of oppression meant to facilitate exploitation and subjugation, Mogens T. Larsen instead assigned to writing, especially in the context of archaic Babylonia, a much more limited and benign role, namely that of an "enabling factor" (Larsen 1988). A similar assessment of the importance of the Uruk script has recently been offered by Christopher Woods:

> Writing played no role in ushering in the momentous socio-economic changes that defined the Uruk period. Rather writing appears during a period of retrenchment, just as the institutions that served as the crucible for its invention begin to falter. What writing did provide, however, was a more robust, flexible, and permanent accounting apparatus that went beyond the simple mnemonic devices that preceded it – the new technology provided unprecedented data storage capabilities that could be exploited for the purpose of economic planning. (Woods 2015: 140)

The Uruk IV–III periods were a time of momentous economic and social changes, as reflected in the appearance of monumental architecture, the enormous spatial expansion of the city of Uruk, and the shift to utilitarian, mass produced pottery. These and other facts strongly indicate that the late Uruk society experienced a kind of industrial revolution: the breakdown of extended family structures in the countryside, with rural population moving *en masse* into Uruk and becoming urbanized, a development not unlike the growth of London in the late eighteenth century. Undoubtedly, these changes led to the establishment of a new social and political order. It was also the time when the so-called "Uruk expansion" had reached its climax – or, more likely, was already in the process of contracting. However, we know absolutely nothing certain about the

---

29 As convincingly argued by Larsen 1988: 185–186, in its range of uses the Uruk script was more akin to the Peruvian *khipu* than to a developed writing system.

political history of that period, or, for that matter, about the then form of govern-ment. This is due to the complete absence of anything that would even remotely classify as written historical records. The only notable exception here is the so-called Jemdet-Nasr city-seal, which records, in two registers, the names of at least eleven Babylonian cities (the original number may have been as high as twenty). See **fig. 1.** The ones that can be identified are Ur, Larsa, Zabalam, Urum, Kesh, BUBUNA, and possibly Kutha or Kiš (R. J. Matthews 1993: 33–40; Steinkeller 2002b; 2002c).

Since all of the toponyms are of the same size, and since there is no hierar-chy in the way they are arranged, the likely message of the seal is that the cities in question were political equals vis-à-vis one another. From this one might plau-sibly infer that, already at that time, Babylonia supported a system of largely in-dependent city-states, which, as certain textual data seem to suggest, formed a loose federation based on religious or ritual principles (Steinkeller 2002b).

In spite of our ignorance of the specifics of the Uruk government, at the very least we know that it had an individualized political leadership. Of this we are assured by Late Uruk art, which contains a very large and highly consistent cor-pus of the representations of a royal figure. As a matter of fact – and this point needs to be emphasized – this royal figure is the central focus of Late Uruk art in general, since such images account for the majority of the surviving Uruk icon-ography. Some of those representations even deserve to be described as monu-mental. The Uruk ruler is always shown wearing the same attire, which consists of a net-like kilt and a characteristic brimmed cap. And he appears in a variety of roles: a high priest, a military leader, and a hunter. See **figs. 2–6, 11–15.** These data demonstrate quite conclusively that his office combined politico-military and ritual powers. Although the title of this royal figure is not known with abso-lute certainty, all the data indicate that it was en, which in Sumerian means "lord" or "ruler" (Akk. *bēlu*), and, in the context of Inana's cult, "high priest." For a detail discussion of this issue, see Appendix 1.

What is astonishing about the representations of the Uruk ruler when one juxtaposes them with the ones from Egypt and Mesoamerica I discussed earlier is that none of them is inscribed. The Uruk ruler is never named. Nor is his royal title ever explicitly specified.[30] He remains completely anonymous; he exists only as a generic type. This is absolutely extraordinary, since the artists who produced these pieces had at their disposal all the necessary means — that is, a developed writing system – to provide such information: to lend the Uruk ruler identity and

---

30 Though it is depicted, but only as a ritual object, on the Warka Vase. See Appendix 1 p. 85.

individuality, to identify his lineage, and to commemorate his achievements. The only explanation of this strange fact is that they purposely chose not to do so.

That the Uruk artists knew cuneiform, and that they occasionally incorporated it into their images is demonstrated by at least one surving example. The case in question is a Late Uruk cylinder seal (see **fig. 18**),[31] which depicts a standing bull accompanied by a number of pictographs: UD, SIG, DINGIR, MUŠ$_3$, and EZEN. These five signs almost certainly are to be read: "the festival (ezen) of the Morning (hud$_2$) and Evening (sig) goddess (dingir) Inana (MUŠ$_3$)." These two designations refer to Inana's astral aspect, when she embodies the planet Venus. As a matter of fact, economic tablets from the Uruk III period refer specifically to the festivals celebrating these two forms of Inana (Szarzyńska 1993).[32] The same sources mention two other avatars of this goddess, Inana NUN, "princely Inana," and Inana kur (Szarzyńska 1987; 1993: 8–9). The second of them (which may be a by-form of the "princely Inana") probably denotes the Venus's invisibility phase, during which, as the ancients believed, the goddess remained in the netherworld (kur) (Steinkeller 2002b: 254 n. 23; 2013b: 468; Boehmer 2014). Here it is of interest that our seal additionally depicts, directly over the bull, a crescent moon, plus three stars, each of which may be read as "deity" (DINGIR). It is possible that the three stars belong to the inscription as well, describing Inana as a "triple deity." This designation of Inana actually appears in other sources. A group of Uruk III tablets record offerings that were collected, apparently in various cities, to be presented to the "triple Inana / deity of Uruk" (Steinkeller 2002b: 252–254).

---

31 From the former Erlenmeyer collection, now in the collection of the Metropolitan Museum, New York. See Nissen, Damerow, and Englund 1993: 17–18 and fig. 18; Cooper 2008: 73–74; Woods, Teeter, and Emberling 2010: 50; Boehmer 2014. More recently, Suter 2014: 557 n. 25 opined that "the authenticity [of this seal] ... is not beyond doubt." However, this artifact undoubtedly is original. It is totally inconceivable that any forger could have come up with these arcane pictographs. Here note that the earliest published discussion of the festivals of the Morning and Evening Inana is Szarzyńska 1993, while the seals from the Erlenmeyer collection had been auctioned in 1992 (Sotheby's 1992: 11 no. 1). The seal itself was first published by Moortgat-Correns, 1989: 34 fig. 1.

32 One of the sources naming these two festivals is ATU 7 W 21671, which I discuss in Appendix 1 p. 96.

5 Early Southern Babylonian Kingship

5.1 Distinctive Characteristics of Southern Babylonian Kingship

Thus I return to my original question: why did the early Babylonians display this peculiar attitude toward history, and why did they use writing and art so differently than the civilizations of Egypt, Mesoamerica, and China?

The answer almost certainly lies in the nature of Sumerian kingship as it existed before the advent of the Sargonic dynasty. Characteristically, that form of rulership was based on the principle of divine election, and not on descent. In other words, it focused on the royal office, and not on the ruler's lineage. Although, in practice, hereditary principle prevailed, in that the father was usually followed by his son, in theory the ruler – usually bearing the title of ensik, "steward" – was elected to his office by the divine owner of the city-state. In this arrangement, the ensik functioned as an earthly representative of the deity, taking care of the human and other resources of the city-state on the latter's behalf, a role somewhat reminiscent of that of the bishop of Rome. In fact, the most characteristic and enduring image of the Babylonian ruler in written sources is that of the deity's trusted shepherd or vicar (sipad in Sumerian, rēʾû in Akkadian). See also Essay 2 pp. 117–120.

Since the office came first, and its holder and his personal qualities and achievements came only second, the ruler, as he appears in written sources, is predominantly a generic type. Although this generic ruler claims a special relationship with the divine realm, in essence he is just like any other member of the temple community. It was only due to his exceptional piety and obedience that he had obtained divine favor. When he is depicted in art, he usually assumes the standard posture of piety. See **figs. 19–22.** He never wears any royal insignia (though he undoubtedly used them in real life), or any special attire for that matter, that would visibly distinguish him from other members of the temple community. It is exceedingly rare that he is depicted as a warrior – as in the "Stele of the Vultures," for example – but even there his martial importance is secondary, the main warrior figure being the deity. Here it is characteristic that the "Stele of the Vultures" sharply separates the profane from the divine, by foregrounding the divine dimensions of the message on its front side, while relegating the human related imagery to its back side (Winter 1985: 13–21).

But these characterizations of the iconography of early Babylonian rulers need to be provided with a caveat. It undoubtedly has not escaped the reader's notice that the representations of the Uruk ruler I have discussed earlier differ significantly from those of Early Dynastic ensiks, since the Uruk ruler, who plausibly bore the title of en, is distinguished by his characteristic garb. Also, unlike the later ensiks, he cuts much more important a figure, as he dominates over other humans. Even more important, he also shares a direct, very intimate relationship with the goddess Inana. This is illustrated by the representations in which he and Inana appear together.[33] In addition, their figures are of the same size and height, which, from a formal perspective at least, makes them practically equals of one another. This kind of imagery finds no parallels in ED art.[34] Unfortunately, we do not have any direct information about the office of this ruler. All we can do is speculate, based mainly on what later tradition imagined this ruler to have been like. Still, there are reasons to think that the Uruk ruler was significantly more important and powerful a ruler than the ensiks of Early Dynastic times. According to later literary sources, the archaic, purely mythical kings of Uruk, such as Mes-kiag-gašir, Enmerkar, Lugal-banda, and Gilgameš, were descended from gods. Possibly, therefore, the archaic ruler of Uruk was believed to be a demigod by his contemporaries. While not a deity properly speaking, he perhaps was imbued with more sacrality than other humans. (For the issue of "sacrality" in early Babylonia, see in detail Essay 2.) It was perhaps this semi-divine aspect of the en, a characteristic no longer shared by the Early Dynastic ensiks, that explains his exceptional and distinguishing attire, as well as his more prominent position in art more generally.

One might even consider that the Uruk ruler was a Dumuzi-like figure.[35] Dumuzi was an exceedingly complex persona, partly human and partly divine, who, according to literary texts, was a lover and ritual attendant of Inana/Ištar. Characteristically, the first millennium version of the "Gilgameš Epic," SB Version, Tablet VI lines 109–110, includes Dumuzi among the human lovers of Ištar. Dumuzi is depicted as a mortal in a number of other sources, which, at the same time, assign to him divine characteristics. Thus the Old Babylonian list of the antediluvian cities and rulers (for which see below pp. 58–65) calls Dumuzi a "shepherd" (sipad), and makes him a "king" of Patibira, the main center of Dumuzi's cult, also identifying him as a deity (by providing his name with the divine determinative DINGIR). There was yet another Dumuzi who shared such

---

33 For a discussion of such scenes, see Appendix 1 pp. 83–90.

34 The corpus of ED III art contains numerous representations of ritual specialists and worshipers presenting offerings to enthroned deities, with the figures of both being of the same size. See Braun-Holzinger 2013: pl. 11 fig. 5, pl. 12 fig. 9, pl. 13 figs. 7 and 8(!), pl. 14 figs. 10 (= our **fig. 26**; discussed below p. 34) and 11, pl. 15 fig. 13; pls. 18 and 19 figs. 1–7; etc. But, in all these instances, divine statues undoubtedly are depicted, thus indicating a significantly lesser level of contact and intimacy between the human and the divine.

35 See Hansen 1998: 49: "this figure may well also be Inanna's consort and lover, Dumuzi." This idea goes back to Jacobsen 1976: 26, who explicitly identified the Priest-King depicted on the Warka Vase as Dumuzi.

mixed human-divine characteristics: a fisherman from Kuwara who is listed, in the SKL lines 109–110, as one of the kings of the First Dynasty of Uruk, and whose name too is marked with a DINGIR sign. Possibly, therefore, there existed a belief that, like Mes-kiag-gašir, Enmerkar, Lugal-banda, and Gilgameš, Dumuzi too was one of the mythical Priest-Kings of Uruk.[36] This hypothetical notion may also have ascribed to Dumuzi the origin of the royal epithet "shepherd," which, as I wrote above, arguably was the most characteristic image of the ruler throughout ancient Mesopotamian history.[37]

The possibility that the Uruk ruler was a semi-divine figure may find indirect support in the fact that the archaic Lu List A, which names the top officials of Uruk's economic and political structure (see below pp. 47–50), excludes the en from its purview. This omission is striking and very puzzling. One way to account for this abnormality would be to assume that the en was thought to stand outside of the normal social system or, in other words, that he formed a category by itself.[38]

5.2 The Cult of the Former Rulers and Priestly Officials

The lack of preoccupation with the ruler's lineage and his individual traits – his legitimacy deriving solely from his office – explains why there is no evidence in early southern Babylonia of a dynastic cult, or more broadly, a cult of royal ancestors centering on lineages, such as existed at Ebla, for example.[39]

What we find there instead is a collective cult of former rulers and high priests and priestesses, which, like the kingship itself, centered on offices, and not on the particular lineages of the holders of those offices.[40] Known as the "sleeping ens," the "gathering of the ens," or the "collegium of Gilgameš,"

---

36 For the role of Dumuzi in the Ur III royal ideology, see Essay 2 pp. 144–145.

37 Wiggermann 2010: 328 writes that "the identity of the priest-king as the en, the ruler of protoliterate Uruk, has become more than plausible, which, of course, does not exclude the possibility of an iconographic overlap with Dumuzi, the god he embodied as husband of Inanna." In this connection, note that the brimmed cap worn by the en of Uruk is later associated with Dumuzi (Wiggermann 2010: 338–339). It is possible, therefore, that this cap had its origins in the headgear worn by shepherds. For the later history of the brimmed cap, which eventually became an attribute of Gudea and Ur III kings, see below p. 34.

38 For a similar suggestion, see Schmandt-Besserat 1993: 210.

39 See Archi 2001; Bonechi 2001.

40 A vague parallel for this practice is provided by the veneration of former Popes at St. Peter's in Rome.

these deceased officials were believed to form a ruling class among the human denizens of the netherworld.[41]

The cult of the "sleeping ens" is particularly well documented at Lagaš, where we find detailed records of it from the Early Dynastic period at least through the Ur III period (2400–2000 BC). This cult focused on a complex of funerary chapels, built over respective tombs, which were contained within one enclosed area. That area very likely was the courtyard of the Eninnu, Lagaš's most important sanctuary. Such funerary chapels housed statues of former ensiks and other high officials, which were attended daily by cultic personnel.[42] Similar complexes of funerary chapels are known to have existed in the neighboring city-state of Umma[43] as well as at Ur.[44]

---

41 In ED Lagaš, they were known as en-en KU.KU-ne, "sleeping lords" (DP 77 v 6), KU.KU-ne, "the sleeping ones" (VAS 14 164 vii 6), or simply en-en-ne$_2$-ne, "lords" (DP 73 ix 1, 77 iv 1; VAS 14 191 i 2–3). Cf. "Ebla Vocabulary" lines 800–801 (MEE 4 289; Archi 2012: 5–6): DINGIR.EN = *ma-'à-um*, DINGIR.EN.EN, *na-u$_9$-lum, du-uš-da-i-i-lu-um*, "the sleeping one(s)," where the verb is *niālu*. For a discussion of the "collegium of Gilgameš," the "gathering of the ens," and the enumerations of the various deceased priestly officials over whom Gilgameš and his deputy Etana ruled in the Netherworld, see Steinkeller 1995a; 1999: 110–111; 2005a: 22–23.

42 These chapels were called ki-a-nag, "the place were the water is libated," lit. "the place where (the dead) are given water to drink." The best known funerary chapel of this type is the one described in Gudea's Statue B, for which, actually, this particular statue of Gudea had been fashioned. While not referring specifically to ki-a-nags, ED sources of Lagaš record garments and various jewelry that belonged to the "sleeping ens," or, more correctly, their statues. See DP 73, 74, 76, 77, 78; VAS 14 163, 164. The existence of such statues implies the presence of funerary chapels of this kind as well. Food offerings for these "lords," called maš-da-ri-a, and consisting of flour, beer, and bread, are referred to in VAS 14 191. In Ur III times, there was a special personnel attached to this cult. Called gir$_3$-se$_3$-ga ki-a-nag en-en-e-ne-ka, "personnel of the funerary chapels of the 'lords,'" and numbering eighteen individuals, this group included four gudu$_4$ priests (one of whom served the deified Gudea), a chief lamenter (gala-mah), a singer of the "lords" (nar en), and various other functionaries and supporting staff (RTC 401 i 13–ii 9).

43 An Ur III topographical plan from Umma (JCS 16 81 HSM 7500) records the dimensions of two adjoining buildings. The smaller of these two structures, measuring over 7 sar (= 247 m^2), was the residence of the lu$_2$-mah, the high priest of Šara. The larger building, measuring 14 sar (= 494 m^2) in size, is labeled as en-en, which allows one to identify it as the place where the funerary chapels of the former "lords" of Umma were situated. It appears certain that these two buildings formed part of the complex of Šara's temple in the city of Umma. According to other Ur III sources from Umma, a large area of agricultural land was set aside exclusively in support of this cult: 825 iku ŠUKU en-en-e-ne (Orient 21 1 iii 6–7; Steinkeller 2017: 563: Text E ii 4'–5'). Umma sources also make frequent mentions of the provisions for these former "lords," called nig$_2$-dab$_5$ en-en-e-ne, which consisted of foodstuffs and sheep (BPOA 2 2647, 2661; MVN 20 69; Nikolski 2 372; etc.).

44 This complex, which formed part of or adjoined the gi$_6$-par$_4$ of Nanna and Ningal, contained the tombs of the former en priestesses of Nanna. In an inscription left by En-anedu, a daughter

5.3 Gudea of Lagaš and His Ideology

A particularly interesting exemplification of these ideas about kingship and its place vis-à-vis the divine realm is presented by the case of an ensik of Lagaš named Gudea, who ruled shortly before the Ur III period.[45] Gudea's reign represented, at least in terms of the ideology he espoused, a total rejection of Sargonic values (of which I will be talking shortly), and a return to the original Sumerian worldview.[46] The numerous and lengthy inscriptions of Gudea deal exclusively with temple-building and ritual matters, making no mention of political events whatsoever.[47] If one were to believe these sources, Gudea and his subjects lived in an immovable ritual continuum, in which humans commingled with gods, and no history of facts ever took place. Although this seems to have been the most radical expression of that ideology ever, similar disinterest in history was typical of the early southern Babylonian culture in general.

It can be shown, in fact, that Gudea had instituted a systematic archaizing program, whose purpose was to restore the conditions that existed in Lagaš prior to the Sargonic take over.[48] Although economic data surviving from Gudea's reign are very meager, we can be certain that this program restored the institution of temple households, which, most significantly, regained the ownership of arable land. Reflections of these archaizing policies are even clearer in texts and art. A careful examination of Gudea's inscriptions reveals that these

---

of Kudur-mabuk of Larsa and an en priestess herself, this locus is described as the "place of the 'destined day' (i.e., death) of the former ens" (ki ud-nam-tar-ra en-en-e-ne libir-ra-me-eš) and the "resting place of the former ens" (ki-na$_2$ en-en-e-ne libir-ra-me-eš) (RIME 4 299–301 Rim-Sin I 20:34–35, 40).

45 It is even possible that Gudea's reign overlapped with that of Ur-Namma, the founder of the Third Dynasty of Ur. See Steinkeller 2013c: 298–302.

46 In a recent article, Claudia Suter (2015) offered a discussion of Gudea's ideology, suggesting that Gudea underwent a "partial" deification, and that he tried to assimilate himself to other deities. In my opinion, these views are fundamentally mistaken. See the following discussion and Essay 2 pp. 112 n. 299, 150 n. 404.

47 There is just one piece of such information, and very unspecific at that. It occurs in Gudea Statue B vi 64, discussed in Steinkeller 2013c: 298–299.

48 The earliest evidence of such efforts dates to the reign of Puzur-Mama, a governor of Lagaš in late Sargonic times, who eventually became an independent ruler of that city-state. See Volk 1992. Puzur-Mama left to us at least one inscription (RIME 2: 271–272 Puzur-Mama 1), in which he calls himself a "king of Lagaš." It is certain that this inscription was composed based on Early Dynastic Lagaš sources, as shown by the fact that it uses the same royal epithets as those materials (ii 1′–12′). Even more revealingly, it assigns to Puzur-Mama as his personal deity Šul-"Utul" (iii 4′–5′), who had been the personal god of Ur-Nanše and his descendants, and who is identified as such in their inscriptions. Cf. Volk 1992: 28–29.

draw directly and very extensively on the votive inscriptions written at Lagaš in Early Dynastic times. This is shown by the use of similar (sometimes identical) phraseology[49] and also certain orthographic conventions that are found only in the ED Lagaš materials and Gudea's inscriptions.[50]

It is certain, therefore, that Gudea's scribes had systematically mined such documentation (some of which, like the inscriptions of Ur-Nanše, were three centuries old by that time) with an objective of bringing the Early Dynastic world and its attitudes back to life.

These archaizing reforms also affected the cult. It is characteristic that Gudea revived the custom of including in the foundation deposits of human-shaped pegs (the so-called *Nagelmenschen*), which were a regular part of such deposits in Early Dynastic times. This custom had been discontinued in the Sargonic period.[51]

Yet another, much more important innovation of Gudea's reign was the revival, in art, of the image of the Early Dynastic ruler. Like his Early Dynastic an-

---

49 Here one may list the following examples: (a) the obscure designation of the sun-god Utu as lugal NI-si$_3$-ga-ke$_4$ is found only in RIME 1 126–140 E-anatum I rev. i 26–27, 36–37 and Gudea Statue B viii 61–62; (b) The passage describing how the Makkan and Meluhha boats submitted themselves to Gudea: Ma$_2$-gan Me-luh-ha kur-bi-ta gu$_2$ giš mu-na-ab-gal$_2$ (Cylinder A xv 8), is patterned after the passage describing how the ships of Tilmun submitted themselves to Ur-Nanše: ma$_2$ Dilmun kur-ta gu$_2$ giš mu-gal$_2$ (RIME 1 103–104 Ur-Nanše 17 v 3–5); (c) the selection of Gudea by Ningirsu (šag$_4$ lu$_2$ 216,000–ta ba-ta-an-dab$_5$-ba-a; Statue B iii 10–11) goes back to the passage describing En-metena's selection by Ningirsu ([šag$_4$ l]u$_2$ 3,600–ta [šu]-ni ba-ta-[dab$_5$]-ba-a; RIME 1 222–223 En-metena 18:1′–3′; cf. also RIME 1 248–265 Urukagina 1 viii 5–6); (d) the passage describing how goddess Gatumdug had planted Gudea's seed in the womb (a-mu šag$_4$-ga šu ba-ni-dug$_4$; Cylinder A iii 8) obviously is derived from the passage describing how the same act was performed by Ningirsu for E-anatum ([rdNin-gir$_2$-su-ke$_4$]' [a] 'E$_2$'-[an]-na-tum$_2$-[ma šag$_4$-g]a [šu b]a-ni-dug$_4$ ... E$_2$-an-na-tum$_2$, a šag$_4$-ga šu dug$_4$-ga ^{d}Nin-gir$_2$-su-ka-da ^{d}Nin-gir$_2$-su mu-da-hul$_2$ (RIME 1 126–140 E-anatum 1 iv 9–12, v 1–5). Note further that many of the royal epithets attested in ED materials, such as lu$_2$ inim-ma si$_3$-ga DN, gidri (mah) sum-ma DN, a$_2$ sum-ma DN, šag$_4$(-ge) pad$_3$-da DN, and dumu tu-da DN, appear in Gudea's inscriptions (see, especially, Statues B and D). Some of this formulary is also used in the inscriptions of his predecessor Ur-Bau (see, especially, RIME 3/1 18–19 Ur-Bau 5).

50 A good example here is the use of the graph -dab$_6$- to express a combination of the commitative infixix -da- and the inanimate agent marker -b-. See sag e-dab$_6$-sig$_3$ (RIME 1 145–149 E-ana-tum 5 iv 24, vi 9′; 149–152 E-anatum 6 v 9), he$_2$-dab$_6$-kur$_2$-ne (Statue B ix 5), and ad im-dab$_6$-gi$_4$-gi$_4$ (Cylinder A v 1).

51 See Muscarella 1988: 306: "It is during the Gudea (neo-Sumerian) period, some two centuries after the last attested archaeological appearance of the *Nagelmensch* figurine, that foundation pegs appear again in the archaeological record, *dramatically reflecting a return to Sumerian custom*" [emphasis added].

cestors, Gudea too wears a simple dress and no royal insignia, and assumes a humble pose of the worshipper, characteristics that make him virtually indistinguishable from his subjects at large. See **figs. 23–25.** But his garb differs in one important respect, for now Gudea sports a brimmed cap (*Breitrandkappe*), which is closely similar to the one worn earlier by the Uruk Priest-King (see above p. 26 and **figs. 2–6, 11–15**).[52] Such caps continued to be used by high priests and priestesses during the following, Early Dynastic times. This is demonstrated by an ED IIIb plaque, which was excavated in the gipar residence of the en priestesses of Nanna at Ur.[53] See **fig. 26.** This object depicts, in the upper register, three women and a naked male officiant presenting offerings to a seated god, who almost certainly is Nanna. The women have long hair and wear long cloaks and brimmed caps.[54] In the lower register, a similar offering is presented in front of a temple.[55] Here the participants are a pair of worshipers, a long-haired female dressed in the same cloak and cap as the three women above, and a naked male officiant. The four women wearing brimmed caps may quite confidently be identified as Nanna's priestesses.[56] This particular representation opens up a possibility that Gudea had used such Early Dynastic images as a model for his cap. Alternatively, he might have drawn on the Late Uruk art directly, examples of which undoubtedly were known to him and his contemporaries. It is characteristic that the same cap was later adopted by the Ur III kings.[57]

More fundamentally, Gudea's art rejects the ethos of the Sargonic age in its entirety. In the words of Henri Frankfort, "in the sculptures [of Gudea] ... the technical achievements of the Akkadian period are utilized, but of the aspirations of that time not a trace remains. Piety replaces vigour" (1954: 93).

---

52 For a possibility that this cap derives from the headgear of the archaic en of Uruk, see Wiggermann 2010: 339. Wiggermann ibid. 338 further notes two Ur III seals depicting Dumuzi, where Dumuzi wears a similar brimmed cap. This evidence provides additional substance to the contention that the en of Uruk was a Dumuzi-like figure. See above pp. 29–30.

53 BM 118561 = U.6831. See Woolley 1926: 376 and pl. 53a; Aruz 2003: 74–75 no. 33; Braun-Holzinger 2013: 173–174 Relief 10, pl. 14 fig. 10. For recent discussions of this piece, see also Winter 2000: 144; J. G. Westenholz 2012: 293.

54 J. G. Westenholz 2012: 293 describes them as "wide-brim headgear." Suter 2007: 331 and n. 49 thinks that this cap is a "flat hairband," but this identification is not supported by the image.

55 This scene precedes the ritual depicted in the relief's upper register. See Winter 2000: 144.

56 It appears that, before the creation by Sargon of the office of the en priestess of Nanna, these priestesses went by the name of zirru. For a discussion of this issue, see Appendix 1 p. 102.

57 See Boese 1973: 15–21 and Essay 2 p. 150.

5.4 Kingship of Early Northern Babylonia

It is important to emphasize that the peculiar attitudes toward history and history writing I have just described, which were typical of Early Dynastic times, and which briefly resurfaced during Gudea's "revival," can be found only in southern Babylonia. We may conjecture that, during the same timeframe, things were significantly different in northern Babylonia, that is the area extending north of Nippur as far as Sippar on the Euphrates and including the Diyala Region. There, no city-states existed, with this whole geographical area rather forming a single territorial state. The form of kingship existing in that state was substantially different as well, since it was considerably stronger and more authoritarian than that found in the south. It may also have embraced the hereditary principle of rulership. Here I am referring to the kingdom of Kiš, which, in the beginning phase of the Early Dynastic period (ED I and ED II), brought under its sway northern Babylonia, the Diyala Region, and probably certain trans-Tigridian territories. It also established hegemony over parts of southern Babylonia. Although, due to the scarcity of relevant historical data, this Kišite entity remains a largely hypothetical construct, it appears that it constituted a territorial state of almost "imperial" size and objectives – thus contrasting sharply with the political organization of southern Babylonia, where city-states were the norm (Steinkeller 1993: 116–127; 2013a: 145–151). In fact, the later tradition, whose beginnings probably belong to the Sargonic period,[58] asserted that it was at Kiš where kingship was introduced for the first time.

A very important datum supporting the existence of this early Kišite kingdom is an inscribed and decorated archaic plaque, which in all likelihood comes from Kiš (Steinkeller 2013a). See **figs. 27–28.** This piece, which dates to ED II or possibly even earlier, is a list of prisoners that were brought from various foreign places to Kiš by an unknown ruler of that city. The inscription recorded on the front side of the plaque lists some 36,000 prisoners, thus offering an eloquent testimony of the might of this Kišite state, and of the geographic scale of its military conquests and political influence. On the back side of the plaque, a group of soldiers bearing arms is depicted. Very significantly, this plaque is the oldest surviving historical source of *truly monumental character* from ancient Mesopotamia, both as regards its text and the imagery represented on it. Because of this particular source, and in consideration of various other data as well (Steinkeller 2013b: 145–151), a strong case can be made that it was this archaic Kišite

---

58 I am referring here to the SKL.

kingdom from which, either directly or indirectly, the Sargonic empire later sprang.

5.5 Kingship of the Sargonic Period

It is only with the Sargonic advent, however, that one witnesses truly revolution-ary changes in the attitudes toward history and history writing. These changes undoubtedly were due to the nature of Sargonic kingship, which was monarchic, highly authoritarian, and based on descent. In addition, beginning with Naram-Suen, the fourth ruler of the dynasty, the Sargonic kings claimed divinity.[59] In other words, they deified themselves. The latter innovation alone made divine se-lection unnecessary. Compared with their Early Dynastic predecessors, the Sar-gonic kings were rulers of an entirely different mould: strong, depending on their own power and abilities alone, forward looking, intent on carrying their might and influence to the very borders of the known world. Theirs was a com-pletely different ethos, which put the divine society in the background, giving priority to personal decision and initiative.

All of these new ideas find ample reflection in the historical sources Sargon and his followers have left to us. These texts are primarily and nearly exclusively about political events, military conquests above all. Their *Leitmotif* is "I went and conquered, no ruler has done it before me." Although the majority of the Sargon-ic historical sources are still couched in the form of dedicatory inscriptions, it is characteristic that most of them begin with an invocation of the ruler, even when the dedication to a specific deity is meant.[60] This fact distinguishes them sharply from the earlier, Sumerian sources, which, as I wrote earlier, invariably name the deity in question at the outset of the text. A good illustration here is the pattern: Royal Name titles *bāni*(ᵇᵃDIM$_2$) E$_2$ Divine Name, "Royal Name, titles, is the build-er of the temple of Divine Name," which appears for the first time in the inscrip-tions of Maništušu,[61] and is employed subsequently by those of Naram-Suen and Šar-kali-šarri.

---

59 For this development, and the Sargonic ideology more broadly, see Essay 2.

60 The exceptions here are some of the inscriptions of Sargon and Rimuš, which begin with the invocation of a deity (RIME 2 Sargon 4 and 9, Rimuš 10–16). The pattern is reversed in the sour-ces of Maništušu, Naram-Suen and Šar-kali-šarri (RIME 2 Maništušu 4 and 5, Naram-Suen 1003, Šar-kali-šarri 9).

61 RIME 2 80 Maništušu 6. This pattern continued to be used into the Ur III period. Of special interest here is an inscription of Šulgi, which commemorates the construction of the temple of Ninazu/Tišpak in Ešnuna. While the Sumerian version of this source follows the traditional,

As we are informed by the adscriptions appended to some of these sources, their originals were provided with rich iconography glorifying the king. They were also, apparently for the first time, systematically displayed in public places, for example, in the courtyard of the Ekur, the temple of Enlil in Nippur, and in the Ebabbar, the temple of Šamaš in Sippar.

The Sargonic stress on individual achievement is also reflected in the contemporary art, which focuses on the figure of the king and his superhuman feats, and assumes truly monumental proportions. Contrasting sharply with the representations of Early Dynastic rulers, these images represent a complete *novum* in Mesopotamian art.[62]

I have already mentioned the chronographic innovations that were made during this period. One of them was the introduction of year-names as a dating method. There are also indications that the first version of the SKL was composed under the Sargonic dynasty (see below p. 40). However, that original version appears to have differed significantly from the later redactions, in that it centered on the dynasty of Kiš as a direct predecessor of the Sargonic kingdom. In other words, it propagated the idea of a single northern monarchy, which commenced in Kiš at the dawn of history, and later continued in Akkade with Sargon and his successors.

5.6 Kingship of the Ur III Period

The Sargonic empire, which, at least in terms of its political and commercial influence, in its heyday stretched from Anatolia in the west to Afghanistan in the east, disintegrated around 2200 BC, and its demise was nearly total. After a passage of roughly one century, during which the south reverted to its traditional, decentralized political organization, and which saw a temporary restoration of the earlier, Early Dynastic ideals under Gudea and his dynasty, Babylonia again had been unified, this time by the rulers of the Third Dynasty of Ur.

In terms of its ideology, the Ur III state represented a return to the Early Dynastic past. In this the kings of Ur followed the trend set first by Gudea. However, this return was highly superficial, since it amounted to not much more than cos-

---

southern Babylonian pattern, its Akkadian counterpart adheres to the Sargonic model (RIME 3/2 135–137 Šulgi 27 and 28). Here note the comments by Van Driel 1973b: 68: "The phrasing of the Old Assyrian (Akkadian) inscriptions, like that of the inscriptions from Mari and of Šulgi's Akkadian inscription from Ešnunna, differs completely from that of the generally Sumerian inscriptions from Babylonia."

62 See Essay 2 for an extensive discussion of this issue.

metic changes. Under the veneer of Sumerian restoration, and the avowed rejection of Sargonic values, the Ur III state was, in many ways, a direct continuation of the Sargonic empire.[63]

The kings of Ur preserved most of the Sargonic innovations. For example, they too became deified. They also retained the Sargonic royal titulary. And, most important, they left in place many elements of the Sargonic economic and administrative structure. Quite characteristically, however, they distanced themselves from Akkade and her kings, tracing their ideological and political descent to the mythical rulers of Uruk instead.[64]

Thus, in many ways the Ur III state was a compromise of sorts. Most visibly, this was reflected in the Ur III concept of kingship, which awkwardly combined the idea of the king's divinity with the principle of divine election. In practice, however, the House of Ur was all about descent and kinship relations, in which, of course, it followed the Sargonic example. In fact, the Ur III kings outdid their Sargonic predecessors in that area, since their state was, for all practical purposes, a family affair, in that, like in the modern House of Saud, nearly everybody of importance in the Ur III society was related by blood to the royal family.[65]

This conflict of ideas can also be detected in Ur III texts and art. While most of the Ur III historical inscriptions adhere to the traditional, Early Dynastic models, there are also examples of texts that clearly were inspired by the monumental display sources of Sargonic kings. A case in point is the collection of Šu-Suen's inscriptions, which survive in copies made from the monumental originals by Old Babylonian scribes (RIME 3/2 295–320 Šu-Suen 1, 3–9). Like the Sargonic display texts, these inscriptions too had originally been accompanied by rich iconography. They also were publicly displayed, in some instances, in courtyard of the Ekur, where the Sargonic monuments were housed as well. While virtually none of the Ur III monumental sculpture survived to our times, we know that there did exist an extensive repertoire of such representations, which appear

---

63 For further discussion of the Ur III royal ideology, historical inscriptions, and art, see Essay 2.

64 To my knowledge, the first scholar to identify this development was J. J. Finkelstein: "Instead [of associating itself with the Sargonic kings], the formal royal rhetoric as well as the cultic pageantry allied the dynastic line with Gilgamesh ... Thus they [i.e., the Ur III kings] quite pointedly demonstrated loyalty to the ideal form of polity exemplified by the hegemony of Uruk in Early Dynastic times ... but with which they in fact had almost nothing in common" (1979: 79). See further my discussion in Essay 2 pp. 141–144.

65 This ambiguous attitude of the Ur III kings toward their Sargonic predecessors is also reflected in the fact that Naram-Suen, as well as Sargon and Maništušu, were worshipped (though marginally) as part of the official Ur III cult. See Essay 2 p. 116 n. 314.

to have closely imitated the Sargonic models. This information comes from Ur III economic sources, which concern the manufacture of royal statues, for example, a statue described as the "king of the four quarters."[66]

In concluding this part of my discussion, I note that, although both the Sargonic and Ur III kings made important inroads in that direction, it was not until the Old Babylonian period (1900–1500 BC) that the hereditary principle was firmly established in Babylonia. In all likelihood, this development is to be ascribed to the fact that most of the dynasties that were founded in Babylonia following the end of the Ur III period were rooted in tribal reality. The founders of those dynasties were predominantly Amorites, though there were also Elamites and Hurrians among them. It appears quite certain that it was these individuals who, because of their social and cultural background, were primarily responsible for making the southern kingship a thing of the past, replacing it with a form of government that was decisively family-centered and monarchic in character.

Similar conclusions about this historical transformation were reached many years ago by W. G. Lambert, who contrasted the southern, Sumerian tradition with the one introduced in Old Babylonian times. As being highly pertinent here, these conclusions deserve to be quoted in full:

> The most striking thing about the Sumerians in this connection [i.e., the prevalence of hereditary principle in the ancient Near East] is the lack of evidence that belonging to a particular family qualified a man for rulership. Son often succeeded father, but this seems to have reflected more a trait of human nature than to have been the result of a theory of kingship. Perhaps the ideal of the Sumerian city ruler as a kind of farm bailiff for the god or goddess of the city prevented the growth of prestige around the person of the ruler ... to judge from the surviving evidence, the idea that this family descent somehow assured the legitimacy of the king arose only with the arrival of the Amorites early in the Second Millennium, after which the idea was appropriated by other dynasties and applied to their own descent. The lack of evidence for the currency of this idea in the Third Millennium is probably not due to the chances of discovery. (1974: 427, 434)

6 The Poverty of Historical Tradition in Early Babylonia

I hope that I was able to demonstrate that there is a direct relationship between the type of kingship a given society has, and its attitudes toward history and history writing. Thus we have seen that the lack of elite display sources and chronographic records in Early Dynastic times was largely due to the absence of a developed dynastic tradition during that time. This situation changed significantly

---

66 UET 3 366:2, 5; Nisaba 15/1 165. For a discussion of this title, see Essay 2 p. 136.

in Sargonic times, when the kingship became hereditary, and when the monarchic principle was introduced. As expected, these transformations led, or at least heavily contributed, to the appearance of true historical sources and monumental art that glorified the ruler and his political achievements. We have also seen how the Early Dynastic and Sargonic worldviews and ideas clashed with one another in Ur III times, resulting in an awkward ideological compromise. That compromise, I submit, is discernible in the Ur III historical sources as well.

With reference to history writing specifically, one may offer a generalization that, prior to the advent of Sargon and his dynasty, the Babylonians showed a remarkable lack of interest in things historical. As we have seen earlier, this attitude toward history briefly resurfaced under Gudea, whose reign represented a return to the Early Dynastic ideals.

To expand more on this point, as far as it can be ascertained at this time, third millennium Babylonia did not produce any extensive historical narratives, nor did it create any sources of chronographic nature. One also looks in vain for any evidence of the local lists of rulers, such as the ones postulated by Jacobsen as part of his efforts to demonstrate the historicity of the SKL.[67]

The only exception to the above is the SKL, and this particular case deserves to be considered in some detail. As we now know with certainty, there existed a version of this list already in Ur III times.[68] The exact date of its composition is less clear. As hypothesized by this author,[69] the original list probably was written down in Sargonic times, with an express objective of demonstrating that, save for a brief interlude involving Lugal-zagesi and perhaps some other kings of Uruk, the Sargonic dynasty was a continuation of the kingdom of Kiš. In other words, this hypothetical list was in its essence a linear history of the northern Babylonian monarchy. If so, this "history" would have been part of the ideological innovations that the Sargonic kings introduced to foster the idea of a unified Babylonian state, thus radically differing from the traditional, Sumerian types of historical records.

---

67 "The actual material from which it [i.e., SKL] has been built up ... comes ... mainly from local lists of rulers, date lists kept in various cities for practical purposes ... Such materials must undoubtedly be considered very reliable sources of information" (Jacobsen 1939: 165–166). No such "materials" have surfaced so far.

68 For an edition and discussion of this source, which probably was written during the reign of Šulgi, see Steinkeller 2003.

69 Steinkeller 2003: 282–286.

If such a hypothetical Sargonic list did in fact exist, one would necessarily have to assume that it was later revised, probably in the early Ur III period, when the information about the Gutian and other post-Sargonic dynasties was added. The product of this redaction would be the Ur III ms mentioned earlier. Yet another revision of the list must be posited for still later times, probably the Isin period, when additional dynasties were introduced.[70] It was at that point that the SKL acquired its final form.

It must have been then that the various anecdotal information about particular rulers also was added throughout the list.[71] That this information is late is shown by the fact that none of it is found in the Ur III version of the SKL. The sources of these anecdotes remain unknown, though the fantastic nature of some of them[72] suggests that most of this information is pure invention.

A more serious problem is presented by the additional dynasties included in the standard version of the SKL. The choice of those particular centers of power and their rulers may have been guided by some considerations of propagandistic or conceptual nature, but those, if they existed, remain uncertain. This applies especially to the dynasties of Awan, Hamazi, Adab, Mari, and Akšak. The only exceptions here are the Uruk I and Ur I dynasties, whose inclusion in the list undoubtedly had been dictated by the politico-ideological pedigree of the Ur III dynasty (which, by extension, constituted the pedigree of the Isin dynasty as well).[73]

It is even more difficult to answer the question as to where the names of the additional rulers listed in the standard SKL came from.[74] Some of them, such as that of Mesanepada of the First Dynasty of Ur, were probably found in votive inscriptions. Others may have been *ad hoc* creations. Still other among them possibly were derived from ancient literary and lexical sources. In this connection, one thinks in particular of the ED "Names and Professions List" (Archi 1981). As I suggested elsewhere,[75] some of the names of the kings of the First Dynasty of Kiš may actually be borrowings of the entries found in that list. If such borrowings

---

70 These are the Isin dynasty and the Early Dynastic dynasties not recorded in the Ur III version of the SKL. These additions also included the list of the antediluvian cities and rulers, which I treat in detail below pp. 58–65.
71 For a discussion and a full listing of these anecdotal notes, see Marchesi 2010: 233, 238–243.
72 Such as the story about the barmaid Kug-Bau, who strengthened the foundations of Kiš (SKL lines 224–226). Here also belong the fuller Su$_8$-sud$_3$-da (line 160), the sailor Ma$_2$-ma$_2$-gal (= "The Great Ship") (line 164), and the stone-worker Na-an-ni-a (line 254), all of whom had somehow been able to join the ranks of royalty.
73 For a suggestion that the Uruk I dynasty was a construct of Isin times, see Mittermayer 2012.
74 For the names of the antediluvian rulers, see below pp. 61–65.
75 Steinkeller 2013a: 151 n. 87.

did indeed occur, this development likely took place in Sargonic times, since two of those particular names appear in the Ur III version of the SKL.[76] But the "Names and Professions List" may have been mined for similar purposes also in later times. This is suggested by the names such as Ba-zi, Zi-zi, and Ba-lu-lu, which are found both in the ED list in question and the SKL.

It becomes clear, therefore, that the authors of the standard SKL had a very limited number of genuine ancient sources at their disposal.[77] As illustrated by the case of Rimuš and Maništušu, whose sequential order had been in doubt already in Ur III times (see above p. 14), there neither existed any permanent collections of historical data by recourse to which such chronological discrepancies could be resolved.

Another illustration of how little the OB and later scholars knew about the third millennium history is provided by the composition "Rulers of Lagaš." Written in OB times, in all likelihood at Lagaš, this text preserves an independent, local tradition about the origins of civilization and kingship.[78] Importantly, this is the only such tradition in existence apart from that presented in the SKL. Closely paralleling the form of the SKL, the main section of the "Rulers of Lagaš" is a "chronological" list of Lagaš kings, to whom similarly fantastically long reigns are assigned. Although the majority of the kings enumerated in it appear to be artificial creations, a handful of them are historical figures, whose names undoubtedly came from building and votive inscriptions. Certain examples here are Ur-Nanše (line 153), E-anatum (written An-ne$_2$-tum$_2$ and incorrectly identified as a son of Ur-Nanše; line 157), En-entarzi (line 164), Puzur-Mama of post-Sargonic times (line 183), Ur-Ningirsu (line 195), Ur-Bau (line 196), and Gudea (line 198). These "real" kings are listed in a correct chronological order,

---

76 Me-en-nun-na-ke$_4$, which appears as En-me/men-nun-na in SKL line 71, and Ur-Zababa (SKL line 247).

77 Cf. Cooper 2010: 330, who suggests that the gross omission of historical data in the SKL is "less intentional forgetting than a simple lack of reliable historical sources."

78 The "Rulers of Lagaš" begins with a lengthy poetic preamble (lines 1–65, followed by a break of ca. 35 lines), whose contents may be summarized as follows. Following the Deluge, mankind was created. The gods An and Enlil subsequently gave a name to mankind and created the "stewardship" (nam-ensi$_2$). Interestingly, the text then notes that, at that time, "kingship" (nam-lugal) had not yet been lowered down from heaven. The following lines describe the state of things existing then: there was no irrigation-based agriculture, though people were able, thanks to rains, to do some cultivation. They were also involved in herding. On the whole, however, it was a time of hunger and suffering. This situation changed when, finally, Ningirsu created the tools of agriculture and introduced irrigation. Unfortunately, the concluding part of this preamble, which probably described the establishment of kingship proper, is not preserved. For the motif of "Deluge," see below pp. 60–61, 74–76.

but both their patronymics and the factual data about them for the most part are erroneous.[79] On the whole, the "Rulers of Lagaš" is a pathetic jumble of factual information haphazardly extracted from earlier materials, which was expanded and embellished by the addition of various ficticious data, generated by processes similar to those that led to the creation of the SKL. And it was probably the latter composition that inspired the writing of the "Rulers of Lagaš." For the modern scholar, the main value of the "Rulers of Lagaš" lies in its demonstrating that its authors had but a few historical records of poor quality at their disposal, and that their own familiarity with the past was probably even worse (not much evidence of a robust oral history in OB Lagaš here!).[80] Rather than a "patriotic satire,"[81] the "Rulers of Lagaš" is simply bad history writing, a desperate and uninformed attempt to produce a local history out of deficient data.

All of this makes it abundantly clear that the Old Babylonian and later scholars had a very small body of written data about early Babylonia available to them to work with. This point is underscored by the fact that, apart from the Sargonic and Ur III royal inscriptions that were accessible in copies in OB times[82] and the "Rulers of Lagaš" just discussed, virtually all the information on early Babylonia one finds in the second and first millennium sources derives directly from the SKL. Here one may list the "Tummal Chronicle,"[83] "Ballade of Early Rulers,"[84] the "Dynastic Chronicle," the "Weidner Chronicle," and "Chronicle of Early Kings,"[85] all of which are dependent on the SKL. In fact, it is impossible to think of *any* instance where a different, attributable to an independent source, information on early Babylonia can be detected in later sources. This is remark-

---

79 Here note in particular the characterization of Gudea as dumu ama-na dumu ad-da nu-me-a, "he was not his mother's son, nor his father's son" (line 199). As observed already by Sollberger (1969: 286 n. 80), this description almost certainly goes back to Gudea's Cylinder A iii 6–8, where, addressing mother-goddess Gatumdug, Gudea rhetorically asserts that "I have no mother – you are mother; I have no father – you are my father; it is you who planted my seed in the womb! It is you who formed me in the 'womb'!" While not denying his human parentage, Gudea acknowledges here that his true mother – like of the entire humanity — is Gatumdug. See discussion in Essay 2 pp. 112–113. This nuance was missed by the author of the "Rulers of Lagaš," who had understood Gudea's words literally.

80 Sollberger 1969: 280 observes that "it is … difficult to imagine a scribe of the Ur-III or Early-Isin periods displaying such a crass ignorance of recent history, and especially of the reign of Gudea." As the other data bearing on the state of historical knowledge in the beginning of the second millennium demonstrate it, such a possibility actually is quite easy to imagine.

81 As this composition was characterized by its original editor. See Sollberger 1969: 280.

82 For these copies, see above p. 38.

83 For this composition, see most recently Michalowski 2006; Steinkeller 2015c: 157, 162–165.

84 Alster 2005: 288–322.

85 For the last three of these chronicles, see Grayson 1975.

able, since ancient inscriptions of all kinds undoubtedly were continuously being unearthed in Babylonia. The scribes and scholars must have known about them, but, characteristically, they chose not to use such evidence to modify or to alter the version of history preached in the canonical "stream of tradition."

For all these reasons, one may justifiably talk of the poverty of historical tradition in early Babylonia. This fact has not been generally recognized in scholarship. In truth, I cannot think of any cogent and extensive acknowledgment of this situation. This is not entirely surprising, since students of early Mesopotamia have generally (and perhaps understandably) been reluctant, for chauvinistic reasons if nothing else, to concede that "their" Sumerians may have been deficient on that score, and that the corpus of early cuneiform sources, which is so rich in all other respects, is not quite on a par with other ancient corpora (even those stemming from later Babylonia and Assyria) as far as historical records are concerned. Rather than accept this fact and its consequences – disappointing as they may be – many of them have tried instead to make more of the surviving historical texts than they in truth really are.

A good case in point is Jacobsen's edition of the SKL (Jacobsen 1939). Few will remember today that, prior to the publication of this work, scholars were quite sober in their assessment of the value of the SKL as a historical document, usually considering it of little use for the historian, especially as regards its treatment of the Early Dynastic period. Typical here is the opinion of B. Landsberger, who, in 1931, wrote as follows:

> Der Wert der Königsliste, der selbst in historisch völlig Perioden wegen ihrer Gepflogenheit, gleichzeitig regierende Dynastien hintereinander aufzuführen, beschränkt ist, ist für diese alten Zeiten noch geringer, wie sich aus den hohen Regierungsdaten, dem Fehlen wichtiger Namen wie Me-silim und Lugal-kisal-si ergibt. Wir haben den Eindruck, dass die in der späteren Zeit durch die Sage berühmt gewordenen Gestalten an beliebiger Stelle als Dynastiengründer untergebracht wurden. Jedenfalls sind hier sehr verschiedenartige Quellen ohne richtige historische tradition kompiliert worden. Daraus ergibt sich dass wir uns von der Königsliste vollständig emanzipieren müssen. (Landsberger 1931: 119)

It was in reaction to such views that Jacobsen had embarked on his SKL project, clearly with an objective of proving the SKL's historicity.[86] While Jacobsen's book is a masterpiece in many respects and a milestone in the history of Sumerian

---

86 Although Jacobsen's avowed goal was merely a "further study" of this composition (1939: 4), his real mission from its inception was to show it to be a genuine historical document. Thus his conclusion that the SKL is "a historical source of high value" (ibid. 167) comes as no surprise at all. For a critical assessment of Jacobsen's edition of the SKL, see now Marchesi 2010.

studies, his edition of the SKL itself is badly flawed, since, guided by the intention of presenting a single connected text, it conflates all the mss of the SKL together, ignoring the fact that some of them represent different, conflicting versions. Even worse, in some instances royal names that assuredly had not been part of the SKL, but which figure in historical inscriptions, were forced by Jacobsen into the text,[87] to fit both the historical sequence he favored and his idea of the SKL as a genuine historical document. While Jacobsen's book fostered the study of third millennium history, it also negatively affected its proper understanding, for it created an overconfident vision of this period, seemingly solid in its periodization and genealogical sequences, but actually deceiving in its concealment of various problems. Because of being so straightforward and persuasive, this vision of third millennium history immediately found broad appeal, especially among the archaeologists, who at times were too eager to accept the SKL as a word of truth. These negative consequences of Jacobsen's reconstruction can be felt even today, particularly in the area of chronology.

As examples of similar efforts to assign to Sumerian historical records considerably more substance and meaning than they actually possess may serve Kramer's presentation of the "Tummal Chronicle" as a genuine historiographic source[88] and Hallo's passionate defense of the authenticity of the "Ur III Royal Correspondence"[89] and similar corpora related to the kings of Isin and Larsa.[90]

How should the modern student of early Babylonia proceed from here? In my view, we have no choice but to acquiesce to the fact that the early Babylonians lacked a developed historical tradition. But such a realization does not constitute an entirely negative outcome. As I will try to show in the following discussion, the acceptance of the early historical tradition for what it really is opens up new heuristic horizons and suggests alternative directions for further inquiry.

---

87 Examples here are A'anepada of Ur and Enbi-Eštar of Kiš, whose names were "emended" by Jacobsen in his edition of the SKL. Cf. Marchesi 2010: 235.

88 Kramer 1963: 46–49.

89 For which see now Michalowski 2011.

90 Hallo 2001: 201; Hallo 2006. Note, especially, the following statement: "In fact, it can be argued that the royal correspondence of all three dynasties represents copies of actual letters originally deposited in the royal archives and selected by later generations of scribes for their bearing on matters of particular interest to them" (Hallo 2001: 201).

7 The Importance of Scribal Lore in Babylonia and Its Relevance for the Question of Early Historical Tradition

7.1 Introductory Remarks

The lack of interest in things historical in early Babylonia is countered by the existence, during the same timeframe, of an exceedingly strong and stable "scribal tradition." By the latter term I mean not only the corpora of lexical, literary, and scientific texts (as this designation is usually understood) but more broadly the cuneiform script itself and its various usages in the context of accounting and record keeping – in short, what I would call the know-how and techniques of administration. That the poverty of historical tradition should somehow be related to the strength of the "scribal tradition" so defined may seem to be a strange and questionable proposition. But, as I will show in the following, these two phenomena not only are closely connected, but also mutually interdependent.

The history of the "scribal tradition" reaches back to the very beginnings of cuneiform, as evidenced most visibly in the fact that already in the Uruk III period there existed a large body of lexical lists. Quite amazingly, copies of several of those lists survive from much later periods, indicating that the Uruk materials continued to be copied and usually further redacted throughout the third millennium. This was done not only in Babylonia itself, but also in northern Mesopotamia, northern Syria, and probably other peripheral areas as well. Of particular interest among those sources is the so-called Lu List A, a list of titles and occupations, which shows an unusually broad temporal and geographic distribution. A detailed discussion of it is offered below pp. 47–50.

In this connection, it is striking – and probably also significant – that the corpus of third millennium lexical and literary sources does not contain a single record of historical or chronographic nature. As far as we can tell, Sumerian scholars made no effort to deal with history in any serious way until the Ur III period, when the Ur III version of the SKL[91] and "The Curse of Akkade" were composed. It was only in early OB times that the "scribal tradition" began to include such sources under its purview. Among the texts copied by the OB scribes one finds a large collection of Sargonic royal inscriptions, a smaller collection of similar Ur III texts,[92] an inscription of Utu-hegal,[93] another one of Gudea,[94] and

---

91 As I noted earlier, there may have existed an earlier version of the SKL in Sargonic times. But the milieu in which that hypothetical version originated and its authors remain unknown.
92 This group is very small, being limited to a few of Šulgi's inscriptions and a larger collection of Šu-Suen's inscriptions.
93 For this inscription, see above p. 11.

the lists of Ur III and Isin year-names. As this listing shows,[95] none of them are earlier than the Sargonic period. Although copied and studied during OB times, this group of sources, which is quite small compared to the entire corpus of lexical and literary texts, did not become part of the later curriculum. Nor did that curriculum ever come to include any *new* historical inscriptions, such as the Middle Babylonian, Neo-Assyrian, and Neo-Babylonian ones. The latter no doubt were composed by scholars, the group of individuals known as *ummânū*, "*literati*, sages." But these scholars never copied them or treated as a subject of scholarly inquiry.[96]

7.2 The Archaic Lu A and Ad-gi₄ Lists

I return now to the question of the list Lu A.[97] As repeatedly observed by scholars, this list is distinguished by its exceptional temporal and geographic distribution. Composed in the Uruk III period,[98] Lu A was copied throughout the third millennium (ED II, ED IIIa, ED IIIb, Sargonic) and well into the second millennium (OB). Its copies were found at a large number of places in Babylonia itself (Ur, Šuruppak, Abu Salabikh, Adab, Lagaš, Nippur, Kisura, and possibly Sippar), as well as in several peripheral locations (Ebla in northwestern Syria, Nagar = Tell Brak in northern Mesopotamia, and Susa in western Iran) (Michalowski 2003). The great prestige that the Lu A enjoyed during the third millennium is illustrated by the fact that the Ebla scribes had used it as a matrix to develop their own version of a Sumerian syllabary.[99] Undoubtedly, to their minds the Lu A was the central and the most emblematic text of the Babylonian cuneiform culture.

The Lu A is a very extensive thematic lexical source, devoted entirely to human professions and titles. Some of its entries appear to have a more abstract

---

94 Wilcke 2011.

95 Here one should also mention the "Ur III Royal Correspondence," but this group of texts is a special case, since, even though some of the information contained in them may go back to the original Ur III prototypes, these alleged "letters" are for the most part pure fabrications.

96 Commenting on Babylonian scholars, Glassner 2015: 131 writes that "one is astonished by the remarkable effort they did in copying official inscriptions, studying royal correspondences, composing chronological lists, [and] chronicles." These characterizations are applicable only to the OB and later periods, and, even in reference to those, are grossly exaggerated.

97 See most recently Veldhuis 2014: 34–36, 72–76, 216–218, who offers an extensive discussion of this source and cites earlier literature.

98 Some of its mss may even date to Uruk IV, but this is far from certain.

99 Archi 1987.

sense, denoting the areas of professional responsibility.[100] The exact number of entries in the Uruk III version remains uncertain, since after line 41 the list is not rigidly standardized and often diverges from the ED version. The latter source, which is most completely preserved in the mss from Abu Salabikh and Ebla, contains 129 entries.

Although the Lu A underwent a degree of redaction over time, such modifications and changes being best detectable in the ED and OB versions, the level of similarity between all its versions is remarkable, if not even astounding. This is particularly true of the ED version, which, as aptly described by Veldhuis, "is by far the most frequently attested lexical text of the third millennium, with the widest geographical spread and the most rigid mode of standardization" (2014: 72). Of all the early lexical lists, the Lu A is the only source showing that high degree of conservatism and textual stability. This fact is even more remarkable when one considers the history of the Lu A's longevity and geographic diffusion.

It is clear that, already in ED times, scribal understanding of many of the signs and terms found in the archaic (Uruk III) version was highly deficient. Although the ED and later scribes tried their best to explicate such obscurities, it is a fair assumption that they more often erred than got it right. For this reason, later redactions, such as these appearing in the ED and OB versions, need to be treated with the utmost caution.[101]

---

100 This applies to the entries beginning with nam_2, for which see Appendix 1 pp. 98–99.

101 An obvious instance of a later misinterpretation is the entry MES-sanga in the ED version line 47, which replaces DUB-sanga in line 48 of the archaic version. Clearly, in this instance the ED scribe had misread DUB as MES. Another such case may be suspected in lines 80–83 of the ED version, which correspond to lines 82–85 of the archaic version:

Uruk III	ED
GAL.ZAG (82)	GAL.ZAG (80)
NESAG.ZAG (83)	NESAG.ZAG (81)
DAG.ZAG (84)	PA.DAG.ZAG (82)
DILMUN.ZAG (85)	DILMUN.ZAG (83)

The ED version contains three additional entries that include the sign ZAG, which do not appear in the Uruk III version: AN.PA.SUD.SIKIL.ZAG (84), PA.SUD.SIKIL.ZAG (85), and IDIGNA.ZAG (86). But these, as probably added in ED times, will not concern us here.

In the corresponding lines of the OB version (SLT 24 rev. ii' 1'–4' = CBS 13493; edited by Green 1984), ZAG is replaced by the syllabic writing $en-ku_3$: $en-ku_3$ gal, $en-ku_3$ nesag-ga_2, $en-ku_3$ da-kalam-ma, and $en-ku_3$ Dilmun-na. It is apparent that the ED scribe interpreted ZAG as an abbreviation/prototype of $ZAG.KU_6$ = enkud, consequently explaining these entries as listing various types of "tax collectors": the chief tax collector, the tax collector of (dues from) "first fruits", the tax collector (of the dues from the trade with) the borders of the Land, and the tax collector of (the dues from) Tilmun (trade). Following Green 1984, this understanding of the Uruk III and ED entries was universally adopted by scholarship (e. g., Taylor 2008: 207–208; Veldhuis 2014: 75).

It is commonly thought that the Lu A shows a hierarchical arrangement.[102] This conclusion is based mainly on the first entry of the list, reading nam$_2$-šita$_2$, which, beginning with Lambert 1981, was explained as designating the supreme ruler or at least the head of the Uruk administrative structure.[103] On this logic, the following titles and occupations were consequently taken by scholars to represent nam$_2$-šita$_2$'s various subordinates. However, if my suggestion that nam$_2$-šita$_2$ rather is a general term for the (cultic) employee of a temple household is correct (see Appendix 1 pp. 96–100), then the listing of titles and occupations in the Lu A probably does not follow any specific order.[104] Such a conclusion is corroborated by the fact that no clear hierarchical relationships can be detected among any of the other entries appearing in this list.

Be that as it may, in its original, archaic form the Lu A is a highly detailed listing of the members of Uruk's officialdom. The Lu A may even offer a global view of all such individuals of importance. The physical reality of these titles

---

However, there are grounds to think that the OB redactor of the list had been mistaken. The main reason here is the fact that, throughout the third millennium, the term enkud described specifically and *exclusively* an official in charge of fisheries and fishermen, and not a tax collector. See Amar-^{d}IB enkud (WF 69 viii), elsewhere identified as enkud šu-ku$_6$ (WF 67 xi, 68 ix 8–9); RIME 1 248–265 Urukagina 1 iii 11–13, viii 21–23; BPOA 1 1206:1–2; BPOA 2 2412; BPOA 6 1004, 1053; Hirose Collection 407; RSO 83 343 5; UET 3 1310; UTI 4 2577, 3284 (all Ur III; for other Ur III attestations consult BDTNS under "enku"). The enkud's preoccupation with fish also demonstrated by the inclusion of the sign KU$_6$, "fish," in the logogram [n.b. Green's suggestion 1984: 94 that KU$_6$ of ZAG.KU$_6$ is a phonetic indicator has no foundation.] It was only in OB times that enkud, for reasons unclear, became a general designation for "tax collector," standing now for Akk. *mākisu* (see CAD M/1 129–130). One can be reasonably certain, therefore, that this is how the glosses found in SLT 24 had originated.
If this section of the list deals with taxation at all, a much more likely explanation is that, in the entries in question, ZAG actually stands for zag-10 (Akk. *eširtu*), "tithe." Interestingly, in the Ur III and OB periods, there actually existed a tithe on the exports from Tilmun, which was paid to the temples of Nanna and Ningal at Ur. See Oppenheim 1954: 7; UET 3 341 (Ur III). Needless to say, this explanation would fit ZAG.DILMUN perfectly. For other examples of zag-10 in Ur III sources, usually paid to temples and priestly officials, see BDTS under "za$_3$-10." Accordingly, one may tentatively conclude that the ZAG section of the Lu A lists officials in charge of tithe collecting: "chief tithe (official)," "(official) of the tithe of 'first fruits,'" and so on. [N.b. the entry DAG.ZAG, which appears in line 84 of the archaic version, is matched by ZAG.GAL.DAG in the Uruk III tablet MSVO 3 61 ii 4.]
102 E. g. Wilcke 2005: 440. Wagensonner 2010: 293 writes that the "structure and possible hierarchy" of this list may "presumably mirror the Urukean human stratification at the time of the list's emergence." Bourguignon 2012: 253 suggests that the list is "'globalemant' hiérarchique."
103 For nam$_2$-šita, see in detail Appendix 1 pp. 96–100.
104 Towards this conclusion also leans Veldhuis 2014: 35–36.

and occupations is confirmed by the fact that many of them appear in the contemporaneous administrative records.[105]

Another Uruk III lexical text that had a similar history of later transmission, though not nearly as extensive as that of the Lu A, is the Ad-gi$_4$ (also known as "Archaic Word List C" or "Tribute List").[106] It is preserved in the mss dating to the Uruk III (Uruk), ED III (Fara, Tell Abu Salabikh, Ebla, and unknown origin); Ur III (Nippur), and OB periods (Nippur and unknown origin).[107] The Ad-gi$_4$ is formally quite different from other Uruk III lists. It was mainly this fact that led Miguel Civil (2013) to interpret it as a narrative text. In view of the enormous difficulties this source presents, Civil's interpretation, though full of excellent ideas, must be considered hypothetical in extreme. With the present knowledge of the archaic script, all that can be said with certainty is that the Ad-gi$_4$ deals with administrative matters and practices. One should possibly see in it an administrative manual, in the tradition of the later "Farmer's Instructions." Toward that solution point the mentions, in its opening section, of ad-gi$_4$, "advice" (line 1); ad-hal, perhaps "confidential" (line 3); ki sag, "capital/important place" (line 2); and abrig (Akk. *abriqqu*), probably identical with the later agrig (Akk. *abarakku*), "head of the temple household" (line 4).[108] When taken together, these lines could mean: "the abrig official (shared) confidential advice in a capital place (possibly referring to Uruk)." A striking (and unique) feature of the Ad-gi$_4$ is that its main and by far the longest section consists of an identical passage cited twice in succession: a listing of various counted items, which is followed by four entries, possibly representing titles (lines 5–32, 33–60). This feature suggests that the Ad-gi$_4$ had a pedagogical intent, such as rote learning, for example. One might even envisage that it served to examine prospective administrators. But, whatever the exact function of the Ad-gi$_4$ may have been, it is clear, I think, that it formed part of the administrative praxis *sensu stricto*.

7.3 Why Lexical Sources?

The histories of the Lu A and the Ad-gi$_4$ just outlined cannot but raise the following questions of broader nature: why this focus on lexical sources in the early

---

105 For the examples, see Bourguignon 2012; Veldhuis 2014: 34–35. See further nam$_2$-uru, found in the archaic Lu A line 5 and MSVO 3 61 i 4; and the various types of sanga officials, appearing both in the Lu A and economic tablets, which I discuss below p. 52 n. 113.
106 Recently edited and studied by Civil 2013.
107 Civil 2013: 51–54.
108 For this identification of abrig, see Civil 2013: 24–25.

"scribal tradition," and, even more important, why this persistent transmission of them both in time and in space? These questions are valid, since lexical lists, while obviously helpful, were not *indispensable* to the process of scribal training. Examples of other ancient literate civilizations that produced texts of all possible genres and types and possessed highly sophisticated systems of scribal training, but never felt a need to compile lexical lists – here Egypt, Greece and China come to mind most immediately – demonstrate this point very clearly. As a matter of fact, lexical lists are historically an exceedingly rare phenomenon, with Mesopotamia being the only ancient culture that created and used them extensively. Since they are so ubiquitous to us Assyriologists, we tend take them for granted, forgetting how unique and special they really are. One might even go so far as to say that lexical lists are one of the most characteristic features of ancient Mesopotamian civilization.

Rather than an essentially educational tool, I would rather see in them an expression of independent intellectual inquiry and, even more so, of *the solidarity of a particular professional and social group.* All of these individuals used writing as part of their work. But their professional training involved much more than the acquisition of cuneiform. In fact, that training concentrated *primarily* on computing and accounting methods, such as land surveying and the use of various measuring systems for solids and liquids. This know-how depended on a good grasp of mathematics, which was an essential (if not the basic) element of administrative curriculum already in Uruk III times.[109] It appears that already then this curriculum also taught applied astronomy, as used in calendrics and to predict and time seasonal events (especially the agricultural ones, such as seasonal floodings, seeding operations, and harvests). Of this we can be virtually certain because of the range of functions associated with the goddess Nisaba, the patron of writing, accounting, and various forms of computing, who famously oversaw astronomy as well.[110]

---

109 There survive two Uruk III sources that may be characterized as true mathematical texts (CUSAS 21 38 and CUSAS 31 8). As demonstrated by Monaco 2011a; 2014: 4–5; 2016: 4–5, these two tablets are sophisticated exercises involving the calculations of land areas. See also Fridberg 1998/99 for other Uruk III sources involving highly complex mathematical calculations.
110 As shown by the following examples: gi-dub-ba kug bar$_7$-a šu im-mi-du$_8$ dub mul an du$_{10}$-ga im-mi-gal$_2$ … e$_2$-a du$_3$-ba mul kug-ba gu$_3$ ma-ra-a-de$_2$, "(Nisaba) held a stylus of flaming metal; on her knees there was a tablet of heavenly stars, she was consulting it … she was calling out for you the holy star (controlling) the building of the temple" (Gudea Cylinder A iv 25 – v 1, vi 1–2); nin an mul gun$_3$-a dub za-gin$_3$ šu du$_8$, "(Nisaba) the lady of colorful heavenly stars, the one who holds a lapis lazuli tablet" (RA 7 107 lines 1–2; Ur III or earlier); munus mul-mul-la, "(Nisaba) the women of the stars" (BRM 4 46:4 + OLZ 7 253–254; Ur III?); an-ne$_2$ kuš$_3$ ra-ra ki eš$_2$ ra-ra, "(Nisaba) measures out the sky with a cubit (measure), she measures out the earth

In fact, it is striking that the mathematics and metrology of the Uruk III period far outstripped, in terms of sophistication and complexity, the contemporaneus writing system.[111] Therefore, it is quite certain that the Uruk IV–III script is to be explained as an outgrowth of mathematics.

That the administrative know-how was mainly concerned with computation and accounting is evident from the history of the term sanga (umbisag).[112] This term designates an important administrator in Uruk III times.[113] As was repeatedly noted by scholars, the sign with which this term is written, i.e., ŠID, depicts a counting device of some kind.[114] The connection of ŠID with counting is confirmed by its later meaning "to count" (šid, Akk. *manû*), and its forming part of

---

with a measuring rope" ("Temple Hymns" line 541). Cf. Klein and Sefati 2014. The antiquity of astronomy in Babylonia is further demonstrated by the Ebla usage of the word nig₂-mul(-an), "thing of the stars," i.e., "astral omen," as a generic term for "message." For the Ebla examples (though with a different interpretation), see Sallaberger 2003.

111 I owe this important insight to Christopher Woods. How advanced and sophisticated that early mathematical thinking was is demonstrated by the presence, in a number of Uruk III tablets, of what may be identified as the earliest examples of "contingency tables." See Woods 2015.

112 When signifying a title, ŠID has the alternative readings sanga and umbisag. The latter is equated with *ṭupšarru*, "scribe," in lexical sources. The original relationship between sanga and umbisag is unclear, though it is possible that both of them designated an accountant. Provisionally, I assume that, by the ED IIIb period, the reading umbisag had become obsolete, with the meaning "accountant, scribe" having been taken over by dub-sar. For dub-sar, see below. Concurrently, sanga came to mean the head of a temple household. Because of these ambiguities, in the context of Uruk III sources, I use only the reading sanga, translating it as "accountant."

113 In reference to the Uruk III sanga, Woods 2017: 436–437 notes the following: "It is plausible that writing sprung from the office of the sanga, possibly at Uruk, whose duties, as the chief administrator and accountant, were bound up with counting, and whose primary tool of the trade, the abacus, came also to represent, pictographically, the office itself."

The archaic Lu A lists several types of the sanga, among them gal-sanga, "chief accountant" (line 47), sanga-dub, "accountant of tablets" (line 48), sanga-simug, "accountant of smiths" (line 31), sanga-suhur, "accountant of carps" (line 72), sanga-kurušda, "accountant of animal fatteners" (line 97), and sanga-ZATU-737xDI (line 41). The "chief accountant" is very frequent in Uruk III economic sources (CUSAS 1 38 ii 2, 149 ii 2, 220 ii′ 1′, 5′; CUSAS 21 53 ii 2, 68; etc.). Even more common is the plural form gal-sanga-sanga, which often appears in the text's concluding section (CUSAS 1 27 end, 78 end, 93 ii, 154 end; et passim in this volume; MSVO 3 6 ii 4, 73 i 5, 75 iv 1, 77 i 1, 79 end; etc.). Other "accountants" listed in the archaic Lu that appear in economic tablets are sanga-dub (CUSAS 1 22:2′, 30 rev., 149 ii 4; CUSAS 21 81 ii′ 2′; ATU 5 pl. 72 W 9579,cf rev., pl. 77 W 9579,dx), sanga-simug (MSVO 4 16 rev. ii′), sanga-kurušda (ATU 5 pl. 14 6738,b), and sanga-ZATU-737xDI (CUSAS 1 81 ii′). Note also sanga-ab₂-udu, "accountant of cattle and sheep" (MSVO 4 32 ii′ 2′; ATU 2 pl. 18 W 20274,1 i 5), who, though not attested in the extant mss of the archaic Lu A, is named in line 99 of the ED version.

114 Probably an abacus or counting board, similar to the Inka *yapuna*. See now in detail Woods 2017.

nig$_2$-ŠID-ak, "an account." These facts demonstrate beyond any doubt that the early sanga (umbisag) primarily was an accountant – though of course he used to write tablets as well.[115]

The same was true of the dub-sar, who, by the ED IIIb period,[116] had replaced the sanga (umbisag) as the accountant par excellence. Although the etymology of dub-sar demonstrates his connection with writing ("tablet writer'"), the dub-sar's role, as it can be gathered from the economic and literary sources (particularly the so-called "Edubba literature"), was that of a certified accountant or manager. An examination of the functions performed by the individuals so titled, especially as reflected in the more complex kinds of economic records, makes it abundantly clear that the writing of tablets represented but one facet of their work. A good example here are the Ur III agricultural estimates from Girsu/ Lagaš, which have the form of balanced accounts.[117] It is apparent that the actual preparation of these records was but a concluding and largely insignificant element of a complex process that involved several measuring and accounting procedures, performed with little if any recourse to writing: the surveying of fields to be cultivated and the assessment of the soil's quality; the estimates of the grain needed as seed and fodder for draft animals and the wages of plowing teams and associated personnel; and the final calculations of grain on hand against its projected expenses. All the know-how needed to perform such operations was part of the Ur III and Early OB administrative schooling,[118] and so the

---

115 The colophons of the ED IIIa lexical and literary texts from Fara and Abu Salabikh frequently mention individuals identified as sangas, who undoubtedly were the authors of the texts in question. As suggested by Biggs 1974: 33 n. 29, some of the Fara sangas so attested seem to appear as dub-sars in the economic tablets from that site.

116 The earliest attestation of this title is found in a display inscription from Kiš, which dates to the ED II period (or possibly even ED I). See Steinkeller 2013a and above p. 35. This title is common in Fara texts, where it seems to interchange with sanga (see the preceding note).

117 See, e. g., CT 7 8 BM 12926; TuT 5; ASJ 3 50 BM 18060.

118 The "Edubba Literature" is particularly informative here, as it shows that mathematics, accounting, and measuring were essential elements of the scribal/administrative curriculum. See the following examples: "Do you know multiplication, reciprocals, coefficients, balancing of accounts, administrative accounting, how to make all kinds of pay allotments, divide property, and delimit shares of fields?" ("Edubba A" line 27); "you have learned perfectly multiplication, inverted numbers, accounting and calculation of volume" ("Dialog 1" line 6); "go to divide a field ... go to delimit a field — but you will not be able to hold the tape and the measuring rod; the pegs of the field you will not be able to drive in and so you will not get (its) 'meaning'" ("Dialog 3" lines 21–23) (all three cited after Sjöberg 1975: 167–168); "I can handle equally well Sumerian, scribal work, tablet content, calculation, and accounting, ... I am going to write tablets now: a tablet with (the volumes of) barley from one bushel to 600 bushels (and) a tablet with (the weights of) silver from one shekel to ten minas" ("Edubba D" lines 37–42 = Civil 1985).

title of dub-sar essentially meant a professional certification, the fact that its bearer successfully completed his education and was fit to be a manager (Michalowski 1987: 62). Once becoming certified "managers," these functionaries would then specialize in specific administrative tasks, such as field-surveying (sag-du$_5$), record-keeping (pisan-dub-ba(-k)), estimating the land productivity (sar$_2$-ra-ab-du), and so forth.[119]

For these reasons, the administrative know-how should be seen as a package combining a number of tools, one of which – but not necessarily the most important one – was writing. However, because of the physical visibility of texts, the importance of those other tools of administration tends to be underappreciated or even ignored.[120] As I argued elsewhere (2004a), many highly developed and successful civilizations operated without the benefit of writing. Other early literary civilizations did not use writing extensively for the purposes of administration, relying instead on various accounting devices (see above). For this question, the case of prehistoric Babylonia is particularly informative. As generally accepted, cuneiform, an "invention" of the Uruk IV period, came to be widely used in administration in Uruk III times. It is evident, however, that already centuries earlier there existed a sophisticated system of accounting and recording methods, which depended on the use of tokens, bullae, abaci or counting boards, and similar para-writing devices. Reflections of these methods survive in the Uruk III measures. As reconstructed by Damerow and Englund,[121] economic tablets of that period employ at least twelve different measuring systems, which are represented in writing by system-specific numerical graphs. Most of them involve volume measures, each being reserved for a specific substance, such as barley, wheat, barley groats, milk, malt, and beer. These graphic conventions must have arisen from a situation in which each of the substances in question was kept in and measured with a size- and shape-specific container. It be-

---

119 This is shown by the fact that such specialized officials are often subsumed as "managers" (dub-sar). See Steinkeller 2013d: 358 n. 52 where one such case is discussed.

120 Typical here is the position of Glassner 2014, who, in his discussion of the Uruk III society, concentrates exclusively on writing, which he imagines to have been a tool of power, used by the political elites to dominate the society. I believe that this opinion is untenable, simply because it is impossible to see how the limited use of written sources at that early time could have been a tool of political oppression – and Glassner does not expand on that point. If anything, it would have been my "administrative package" – and not just writing – that served such ends. In the following I suggest that at least some of the Uruk III texts indeed had a meta application, but its nature was quite different from that argued by Glassner. Glassner's ideas undoubtedly derive from Lévi-Strauss' concept of writing as the technology of repression, which I address earlier in this essay.

121 Damerow and Englund 1987.

comes obvious, therefore, that the Uruk III measure-graphs duly reproduce the units of measure used in real life. Given the conservative nature of measures, one can be certain that the history of these systems was very ancient, going back at least to Uruk IV, and probably much earlier.

The use of these multiple measuring systems in writing must have been incredibly cumbersome, and so highly impractical as well. Thus, already in the ED IIIa period (if not earlier), these systems were streamlined and simplified, with the old volume measures having been reduced to just two: one for solids and another one for liquids. This development shows that the introduction of writing significantly impacted the administrative praxis, mainly by expanding its conceptual range, and by fostering abstract thinking. Most important, it has now become much easier to engage in various forms of prognostication. This made administrative operations more efficient, in turn increasing economic productivity.

Still, even in the late third millennium the use of written records in administration by was no means automatic. Whether or not writing was employed generally depended on the complexity of the economic system: the more centralized and complex it was, the more written documentation was produced. In a completely decentralized situation, however, one could still get by without written records, by using traditional para-writing methods, such as tokens and counting devices.

These somewhat disparate observations about accounting, writing, and administrative practices have hopefully convinced the reader that the authors of the Lu A, the Ad-gi$_4$ and other early lexical lists were administrators first and foremost. This fact is often lost on Assyriologists, who, because of their concern with the written, too often think of these individuals solely as scribes. Equally inappropriate is to envision them as a sort of *savants* or *érudits*, who, in the fashion of the regulars of Café de Flore, spent their days discussing esoteric problems. This they did too, of course, but one should keep a sense of proportion.

To paraphrase the famous Baconian axiom, administrative knowledge is power, and the group that controlled this type of knowledge in early Babylonia seems to have safeguarded it and their social position very closely.[122] It appears

---

122 As put succinctly by Max Weber: "Bureaucratic administration means fundamentally domination through knowledge. This is the feature of it which makes it specifically rational. This consists on the one hand in technical knowledge which by itself, is sufficient to ensure it a position of extraordinary power. But in addition to this, bureaucratic organizations, or the holders of power who make use of them, have the tendency to increase their power still further by the knowledge growing out of experience in the service. For they acquire through the conduct of of-

that one of the ways in which they derived their legitimacy was by tracing their know-how all the way back to the prehistoric age. This they accomplished most palpably by recopying the Lu A, the Ad-gi₄ and other archaic lists generation after generation, at the same time making certain that the archaic character of these sources was preserved as closely as possible. By so doing they were able to demonstrate to their political leaders that, before there were kings and dynasties, bureaucrats had ruled supreme.

In this light, the Lu A emerges as a founding charter of the Managerial Class, which, by virtue of its enormous antiquity and prestige, legitimized the political claims of this social group, many of whose members could actually find their own particular titles and occupations in this charter. As we shall see subsequently, identical concerns preoccupied the later generations of the Managerial Class as well, prompting them to invent other types of sources that legitimized their social standing and furthered their political ambitions.

A similar, though not as far reaching in its conclusions, assessment of the Lu A was offered by Veldhuis:

> The relevance of ED Lu A in the third millennium and beyond is not located in its vocabulary but in its archaic character, connecting scribes with their ancient predecessors. As such ED Lu A is probably the most powerful symbol of scribal identity that was available in the third millennium. (2014: 76)[123]

As a distinctive and solidly entrenched social group, the Managerial Class of Babylonia must have had its own political agenda, which probably more often than not was at odds with the politics of the king. As I define it, this group included some of the highest officials of city-states, such as sanga and sabra, the heads of temple households, who yielded enormous power, both economic and political. In some of the smaller city-states and many of the major cities, for example in Isin, Larsa, Keš, Karkar, Zabalam, and Girsu, the sanga in fact was the main administrative official.[124] These functionaries undoubtedly were vested in

---

fice a special knowledge of facts and have available a store of documentary material peculiar to themselves" (1978: 225).

123 Such an understanding of the character of the Lu A was anticipated already by R. D. Biggs and H. J. Nissen, MSL 12, 4: "Since some of the signs and entries of the list already appear to be anachronistic in the Fara period, there is good reason to ask whether some unknown cultural value, other than the mere lexicographic one, contributed to its prestige."

124 In ED times, the sanga of the temple household of Inana in Zabalam and that of the temple household of Ningirsu in Girsu operated almost independently of the ensiks of Umma and Lagaš respectively. Among other things, this is shown by the use of dating formulae in which both the ensik and the sanga are named. For Umma and Zabalam, see Monaco 2011b: 6–8. For Lagaš and

the preservation of the traditional system of political organization, in which the real power rested with the temple households operating as largely independent and self-sufficient socio-economic institutions. A tension and rivalry between this group and the king can be detected in Lagaš during the reign of Urukagina, whose famous "reforms" aimed to reduce the influence of precisely such officials. We witness their influence again at Lagaš during the reign of Šar-kali-šarri, when these high officials, named *bēlū parṣī*, "temple(-household) administrators," sold the landed possessions of the main temple households of that city-state to the king of Akkade.[125] It makes sense to assume that the Managerial Class so understood was naturally inclined to oppose the principle of hereditary dynastic rule, thus constituting a force that consistently frustrated attempts to bring strong kings to power.

Is the absence of historical inscriptions and chronographic sources I talked about earlier attributable to that disconnect between the political objectives of the Managerial Class and those of the kings? Did the Managerial Class purposely obstruct the development of historical and chronographic sources? Did they perhaps even conspire to blot out historical memory, or at least to bend it to their own particular ends? Given the hostility of this group toward the dynastic rule and the ideology that went along with this form of government, I think that such a possibility should be considered very seriously.

At the very least we know that, in one particular instance, the Managerial Class was able to impose their own vision of history on the official line. The case I am referring to is the Old Babylonian list of the antediluvian cities and their rulers.

Girsu, see RTC 16 vi 3 – vii 3, whose date-formula names the ensik En-metena and the sanga En-entarzi. See further RIME 1, 231–234 Enmetena 27–29, which concern En-metena and the sanga of Ningirsu named Dudu (who probably was En-entarzi's predecessor). This Dudu is likely identical with the dub-sar Dudu, who dedicated his statue to Ningirsu (Strommenger 1962: figs. 86 and 87). If so, we would find here an instance of the "manager" becoming eventually a sanga. Some of these sangas (Il of Zabalam and En-entarzi of Girsu) were so powerful that they succeeded in becoming ensiks themselves.
125 Steinkeller 1999b: 555–565.

7.4 The Antediluvian King List

The list of the antediluvian cities and rulers (henceforth AKL) forms the beginning section of the SKL (lines 1–38).[126] This list is reproduced almost *verbatim* in the first millennium "Dynastic Chronicle."[127] The names of the antediluvian rulers, as they appear in the SKL, are also cited in the Hellenistic version of the "Story about the Seven Sages."[128] Yet another, but considerably altered, version of the SKL is incorporated into the second book of "Babyloniaca."[129]

The AKL lists five cities, which are Eridu, Patibira, Larak, Šuruppak, and Sippar. One of its mss (UCBC-9–1819) names Kuwara instead of Eridu, but this is a point of no significance, since Kuwara was Eridu's satellite. A more significant deviation is presented by the addition of Larsa in W-B 62. As usually explained, this addition probably reflects the "local patriotism" of the author of that particular ms (so already Jacobsen 1939: 72).

The AKL begins with the statement: "when kingship was lowered down from heaven" (nam-lugal an-ta e_3-de$_3$-a-ba; line 1). Five cities, their respective rulers, and the lengths of the latter's reigns are then enumerated. The essentials of this listing may be summarized as follows:

Eridu	Alulim[130]
	Alalgar[131]
Patibira	En-me(n)luana[132]
	En-me(n)galana[133]
	Dumuzi (sipad)

---

126 For a recent, very exhaustive study of this source, see Chen 2013. To the mss cited there (ibid. 183), add George 2011: 199–205 nos. 96, 97, and 98. The sigla of the mss of the AKL used in the present study follow Chen ibid. 183.

127 Grayson 1975: 140 lines 1′–14′.

128 SpBTU 2 8, discussed below pp. 71–73.

129 Burstein 1978: 18–19. This account names ten antediluvian "kings," assigning them to Babylon, Patibira (Pautibiblon), and Larak (Laragchos). As secondary and therefore unreliable, these data are exluded from the following discussion.

130 Spellings: A-lu-lim and A$_2$-lu-lim. Appears as A-a-lu in BagM Beih. 2 89:1 and as A-lu-lu in "The Ballade of Early Rulers" line 9 and various other sources (see below pp. 61 n. 143, 64).

131 Spellings: A-lal$_3$-gar, E-lal$_3$-gar, and E-lal-gar. Appears as A-la$_2$-al-gar in BagM Beih. 2 89:2.

132 Spellings: En-me-en-lu$_2$-an-na, [En]-ˈmenˈ-lu-an-na, Am-me-lu-an-na, and Am-mi-lu$_2$-an-na. Appears as Am-me-lu-an-na SpBTU 2 8:3. For the interchange of men and me-en with me in early onomasticon, which appears in this name and in En-me(n)galana and En-me(n)durana/En-me)nduranki, see Steinkeller 2015b.

133 Spellings: En-me-en-gal-an-na, En-me-gal-an-na, and Am-me-gal-an-na. Appears as Am-me-gal-an-na in BagM Beih. 2 89:4.

Larak   En-sipadziana[134]
Šuruppak   Ubur-Tutu[135]
          Ziudsudra (only in some mss)
Sippar   En-me(n)durana/En-meduranki[136]

The AKL concludes with the statement: "the Deluge (then) swept over" (a-ma-ru ba-ur₃; line 39).[137] Immeditaly following, the introduction of dynastic history proper is described: "after the Deluge swept over, kingship was lowered down from heaven" (a-ma-ru ba-ur₃-ra-ta / nam-lugal an-ta e₃-de₃-a-ba; lines 40–41).

As universally agreed by all the modern students of the SKL, the antediluvian section represents a later addition. This is confirmed by the fact that the AKL is not part of the oldest surviving ms of the SKL, which was written down in Ur III times (likely during the reign of Šulgi).[138] The precise date when this section was added to the SKL cannot be ascertained with certainty. However, the fact that the AKL is closely connected with the Deluge tradition, whose earliest attestations seem to belong to the twentieth century BC (see below), indicates that this happened either in the Isin-Larsa period or sometime later in OB times.

That the AKL is a secondary development, which was grafted on the SKL by using the latter's internal logic and formal pattern, is demonstrated most clearly by the fact that the introductory line of the AKL, "when/after kingship was lowered down from heaven (kingship was in Eridu, and so on)," is a borrowing of line 41 of the SKL. Apart from proving that the AKL is a derivative of the SKL, this borrowing is also crucial for understanding of the AKL's intent, which is to show that there were two separate appearances of kingship in Babylonia: the original one, which resulted in the founding of five antediluvian cities and was terminated by the Deluge; and another one, which took place following the Deluge and led to the founding of other cities and the advent of what may be described as dynastic history *sensu stricto*. In other words, dynastic history

---

134 Spellings: En-sipad-zi-an-na and ʼAm-me-sipad-zi-anʼ-na. Appears as E[n-m]e-ušum-gal-an-na in BagM Beih. 2 89:5.

135 Spellings: Ubur-Tu-tu and Ubur-Du-du. For this name, see below n. 142.

136 Spellings: En-me-en-dur₂-an-na, Am-me-dur-an-na, En-me-dur-an-ki, and Me-dur-an-ki. Appears as En-me-dur-an-ki in SpBTU 2 8:7, the "Enmeduranki Text" (see below p. 63), and a number of other late sources. The spellings with -dur-an-na almost certainly are original. This is shown by the fact that there was a zikkurat of Šamaš at Larsa called E₂-dur-an-na (George 1993: 80 no. 220). [Nb. the same structure is elsewhere, erroneously, identified as E₂-dur-an-ki, see George 1993: 80 no. 219.] On the other hand, Dur-an-ki was traditionally associated with Inana/Ištar and Nippur. For this opinion, see already Jacobsen 1939: 75.

137 In the following discussion, I refer to this catastrophic event as "Deluge," to distinguish it from the regular seasonal floods that are designated by the same Sumerian term a-ma-ru.

138 See above pp. 40–41.

was preceded by a sort of "history before history" or "pre-history," the two being separated by the Deluge. This point is made explicit by one of the mss of the AKL, which concludes with a note that "(after) the Deluge had descended(?), kingship was lost" (George 2011: 201 no. 97:27).

An account closely similar to the AKL is preserved in the Sumerian "Deluge Story" lines 88–98. The latter composition lists the same five cities in identical order, but makes no mention of their rulers, though it adds the names of their respective divine masters. Like the AKL, this account too places the founding of the five cities after the anonymous lowering of kingship from heaven. In contrast to the AKL, however, it attributes the founding activity to a divine agent whose name is not preserved, but who can plausibly be identified as Enlil. Enlil not only established the five cities, but also gave them their names and assigned to them their divine masters. Although not mentioned here, Ziudsudra of Šuruppak, identified as "king" (lugal) and a gudu$_4$ priest, makes an appearance later in the story (lines 145, 209, and 257). The Deluge follows then, demonstrating that, as in the AKL, the five cities in question belonged to the antediluvian past.

The motif of a cataclysmic Deluge that destroyed Babylonia at some point in her early history is central both to the AKL and the Sumerian "Deluge Story." A closely similar Deluge narrative appears in the OB story about Atra-hasis. Various allusions to it are also found in a number of Sumerian literary compositions, which usually take the form of an introductory phrase "after the Deluge wept over," emphasizing the temporal remoteness of a particular event. As is generally recognized by scholarship,[139] there is nothing in the surviving corpus of Sumerian and Akkadian sources of all genres that would allow us to detect the existence of the Deluge motif during the third millennium. Here it is additionally significant that the Ur III version of SKL, which preserves the beginning of this composition, makes no mention of the Deluge in this context. With the evidence presently available, it is fair to conclude that this motif is a product of the Old Babylonian period.[140] Equally uncertain remains the question of the linguistic and cultural background of this motif. Since the "Deluge Story" takes place in Sumer and involves Sumerian rulers and deities, an assumption of its Sumerian origins is usually favored. But the existence of the OB "Atra-hasis Story", which, in terms of its witnesses, is a contemporary of its Sumerian counterpart, leaves open a possibility that the Deluge motif actually comes from elsewhere (either

---

139 See most recently Chen 2013.
140 The earliest example of the phrase "after the Deluge swept over" appears in a hymn dedicated to Išme-Dagan of Isin. See Civil in Lambert 1969: 139. Unless this attestation results from a later OB redaction, this would permit us to date its appearance to ca. 1950 BC.

from the Akkadian cultural milieu or perhaps even from some other, foreign tradition). It cannot even be excluded that the Deluge narrative was an *ad hoc* invention, which was perpetrated by the OB scribes to advance the same propagandistic causes that led to the creation of the AKL.

7.5 The Antediluvian Kings

As I hope to demonstrate it fully in the following discussion, the most striking fact about the antediluvian "kings" as they appear in the AKL is that they were no ordinary rulers. One should rather identify them as sage-kings, not unlike those of the Confucian tradition, who were thought to be "ideal rulers of antiquity who by combining the virtue and wisdom of a sage with the power of a king exemplified perfection in government."[141]

In order that this point may become fully apparent, a detailed examination of the names and identities of the nine personae in question is required. The first observation emerging from such an investigation is that none of them can be traced back to the third millennium. The only exception here is Ubur-Tutu, the ruler of Šuruppak and (but only in some versions of the AKL) the father of Ziudsudra, whose name can plausibly be traced back to the ED version of the composition "Instructions of Šuruppak."[142] This fact alone is sufficient to conclude that all nine of these antediluvian "kings" are artificial creations.

Like the name of Ubur-Tutu, those of Alulim and Alalgar of Eridu may also have been derived from ancient material, but there is no assurance of that.[143] The

---

141 Quoting the definition of Merriam-Webster Dictionary, online version.

142 One may be reasonably certain that the name Ubur-Tu-tu/Du-du was derived from the phrase Šuruppak ušbar$_x$(UR$_2$.RUM), "the one of Šuruppak, an ušbar$_x$," which is found in the ED version of "Instructions of Šuruppak" line (Alster 2005: 176, 196). In this example, ušbar$_x$ means either "weaver" or "father-in-law." While the source of the element Tu-tu/Du-du is unclear, ubur in all likelihood is an OB interpretation of the ED ušbar$_x$. It may be envisioned that the ED Šuruppak ušbar$_x$ became, in the AKL, Šuruppak^{ki} Ubur-Tu-tu, "in Šuruppak, Ubur-Tutu (was 'king')." This passage was then misinterpreted as "Šuruppak *of* Ubur-Tutu," resulting eventually in Šuruppak dumu Ubur-Tutu, "Šuruppak, son of Ubur-Tutu," which is found in the OB "Instructions of Šuruppak" line 7 (Alster 2005: 57). The final product of this development was Šuruppak dumu Ubur-Tu-tu ... Zi-ud-sud-ra$_2$ dumu Šuruppak-ke$_2$, "Šuruppak, son of Ubur-Tutu ... Zi-ud-sud-ra$_2$ son of Šuruppak," which appears in the ms. W-B 62 of the AKL (Chen 2013: 140).

143 While no direct parallels for Alulim can be found, his alternative name A-lu-lu, which is found in the "Ballade of Early Kings" line 9 and various first millennium sources (see p. 64) appears in Fara and Pre-Sargonic sources as A-lu-lu (Pomponio 1987: 7; CUSAS 11 364 i 2) and A-lu$_5$-

largest group of names in this group conforms to the pattern beginning with En-"Lord" and ending with -ana(k), "of heaven/An." Here belong:

> En-me(-en)-lu$_2$-an-na of Patibira
> En-me(-en)-gal-an-na of Patibira
> En-sipad-zi-an-na of Larak
> En-me(-en)-dur-an-na of Sippar

The name pattern in question is typical of ceremonial priestly names, a tradition that began with En-he$_2$-du$_7$-an-na, en priestess of Nanna and daughter of Sargon,[144] and continued into the reign of Ibbi-Suen with the following examples[145]:

> En-men-an-na, en priestess of Nanna and daughter of Naram-Suen[146]
> En-nir-zi-an-na, en priestess of Nanna (year-name Šulgi 15)
> En-ubur-zi-an-na, en priestess of Nanna (year-name Šulgi 43)
> En-me-zi-an-na, the cultic name of Ur-Ningirsu, the en and the šennu priest of Nanše during the reigns Šulgi – Ibbi-Suen[147]
> En-mah-gal-an-na, en priestess of Nanna (year-name Amar-Suen 4 and UET 1 64)
> En-unu$_6$-gal-an-na, en priest of Inana (year-name Amar-Suen 5)
> En-nun-gal-an-na, en priestess of Enki (year Amar-Suen 8)
> En-am-gal-an-na, en priest of Inana (year-name Ibbi-Suen 4)
> En-nir-zi!-an-na, en priest of Inana (year-name Ibbi-Suen 10)[148]

It appears quite certain that it was precisely this body of onomastics that served to generate the four antediluvian names in question. By using this name pattern, the authors of the AKL referenced the high priests of Sargonic and Ur III times, who happened to be linear descendants of the Priests-Kings of Uruk as well. In

---

lu$_5$ (BIN 8 349:34). For Alalgar, which is spelled A-lal$_3$-gar or E$_2$-lal$_3$-gar, compare the Fara names A-lal$_3$ and E$_2$-lal$_3$ (Pomponio 1987: 7, 83).

144 As demonstrated by En-šag$_4$-kuš$_2$-an-na, the name of a late Pre-Sargonic king of Uruk, such names were known, and probably used by the en priests of Inana, already in ED times. In this connection, note also En-suh-keš$_2$-an-na, the name of a mythical king ruler of Aratta, who competes with Enmerkar for Inana's attentions in the composition "Enmerkar and En-suhkeš-ana". While En-suh-keš$_2$-an-na obviously is an artificial creation, it shows that the author of this composition associated this name-pattern with the early history of Uruk.

145 The only name of this category that diverges from this pattern is En-an-ne$_2$-pad$_3$-da, the en priestess of Nanna and the daughter of Ur-Bau of Lagaš. See Steinkeller 1999a: 127–128.

146 Sollberger 1954/1956: 26–28. She is also mentioned, in a broken context, in an Ur III tablet from Ur (UET 3 864:15; date not preserved), where her posthumous cult apparently is meant.

147 See Steinkeller 1999: 119.

148 Attested only in UET 1 295 i 5, where the sign looks like SUM but probably is a misshapen ZI. If SUM indeed was meant, read si$_3$ for zi.

this way, they were also able to link their antediluvian inventions with the most ancient manifestation of Babylonian kingship.

Apart from being modeled after the high priests of yore, who were leaders of a distinctly different kind, the four antediluvian "kings" in question show other characteristics that place them within that same ancient cultural and political tradition, and identify them as sage-kings. Both En-me(n)luana and En-me(n) galana are known to have been forms of Dumuzi the shepherd, their successor in Patibira.[149] The same was true of En-sipadziana of Larak.[150] As I hypothesized earlier,[151] there likely existed a belief that made Dumuzi one of the archaic rulers (en) of Uruk, on par with Lugal-banda and Gilgameš. If such a tradition indeed existed, he and his avatars En-me(n)luana, En-me(n)galana, and En-sipadziana would be fitting examples of the "semi-divine 'cultural heroes,'"[152] the wise leaders of old who were priests and rulers alike.

A connection with wisdom and learning is even clearer in the case of En-me-durana/En-meduranki of Sippar. According to a first millennium source known as the "Enmeduranki Text,"[153] this antediluvian "king" received extispicy and other divinatory arts, as well as mathematics,[154] directly from Šamaš and Adad, the gods of divination. These intellectual gifts En-meduranki then shared with other Babylonians. The text subsequently goes on to describe in great detail the characteristics qualifying one to become a member of the diviners' guild, making it crystal clear that its function was to demonstrate the antiquity of this professional group, and so to legitimize its socio-political position. For these reasons, the "Enmeduranki Text" may be characterized as a founding charter of the diviners' guild, whose intent was quite similar to that of the Lu A list I have discussed earlier.

Since Sippar was home of Šamaš, there is a strong likelihood that the tradition connecting En-me(n)durana/ki with divination and other areas of knowl-

---

149 See Lambert 1969: 26–27.
150 See Lambert 1969: 26–27. Two versions of the AKL (UCBC 9–1819 and Ni. 3195) assign him to Patibira instead, probably precisely because of the Dumuzi connection.
151 Pp. 29–30 above.
152 The term used by Hallo (1970: 63) in reference to Sanchuniathon, a legendary Phoenician sage, priest, and author.
153 See Lambert 1967: 132–133; 1998. A similar tradition about En-me(n)durana/ki is preserved in the bilingual composition known as the "The Seed of Kingship" (Lambert 1967: 128–131; 1974: 434–440; Chen 2013: 150), where Nebuchadnezzar I is described as "distant seed of kingship, seed preserved from before the Deluge, offspring of Enmeduranki, king of Sippar, the one who set up the pure bowl and carried cedar (oil), who sat in the presence of Šamaš and Adad, the divine judges" (lines 8–10).
154 arâ(a.ra₂)ᵃ šu-ta-bu-l[u] (line 18).

edge existed already in OB times. Interestingly, "Babyloniaca" identifies Sippar as the place where antediluvian knowledge, written on tablets, had been stored prior to the Deluge, to be subsequently recovered by the Deluge's survivors.[155] Somewhat contradictorily, another late source ("Erra Epic" IV 50) describes Sippar as the only city that was not destroyed by the Deluge. Irrespective of this inconsistency, these accounts attest to Sippar's reputation as a city of learning and great antiquity.

A very similar reputation was shared by Šuruppak, a renowned ancient city in its own right and home of the antediluvian "kings" Ubur-Tutu and Ziudsudra. I have already shown that Ubur-Tutu was created out of the anonymous sage of Šuruppak, the alleged author of sayings of wisdom collected in an ED source, which, together with their author, were redacted in OB times into a composition titled "Instructions of Šuruppak." As for Ziudsudra, extant Sumerian sources do not describe him as a sage. But he must have been known as such, since the Akkadian version of the "Deluge Story" names him Atra-hasis, "Exceedingly Wise." There was a cultic side to Ziudsudra as well, since the Sumerian "Deluge Story" identifies him as a gudu$_4$ priest (for this official, see Appendix 1 pp. 86–87). This, too, shows that he was a "king" of a very special mould.[156]

It is superfluous to say that the characteristics just described attach also, and in a much greater measure, to Eridu, the first antediluvian city appearing in the AKL. As the ancients believed, Eridu was *the* source of Babylonian knowledge, which emanated from Enki and his shrine Abzu, and which was further disseminated by Enki's various companions and attendants, such as the sages (abgal), of whom Adapa is best known. Unfortunately, the identities of the two antediluvian "kings" of Eridu, Alulim and Alalgar, remain largely unknown. But we can be practically certain that they were sage-kings as well. The first of them appears in two first millennium incantations, where, under the name of A-lu-lu, he is presented as a magician, expert in controlling field pests.[157] Another late source implies that he obtained this knowledge from the sage Adapa.[158] Alulim's connection with Adapa is also recorded in BagM Beih. 2 89,[159] where, as A-a-lu, he is paired with U$_4$-an-na, an alternative name or form of Adapa. Very likely, therefore, both Alulim and Alalgar were Adapa-like figures. It undoubtedly was for all these reasons that the authors of the AKL chose to

---

155 Cited below p. 75.

156 For an extensive discussion of the role of Ziudsudra in the Babylonian wisdom tradition, see Beaulieu 2007: 3–7.

157 George and Taniguchi 2010: 136–137.

158 STT 176+185. See Lambert 1969: 27 under (f); George and Taniguchi 2010: 136.

159 For this source, see below pp. 72–73.

begin their antediluvian history – which, as I believe, is a history of early Babylonian learning – with Eridu, making Eridu its original source but also the place from where over time that learning was transmitted to other places.

These conclusions – or speculations, to be more exact – about the nature of history treated by the AKL find a nice corroboration in one of its mss (George 2011: 201 no. 97), where the names of Eridu and Sippar are written with the signs NUN.ME = abgal, "sage," instead of the standard spellings with a single NUN sign. I believe that these spellings are intended, their purpose being to identify these two cities as the seats of wisdom, and so to implicate their rulers as sage-kings.[160]

7.6 The Figure of abgal, *apkallu*

The last point brings us to the question of sages proper (abgal, *apkallu*), who, at least in the view of the first millennium literary tradition, were closely linked to the antediluvian cities and their rulers.

I begin with the history of the abgal. The term abgal = NUN.ME figures already in the archaic Lu A list line 15.[161] This is how this lexeme is written in all later sources, except in ED IIIb Lagaš texts and Gudea, which consistently use the writing abgal$_2$(NUN.ME.KAxŠE$_3$) instead.[162] A possible syllabic spelling ab$_2$-gal appears in an ED IIIb text from Nippur.[163]

Persons bearing the title of abgal appear in Fara economic tablets, but no indication is given in them of those persons' particular duties, except perhaps in TSS 558 (distribution of field plots to various named individuals), which suggests that these individuals wrote cuneiform tablets. The final column of this text contains a single abgal sign, which possibly identifies the tablet's author.

More informative in this respect are two incantations, also of ED IIIa date, which show that the abgal was involved in the construction of temples. In

---

160 George 2011: 201 speculates similarly (but somewhat more prosaically) that "this mistake probably arose from an intrusion in the writer's mind of the mythological tradition that placed the sages in the antediluvian era."

161 This title appears also in Uruk III economic tablets. See, especially, MSVO 1 145 iii 1 and CUSAS 31 185 v 5, which mention abgals in association with the en official.

162 For examples, see PSD A/2 175. Line 53 of the Archaic Lu A list has a title NUN.KAxŠE$_3$, which appears as NUN.ME.KAxŠE$_3$ in line 52 of the ED version. One may suspect that the authors of the ED list had erroneously identified NUN.KAxŠE$_3$ (which, apparently, is unrelated to abgal) as abgal$_2$ = NUN.ME.KAxŠE$_3$. This would explain why this title appears twice in this version (as abgal in line 15 and as abgal$_2$ in line 52).

163 6 PNs ab$_2$-gal-me (ECTJ 16:1–8).

both instances the text says that the en official erected the temple, while the abgal treated it in some way: e$_2$ en-ne$_2$ i$_3$-du$_3$ e$_2$ en gal-le i$_3$-du$_3$ abgal-le šu be$_2$-ak, "the en erected it, the great en erected the temple, the abgal treated it" (Krebernik 1984: 146 no. 27 E); e$_2$ en in-du$_3$-gim enkum$_x$(EN.PAP.SIG$_7$) si bi$_2$-sa$_2$-gim enkum$_x$ abgal-gim u$_9$-gub, "as the en erected the temple, as the enkum put it in (cultic) order, as the enkum (and) the abgal set it up (properly)" (ibid. 146 no. 27 1 (b)).[164] This role of abgal is reflected also in "Amar-Suen A" line 16, which describes Amar-Suen's prolonged (and eventually failed) efforts to rebuild Enki's temple in Eridu: abgal-e dug$_4$-ga ⌜u$_3$⌝-na-dug$_4$ giš-hur e$_2$-e pa e$_3$ nu-mu-un-ak-e, "the abgal gave him the instructions, (but) he still was unable to display the plan of the temple." Given his connection with cleansing rites (see below), the abgal may have been specifically responsible for the laying down of the temple's foundations and the associated purification rites. Characteristically, temple foundations and the ritual deposits inserted into them were believed to be linked to the Abzu – and so with Enki and his cultic associates as well. See further Gudea Cylinder A xxii 11–17 (discussed below), which suggests that one form of the foundation deposits was called abgal.

A literary text from Abu Salabikh (OIP 99 114 v 10'-13'), likewise dating to ED IIIa times, mentions an abgal in a context suggesting that these functionaries performed extispicies as well (abgal LAGAB ... maš šu mu-gid$_2$).

ED IIIb sources from Lagaš show the abgal acting in funeral contexts[165] and associate him specifically with Nanše.[166]

He is unknown in Sargonic and Ur III texts, except for the mention of Lu$_2$-^{d}Nanna abgal in OIP 121 352:3, a Puzriš-Dagan tablet dating to the eighth year of Amar-Suen. This example is highly interesting, since it immediately brings to mind the abgal Lu-Nanna associated with Šulgi in a first millennium story about the Seven Sages,[167] and the alleged author of the "Etana Story" of that same name, who appears in the late catalogue of texts and authors edited by W. G. Lambert.[168] He is also mentioned in the colophon of K. 8080, a list of magical poultices.[169]

---

164 The enkum was a member of Enki's entourage. See Wiggermann 1992: 71 and below p. 67.
165 PSD A/2 175 1.2.
166 NN abgal$_2$ ^{d}Nanše (six attestations). For these examples and other attestations of the abgal$_2$ in texts dealing with Nanše's cult, see Foxvog 2007.
167 SpBTU 2 8 i 1–29, discussed below p. 71–72.
168 Lambert 1962: 66 VI 11.
169 ni-ṣir-ti Lu$_2$-^{d}Nanna abgal Urim$_2$^{ki}, "secret of Lu-Nanna, sage of Ur," cited by Lambert 1957: 7 and n. 27.

While the abgal priests/functionaries are frequently mentioned in OB and later literary sources, I am not aware of any attestations of this title as designating a *real* functionary subsequent to the Ur III period.[170] Although the word abgal/*apkallu* is occasionally applied to the first millennium scholars and literati (*ummânū*), when used in this way abgal/*apkallu* serves as an honorific title only, without any indication that there existed a priestly office of this nature at that time.[171] For that particular usage of abgal/*apkallu*, see below p. 71.

Literary sources of OB and later times identify the abgal as a ritual specialist performing purifying rites and exorcisms and reciting incantations. The same sources also consistently connect the abgal with Eridu and its lord Enki, the master of learning, lustrations, incantations, and magic par excellence. A similar connection is made with Enki's son Asarluhi, lord of Kuwara, who shared many of his father's characteristics. It is not surprising, therefore, that both Enki and Asarluhi are themselves occasionally described as abgals. These two gods had in their employ a slew of semi-divine abgals, among whom Adapa of Eridu was the most famous.[172]

The connection of the abgal with Eridu and Enki goes back to the Uruk III period. This is evident from the term abgal itself, whose component NUN references both Enki (as nun, "Prince") and his city Eridu.[173] Here note that NUN is a marker of Enki and Eridu also in Uruk III art.[174] This is further confirmed by the fact that a number of other functionaries in Enki's employ bore titles that include the NUN sign: enkum, ninkum, and abrig.[175] The abgal's association with Enki is also implied by his being, in ED IIIb Lagaš, one of the cultic attendants of goddess Nanše (see above), Enki's daughter and, like Asarluhi, a member of his immediate divine circle.

---

170 The abgal/*apkallu* is mentioned in the first millennium *Mīs pî* rituals (Walker and Dick 2001: 143–144 lines 92a-92b, 164 lines 34a-34b, 181 lines 15a-15b), but these attestations undoubtedly involve his mythological apparition.

171 As far as I know, the earliest example of this usage is found in a Middle Babylonian incantation from Emar, which was written by a "scribe and *apkallu*" named Madi-Dagan (DUB.SAR ᵃABGAL) (Tsukimoto 1999). Madi-Dagan was a well-known Emar scribe, who also bore the unique title of "Chief Scribe" (LU₂.GAL DUB.SAR) (Y. Cohen 2009: 37, 189–194). Since there is no indication that Madi-Dagan was a ritual specialist of any kind, his designation as *apkallu* probably was purely honorific, emphasizing his elevated status among the Emar scribes.

172 "Adapa Story" from Me-Turan lines 110 and 119 (Cavignaux 2014); CAD A/2 172 under 2'.

173 See Steinkeller 1998: 88.

174 See the Late Uruk cylinder seals Frankfort 1939: pl. 3 fig. d, pl. 6 fig. a; Schmidt et al. 1972: pl. 42 fig. a; ATU 7 pl. 95 no. 1.

175 For abrig(NUN.ME.DU), who is probably the same as agrig, see above p. 50.

As for the physical appearance of the early abgal,[176] literary sources consistently paint him as having long hair hanging down his neck.[177] This characteristic conceivably is reflected also in visual art, as is suggested by Gudea Cylinder A xxii 11–17 and the related archaeological data:

> temen Abzu-bi dim gal-gal ki-a mi-ni-si-si
> ^{d}En-ki-da E_2-an-gur$_4$-ra-ka
> šag$_4$ mu-di$_3$-ni-ib$_2$-kuš$_2$-u$_3$
> temen an-na ur-sag-am$_3$ e$_2$-e im-mi-dab$_6$
> ki-a-nag dingir-re<-ne>-ka im-nag-nag-a
> E_2-ninnu dim gal mu-gi
> abgal$_2$-bi mu-du$_3$,

> The foundation deposits of the Abzu (i.e., reaching into the Abzu), (which are like) great mooring stakes, he sunk into the ground;
> they (now) take counsel with Enki in the Engur.
> The upper foundation deposits – they are heroes indeed! – he positioned around the temple;
> they (now) drink water from the (underground) libation pipes of the gods.
> He made the Eninnu firm (like) a great mooring stake,
> its abgal$_2$ (foundation pegs) he set up.

I suggest that the word abgal$_2$, as it appears in this passage, is a generic term for the foundation peg topped with a human figure (the so-called *Nagelmensch*).[178] It may be hypothesized that the origin of this usage goes back to the beardless male figures with clasped hands and long hair, which appear on foundation pegs from ED II–III Lagaš.[179] The coiffure worn by these figures has two distinctive styles. The first, attested on the uninscribed pegs predating Ur-Nanše and those belonging to his reign, has small plaits over the forehead; the hair falling over the back is heavy and neatly arranged in horizontal strands. See **fig. 29**.[180]

---

176 For the appearance of the later mythological abgals, see below p. 71.

177 For the examples, see PSD A/2 176 4.

178 A similar broad interpretation was offered by Jacobsen 1987: 416–417 n. 113. Jacobsen likewise concluded that the abgal$_2$ objects mentioned in Cylinder A xxii 11–17 (which he translated "wizards") are the anthropomorphic nails/pegs of the foundation deposits. But, rather than connecting them with the long-haired figures of the ED period, he compared them with "a fully human figure steadying the peg with both hands," which is typical of the foundation deposits of Gudea's time. Edzard, in RIME 3/1 83, adopts Jacobsen's translation of abgal$_2$, though rendering it "praying wizard," on the assumption that abgal$_2$ represents abgal(NUN.ME) plus šud$_3$, "to pray." But, as I noted earlier, NUN.ME.KAxEŠ$_3$ = abgal$_2$ is the regular writing of this vocable in ED IIIb sources from Lagaš. PSD A/2 176 5 likewise assumes that the figurines of abgal$_2$ are meant here.

179 See Ellis 1968: 50–54; Rashid 1983; Muscarella 1988: 303–313.

180 For other examples, see Marchesi and Marchetti 2011: 320 figs. 3–6.

In the other style, which appears on the pegs of En-anatum I and En-metena,[181] the hair is equally heavy, but it is parted in the middle, falling down over the back in two large strands, arranged into plaits.[182] See **figs. 30–33.** Similar long hair is worn by the male figure that accompanies the Priest-King on the Warka Vase,[183] on a number of Late Uruk cylinder seals,[184] as well as on the so-called "Blau Plaque," front side, which likewise belongs to the Uruk III period.[185] It is tempting to think that both the ED foundation pegs from Lagaš and the Late Uruk examples just cited depict the abgal priest. This hypothesis is corroborated by the evidence of literary sources (see above), according to which the abgal had characteristically long hair, which fell loosely down his back.[186]

To summarize, the abgal was a real figure, which can be documented as such from the archaic Uruk III period through Ur III times. It appears that the abgal's office disappeared at the end of the third millennium, surviving only as a designation of mythical sages and as an honorific title of the first millennium scholars (*ummânū*). The abgal was an important cultic official and a ritual specialist, who

---

181 For the pegs of En-anatum I, see Hansen 1970. For the ones of En-metena, see Muscarella 2003: 80 no. 39 = RIME 1 215–216 En-metena 13.

182 The figures with this coiffure have two protrusions on front of the head, which were interpreted as horns by scholars. See, e. g., Muscarella 2003, who thinks that the alleged "horns" indicate the "divinity" of the figure in question. Cf. also Ellis 1968: 52; Hansen 1970: 246; Van Driel 1973a: 70; Braun-Holzinger 2013: 23. But this explanation is unlikely, since the protrusions are very short and rounded. It is virtually certain that these are front sections of the coiffure, which have been coiled up into two small locks or some type of an elaborate pompadour. This can be seen quite clearly in the side-views of the pegs in **figs. 31–33,** and in the front view of the peg in **fig. 33.** In ED and Sargonic art, the horns sported by deities are fully articulated and always forming part of crowns (see the images collected in Braun-Holzinger 2013).

183 See Appendix 1 p. 84 and **figs. 7** and **8.**

184 See Heinrich 1936: pl. 17 fig. b; Vogel 2013: 143 fig. 20:5 (= our **fig. 3**); Buchanan 1981: 43 fig. 134a, 44 fig. 135; Marchesi and Marchetti 2011: pl. 48 fig. 4.

185 See Gelb, Steinkeller, and Whiting 1991: Text Volume 41–43 no. 11, Plates Volume pl. 12 no. 11. Note that, in this image, the figure in question has clasped hands, in the manner of the ED representations of the *Nagelmensch.*

186 During the excavations at Al-Hiba (= ancient Lagaš) ten foundation deposits were recovered. Seven of them consisted of a copper figurine and a stone tablet while three contained only the tablet. All of these objects bear an identical inscription of En-anatum I mentioning his personal god Šul-"UTUL" (Hansen 1970: 246). For the inscription, see ibid. 246–247 and RIME 1: 175–177 En-anatum I 5 ex. 4. Based on this mention, Hansen confidently concluded that the pegs depict Šul-"UTUL." But this assumption is spurious, since Šul-"UTUL" is routinely invoked in ED Lagaš building inscriptions (Ur-Nanše through En-anatum II) irrespective of their shape and form (as shown best by the stone tablets included in the Al-Hiba deposits). Cf. Van Driel 1973b: 70–71. Therefore, since the mention of Šul-"UTUL" is not an exclusive characteristic of the pegs of the *Nagelmensch* type, there is no reason to identify the figure in question as such.

was involved in a wide range of cultic activities. It is significant that the Fara and Abu Salabikh sources present him as a scholar, who performed extispicies and perhaps even wrote cuneiform tablets. From the very beginning the abgal was closely connected with Eridu and Enki's cult. The abgal may be represented in art (Uruk III, ED Lagaš), where, if these identifications are correct, he wears characteristic long hair.[187]

7.7 The "Story about the Seven Sages"

A number of literary texts dating to the first millennium preserve a mythological story about the Seven Sages, fish-like creatures who were born in the sea. Although not stating it explicitly, the story seems to imply that these creatures brought the arts of magic to Babylonia, apparently acting in this role as the agents of Enki. So at least says the version of this story preserved in "Babyloniaca," which, while not mentioning Enki or any other deity, makes the fish-like Oannes responsible for the teaching of all the aspects of civilization to the Babylonians.[188] Since Enki lived in the underground sweet-waters of the Abzu, a belief that his servants and representatives were partly human and partly piscine is easy to understand. A similar product of this logic is Enki's famous goat-fish (dara$_3$-Abzu, *suḫurmāšu*), which, in late iconography, combines the front part of a goat with the back part of a fish.[189]

Before we consider this story in detail, some words need to be said about its historical background and cultural setting. The earliest documented mention of the Seven Sages is found in "Temple Hymns" line 139, where, in a hymn devoted to Kuwara and its god Asarluhi, seven abgals are explicitly mentioned: abgal imin-e sig nim-ta šu mu-ra-ni-in-mu$_2$-uš, "the Seven Sages enlarged it (i.e., the temple) for you (with the supplies? coming) from the south and north." Since it is known that "Temple Hymns" were composed (or at least redacted) in the Ur III period, it is possible that the Seven Sages were known already at that time. This is by no means certain, however, since this mention could conceivably be an Old Babylonian addition. But, even if one chooses the latter alternative, we

---

187 Here it should also be noted that the statue of Ur-Ningirsu, the en and the šennu priest of the goddess Nanše during the reigns of Šulgi – Ibbi-Suen, shows similar long hair. See Braun-Holzinger 1991: 275 St 157, pl. 18. This example is interesting, since, as I noted earlier, Nanše belonged to Enki's divine and cultic circle.

188 Burstein 1978: 13–14.

189 A. Green 1986: 25–26, pls. 5 and 6.

may be confident that some tradition about the Seven Sages did exist already during the first half of the second millennium.

This group of seven characters is not attested textually during the remainder of the second millennium, becoming visible in texts only in the "Story of the Seven Sages." But we can discern them in art. Males wearing fish-like garb, performing lustration rites, and accompanying Enki/Ea are amply documented in the first millennium art.[190] See **fig. 34.** Revealingly, the earliest depictions of these personages, who can confidently be identified as the abgals of the story in question, appear on a number of Kassite seals.[191] No representations of this kind are known from the third millennium; nor are they documented in the Old Babylonian period. This agrees with the fact that, as I noted earlier, the third millennium abgal had a distinctively different appearance. All these facts argue that the introduction of the fish-like garb iconography was closely connected with the development of the late tradition about the Seven Sages, which describes them as fish-like creatures. Given the presence of such creatures on the Kassite seals I cited earlier, it is likely that it was in Kassite times that the literary tradition about the fish-like Sages was created – or least was given its earliest formulation.

The "Story about the Seven Sages" is known essentially from two first millennium sources.[192] The first of them forms part of the third tablet of the series *Bīt mēseri*,[193] and is technically an incantation (as shown by the introductory label en$_2$ and the concluding ritual instructions). It begins with a listing of seven named abgals, followed by a statement identifying them as "pure carp,

---

190 Among such representations, see especially the Neo-Assyrian water basin from Assur, which is decorated with multiple depictions of Ea flanked by the abgals (Klengel-Brandt 1997: 132 fig. 141 = our **fig. 34**), and two Neo-Assyrian seals, both showing an abgal standing behind Ea, who is mounted on his goat-fish (Forte 1976: no. 39; Collon 1987: 174 no. 817). For other representations and discussion, see Forte 1976: nos. 40 and 54; Muscarella 1981: 143 fig. 104; Klengel-Brandt 1997: 130 fig. 137, 132 fig. 143; A. Green 1983: 88–90 pl. 10 figs. a, b, c, and d; 1986: pl. 10 fig. a; Wiggermann 1992: 76–77.

One of the ED Lagaš sources pertaining to Nanše's cult and involving an abgal$_2$ (for which see above n. 166) also mentions 2 gala eštub^{ku6}–di (DP 222 iv 6), whom Foxvog 2007 ingeniously interprets as "carp-actor gala's." Even if this term, which possibly also appears as GUD-di in the list ED Lu B line 5 (so Foxvog), does in fact refer to some carp-involving ritual action, this evidence does not directly bear on the abgal's appearance. But, if this interpretation is correct, we would find here an indication that the fish-like garb or similar paraphernalia were part of Nanše's (and therefore also Enki's) cult already in ED times.

191 See D. M. Matthews 1990: nos. 142–144, 196.

192 Reflections of it are also found in "Babyloniaca" and in a number other sources.

193 SpBTU 2 8 i 1–29; Reiner 1961: 1 K. 5119 + other mss.

the carp of the sea, seven of them; the seven abgals, born in the river, the regulators of the designs of heaven and earth/netherworld."[194]

A listing of four other named abgals then follows. Although the text does not say it, these four belonged to postdiluvian times. This is demonstrated by the fact that two of them are said to have been associated with "historical" figures: Nungal-piriggaldim (no. 1) was an abgal of Enmerkar, while Lu-Nanna (no. 4) lived during the reign of Šulgi. Abgals nos. 2 and 3 were natives of Kiš and Adab respectively, with the text probably referring to the Kiš and Adab dynasties listed in the SKL. This group of the abgals is summarized as "four abgals of human descent, whom lord Enki/Ea provided with broad knowledge."

The text concludes with ritual instructions, which name a number of incantations to be recited as part of healing procedures, in the presence of the figurines of the seven fish-like abgals (thus excluding from further consideration the four abgals of human descent).

The other source preserving the "Story about the Seven Sages" is a late text from Hellenistic Uruk, dating to 147th year of Antiochus V = 164 BC.[195] Dubbed "Uruk List of Kings and Sages" by A. Lenzi (henceforth ULKS), this version of the story fuses the listing of the seven abgals appearing in SpBTU 2 8 with the AKL, by assigning to each "king" a particular abgal: "during the reign of king X, the abgal was Y."

Like SpBTU 2 8, the ULKS then lists additional, postdiluvial abgals. In this case, however, the listing is more extensive and follows the pattern of the first part of the text, in that it pairs sages with particular kings. The listing aspires to be truly historical, since it follows a chronological order and names mostly authentic rulers. It begins with Enmerkar (who is placed after the Deluge, if Lenzi's reconstruction is correct) and Gilgameš, the mythical kings of the First dynasty of Uruk, as it appears in the SKL. Listed then are the "real" kings Ibbi-Suen, Išbi-Erra, Abi-ešuh, [NN], Adad-apla-iddina, Nebuchadnezzar I, Esarhaddon, and possibly Nikarchos.[196]

Of special interest for our purpose are the names of the kings and sages appearing in the first part of the ULKS. Except in one case (involving king no. 5), the names of the kings are identical with those in the AKL. Save for some spelling variations, the names of the sages are exactly the same as the ones appearing

---

194 This description is echoed by "Erra Epic" I 162: "the seven *apkallū* of the Apsu, pure carp, who are endowed with great knowledge like their lord Ea."

195 BagM Beih. 2 89, edited and discussed by van Dijk 1962: 44–52. It was subsequently re-edited and discussed by Lenzi 2008a: 144–147. See also Lenzi 2008b: 107–109.

196 As suggested by van Dijk 1962: 52 and Lenzi 2008a: 163–165.

in SpBTU 2 8. The relationship between the names of the kings and those of their respective sages is clearest in entries nos. 3, 4, and 5:

Am-me-lu-an-na	En-me-dug$_3$-ga
Am-me-gal-an-na	En-me-galam-ma
E[n-m]e-ušum-gal-an-na	En-me-bulug$_3$-ga$_2$

It is highly probable that En-me-dug$_3$-ga,[197] En-me-galam-ma,[198] and En-me-bulug$_3$-ga$_2$ were derived from the names of the kings,[199] specifically from the En$_2$-me(-en)- forms found in the AKL. This is obvious in the case of En-me-galam-ma (no. 4), which almost certainly goes back to En-me(-en)-gal-an-na. The connection between the other two pairs of names is less obvious.

Other names deserving attention are entries nos. 1 and 2:

A-a-lu	U$_4$-^{d}60 (U$_4$-an-na in SpBTU 2 8)
A-la$_2$-al-gar	U$_4$-^{d}60-dug$_3$-ga (U$_4$-an-ne$_2$-dug$_3$-ga in SpBTU 2 8)

As it was established many years ago by Lambert (1962: 74),[200] U$_4$-an-na (read by him as the Akkadian *Uma-an-na*) is identical with Oannes, the fish-like creature appearing in "Babyloniaca," and the grantor of civilization to the Babylonians.[201] According to a somewhat earlier tradition, U$_4$-an-na was an *alter ego* of the sage Adapa, the exact nature of the relationship between the two remaining uncertain.[202] This is of no concern to us, however, since our interest lies in U$_4$-an-na's name only. U$_4$-an-na appears to be related to U$_4$-an-ne$_2$-dug$_3$-ga, thus suggesting a common derivation of both of them. The second name may in turn show a connection with the earlier discussed En-me-dug$_3$-ga. If this is correct, one could then envision a development by which En-me-dug$_3$-ga / *Am-me-

---

197 En-me-dug$_3$-ga appears as an author in the list of authors published by Lambert 1962: 66 IV 11, discussed ibid. 74.

198 Hallo's idea (1963: 176) that En-me-galam-ma is named in the first line of "Ur-Ninurta B" may be safely discarded, in my view.

199 Cf. Wiggermann 1992: 77, who too thinks that the names of the abgals developed "partly from the names of the antediluvian kings."

200 The same conclusion was reached independently by van Dijk 1962: 47–48.

201 Burstein 1978: 13–14.

202 Lambert's idea (1962: 74) that U$_4$-an-na was the real name of the sage in question, with Adapa representing only his title, is unconvincing. Here note that Adapa, designated as an abgal, appears already in the OB version of the "Adapa Story" from Me-Turan, lines 110 and 119 (Cavigneaux 2014). This indicates that his identification with U$_4$-an-na is a late development and that, therefore, U$_4$-an-na is a secondary phenomenon. Similar conclusions were reached by Cavigneaux 2014: 37.

dug$_3$-ga gave rise to U$_4$-an-ne$_2$-dug$_3$-ga, from which eventually U$_4$-an-na was generated.

These facts suggest that at least some of the abgal names were derived from the names of the "kings." What is not in doubt is that all seven of them are late artificial creations.

7.8 Summary and Conclusions

The preceding discussion of the antediluvian tradition, as it is reflected in the various sources dating to the second and first millennia, permits us to draw a number of conclusions. The list of the antediluvian cities and their rulers (AKL) undoubtedly is a secondary addition to the SKL, which was created either the Isin-Larsa or the OB period. The names of the "kings" found there were either borrowed from earlier sources or artificially formed by resort to third millennium name patterns. The inclusion in the AKL of figures associated with knowledge (Ubur-Tutu, Ziudsudra, En-medurana/En-meduranki) or archaic kingship (Dumuzi the shepherd) assures that these individuals were conceived of as sage-kings.

By inventing the tradition of five antediluvian cities and their rulers, the authors of the AKL created their own version of history before history. This "pre-history" involved a form of rule dramatically different from the dynastic history treated in the SKL. To emphasize this difference and to make the antiquity of the sage-kings even more apparent, the authors separated the two by the sharp caesura of the Deluge, a motif that was closely interwoven with the development of the tradition of the antediluvian form of rule. It is possible (though not provable at this time) that the Deluge motif itself had been invented to serve those same ends as well.[203]

The sage-kings of the antediluvian cities thus emerge as the guardians of the most ancient manifestations of knowledge and arts, more broadly, of human civilization. They were also believed to have been responsible for the civilization's original establishment and its further refinement. This foundational role of the sage-kings is made explicit in the SB "Gilgameš Epic," where the Seven Sages,

---

203 It is possible, of course, that the Deluge motif preserves a memory of some cataclysmic natural event that occurred in Babylonia's remote past. But, if such a memory existed, it might have equally well recalled a historical occurrence. There are many reasons to think that the end of the Uruk period was catastrophic, with a nearly total collapse of the society, economy, and culture. When this debacle was over, all had to be rebuilt and recreated from scratch. To the people who had gone through this experience, it must have seemed as they indeed had survived a flood.

here identified as *muntalkū*, "wise men," are said to have been the original founders of Uruk's famed city-wall, a building project subsequently completed by Gilgameš.[204]

Although it is possible that, already when the AKL had come into being, there existed a notion that the arts and tools of civilization actually were brought to Babylonia by the Seven Sages, the servants of Enki (as narrated in some first millennium sources, especially "Babyloniaca"), we have no evidence of that. On the other hand, the story of En-meduranki, who obtained his knowledge *directly* from Šamaš and Adad, speaks against the existence of such a notion rather strongly. A similar case is presented by the sage Adapa, who was presented the arts of magic by his master Enki. These facts suggest that, according to the original, Old Babylonian tradition, the sage-kings acquired their knowledge from the divine realm without any mediation of the Seven Sages.

Already in the OB period it was believed that this ancient knowledge was lost due to the Deluge, and that it had to be recovered – or actually excavated – subsequently.[205] Of this we can be certain thanks to the Sumerian composition "Death of Gilgameš," which describes how Gilgameš obtained that lost knowledge from Ziudsudra.[206] The implication is that Ziudsudra transferred that knowledge to Gilgameš in a *written* form, likely that of clay tablets. Such a view is held at least in "Babyloniaca," which describes how Xisouthros = Ziudsudra saved the tablets by burying them in Sippar, and how they were excavated after the Deluge by his ancestors:

> Therefore, he [i.e., Kronos = Marduk] ordered Xisouthros to bury the beginnings and the middles and the ends of all writings in Sippar, the city of the Sun. [Following the Deluge, its survivors were told by the "voice" that] they were to return to Babylon and that it was declared that they were to dig up the writings from (the city) of the Sipparians and distribute them to mankind ... When these people came to Babylon, they dug up the writings at (the city of) the Sipparians and founded many cities and rebuilt many shrines and founded anew Babylon" (Burstein 1978: 20–21).

---

204 *uššīšu la iddû 7 muntalkū*, "have not the Seven Wise Men laid down its foundation?" (SB "Gilgameš Epic" I 21, XI 326).

205 Cf. Chen 2013: 150–151.

206 "Death of Gilgameš" Me-Turan version Segment F lines 15–17: "you (Gilgameš) have reached Ziudsudra at his dwelling place; having brought back to the Land the divine powers of Sumer, which at the time (of the Deluge) had been lost forever – as well as the instructions (and) divine rites, (you then put in order cleansing rituals)." Cf. SB "Gilgameš Epic" I 8: "he brought (back) the knowledge *(ṭēmu)* from before the Deluge." Cf. Beaulieu 2007b: 160.

Echoes of this belief also survive in the annals of Assurbanipal, who claims to have read "the cuneiform inscriptions on stone before the flood,"[207] whose author, as Assurbanipal believed, was none other than the sage Adapa: "the work of Adapa I acquired, I learned the hidden treasure of all scribal knowledge, the signs of heaven and netherworld, I am able to discuss them among scholars."[208] Sages are associated with the antediluvian knowledge in other sources as well.[209]

It is self-evident that, throughout Mesopotamian history, people were familiar with archaic cuneiform tablets (such as those dating to Uruk III), both through their preservation in scribal schools and by finding them regularly in their cities, in various forms of excavations and earthworks. Those among them who could read them (or at least pretended to possess this ability) were of course the members of the Managerial Class I described earlier. It was surely in the interest of that group to promote the antiquity and importance of such records, especially vis-à-vis their rulers. To give them even more importance, they presented them "as coming from before the Deluge" — thus invoking a tradition they themselves had likely created for similar self-serving political purposes. Significantly, this type of knowledge is described (especially in the SB version of the "Gilgameš Epic") as sealed off and inaccessible to the uninitiated.[210]

As the foregoing discussion must have made it clear, I attribute the creation of the AKL to the Managerial Class. I have already shown that the AKL was added as a preamble to the SKL to demonstrate that, long before the beginning of dynastic history, there existed a different kind of political power, which was vested in the sage-kings of the cities of Eridu, Patibira, Larak, Sippar, and Šuruppak. Significantly, none of those cities had ever been a seat of royal power, and so the composition of this source could not have been inspired by the political aims of any Old Babylonian ruler. Therefore, it is certain, I believe, that the AKL advances the interests of the Managerial Class. By selecting cities that never were political centers of any significance, though were renowned as the ancient seats of culture and learning, the authors of the list are saying – and

---

207 ḫītāku miḫišti(GU₂.SUM) abnī ša lam abūbi (Streck 1916: 256 i 18).
208 šipir apkalli Adapa āḫuz niširtu katimtu kullat ṭupšarrūte ittāt šamê u erṣeti amrāku šutad-dunnāku ina puḫur ummâni (Streck 1916: 254 i 13–14). Here note that the Neo-Assyrian kings are commonly compared to Adapa in the letters addressed to them (Pongratz-Leisten 1999: 309–319).
209 See, especially, the medical text AMT 105:21–24: ša pī apkallī labīrūti ša lam abūbi, "(instructions) from the mouth of the ancient sages from before the Deluge (which, in Šuruppak, in the second year of Enlil-bani, king of Isin, Enlil-muballiṭ, sage of Nippur, composed?)." Cf. Lambert 1957: 8.
210 As Christopher Woods points out to me in a personal communication.

thus reinforcing the message of the Lu A – that it was the wise men like them that were the ultimate source of political power in Babylonia.

The Managerial Class faced a major crisis during the time after the fall of the Ur III dynasty, which saw dramatic transformations of kingship and economy, caused mainly by the appearance on the scene of new political elites of foreign origin and different cultural traditions. One of those changes was the introduction of a truly hereditary form of kingship. Another important change, which affected the Managerial Class most directly, was the waning importance of temple households as communal socio-economic institutions, the traditional focus of its influence. This development was countered by the rise of the palace and the private sector as the dominant centers of power. For the Managerial Class this period of change meant uncertainty and the need to re-orient itself in the new socio-political reality. Having lost their former influence, members of the old Managerial Class now tried to become advisors to the king and his immediate circle, and so to secure for themselves a place in the new poltical order. Hence their attempts to demonstrate to the new (mostly Amorite) rulers the great antiquity of their class, the importance they played in the past, and, perhaps most important, their role in running the government and advising the king.

I believe that the anxiety this group felt as the old order was crumbling around them finds an expression in the group of literary texts known as "City Laments." Composed shortly after the fall of the Ur III empire, these compositions offer a vivid and highly pessimistic picture of the destruction that marked the end of that glorious period. The motivation behind the creation of these compositions is a puzzle. It is hard to imagine that the Isin kings would have had a direct interest in composing this group of texts. Although "City Laments" may have had a ritual application, especially in the rebuilding of temples,[211] it is unlikely, in my view, that official sponsorship played a significant part in their creation. The voice of these compositions, which read almost like responses to the Holocaust of more recent times, is just too personal and emotional for that. Therefore, I would argue that, rather than as a product of official propaganda, the "City Laments" should be seen as a spontaneous reaction of the Managerial Class, their outcry at what had happened, and their mourning of the world that had been lost forever. In wailing over that gone world, they also (or perhaps in the first place) bemoaned the loss of their own social position and all that went along with it. They understood that their lives had been changed forever, and they feared the future.

---

211 As speculated by Hallo 2001: 202–203.

But the message of the AKL was not explicit enough to serve the political ends of the Managerial Class, which, by the mid second millennium, had been reduced to not much more than a guild of scholars. Therefore, in order to emphasize their connection with ancient knowledge and the role they allegedly used to play in the running of government, the heirs of this social group later felt it necessary to invent independent, autonomous sage figures, which they assigned to the antediluvian rulers as their respective advisors. The final product of this propagandistic line of thought is the ULKS, which offers a rigorous historical argument that, from the very beginning of Babylonian history till present day, all rulers always had sages as their advisors.[212]

This understanding of the Seleucid list nicely agrees with the conclusions of Lenzi 2008a, who too interprets this text as a piece of political propaganda, which was meant to advance the cause of the "sages" as political advisors to the Seleucid kings. See, in particular, Lenzi's following statements: "I interpret the ULKS as a tendentious document written by scholars who needed to reassert their importance to the community leadership in order to advance their cultic-political agenda" (ibid. 139); "Invoking the association of scholarship with memorable kings and their mythical sages or famous human scholars in the ULKS attributes to the Seleucid-era scholarly professions a venerable history, which in turn implies the scholars deserved a higher level of political influence or support than in fact they were enjoying at the time" (ibid. 161).

Lenzi subsequently asks the following two questions: "But are the scholars who created and copied this list really trying to manipulate the Seleucid court? Are they trying to insinuate that the traditional association of kings and scholars should continue under a non-native king?" (ibid. 162). I believe that the answer to both these questions is an unequivocal "yes." The Seleucid era was in many ways similar to the Isin-Larsa period, in that both of them were transitional phases, which in either case witnessed dramatic changes in the social and political conditions, marked especially by the establishment of foreign dynasties. Like the members of the Managerial Class, who, following the collapse of the Ur III empire, desperately needed to reassert their position in the new order, and who, toward that end, created fictitious documents demonstrating the an-

---

212 Cf. Beaulieu 2007a: 15–17; 2007b: 160–162. See, in particular, the following statement: "In the late periods of Mesopotamian civilization ... scribes, scholars, and royal advisors gained an influential place at court and invented traditions that put them on a par with the king in the intellectual and religious leadership of their culture, a role that became even more prominent with the demise of the last native Mesopotamian monarchy in 539 B.C.E." (2007a: 17). As Beaulieu notes (2007: 15 n. 37), the *ummânū* are paired with kings also in certain Neo-Assyrian king lists.

cient origins of this social group and its role in advising the rulers, their Seleucid descendants faced very similar challenges, coming up with similar responses.[213]

Are there any other compositions of broadly "historical" content in which the voice of the Managerial Class may be detected? One such source, I submit, is "The Curse of Akkade." This unusual text in the tradition of the later "admonishing" literature, whose closest relatives are the OB and later Akkadian texts dealing with the reign of Naram-Suen,[214] is a capsulized, highly poetic history of Sargonic times. As the "Curse" understands this period, thanks to divine protection the reign of Sargon was a time of success, during which the capital city of Akkade enjoyed great prosperity. This state of things changed dramatically during the reign of Naram-Suen, when, by the decision of Enlil, the head of the Babylonian pantheon, Akkade suddenly was deprived of divine support. Naram-Suen tried to correct this situation, by embarking on a plan to rebuild Enlil's temple Ekur, and so to regain Enlil's favor. These attempts failed, however, since Naram-Suen had repeatedly been denied favorable omens from the divine realm. Ignoring this message, Naram-Suen proceeded with his original plan anyway, tearing down the old temple in preparation for the new construction. Since this action, which the "Curse" depicts as an "attack" and "destruction,"[215] represented a total violation of the divine rules, Naram-Suen was duly punished. The tool of Enlil's retribution was the barbaric Gutians, who, by Enlil's command, invaded Babylonia and destroyed Akkade. The final act of this mini-history of the Sargonic age, as presented in the "Curse," was the gods' decision that Akkade should never be rebuilt.

Although the reason behind Naram-Suen's reversal of fortune is not spelled out in the "Curse," one may plausibly conclude that it was the decline of Nippur as a center of power, a development that the elites of Nippur (where the "Curse"

---

213 It is a good guess that these political efforts were related to the archaizing ideological program aiming to bring to prominence in Uruk the cults of An and Antum, which began in the late Persian period and culminated in Hellenistic times. See Beaulieu 1992; 1994.

214 Such as the various recensions of the "Naram-Suen and the Enemy Hordes," for which J. G. Westenholz 1997: 263–368.

215 As I argued elsewhere (Steinkeller 1993b: 142), this "attack" on the Ekur and its "destruction" are purely metaphoric, referring to the alleged neglect of Nippur and Enlil's cult by Naram-Suen. The demolition of an old temple per se was a necessary procedure before the new one could be erected and, as such, was free of negative connotations. What was wrong about it in this case is that it was carried out without the divine approval, which, as many sources demonstrate it very clearly (e. g., Gudea Cylinder A), was a condition *sine qua non* for such an action to take place. As for the Ekur, we know that, actually, it was rebuilt by Naram-Suen and Šar-kali-šarri, who also lavished magnificent gifts on it (A. Westenholz 1987: 24–27; Steinkeller 1993b: 142).

apparently originated) must have attributed directly to Akkade's having become the capital of the united Babylonia, the position belonging earlier (at least in religious and cultural terms) to Nippur. In other words, Naram-Suen's original sin was that he neglected Nippur in favor of Akkade[216] and, even more important, that he made himself a god of Akkade, which diminished the role of Enlil. Hence Enlil's wrath, Naram-Suen's inability to correct the situation, and the ensuing punishment.[217]

Since the "Curse" was composed in Ur III times, probably at Nippur,[218] it is natural to think that the motivations behind the creation of this composition lie in the realities of that period. On this assumption, I suggest that the "Curse" is a cautionary tale, which was written by the Nippur members of the Managerial Class,[219] and which is obliquely addressed at the Ur III kings. As I read it, the "Curse" is a veiled warning about the dangers of going too far with the unification of Babylonia and the deification of kings, the policies that had earlier and with disastrous results (at least as the "Curse" views them) been implemented by Naram-Suen, and which now, though in a less radical form, were being practiced by Šulgi and his successors. Needless to say, it was the Managerial Class that had most directly been affected by Šulgi's reforms. One thinks here above all of his policies regarding temple households, as a result of which these institutions were put under the direct control of the crown and so deprived of their former influence.

I conclude by pointing out that "The Curse of Akkade" is not an isolated case. There exist a number of other, later sources in which the political and economic motivations of the Managerial Class are reflected – and even in a more obvious and direct way. Among them is the "Cruciform Monument" of Maniš-tušu,[220] a fictitious Neo-Babylonian source that was fabricated, through the

---

216 The "Chronicle of Early Kings" lines 18–23 (Grayson 1975: 153–154) attributes a similar misdeed to Sargon, in accusing him of building a replica of Babylon (read Nippur) in Akkade. This angered Marduk (read Enlil), who consequently wiped out Sargon's people with famine, caused his subjects to rebel against him, and afflicted him with insomnia. In this case too a metaphor is employed, since the creation of a "replica" of Babylon obviously means the making of Akkade a political counterpart of Babylon = Nippur. A similar narrative is found in the "Weidner Chronicle" lines 49–52b (Grayson 1975: 149; Al-Rawi 1990: 6). Note that Grayson 1980: 180 characterizes the latter source as "a blatant piece of propaganda written as an admonition to contemporary and future monarchs to pay heed to Babylon and its patron deity."

217 Cf. also Steinkeller 1993b: 142.

218 Cooper 1983: 11.

219 Cf. Finkelstein 1979: 77, who suggested that "The Curse of Akkade" was a "creation of the priests of Nippur."

220 Sollberger 1968; Al-Rawi and George 1994: 139–148.

use of Maništušu's original inscriptions, to demonstrate the antiquity of various privileges of the priests of Šamaš of Sippar. Another successful re-establishment of the benefices of the same priests is described in the so-called "Sun-God Tablet of Nabu-apla-iddina."[221] This outcome too resulted from the manipulation of ancient relicts, in this case, a relief depicting Šamaš, which allegedly had been discovered on the west bank on the Euphrates, and then shown to king Nabu-apla-iddina by a *šangû* priest of Šamaš and a diviner ([lu2]HAL), scion of another individual bearing the same titles.[222] In presenting ancient sources to their rulers in support of their economic claims, the authors of these two inscriptions (who obviously were the said priests themselves) acted very much like the "sages" responsible for the composition of the AKL and the Hellenistic version of the "Story of the Seven Sages" I discussed earlier.

---

221 For the most recent edition and study of this text, see Woods 2004.
222 See Woods 2004: 85 iii 19 – iv 11, discussed ibid. 42.

Appendix 1: The Priest-King of Uruk Times

1 Introductory Remarks

The main question to be considered here is the identity of the royal figure represented in Late Uruk art. This figure has commonly been described as "Priest-King" by scholars. It needs to be emphasized that this designation is based exclusively on the iconography, which depicts the Uruk ruler as a priestly official, warrior, and hunter. As encapsulating those various roles, this term is a convenient label that emphasizes the uniqueness of this Uruk royal, differentiating him from the kinds of rulers one encounters in later Babylonian history.[223] Consequently, I will be using this designation throughout my discussion.

Having examined the pertinent iconographic evidence, which, as I hope to show, strongly suggests that the Uruk ruler bore the title of en, I will consider the Uruk III written data involving the en official, as well as later evidence bearing on the archaic kingship of Uruk. Finally, a brief history of the office of the en and its various later transmutations will be offered.

I promise that I will *not* discuss the notorious "sacred marriage" in this connection. This ritual, if it existed at all, is comparatively late (at least from the perspective of archaic Uruk) and exceedingly poorly known. Because of this, any speculation about the existence of this rite in archaic Uruk is completely futile. As such, it should be avoided. Regrettably, the mystique of the "sacred marriage" continues to allure archaeologists and philologists alike, leading them again and again to seek the evidence of this ritual in Late Uruk art (see, most recently, McCaffrey 2013). Their efforts in this area usually produce but new misunderstandings, which further confuse the issues involved. The archaic kingship of Uruk is a fascinating subject by itself. It certainly deserves better.

2 Priest-King Iconography

Most of the surviving images of the Priest-King show him in ritual roles. In such instances he almost invariably appears either together with Inana or in association with her symbolic representations, the $MUŠ_3$ emblem and the rosette.[224] An-

---

223 This point is missed by Suter 2014: 554, who does not find this designation "tenable," but without justifying her judgment.
224 For these two symbols, see below.

DOI 10.1515/9781501504778-003

other large group of images depict him as a warrior and hunter.[225] In those, neither Inana nor her symbols are ever depicted. There also survive a few representations of the Priest-King in round sculpture. An extensive, though not fully comprehensive listing of this iconography is found in Braun-Holzinger 2007: 8–16, pls. 1–15. Cf. also Schmandt-Besserat 1993. For good discussions of the Priest-King's various roles, see Schmandt-Besserat 1993: 214–217; Hansen 2003: 22–24. The present study considers exclusively the images illustrating the Priest-King's ritual aspect.

2.1 The Warka Vase

Of primary importance for the question of the identity of the Priest-King is the celebrated Warka Vase.[226] See **figs. 7–9.** As aptly described by Irene Winter (1983; 2007: 125–131), the imagery of the Warka Vase forms a coherent, highly sophisticated visual program, which, both in its formal organization and the message it carries, is a celebration of agricultural abundance. This effect is achieved by the presentation of abundance as a continuous process, in which one natural element turns into another, in a never-ending chain. This process begins in the bottom register of the vase with a cursively drawn river or canal, at the bank of which spring up cereals and other plants.[227] These subsequently "become," in the next register, sheep and goats. The process continues in the vase's middle register, where the plants and animals turn into various foodstuffs, which are carried in baskets by a chain of naked attendants. The climax of this visual program and the culmination of its symbolic message happens in the top register,

---

225 Usually overlooked here is the basalt stele from Uruk, which had been found by Loftus, and became subsequently lost during its transportation to Europe (Reade 2002: 258–259 and fig. 1). This large object, measuring 77.5 cm in height, depicts the Priest-King wielding a spear, probably as part of a hunting scene.

226 Excavated at Uruk, in a building dating to Uruk IIIa, as part of the so-called "Sammelfund." See Heinrich 1936: 2–6. For an excellent description and analysis of this artifact, see Porada 1995: 130–135.

227 Two distinctive types of plants are depicted, one of which almost certainly is an abstract representation of wheat. Cf. the representations of wheat on the Late Uruk seals Frankfort 1939: pl. 5 fig. b; Buchanan 1981: 44 fig. 135. A recent study tried to explain it instead as a date-palm sampling (Miller, Jones, and Pittman 2015), but I find this identification highly unconvincing. The other plant is possibly flax (as argued by the same authors). However, given the schematic nature of these representations, this identification too is not beyond doubt.

where the foodstuffs are, finally, delivered by the Priest-King to Inana, possibly in connection with one of Inana's festivals or a similar ritual event.[228]

The Priest-King (of whom only traces survive, but which are sufficient to identify him as such) walks to the right, being preceded by a naked male holding a basket overflowing with food. Another male attendant, long-haired and wearing a short tunic,[229] follows behind the Priest-King, holding a train of his dress or belt. These three figures approach the standing Inana, dressed in a long garment, who greets them with her raised right hand. The goddess wears headgear that may plausibly be interpreted as a type of crown. Behind the goddess, there are two large standing emblems, which are identical, formally and functionally, with the sign MUŠ₃, the graph of Inana's name.[230] These two emblems, which appear to flank the goddess at her both sides, reference her as Inana, in the manner of symbols and written labels that identify deities in later Mesopotamian art.

To the right of the MUŠ₃ emblems, there stands a large stepped altar, which is supported by a pair of rams.[231] On top of the altar, there are depicted, upright and

---

228 A very similar message is communicated by the Late Uruk seal Woods et al. 2010: 53 fig. 6, which combines the representations of a waterway, farm animals, wheat plants, and Inana's emblems (MUŠ₃).

229 The same figure accompanies the Priest-King on a number of Late Uruk seals. See Heinrich 1936: pl. 17 fig. b; Vogel 2013: 143 fig 20:5 (= our **fig. 3**); Buchanan 1981: 43 fig. 134a; Buchanan 1981: 44 fig. 135; Marchesi and Marchetti 2011: pl. 48 fig. 4. For a suggestion that this individual may be the abgal priest, see above p. 69.

230 As I argued elsewhere (Steinkeller 1998), the MUŠ₃ emblem was a large, totem pole-like object made of reeds, to whose top there was attached a scarf or streamer made of textile. This interpretation is based on a literary source of ED IIIa date (ARET 5 20, 21; OIP 99 278) that identifies Inana's emblem as a lapis lazuli "scarf" (bar-sig), which binds Inana's neck. As I point out there, reed emblems of this kind, further examples of which are the NUN of Enki and the ŠEŠ of Nanna, are described in Sumerian by the term urin or urin-gal (Akk. urinnu, uriggallu). Because of this, they should be distinguished from standards proper, which are called šu-nir in Sumerian (Akk. šurinnu). A specimen of such a reed urin (probably of Inana) actually was excavated at Uruk, in the level Uruk V. See Eichmann 2013: 123 fig. 16.7.

Suter 2014: 551 writes that the MUŠ₃ emblem "closely resembles Inana's pictogram." This statement fails to recognize that the sign MUŠ₃ and the emblem of Inana are, as typical of pictographic writing systems (cf. the Egyptian and Mayan ones), *one and the same thing*. The same is true of the graphs/symbols NUN and DINGIR/AN.

231 That the object in question is an altar is shown conclusively by its other representations in Late Uruk and later art. See the following cylinder seals: (a) Marchesi and Marchetti 2011: pl. 48 fig. 9: an altar mounted on a lioness (which clearly refers to Inana's martial aspect), on whose top there is a standing attendant (similar to the figures on the altar depicted on the Warka Vase) flanked by two MUŠ₃ emblems, with another MUŠ₃ emblem standing to the left; (b) Amiet 1961: pl. 46 fig. 654: an altar mounted on a bull, topped with two MUŠ₃ emblems, two large baskets and the Priest-King standing to the left; (c) Heinrich 1936: pl. 17a: a boat carrying an altar,

facing left, two female(?) long-haired attendants, who are dressed in long garments. Behind them stands another MUŠ₃ emblem but smaller than the ones
flanking Inana, which marks these two figures (and the altar itself) as belonging
to Inana's cult. The attendant standing in the back raises her/his hands as in
blessing; the one in front holds up with both hands an object whose shape is
identical to the sign EN.[232] The identity between the two is particularly clear in
the Uruk III tablet MSVO 4 73, where the sign EN replicates the object in question
in every detail. See **fig. 10**.[233] It appears that the attendant shows – or probably
even offers – this object to the Priest-King. In fact, in his original state of preservation, the Priest-King probably would have been able to see it over Inana's
head. Be that as it may, it is clear that the presentation of the EN object to the
Priest-King by Inana and her attendant and the presentation of food offerings
to the goddess by the Priest-King and his naked attendant are symmetrical, reflecting a relationship of reciprocity: by bestowing foodstuffs on Inana, the
King-Priest is rewarded with the EN object. Therefore, there is every reason to
think that the object in question symbolized the office of the en, specifically,
the role this official played in Inana's cult. As for the nature of this object, it appears that it was some kind of a ceremonial vessel. The sign EN as it appears in
MSVO 4 73 (see **fig. 10**) suggests that this vessel consisted of a flat base on which
there were mounted, in a tree-like manner, five cups; another, free standing cup
was positioned on the other side of the base. The open mouths of the cups are
clearly depicted in MSVO 4 73.

   Immediately to the right of the altar with the two attendants, various offerings and containers are depicted. These include two large baskets overflowing
with foodstuffs[234] and, between them, a bull's head and two objects of uncertain

---

which is mounted on a bull and topped with two MUŠ₃ emblems; to the left of it stands the
Priest-King facing right (plus an oarsman and a sitting male figure); (d) Buchanan 1981: 47
fig. 138, an altar mounted on a bull and topped with two MUŠ₃ emblems, with another MUŠ₃ emblem standing to the left. For the representations of very similar altars in later art, see the Old
Akkadian seal Boehmer 1965: pl. 32 fig. 387: an altar on top of which there is a ram's head and a
footed cup with smoke rising from it; and the clay altars from the archaic temple of Ištar at Assur
(Harper 1995: 35–36).

232 The identification was proposed already by Heinrich 1936: 16. See also Wilhelm 2001: 478 n.
3; Cooper 2008: 73.

233 The contents of MSVO 4 73 are discussed below p. 95.

234 Identical baskets are shown on the Late Uruk seal Vogel 2013: 143 fig 20:5 (= our **fig. 3**),
which depicts the Priest-King presenting food offerings in front of two MUŠ₃ symbols. Like on
the vase, the Priest-King is accompanied by a long-haired attendant. As I note in the following
three footnotes, various other paraphernalia found on the vase appear also on that seal, indicat-

nature. Over these items, another group of objects is found: (a) two tall, elongated vessels;[235] (b) two stands shaped as a gazelle and a lioness respectively;[236] (c) two footed plates with what appears to be breads.[237]

The final feature of the vase's iconography that needs to be discussed is the ministrant proffering foodstuffs to Inana. This figure is identical to the food carriers depicted in the middle register of the vase. He must, therefore, be identified as a member of that group. All of these individuals are shown completely naked, with their heads shaven as well. Similar naked figures are depicted on two Late Uruk seals (Frankfort 1939: pl. 3 fig. d; Schmidt et al. 1972: pl. 42 fig. a),[238] which show them in the process of delivering various cultic objects to a temple that, because of the presence of NUN emblems in both instances, may be identified as that of Enki. As the third millennium texts and art make it clear, the access to the sanctuary's cella where the statue of the deity was housed was limited to two types of ritual specialists only: the chief priest or priestess and the officiants whose function was to feed the statue and probably also to manipulate it ritually in other ways as well, through the actions of waking the statue up, dressing it and undressing, laying it back to sleep, etc. These officiants, likewise naked and with shaven heads, appear in a number of ED III images, where they are depicted standing before a divine statue or, exceptionally, in front of a temple. See Braun-Holzinger 2013: pl. 11 fig. 5, pl. 13 figs. 7 and 8(!), pl. 14 figs. 10 (= our **fig. 26**) and 11, pl. 15 fig. 13, pl. 16 fig. 16. In all likelihood, the functionaries in question bore the title of gudu$_4$, Akk. *pašīšu*. As indicated by the word *pašīšu*, "the anointed one," lit.: "the smeared with oil," because of his physical contact with the divine, this functionary needed to remain ritually pure in order to prevent the statue's pollution. This meant that all his head and body hair had to be

---

ing that these two images involve a closely related ritual event, whose referent in either case was Inana.

235 The shape of these vessels is identical with that of the vase itself. The same vessels are depicted on the Late Uruk seals Vogel 2013: 143 fig 20:5 (= our **fig. 3**) and Buchanan 1981: 44 fig. 136c (= MSVO 4 pl. 41 no. 78). See further the "Blau Plaque," front (Gelb, Steinkeller, and Whiting 1991: Text Volume 41–43 no. 11, Plates Volume pl. 12 no. 11), on which the Priest-King holds up an object that very likely represents this vessel as well.

236 Similar zoomorphic stands appear on the Late Uruk seal Vogel 2013: 143 fig 20:5 (= our **fig. 3**).

237 The same footed plates are depicted on the Late Uruk seals Vogel 2013: 143 fig 20:5 (= our **fig. 3**) and Marchesi and Marchetti 2011: pl. 48 fig. 9.

238 The first seal (Frankfort 1939: pl. 3 fig. d) includes in addition a male that wears a short tunic and seems to have long hair falling down his back. He likely is the same person as the Priest-King's attendant appearing on the Warka Vase, whom I tentatively identify as the abgal official. See above p. 69.

removed, and that his entire body then be smeared with the cultically "pure" (Sumerian kug) oil.[239] It is certain, in my view, that the naked figures appearing on the Warka Vase represent precisely this kind of ritual functionaries. However, as the Uruk III texts do not contain (as far as I know) any mentions of the gudu$_4$, their title remains unknown. Be that as it may, these data add further substance to the conclusion that the top register of the Warka Vase depicts a ritual, which takes place in the cella of Inana's sanctuary (eš$_3$), and shows the act of feeding the goddess (or her statue).

A novel interpretation of the top register of the Warka Vase was suggested by Daniel Hockmann (2008), who claimed that the scene in question includes a number of city names. It was those cities, in Hockmann's view, that were responsible for the delivery of foodstuffs depicted in this scene. Hockmann's prime "identification" is the name of Nippur, which he creates out of the EN object (for which see above) and the stepped altar on which the figure holding the EN object and her/his companion are standing. Hockmann imagines this altar to be a *Sockel*, interpreting it as the sign KID. In his opinion, the EN object and the alleged KID belong together, forming the toponym EN.LIL$_2$ = Nibru. However, the altar in no way looks like the KID sign (ZATU-291) or, for that matter, as E$_2$, which would be the correct component of Nibru (= EN.E$_2$) in that period. As I note above in n. 231, this object is simply an altar, several examples of which are depicted in Uruk art.[240] Incredibly, Hockmann then goes on to interpret two very similar altars shown on Late Uruk seals as the signs AB and URU, producing more "toponyms" of this kind. Needless to say, these identifications are baseless. As for the other "readings" suggested by Hockmann, the bull's head appearing as part of the scene (2008: 330 and fig. 3) indeed is formally identical with the archaic sign KIŠ/ALIM sign (see Steinkeller 2004b), but, given the context, it undoubtedly is a real bull's head, which formed part of the offerings. For similar depictions of animal body parts presented as offerings, see Vogel 2013: 143 fig 20:5 (= our **fig. 3**) and the Old Akkadian seal Boehmer 1965: pl. 32 fig. 387, the latter depicting a ram's head on top of an altar. Regrettably, Hockmann's interpretation has uncritically been embraced by a number of archaeologists / art historians. See, e. g., Marchetti in Marchesi and Marchetti 2011: 190–191 and n. 27; McCaffrey 2013: 238–239.

---

239 Interestingly, Jacobsen (1963: 477 n. 11) interpreted UH.ME, the constituent signs of gudu$_4$, as a combination of uh(u), "lice, vermin," and išib(ME), "anointed," that is, "lice-cleansed." As he further elaborated, "anointing served specifically as a means to rid oneself of lice; conceivably the oil used contained petroleum or some other effective bituminous ingredient ... this connotation of delousing underlies the term gudu" (ibid. 477 n. 11).

240 For this identification, see already Hans H. von der Osten 1934: 16 no. 22, 116 and fig. 11.

2.2 Five Uruk Seals Depicting the Priest-King and Inana

A scene closely similar to the one represented on the Warka Vase, likewise involving the Priest-King and Inana and illustrating a close and intimate relationship between the two, is found on five Late Uruk cylinder seals (Heinrich 1936: pl. 17 fig. d, pl. 18 figs. a, b, c, and d; discussed ibid. 29–30).[241] See **figs. 11–15.** Four of these artifacts, together with the Warka Vase and three other Uruk III cylinder seals pertaining to Inana's cult,[242] formed part of a deposit (the so-called *Sammelfund*) excavated in the latest phase of level III of the Eanna precinct, Inana's temple at Uruk.[243] This fact is highly significant, since it suggests that this group of objects, which obviously constituted a treasured heirloom, had been selected and buried in that particular location because of their connection with and the paramount importance for Inana's cult.

The image borne by the five seals in question is practically the same in each instance. It shows the Priest-King and Inana facing each other; they are separated by two large baskets with food offerings. These are closely similar to the ones pictured in the top register of the Warka Vase, to the right of the altar supported by two rams. In one instance, Inana follows the Priest-King, who faces the baskets (Heinrich 1936: pl. 18 fig. b = our **fig. 13**). The goddess wears headgear that closely resembles that shown on the Warka Vase. She is accompanied by the MUŠ$_3$ emblem, which explicitly identifies her as Inana (Heinrich 1936: pl. 17 fig. d, pl. 18 figs. a, b, and d = our **figs. 11, 12, 13 and 15**). Her connection with it is underscored by the fact that, in Heinrich 1936: pl. 17 fig. d, pl. 18 figs. b and d (= our **figs. 11, 13, and 15**), she actually *holds* the emblem, more precisely, the scarf forming part it. Here it is significant that, in two cases, Inana wears a very similar scarf herself, which falls down over her back (Heinrich 1936: pl. 17 fig. d, pl. 18 fig. d = our **figs. 11 and 15**).[244] The Priest-King carries in his hands a grain stalk (Heinrich 1936: pl. 17 fig. d, pl. 18 fig. b, c, and d = our **figs. 11, 13–15**).

---

241 The most recent extensive discussion of these seals is by Marchesi in Marchesi and Marchetti 2011: 190.

242 Heinrich 1936: pl. 17 figs. a and b, pl. 19 fig. a.

243 See Heinrich 1936: 2–6; Marchesi in Marchesi and Marchetti 2011: 189–190.

244 If correct, this point would lend further support to my identification of Inana's emblem. See above n. 230.

2.3 Summation

It is certain that the scene represented on the seals just discussed is an abbreviated version of the top register of the Warka Vase, both of them depicting a delivery of food offerings to Inana by the Priest-King, possibly as part of her ritual observances. The identity of these observances remains unknown, though it may have been one of Inana's regular festivals (ezen), such as the "festivals of the Morning and Evening Inana," which are mentioned in the archaic tablets from Uruk.[245] It is equally possible, however, that what the Warka Vase and the seals present to us is a generalized definition of the relationship that existed between the Priest-King and Inana, without referring to any of her observances in particular. This relationship was reciprocal, with the Priest-King feeding Inana on behalf of the community he ruled over, and with Inana providing the Uruk community with agricultural abundance and protection in return, and making the Priest-King her chosen representative. The relationship between the Priest-King and Inana may even have been symbolically spousal – as suggested by the later Babylonian tradition and the comparative data demonstrating the common existence of such arrangements between rulers and goddesses – but there is no reason to suspect that some sort of a "sacred marriage" ritual is meant in this particular instance.

Both the Warka Vase and five seals in question firmly associate the Priest-King with Inana, thereby establishing beyond any doubt that he was Inana's chief ritual official. This association is confirmed by various other Late Uruk images, in particular, the cylinder seals on which the Priest-King appears as a caretaker of Inana's herds. Among those, of special importance are Heinrich 1936: pl. 17 fig. c and Klengel-Brandt 1997: 63 fig. 47 (= our **fig. 4**), where the Priest-King offers rosettes to the cattle and goats respectively. As is well known, the rosette, which is simultaneously a representation of the star – thereby meaning "deity" (dingir) and "heaven" (an) – is Inana's alternative symbol.[246] In both instances, the MUŠ$_3$ emblems are included in the image as well.

The grain stalk that appears as an attribute of the Priest-King in several Uruk III seals (Heinrich 1936: pl. 17 figs. b and d, pl. 18 fig. b, c, and d; Strommenger 1962: fig. 16 bottom) obviously indicates this official's responsibility for cereal production, perhaps even representing one of his symbols (Marchetti in Marchesi and Marchetti 2011: 190, 192). On the other hand, his involvement in animal husbandry, as depicted on some other seals, shows that he was Uruk's chief shep-

---

245 See above p. 27.
246 See Steinkeller 2002a; Szarzyńska 2011.

herd as well. As is strongly suggested by the inclusion of the pictogram EN among the imagery of the Warka Vase, the title of this official in all probability was en.

2.4 Further Remarks and Final Conclusion

This interpretation of the Priest-King iconography, while providing new data and insights, and clarifying, hopefully, some of the outstanding problems, in its essence represents what has been the traditional *communis opinio* regarding this matter. Two recent studies, however, question some of the basic assumptions of this position. It is necessary, therefore, to address these contrary opinions in some detail.

In a book co-authored with Gianni Marchesi, Nicolò Marchetti denies that the Priest-King is a mortal, identifying him as a god instead (Marchesi and Marchetti 2011: 186–196).[247] Marchetti's sole argument here is the fact that the imagery of the Priest-King is limited to the Uruk III period, disappearing subsequently (ibid. 187). An obvious explanation of this situation is the possibility that the office of the en underwent an evolution over time, by the Early Dynasty period morphing into that of ensik, which differed significantly from the Uruk prototype, especially in that it no longer comprised any specifically priestly functions. See my discussion of this problem below pp. 103–104. That the Priest-King is not a god is shown conclusively by the images depicting him, in the contexts entirely devoid of any religious character, as a warrior and hunter (see above). In his search for a candidate for that hypothetical male deity, Marchetti settles on ᵈInana kur, one of Inana's avatars mentioned in Uruk III economic documents, whom he identifies, against all evidence and logic, as a male form of Inana (ibid. 192).[248] Equally unconvincing is Marchetti's interpretation of the human figure appearing on the ED II "Figure aux plumes," which he explains as another depiction of the Priest-King, and which, in his view, must necessarily "show the god celebrated in the inscription [i.e., Ningirsu]" (ibid. 195). But the figure in question resembles the Priest-King of Uruk art only vaguely. Nor is there any

---

247 Marchetti is responsible for the chapters dealing with archaeological and art-historical matters; Marchesi wrote the ones dealing with philology and purely historical issues.

248 In all likelihood, the deity in question is a netherworld form of Inana. See above p. 27. A much more reasonable candidate for such an interpretation would have been Dumuzi, as speculated by Jacobsen 1976: 26. But the fact that the Priest-King appears as a warrior and hunter in Late Uruk art excludes Dumuzi from consideration as well, at least in his purely divine form.

compelling reason to think that this figure is a god. As generally believed, in all likelihood this is a depiction of the ruler of Lagaš of that particular period.

While Marchetti's idea obviously is false, a caveat needs to be offered in this connection. As I wrote earlier (see above pp. 29–30), there is a distinct possibility that the Priest-King of Late Uruk times enjoyed a semi-divine status, being a Dumuzi-like figure of sorts, in which he differed quite significantly from the later ensiks, his linear successors. If true, this would consequently mean that his office was charged with a high degree of sacrality. But there is no indication that the Priest-King was a divine king *sensu stricto*. I return to this problem in Essay 2.

The other contrary opinion I alluded to earlier is found in an article by Claudia Suter (2014), who argues that the female figure represented on the Warka Vase and the seals in question – who, in our view, is Inana – actually is a mortal.[249] The main argument Suter offers in support of this idea is the fact that, allegedly, no anthropomorphic representations of deities are documented before the ED III period. However, this argument is circular, since, if the Uruk images in question do depict Inana (as generally thought), this evidence proves that such images existed already in Late Uruk times. Even more important is the fact that statues of Inana are actually mentioned in Uruk III sources. There survive at least four references to such images:

(1) 80 (units of barley) for TAK$_4$.ALAM ^{d}Inana hud$_2$, "statue of the Morning Inana" (MSVO 3 28 i 1);
(2) 1 (unit of barley) for TAK$_4$.[AL]AM Inana (ATU 2 pl. 21 W 20274,11 iii 1);
(3) 3 (units of barley) for TAK$_4$.ALAM ^{d}Inana; (out of this) 1 (unit of barley was spent) for ZATU-649? (probably a location), 1 (unit of barley was spent) for the "cattle pen" (tur$_3$-a), and 1 (unit of barley was spent) for the "shrine of the Evening Inana" (eš$_3$ Inana sig) (ATU 2 pl. 22 W 20274,16 i 3);
(4) 1 (unit of barley?) for [TAK$_4$].ALAM Inana (ATU 2 pl. 32 W 20327,4 i 2′).[250]

For TAK$_4$.ALAM, "statue," see TAK$_4$.ALAM = *la-ʾà-núm* (= alam/alan; cf. *lānu*, "figure") ("Ebla Syllabary" line 52 = Archi 1987: 95); TAK$_4$.ALAM = *šè-tum* ("Ebla Vocabulary" line 1275′ = MEE 4 333), where *šēdu*, "protective spirit/statue" apparently

---

249 This speculation revives the earlier suggestion made by Asher-Greve 1985: 7–8, who sought to identify this figure as a priestess of Inana.

250 Further evidence of the existence of such statues is provided by two Uruk III tablets, which refer to Inana's bedroom (e$_2$-na$_2$ Inana) at Uruk (ATU 2 pl. 30 W 20274, 36 i 1; ATU 7 pl. 47 W 20274,54 ii 1, iii 1). The second of them mentions also "one bed" (1 na$_2$; iii 2). See further 1 MUŠ$_3$ na$_2$ Inana, "1 MUŠ$_3$ (emblem or scarf) for the bed of Inana" (ATU 5 pl. 90 W 9656,af ii 2′–3′), and e$_2$-na$_2$ (ATU 2 pl. 32 W. 20327,4 i 5′). Obviously, these data imply the presence of Inana's statues as well.

is meant. Cf. DUL$_3$ = *lu-ma-'à-sum*. "protective spirit/statue" ("Ebla Syllabary" line 49 = Archi 1987: 95). See further TAK$_4$.ALAM-ni nam-ti-la-ni-da he$_2$-na-da-gub, "may his statue stand for/before DN, for the intention of his life" (Steible 1982: 342 Anonym 3:5–7, an upper half of the ED III statuette of a male worshipper; Walters Art Museum, Baltimore, 21.5; Braun-Holzinger 1977: 74, 83). An official gal-TAK$_4$.ALAM, who appears in ED Lu A line 122 (also in archaic Lu 122 = ATU 3 84), probably supervised sculptors.[251] This is confirmed by Diri VI B 86 (= MSL 15 192), which translates URUDU.SIG$_7$.TAK$_4$.ALAM as *gurgurru*, "sculptor" (usually corresponding to tibira).[252] SIG$_7$.ALAM = *nabnītu*, "appearance, stature," appears to be related as well; it is possible that SIG$_7$.ALAM is a misinterpretation of the original TAK$_4$.ALAM.

A likely example of a Late Uruk statue of a deity is the spectacular female head of marble from Uruk, the so-called "Lady of Warka,"[253] which almost certainly is a depiction of Inana. See **fig. 16**. This conclusion is supported by the fact that the top of this head is provided with indentations and groves that must have supported either a hairdo or a crown. The second option is more likely, since the ED IIIB texts from Lagaš specifically mention a silver crown that "fills / fits into the head (of a statue)," specimens of which belonged to the statues of the goddesses Nanše and Nin-MAR.KI.[254]

Here it should also be noted that the anthropomorphic representations of deities are documented already in ED II art, thus much earlier than "the last phase of the Early Dynastic period," as Suter asserts (2014: 551). The best examples of such images come from a group of cylinder seals depicting the construction of stepped towers, which show seated deities wearing crowns (Braun-Holzinger 2013: pls. 39–40 figs. 128, 129, 132, 139 and 142; discussed ibid. 124–130, 208–211). [255] There may survive an even earlier image of a deity in human form. A Jemdet Nasr seal shows a human face (evidently female) flanked by three rosettes, which hovers over a temple facade with gateposts (Frankfort

---

251 TAK$_4$.ALAM designates "sculptor" in the ED IIIb texts from Lagaš. See Nikolski 1 108 ii 1–2; VAS 14 106 iii 2.

252 The tibira/*gurgurru* was an elite craftsman, who used metal and wood to manufacture statues, high quality furniture, and various other types of inlaid objects. See, in particular, CT 7 16 BM 17765 ii 21 and SAT 1 63:8 (both from Girsu/Lagaš), which refer to the tibira working on royal statues.

253 This object was found in the level Uruk III of the Eanna precinct (Lenzen 1940: 19–21). According to the excavators, its deposition occurred not later than Uruk IIIa (ibid. 20).

254 men-sag-si-ga (kug luh-ha) ... ^{d}Nanše (VAS 14 13 ii 1–3; DP 70 i 5 – ii 2, 71 i 2–4, 72 i 1 – iii 2); men-sag-si-ga ... ^{d}Nin-MAR.KI (DP 69 i 2–4).

255 A related seal, likewise depicting a construction and a horned seated deity, is Pittman and Aruz 1987: 55 fig. 19. Although dated to ED IIIa by the authors, its date is more likely ED II.

1955: pl. 84 fig. 880). See **fig. 17**. Given the presence of rosettes, Inana's symbols, this plausibly is a representation of Inana.

To bolster her idea that the female companion of the Priest-King is a mortal, Suter needs to neutralize any evidence that might indicate this person's divinity. Thus she argues that the fact that Inana's emblem may appear repeatedly in the same image (as on the Warka Vase) "speaks against the interpretation of reed standards as icons of the respective deity [i.e., Inana] in symbolic form" (2014: 552). Further evidence of this, in her view, are the images where Inana's emblems appear without the female figure in question (ibid. 552). To minimize the connection between Inana and the MUŠ₃ emblems, Suter subsequently claims that, on the seals depicting the Priest-King and Inana – contrary to what these images actually show (see above p. 88) – "Inana's standard *only is touched* by the same female as the one depicted on the Uruk Vase [emphasis added]" (ibid. 552). All this evidence convinces her that Inana's emblems are merely "markers of numinosity" (ibid. 552). Hence her conclusion that "this function of reed standards precludes that the female on the Uruk Vase depicted the goddess" (ibid. 552).

These speculations are without any substance. As Mesopotamian visual art demonstrates very clearly, divine symbols function as alter-egos of the deities they stand for irrespective of whether or not those are concurrently depicted in anthropomorphic form. Thus, the anthropomorphic Inana/Ištar is often accompanied by a lioness, her avatar as the goddess of battle, Iškur/Adad is depicted with his lightning, Gula is shown together with her dog, and so forth. In the same way, in Late Uruk art Inana is most commonly represented by the MUŠ₃ emblem,[256] which may appear either alone or together with her anthropomorphic apparition. Here it is completely irrelevant how many symbols are depicted in one image. As we have seen earlier, the Warka Vase depicts three MUŠ₃ emblems: two of them flanking the goddess, and another, smaller one, on top of the altar behind her. The function of all three of them is identical: to reference the goddess, either directly – as do the large emblems next to her, or indirectly – as does the smaller emblem, which identifies the altar and the two persons standing on it as belonging to Inana's cult. Needless to say, this whole issue has little to do with "numinosity," which simply indicates a divine presence when the deity remains invisible. In the case of the MUŠ₃ emblems of Inana, one indeed could say that these indicate Inana's "numinous" presence when she is not depicted in her anthropomorphic form. But it is absurd to claim that such "numinosity" cannot co-exist with anthropomorphic representa-

---

256 Though Inana is also symbolized by the rosette and the lioness, both of which were her alternative avatars.

tions. This is clearly shown by the earlier-cited cases where both the anthropomorphic representation and the symbol appear together.

Suter thinks that the female appearing on the Warka Vase and the seals in
question is some "elite woman linked to Inana," such as, for example, the ruler's
wife (2014: 555). However, in view of the transparent importance and high sym-
bolism of the scene represented on the vase, it is difficult to see how the recipient of Inana's ritual offerings, delivered with such pomp and circumstance by
the ruler of Uruk on behalf of the whole community, could be one of her representatives, rather than the goddess herself. This impression is strengthened by
the regal and commanding gesture with which the female figure greets (or bless-
es) the Priest-King, which is exactly the same as that used by deities in later Mesopotamian art. Moreover, this figure is accompanied by two cultic attendants –
in the same way that the Priest-King has his own two attendants, making the
scene perfectly symetrical – which suggests that she is more than just a priestess.
The encounter between the Priest-King and the female figure, which is the climax
of the visual program of the vase, is so dramatic and charged with such intense
religious emotion that the viewer is *forced* to conclude that the figure in question
is a deity. This has been the usual – and I would say the natural – response to
this image. Apart from these arguments, which rest on essentially esthetic considerations, another reason why Suter's hypothesis lacks conviction is the fact
that no priestesses of Inana of any importance are attested in later times. Therefore, the possibility that such officials did exit in Uruk times, though they for
some reason disappeared later, is not very likely.

3 The en Official in Uruk III tablets

The en functionary is mentioned very often in Uruk III economic documents,
both those from Uruk itself and the ones stemming from other sites, such as Jemdet Nasr and Tell Uqair, as well as in tablets of undetermined origin. Even more
importantly, many of such attestations present him as an official of very high status. This is underscored by the fact that the title of en often appears in the tablet's colophon.

The en of Uruk may specifically be referred to in three texts of uncertain origin.[257] Tablets from Jemdet Nasr, a northern Babylonian site whose archaic name

---

257 CUSAS 1 20 ii 1; MSVO 3 21 i 2; CUSAS 31 185 iii 3′. In each case, these tablets record expenditures of commodities for en Unug.

probably was NI.RU (Englund 1996: 12), mention an en of NI.RU,[258] evidently the ruler of that city. Similarly, in the documentation from Tell Uqair, the title of en is associated, usually in the concluding section of the document, with the signs (ME.)HA.UR₂.RAD (appearing in different combinations),[259] which almost certainly are to be read $Urum_x$, and explained as the archaic spelling of Urum (Green 1986; Gelb et al. 1991: 40–41; Englund 1996: 12 n. 22; Steinkeller 2002b: 252–254), a northern Babylonian city well known from later periods. Here too, apparently, we find a city ruler. These facts suggest that, during the Uruk III period, en served as a generic designation of the city-state ruler throughout Babylonia.

Above anything else, the paramount importance of the en is demonstrated by the fact that, in a number of sources, he is assigned very large areas of agricultural land. Here one may single out MSVO 1 2, 3, and 4, from Jemdet Nasr, and MSVO 4 57, which possibly stems from Larsa (Steinkeller 1988: 13–14; Englund 1996: 17; Fridberg 1997/1998: 19–32). Among these sources, MSVO 1 2 credits the en with a total of 3,852 iku (= 1,387 ha) of land. According to MSVO 4 57, in another instance the en held 720 iku (= 259 ha) of land, which was part of a larger area (1,824 iku = 657 ha) held by five towns or townships (uru).[260]

The en also appears as a recipient of large volumes of barley and various commodities. See, e.g., MSVO 1 4, 7; MSVO 3 83; MSVO 4 1, 3, 4, 19, 22, 24, 25, 28, 41, and 54. In other sources, he is identified as a possessor of sheep (e.g., CUSAS 31 60 rev., 65 i 2, 75 iv 3, v 3) and donkeys (e.g., CUSAS 21 53 i 2).

Uruk III sources frequently mention officials, craftsmen, and laborers associated with the en. One may plausibly infer that these were his various subordinates. However, due to the paramount difficulties presented by the archaic script, this point usually cannot be confirmed with certainty. One of the instances where such a determination is possible is MSVO 4 73, which is a listing of the en's cooks:

i	1)	1 muhaldim en	one cook (for) the en,
	2)	1 muhaldim eš₃	one cook (for) the shrine,
	3)	1 ŠUM.X.DI	(and) one (cook for) ŠUM.X.DI
	4)	DA	(were) assigned (to work);
ii	1)	gal-muhaldim en	(these are) chief cooks of the en;
iii	1)	3 gal-muhaldim en DA	three chief cooks of the en were assigned (to work).[261]

---

258 MSVO 1 159 and 235.

259 MSVO 4 1, 2, 3, 4, 10, 22, 24. 25, 26, 28, 34, and 35.

260 Cf. also CUSAS 1 25 I 1 – ii 2, which reads: [x] gana₂ en šag₄ Ama-men ru-a, "[x] land, the en donated (or: was donated to him) in the (field) Ama-men"; 4(bur₃) gana₂ šu en ʼx?ʼ.

261 The assumption that the sign DA means here "to assign" is only conjectural, of course. Since DA means later "side" in Sumerian, it could equally well refer to the placing of the cooks "aside," in order to perform other duties.

There are also instances where the en appears in connection with ritual observances. A good example here is ATU 7 pl. 77 W 21671, from Uruk, which records expenditures of woolen garments, linens, and covers in connection with the festivals of the "Evening and Morning Inana" (^{d}Inana sig, ii 1; ^{d}Inana hud$_2$; ii 10), which, in this particular case, appear to have taken place at Ur. In two instances, the recipient of these items was a carpenter of the en, present at Ur (nagar en Urim$_x$(ŠEŠ); ii 5–6, iii 8). The en himself appears in the tablet's concluding sections. There, all the items enumerated earlier are summarized under his title, and he is described as participating in these festivals: en ezen dingir dug$_3$ 'ZATU-743' Urim$_x$(ŠEŠ), "the en, (acting) at the festivals of the Sweet Deity (i.e., Inana), at Ur, ..." The same ritual event is mentioned in another Uruk tablet: 8 SAL+KUR en ezen dingir dug$_3$ Urim$_x$(ŠEŠ) ZATU-774, "eight slave women (assigned to) the en (for) the festivals of the Sweet Deity at Ur, ..." (W 23999,l iii 1 = Englund 1995: 132).[262]

Another indication of the high status of the en is the fact that the sign EN forms part of a number of the archaic names of occupations, such as engiz (EN.-ME.GI) and endib(EN.ME.MU), both describing ritual cooks. It is likely that these functionaries were the en's subordinates, whose title gave rise to their own particular designations. A similar development may have taken place also in the case of the title ensik, the designation of the city-state ruler in late ED times, which too conceivably derives from the word en. See below pp. 103–104.

4 The Question of nam$_2$-šita$_2$

Since it has been speculated that the Priest-King of Late Uruk art actually bore the title of nam$_2$-šita$_2$,[263] which appears in line 1 of the Uruk III version of the Lu List A,[264] it is necessary to examine this issue systematically.

---

262 See also CUSAS 1 150 i 1–3, which records commodities for ezen en sag, possibly to be interpreted as "chief festival of the en." A group of tablets from Uruk (ATU 2 pls. 19–22 W 20274,5, W 20274,10, W 20274,11, W 20274,13 [= ATU 7 pl. 40], W 20274,16, pl. 32 W 20327,4, pl. 55 W 20511,1) mention the en in connection with Inana's observances, always in the sign-group en eš$_3$ dug ZATU-686.

263 This vocable is commonly cited as "namešda" in literature. This transliteration is based on the value of ŠITA$_2$ as given in some lexical sources: eš-da ŠITA.GIŠ.NAM$_2$ (Lu I 26 = MSL 12 93); eš-da ŠITA.GIŠ (Ea II 36 = MSL 14 248); eš$_6$-ta ŠITA (CT 51 pl. 59 iv 1). This value is a secondary development, which obviously derives from the *phonetic* shape of nam$_2$-šita$_2$ that resulted from the contraction of this compound: [námšita] > [naméšta]. Since the basic value of ŠITA$_2$ is šita (Diri II 257), the compound in question is to be transliterated nam$_2$-šita$_2$.

The idea that nam$_2$-šita$_2$ was the highest-ranking official in archaic Uruk, and that he was identical with the Priest-King of Late Uruk art, was first suggested by Lambert 1981: 94–97. Lambert's evidence in that regard was twofold:

(1) The fact that, in the ED IIIb text ECTJ 173 i 8 = ii 8, which uses an orthography known as UD.GAL.NUN, the sign NAM$_2$ replaces EN in the writing of Enlil's name. This particular spelling, together with the testimony of a Middle Babylonian lexical list that equates NAM with *bēlu* (CT 51 168 iv 52), convinced Lambert that nam$_2$ corresponds to *bēlu*, "lord";

(2) The evidence of the late lexical list Lu = *ša*, which, in Tablet I lines 25–26 (MSL 12 93), translates both šita and nam$_2$-šita$_2$ as *šarru*, "king." As Lambert (probably correctly) concluded, in these two entries the word šita, one of whose meaning is "mace, weapon" (*kakku*), probably is a metaphor for "king."

Hence Lambert's final conclusion that nam$_2$-šita$_2$ is the "lord of the mace," and therefore, that this term denotes the archaic ruler of Uruk (Lambert 1981: 94). This hypothesis was subsequently accepted by numerous scholars (see, e. g., Nissen 1986: 329; Selz 1998: 300–301, 306; Glassner 2000b; Charvát 2012; Bourguignon 2012: 250). Lambert's hypothesis appeared particularly attractive because nam$_2$-šita$_2$ is listed in the opening line of the Lu A. This suggested to some that this source uses a hierarchical arrangement, with nam$_2$-šita$_2$ indeed designating the top official of Uruk.

The main problem with Lambert's hypothesis is that, in the UD.GAL.NUN orthography, which was used during the ED III period, the correspondent of EN regularly is GAL. In light of this, the occurrence of NAM$_2$ as a variant of EN in ECTJ 173 is completely aberrant, and, accordingly, it almost certainly is wrong. Furthermore, there is no reason to think that the UD.GAL.NUN orthography existed already in the Uruk III period.[265] As for the second millennium interpretations of nam$_2$-šita$_2$ and šita as *šarru*, "king," they either are metaphorical (by associating

---

264 The term nam$_2$-šita$_2$ is also found in the Uruk III List "Officials" line no. 23 (Englund and Nissen 1993: 86–89). nam$_2$-šita$_2$ is further mentioned in ED IIIa sources. Here note especially the mentions of nam$_2$-šita$_2$ Larsam(UD.UNUG) and nam$_2$-šita$_2$, which appear following gal-šidim Unug, "chief mason of Unug" (SF 57 vii 8–9 = OIP 99 46 vi 3–5, 53 iii′ 6′–7′). See also nam$_2$-šita$_2$ 600, "(a group of) 600 nam$_2$-šita$_2$," (OIP 99 142 xi 4′, 13′); šita$_2$ 600 "(a group of) 600 šita$_2$," (OIP 99 306 iii′ 1′, which joins OIP 99 129). Charvát 2012: 267–269 seeks nam$_2$-šita$_2$ in a sealing from archaic Ur (UE 3 no. 429), alleging that the inscription in the upper register of this sealing begins with ŠITA+GIŠ+NAM$_2$. However, this reading is completely fantastic. All one can read there is X ⌜X⌝ UD Nibru(EN.E$_2$) X.

265 Referring to the archaic list Ad-gi$_4$, Civil 2013: 16 states that this text "shows many features of the UD.GAL.NUN" system, but without offering any specific examples. Although Civil could be right, I am not aware of any *certain* evidence to that effect.

the meaning "mace" of šita with "king") or are mistaken.[266] These facts render Lambert's hypothesis untenable.

That nam_2-$šita_2$ was not the title of the Priest-King of Late Uruk art is equally emphatically demonstrated by Uruk III economic sources. Although nam_2-$šita_2$ does appear in these materials, such attestations are very rare. Green and Nissen 1987: 197, 252, list 464 examples of en in the administrative texts from Uruk, against nineteen examples of nam_2-$šita_2$. Similarly, the indexes of an edition of the Uruk III texts from Jemdet Nasr (Englund and Grégoire 1991) show only three attestations of nam_2-$šita_2$, while those of en number over 140. Moreover, none of the extant occurrences of the nam_2-$šita_2$ official suggest that he was a functionary of special importance.[267] Such evidence certainly is not the fact that nam_2-$šita_2$ occupies position no. 1 in the archaic Lu A list, since, as I noted earlier (see above p. 49), this source does not appear to follow a hierarchical order. In this connection, it is significant that the "Officials" list (Englund and Nissen 1993: 86–89), the other Uruk III source mentioning this title, assigns to nam_2-$šita_2$ position no. 23.

In my view, all these facts preclude any possibility of nam_2-$šita_2$ being the title of the Priest-King.

As for the term nam_2-$šita_2$ itself, one needs to begin with an observation that the initial element nam_2 appears in nine other entries of the Lu A list: nam_2-KAB/ TUKU (2),[268] nam_2-DI (3), nam_2-umuš (4), nam_2-uru (5),[269] nam_2-EREN (6), nam_2- apin/engar (8),[270] nam_2-PA.RAD (10),[271] nam_2-ŠAB (26a), and nam_2-PA.KIŠ/ALIM (26b).[272] Without any doubt, this nam_2 is a variant spelling of the formant nam, which serves to create abstract concepts in Sumerian.[273] As a matter of fact, this spelling appears occasionally in the ED III and later sources.[274] This evidence

---

266 For this possibility, see Veldhuis 2014: 36: "It is well possible that in later periods items of Lu A were reinterpreted, and the translation NAMEŠDA = šarru (king), for instance, may be based on the assumption by Old Babylonian scholar scribes that the king should head a list like this."

267 Cf. Veldhuis 2014: 36, who, referring to the tablet ATU 6 W 15897, c8, concludes as follows: "Neither his position on the tablet nor the quantity of food received by NAMEŠDA suggests that he is in a position of supreme power."

268 Found also in CUSAS 31 43 ii 3, 4; ATU 5 pl. 40 W 9168,h+ ii 2; pl. 86 W 9656,g i 2; etc.

269 Found also in MSVO 3 61 i 4; ATU 5 pl. 74 W 9579,de.

270 Found also in ATU 5 pl. 73 W 9579,co.

271 Found also in CUSAS 31 184 ii 3'.

272 This title also appears in an unpublished ED II inscription (Steinkeller 2013a: 140).

273 For this conclusion, see already Lambert 1981: 84: Wilcke 2005: 442.

274 See, e. g., nig_2-nam_2 for nig_2-nam and na-nam_2 for na-nam in the ED Adab version of "Instructions of Šuruppak" lines 28 and 30 (Alster 2005: 62); nam_2 ʼmuʼ-tar (OIP 99 131 vi 12'); nam_2-

leads one to the conclusion that nam₂-šita₂ and the other entries composed with nam₂ are abstract terms, which, rather than being titles or occupations *per se*, identify either the areas of professional responsibility or the officials collectively responsible for particular aspects of the government and economy.[275] In this way, nam₂-umuš possibly means "counseling, advising" or the "consulting body";[276] nam₂-uru may describe the duties related to or the officials responsible for city administration;[277] and nam₂-apin/engar certainly means agricultural concerns or the functionaries collectively responsible for agriculture.[278] By analogy with these terms, nam₂-šita₂ may be expected to be a similar general/collective designation.

A possible clue to the meaning of nam₂-šita₂ is provided by the lexeme šita, which is written with a simplified ŠITA₂ sign (i.e., ŠITA), and which likely represents the same word as šita₂. All the meanings of šita are connected with cult.[279] Here one finds the meaning "ritual, prayer" (Akk. *ikribū, riksu*). The word šita also describes various types of priests, such as šita-eš₃-sa₂, "šita of the shrine,"[280] šita-ab-ba, "šita of the Sea,"[281] šita-Abzu, "šita of the Abzu temple," šita-ᵈInana,[282] and šita-gal, "chief šita."[283] A related meaning of šita is "cultically pure" (*ramku, ellu*), which too functions as a priestly designation.

---

nun-e (nam₂-nun-e) in lines 1–3 of the OB "Keš Temple Hymn," corresponding to [na]m-nun-ne₂ [na]m-nun-ne₂ in its ED version (Biggs 1971: 200 A i 1); nam₂-nun-e nam₂-nun-e (TCL 15 17:10; nam₂-nun-ne sag na-an-il₂-ta (TCL 15 28:35) = nam-nun-e sag na-il₂-ˈxˈ (UET 6 123:24) (the last two references are cited courtesy of G. Marchesi).

275 So also concludes Wilcke 2005: 442. Since the entries beginning with nam₂ are confined to the beginning section of the list (lines 1–10, excluding the additional entries in lines 26a and 26b), it is possible that, as Christopher Woods suggests to me, these designations identify the principal spheres of professional responsibility in which the scribal class was active.

276 See Glassner 2000a: 204, 268; Wilcke 2005: 443.

277 Cf. Wilcke 2002: 443, who translates it "Stadt-Amt."

278 Cf. Wilcke 2005: 443, who translates it "Pflüger-Amt."

279 I exclude here the meaning *šarru*, "king," which, as I argued earlier, is either erroneous or derived from the meaning "mace, weapon" of šita, as describing royal insignia.

280 Ur-SAR₂xDIŠ / šita-eš₃-sa₂ ᵈInana (Boehmer 1965: pl. 19 fig. 211; Sargonic). See also PN šita-eš₃ (Pomponio 1987: 230; ED IIIa); Sal-le šita-eš₃ (UET 3 101:5, 378:7; Ur III); šita-eš₃-a ("Nanše Hymn" line 117).

281 This priest served the goddess Nin-MAR.KI, whose home was at Gu₂-ab-ba, on the coast of the Persian Gulf. See RIME 3/1 8–9 Ur-Ningirsu I 2.

282 Fot his title, which is found in ED IIIa and later lexical sources, see Civil 1987.

283 For these and other types of šita priests, see Renger 1969: 129–132. Here it should be noted that šita appears already in line 7 of the Uruk III lexical list "Officials" (Englund and Nissen 1993: 86–89). Note also gal-šita in ATU 2 pl. 18 W 20274,1 i.

There is also a term nam-šita, which is formally identical with the Uruk III nam$_2$-šita$_2$. Like šita alone, nam-šita likewise means "ritual, prayer."[284] The lexical list Lu = ša equates nam-šita with Akkadian *kāribu*, a performer of ritual acts. Very significantly, the same source further explains nam-šita as a synonym of lu$_2$-garza = *bēl parṣi*, an official in charge of cultic matters:

[lu$_2$]-garza	=	*bēl*(EN) *pár-ṣi*
[nam]-šita	=	ŠU-*u*
nam-šita	=	*ka-ri-bu*
		(Lu = ša IV 95a, 95b, 96 = MSL 12 131)

As a matter of fact, both lu$_2$-garza (written lu$_2$-mar-za) and *bēl parṣi* are documented in third millennium texts, where they describe members of the highest echelon of the temple-household officialdom (Steinkeller 1999b: 562–564). These facts argue that the Uruk III nam$_2$-šita$_2$ is a collective designation of high cultic functionaries within a temple household. A confirmation of this supposition is provided, in my view, by the existence of the term nam-šita$_4$(U.KID), which, though employing a different writing of [šita], likewise denotes a type of temple functionary. The nam-šita$_4$ officials are well documented in OB times. We find them in the Ekišnugal temple at Ur (Charpin 1980: 47–49; 1986: 257–260), and there is an interesting mention of this office in connection with the Eanna, Inana's temple at Uruk: nig$_2$ mu 1-kam ud 10-kam nam-šita$_4$ E$_2$-an-na iti-nesag^{sag} ki ^{d}*Suen-ma-ilum*(DINGIR) u$_3$ *Bīt*(E$_2$)-*še-mi* ^{d}Nanna-i$_3$-mah in-ši-sa$_{10}$, "Nanna-imah bought from Suen-ma-ilum and Bit-šemi (the usufruct of the office of) nam-šita$_4$ of the Eanna, over a period of one year and ten days, (beginning in) the month Nisannu" (YOS 8 130:1–7; Larsa).

5 Later Data Bearing on the Archaic Kingship of Uruk

The conclusion that the archaic ruler of Uruk bore the title of en finds further support in various later data that either directly or obliquely refer to this individual and his office. This evidence shows that, during the second half of the third millennium BC, Babylonians consistently associated the title of en with the early

---

284 As far as I know, the earliest examples of nam-šita used in this sense come from the ED IIIb texts from Lagaš and Uruk. See ^{d}Ba-u$_2$ nam-šita Uru-ka-gi-na-ke$_4$ ba-DU (Sollberger Corpus Ukg. 53:1–2); PN Nam-šita-mu-bi$_2$-dug$_4$ (HSS 3 15 vii 15, 16 viii 5, 21 vi 14); ^{d}En-lil$_2$ lugal kur-kur-ra-ke$_4$ An a ki-ag$_2$-ni nam-šita-mu he$_2$-na-be$_2$ (RIME 1 433–437 Lugalzagesi 1 iii 14–18).

history of Uruk. The following is a listing of the most important data in this regard:

(a) During the ED IIIb period, there existed in Lagaš a cult of former rulers and high priests. As I wrote earlier (see pp. 30–31), these deceased individuals were collectively described as "lords" (en-en-e-ne). Here it is important that the word en is not otherwise used in the Lagaš sources in reference to rulers or priestly officials. It becomes obvious, therefore, that this usage preserves the memory of an earlier application of this title, when en described a functionary whose office combined ritual functions with political ones.

(b) ED IIIb sources from Ebla and Tell Beydar in the Habur region employ the logogram EN as a designation of rulers in charge of territorial states and larger cities (Marchesi in Marchesi and Marchetti 2011: 104–105).[285] This fact demonstrates that, at the time when these borrowings took place – which at the latest was the ED IIIb period, though an earlier date (ED IIIa or ED II) appears much more likely – Babylonian rulers indeed were called en.[286] This tradition is also reflected in the much later compositions "Enmerkar and the Lord of Aratta" and "Enmerkar and En-suhkeš-ana" (which probably were composed in Ur III times), where the ruler of Aratta likewise is identified as an en.

(c) One of the titles used by the Ur III kings is en Unug^{ki}. As argued by this author, this title defines the role of the king as a ruler of Uruk (Steinkeller 1999a: 110, 117–118). When acting in this role, the king superseded the en of Inana (invariably one of his sons), who served as the chief priest of Inana of Uruk in Ur III times. It is virtually certain that the Ur III title of the "en of Uruk" reproduces the one that had earlier been borne by the ED rulers of Uruk. A documented instance of this is Lugal-kigine-DU.DU, who held the title of the en of Unug, at the same time being the "king" (lugal) of Ur (RIME 1 413–414 Lugal-kigine-dudu 1). One of his successors, named En-šag$_4$-kuš$_2$-an-na, calls himself instead a "lord of Sumer" (en Ki-en-gi) and a "king of the Land" (lugal kalam-ma) (RIME 1 429–432 En-šakuš-ana 1 and 3), probably to add more importance to his office. However, En-šag$_4$-kuš$_2$-an-na's name reveals that he was the en of Inana (and therefore also of Uruk) as well. As I pointed out earlier, the name-pattern beginning with En- and concluding with -an-na is characteristic of ceremonial priestly names, most commonly associated with Inana and Nanna, which were used in Sargonic and Ur III times (see above p. 62). One may confidently assume that these names are patterned after the ones like En-šag$_4$-kuš$_2$-an-na, which, as

---

285 The actual words used differed, of course, depending on the local idom. At Ebla, the native term for "ruler" apparently was *maliku*.

286 For other examples of the title of en describing ED rulers, see Marchesi in Marchesi and Marchetti 2011: 106–108.

there is very good reason to think, allude to that fact that the ED rulers of Uruk were also the en priests of Inana. It is highly probable, therefore, that the ED kings of Uruk were both the ens of Uruk and the ens of Inana, thus closely replicating the case of the archaic ruler of Uruk.

(d) As is well known, Sargon, the founder of the Sargonic dynasty, appointed his daughter, named En-heduana, to the office of the en priestess of the moon-god Nanna at Ur. This appears to have been a new development, whose purpose was to counterbalance the position of the en of Inana/Uruk, and so to provide Sargon with an ideological and political base in southern Babylonia (Steinkeller 1999a: 124–128). Although it is quite certain that there was a priestess of Nanna at Ur before the time of Sargon,[287] this priestess (or priestesses) apparently bore the title of zirru, and not that of en (Steinkeller 1999a: 121–122, 124–125).[288] Accordingly, the most likely explanation of these facts is that the title of the en of Nanna was an innovation,[289] which had been created by Sargon as a replica of that of the en of Inana.[290] If true, this fact underscores the great importance and prestige that the office of the en of Inana/Uruk enjoyed at Sargon's time.

(e) Various historical sources and literary compositions written in the early second millennium BC identify the archaic rulers of Uruk as ens. Here belong Mes-kiag-gašir (SKL lines 96–97), Enmerkar, Lugal-banda, and Gilgameš, the last called the en of Kulaba. While some (if not all) of these characters may have been purely mythological, the fact that the authors of these compositions associated the title of en with the archaic kinship of Uruk appears to be significant.

---

287 As suggested, e. g., by the ED IIIb plaque from Ur, which depicts four women who may confidently be identified as Nanna's priestesses. See above p. 34 and **fig. 26.**

288 J. G. Westenholz 2012: 297 maintains that there existed an en priestess of Nanna already in Uruk times. However, none of the alleged attestations of this title in the archaic texts from Uruk Westenholz cites may confidently be interpreted as such. Some of them do not exist, while others in all probability refer to the en of Uruk. Here it should also be noted that J. G. Westenholz, ibid. 299, misrepresents my position in part (as presented in Steinkeller 1999a: 121–126). Especially, I never claimed that "only male en's existed as consorts of gods" (as she ascribes it to me). What I said in that publication is that the *original* priestly en was that of Inana of Uruk, who happened to be male.

289 Sargon may have re-organized this office as well. If there originally had been several zirru priestesses serving Nanna concurrently (as one may plausibly infer from the Ur plaque I refer to above n. 287), this would mean that Sargon had consolidated it, thereby adding even more importance to it.

290 Once the scope of the title of en had been expanded in this way, en came to denote other types of high priests. See Steinkeller 1999a: 126–128.

6 The Priest-King of Late Uruk Times and the Early History of the En

To summarize the preceding discussion, the Priest-King of Late Uruk art was the political leader of Uruk and the high priest of Inana. As is suggested by the Warka Vase, and extensively confirmed by the Uruk III economic tablets, the title of this official was en. Since the Uruk III written sources mention en officials in connection with other Babylonian cities as well, it appears that, during that period, en was a generic designation of the rulers of city-states.

At least during the earlier phase of the Early Dynastic period, en continued to serve as a title of Babylonian rulers. It was, apparently, at that time that this title was borrowed by the various neighbors of Babylonia, becoming (but only in its *logographic* sense) a term for the rulers of these foreign localities.

It appears that the only place where the en retained his former ritual functions (in the capacity of the high priest of Inana) was Uruk. This dual character of the office of the en of Uruk seems to have persisted at least till the end of the ED period. The office of the en of Inana of Uruk may have existed in Sargonic times, but this remains uncertain. It is documented in Ur III times. The Ur III kings also revived the title of the en of Uruk, which subsequently was used by the rulers of Isin as well.

In other Babylonian cities, the title of en was abandoned, being replaced by that of ensik (Steinkeller 1999a: 112–116). To offer a more precise description of this development, the en evolved into the ensik, with the latter retaining only the political and administrative roles of the en. The en's purely ritual functions had been taken over by various specialized cultic functionaries, such as, for example, the šennu priest of goddess Nanše. In all probability, these transformations took place during the ED II period.

It is possible that the title of ensik developed from the word en. One may envision that this official had originally been one of the en's subordinates, thus serving as a specialized type of en, in the manner of the engiz and endib functionaries I mentioned earlier. The word ensik is a genitival construction, which appears to be composed of the word en and an element that may best be identified as še, the Sumerian word for "barley" and "grain." If so, this hypothetical *en-še-ak (Akk. *iššia'kku*) would mean "lord of grain," perhaps describing the official in charge of cereal production. In this connection, note that the stalk of grain is a characteristic attribute of the Priest-King of Late Uruk times, possibly even representing one of his symbols (see above pp. 88–89). That the ensik was, originally at least, an official responsible for cereal production might also be indicated by Ninurta's title ensi$_2$-gal ^{d}En-lil$_2$, "great ensik of Enlil," which conceivably defines Ninurta, god of the plow and agriculture, as Enlil's chief farmer

(Marchesi in Marchesi and Marchetti 2011: 109). Another reflection of this could be the OB and later usage of *iššia'kku* as a designation of privileged farmers (CAD I/J 264–266).

The final stage of this development occurred in the beginning of the Sargonic period, when Sargon, by drawing on the tradition of the en of Inana of Uruk, created, at Ur, the title of the en of Nanna. Once the scope of en had been expanded in this way, this word came to denote other types of high priests (see Steinkeller 1999a: 125).

Essay 2

The Divine Rulers of Akkade and Ur: Toward a Definition of the Deification of Kings in Babylonia

When Alexander had defeated Darius and taken over the Persian empire he was very proud of his achievement. Feeling himself raised to the level of divinity by the good fortune which had now overtaken him, he sent an introduction to the Greeks to vote him divine honors. This was ridiculous; he could not acquire on demand from the rest of mankind what nature had not endowed him with. The cities passed various decrees, and the Spartans resolved as follows: "Since Alexander wishes to be a god, let him be a god."

Aelian, *Varia Historia* Book 2.19

1 Preface

This essay discusses the deification of living kings in ancient Mesopotamia, a phenomenon involving two, nearly consecutive episodes of brief duration. Lasting together no more than 120 years, these two experiments occurred toward the end of the third millennium BC, during the Sargonic and Ur III periods respectively. The briefness of this phenomenon becomes even more apparent when one considers that the political history of ancient Mesopotamia is textually documented over a period of three millennia – if not significantly longer.

This topic has attracted a good deal of attention during the last decade or so. Here one should single out the collection of papers from a conference held in 2007 at the University of Chicago's Oriental Institute, which addressed the question of the divine kingship in Mesopotamia and other parts of the ancient world (Brisch 2008). There subsequently appeared articles by Nicole Brisch (2013), Tallay Ornan (2013), and Anne Porter (2013), which likewise take up the subject of Mesopotamian divine kings.

A common thread that runs through these recent discussions is the tendency to minimize the exceptionality of the divination of the Sargonic and Ur III kings, or, in other words, to relativize it. Many of these authors find evidence, either before or after the two episodes in question, of allegedly similar expressions of the divinity of rulers. According to those views, the divination of the Sargonic and Ur III kings was but a more radical manifestation of a trend that was an integral part of the politico-religious ideology throughout the history of ancient Mesopotamia. In particular, scholars such as Gebhard Selz (2008), Irene Winter (2008: 81), and Tallay Ornan (2013) think that, already in Pre-Sargonic times, one finds prefigurations or foreshadowings of the divine ruler. The evidence cited

DOI 10.1515/9781501504778-004

in support of this contention are the epithets used by certain Pre-Sargonic kings, which allegedly describe them as being "born" by various deities. As argued by Selz (2008: 20), these epithets "testify to a certain divinity of these kings." Tallay Ornan (2013: 572) is even more assertive about this point, stating that the Pre-Sargonic written sources from Lagaš portray kings as being divine. While not going that far, Walther Sallaberger (1999: 153) submits that the use of such epithets makes the Pre-Sargonic ruler practically a member of the divine family.[291]

Anne Porter takes an even more radical position on the question of divine kings. In an article that denies the very existence of the Sargonic empire (2013),[292] Porter also questions the historicity of Naram-Suen's deification. This — sorry to say — misinformed, confused, and pretentious piece might perhaps be excused as an unfortunate foray of a misguided archaeologist into the matters of history. At the same time, while extreme in its conclusions and even bizarre at times,[293] Porter's opinions in many respects are symptomatic of some of the current thinking about the divinization of kings in Babylonia. For this reason, it will be instructive to quote the basic premise of her article:

> Although there is by no means unanimity, there is a general acceptance of the idea that Naram-Sin was indeed deified during his life time ... I am not of such opinion. Naram-Sin's apotheosis to godhead may be challenged on a number of fronts, not least of which is its incompatibility with indigenous conceptions of what was possible and was permissible in this regard. Moreover, each detail of the evidence – the precise meaning and usage of the divine determinative, dingir; the origins and chronology of its application to Naram-Sin; the historicity of the one direct allusion to Naram-Sin's divinization; and the significance of the horned cap he wears on the Victory Stele – is insecure. (2013: 602)[294]

---

291 "Der Herrscher ist Kind, Geliebter, Bevorzugter, Erwählter, Beschenkter der Götter in Inschriften ab altsumerischer Zeit, steht damit den Göttern bis hin zur Einbindung in die Familie nahe."

292 Porter even denies the existence of Sargonic territorial expansion. See especially ibid. 609: "royal inscriptions registering campaigns in an area do not mean those areas were necessarily incorporated into the kingdom – they do not even mean there were campaigns!" Although it is likely that most of the foreign lands conquered by Sargon and his successors were never incorporated into Babylonia, with the Sargonic kings retaining only a loose control of those territories, their interest there being mainly of a commercial nature, to claim that they never campaigned in the periphery is absurd. Even a cursory reading of the Sargonic historical records (as edited, e.g., in RIME 2) shows that this view is patently wrong.

293 This pertains particularly to Porter's idea that, rather than conquering foreign lands, Sargonic rulers were merely marking their presence there, by gifting their monuments and other artifacts to those lands (meaning that there was no territorial expansion of any sort).

294 In agreement with her general thesis, Porter also questions the divinity of Ur III kings (2013: 599 n. 4).

One reads this exposé with disbelief, since no reputable scholar working today in the field of third-millennium history, religion, and culture would seriously question the fact of Naram-Suen's deification. Moreover, no insecurity attaches to any of the points raised by Porter: the use of the divine determinative DINGIR in reference to mortal kings; the facts and the historical background of Naram-Suen's deification; and the significance of the divine crown he wears in two of his representations. As generally accepted, all of these are solidly established and well-understood facts. Porter's only valid observation is that Naram-Suen's deification was incompatible with the existing ideology. But it was precisely *because it violated the very order of things* that Naram-Suen's godship constituted such a revolutionary (as well as highly controversial) politico-religious development. See in detail below pp. 123–124, 130–131.

That such opinions could be voiced in this time and age is surprising, demonstrating how little is known in terms of factual information about the phenomenon of deified kings in the field of Mesopotamian studies. This situation calls for a systematic examination of the evidence bearing on this issue. Hence the present study.

Before I get down to my task in earnest, however, some general observations about the divine kingship are necessary. To begin with, throughout recorded history kingship – any kingship – always had an element of sacredness attached to it, in that kings universally were believed to share a special relationship with the divine realm. As the renowned anthropologist Edward Evans-Pritchard has put it, "kingship everywhere and at all times has been in some degree a sacred office" (1962: 210). Evans-Pritchard then goes on to cite the famous medieval maxim which says: *Rex est mixta persona cum sacerdote.* This sacred dimension of the royal office is usually described by the term "sacrality." Sacrality, however, is fundamentally different from the phenomenon of divine kingship.[295] In fact, it will be correct to say these are two different *ontological* categories. If I am allowed to make a glib analogy, to be a divine king is like being pregnant: you either are pregnant or you are not. And this is why certain individuals, exceedingly rarely and under very specific historical circumstances, chose, for political rea-

---

295 A classic study of the sacrality of kingship is Kantorowicz 1957. In reference to the political theology of medieval times, Kantorowicz argued that the king was believed to have two separate bodies: a mortal body as well as a spiritual one (or a body politic). The latter served as a vessel of the sacred dimensions of his office and was transcendent, in that it could be passed on to his successors. The ruler's divine attributes were especially prominent in France, where kings were thought, among other things, to have the ability to cure scrofula with a touch of their hands (Giesey 1997).

sons, to be divine, their motivation being to place themselves in a completely separate category, to be entirely different from everybody else.

2 The Question of the Alleged Divinity of Pre-Sargonic Rulers

As for the evidence that gave rise to the speculation about the divine status of Pre-Sargonic kings, there indeed survive several examples where a ruler is said to have been a child "born" (tud-da) by a deity:

> En-an-na-tum$_2$ dumu tud-da ^{d}Lugal-Urub$_x$(URUxEŠ$_2$) (*male deity!*) (RIME 1 170–173
>   En-anatum I 2 ii 7–8; 187–188 15 i 14–15; 189 17 i 6–7)
> En-mete-na dumu tud-da ^{d}Ga$_2$-tum$_3$-dug$_3$ (RIME 1 226 En-metena 22:9–10)
> Lugal-an-da dumu tud-da ^{d}Ba-u$_2$ (RIME 1 242–243 Lugal-anda 2 i' 6'–7')
> Lugal-zag-ge-si dumu tud-da ^{d}Nisaba (RIME 1 433–437 Lugal-zagesi 1 i 26–27)[296]

While the Sumerian verb tud means "to give birth," it also has a more general sense of "to create" and "to form." In fact, tud is used to describe the process by which a stone statue is sculpted.[297] It is apparent, therefore, that in the above examples tud-da is to be translated as "formed" or "created."

---

296 See also ^{d}Ba-⌜u$_2$⌝ … Uru-ka-gi-na nam-sipad-še$_3$ mu-tud, "Bau formed/created Urukagina to be the shepherd (of Lagaš)" (Steible 1982: 354–355 Urukagina 51:1–2).

297 In the Pre-Sargonic inscriptions from Lagaš, tud is regularly used in reference to the manufacture of statues, both of humans and deities. For the examples, see Steible 1983: 333–334. Gudea's statues also were made through the process of tud. See Statue B and passim in the inscriptions on his statues. Otherwise, statues are said to be "fashioned," where the verb dim$_2$ (*banû* or *epēšu*) is used. It is possible that tud refers specifically to the carving of stone statues, a process that perhaps was viewed as more natural than the manufacture of statues by overlaying (see below), and therefore conceptually akin to the formation of a child in the womb. In fact, all of Gudea's statues are made of stone. It is also important that these statues are invariably described as made of *stone* (na): ^{na4}esi im-ta-e$_3$ alam-na-ni-še$_3$ mu-tud, "he brought down diorite and made it into a stone statue of himself" (Statue A iii 1–3; Statue C iii 15–17; Statue H ii 6–8; Statue K ii' 3'–5'). That alam-na-ni represents /alam-na-ani/ rather than /alan-ani/ (as commonly thought) is shown by the examples where the element na clearly is not a resuming complement of alam: alam-na inim-še$_3$, im-ma-dab$_5$, "he installed the stone statue (in order to convey) instructions" (Statue B vii 47–48); alam-na-e mu-tud, "he formed a stone statue" (Statue I v 1–2). Moreover, in most instances the statement in question reads alam-na-še$_3$ mu-tud, "he made (the diorite) into a stone statue" (Statue B vii 12–13; Statue D iv 17 – v 1; Statue E viii 19–20; Statue G iii 3–4; Statue Z i' 4'–5'). As it happens, Gudea actually emphasizes the point that one of his statues was made of stone: alam-e u$_3$ kug-nu za-gin$_3$ nu-ga-am$_3$ u$_3$ uruda-nu u$_3$ an-na-nu zabar-nu kin-ga$_2$ lu$_2$ nu-ba-ga$_2$-ga$_2$ ^{na4}esi-am$_3$, "this statue is not of silver; and it is not of lapis; nor is it of copper or tin (bronze) or (arsenic) bronze; nobody overlaid it through the (standard) manufacture; it is of diorite!" (Statue B vii 49–53). A similar statement appears in

More fundamentally, this issue must be seen within a context of the Sumerian views about human creation. As the Sumerians imagined it, the true mother of all humanity, kings and commoners alike, was the birth-goddess, variously known as Ninhursag, Ninmah, Nintu, and Gatumdug. It was this goddess who planted the human seed in the womb, subsequently formed the fetus, and eventually brought about the child's birth. The birth-goddess would finally determine the child's destiny. While the birth-goddess presided over the conception and birthing *ex officio* so to speak, various other goddesses could appear in these roles as well. See the following example, involving the grain-goddess Nisaba[298]:

a dug$_3$-ga šag$_4$-ga gar-ra-me-en
u$_3$-tud-da šag$_4$-ga-a peš-peš-a-me-en
ama dumu-ni ki-ag$_2$ sum-sum-mu-de$_3$

You (Nisaba) place sweet seed in the womb,
having formed it, you make it fat,
(in order) that you may give to the mother her beloved child.
("Išbi-Erra E" lines 49–51; a hymn to Nisaba)

Accordingly, the claims of having been "created" or "given birth" by a particular deity are simply reflections of the fundamental belief that all humans owe their creation and birth to a divine agency. Among the various data that bear out this point one may single out an Old Babylonian birth incantation, where the birth-goddess is described as a creatrix and midwife of all humanity: *wa-aš-ba-at-ku-*⌜um⌝ *[ša]-*⌜ab⌝*-su-tum ba-ni-a-at [r]i-mi-i-im ba-ni-a-at ka-li-i-ni*, "there sits by you

---

two inscriptions of Puzur-Inšušinak (Gudea's contemporary), which likewise are found on stone statues: *ù-la* KUG.BABBAR *ù-la* URUDU DUL$_3$-*su a-bi-lum* (for *awīlum*) *a-na a-mu-te ù-la e-bi-iš*, "it is not of silver or copper; nobody made it for overlaying?" (MDP 2 63 ii 1–6; MDP 14 20 ii 2′–6′). The manufacture of standard statues, which consisted of a wooden core overlaid with metals and semiprecious stones, is regularly described by the verb dim$_2$, "to fashion." The term for overlaying/inlaying is gar/ga$_2$-ga$_2$ (Akkadian *šakānu*).

The idea that statues (especially the cultic ones) were "born" finds reflection also in Akkadian, as shown by an inscription of Esarhaddon, which says that the statues of several deities "were correctly born" (*ki-niš im-ma-al-du-ma*), a statement referring to their faithful ritual restoration (RINA 4 103–109 no. 48:87). Cf. Walker and Dick 1999: 116–117. One encounters closely similar concepts in ancient Egypt, where "The statues were not made, but 'born.' This was not said only in the case of the creator god Ptah; in royal inscriptions, 'to bear' is practically a technical term for the fashioning of a cult statue, but even simple craftsmen or artisans say of themselves that they 'bore' the statues of deities or the deities themselves. The profession of sculptor was designated 'one who makes live,' that is, 'quickener' ..." (Assmann 2001: 46).

298 Among other goddesses performing same functions were Gula and Nungal. See Steinkeller 2016: 12 n. 40.

(i.e., the pregnant woman), the (divine) midwife, the creator of the womb, the creator of us all" (YOS 11 86:18–20). In the same vein, Ninhursag is called "mother of all children" (ama dumu-dumu-ne) (Gudea Statue A i 3).

That the statements about divine parenthood of rulers are but poetic metaphors is best illustrated by the evidence of Gudea's inscriptions.[299] In Cylinder A iii 6–8, Gudea, while paying a visit on the goddess Gatumdug in his efforts to garner support for the rebuilding of Ningirsu's temple Eninnu, addresses her in the following words:

> ama nu-tuku-me ama-mu ze_2-me
> a nu-tuku-me a-mu ze_2-me
> a-mu $šag_4$-ga šu ba-ni-dug_4[300] unu_6-a i_3-tud-e

---

299 Referring to these sources, Claudia Suter has recently argued that they "imply a certain degree of [Gudea's] divinity by claiming divine parentship on the one hand, and by assimilation to gods on the other" (2010: 522). As I am demonstrating in the following, the references to Gudea's divine parentage are purely figurative. Neither is there any evidence of Gudea's "assimilation" to deities. Here Suter thinks specifically of Gudea's personal god Ningišzida, asserting that "Gudea's relationship with Ningishzida as portrayed in his inscriptions bordered on partial or virtual identity" (ibid. 507). This is also incorrect. To be sure, Gudea shared an intimate connection with Ningišzida, and sometimes compared himself to Ningišzida, but this close relationship was simply a function of the role that personal gods played vis-à-vis their human charges. Both in texts and in art, the two figures – the human Gudea and the divine Ningišzida – are rigorously and consistently kept apart from one another. For the visual demonstrations of this point, see **figs. 24 and 25**. As I note in Essay 1 p. 32 n. 46, in my view, Suter fundamentally misunderstands the nature and historical significance of Gudea's ideology.

300 The precise meaning of šu ... dug_4 in this context is difficult to pin down. The basic sense of this verb is "to treat with a hand," hence "to handle" or "to manipulate." Akkadian lexical sources equate šu ... dug_4 with *lapātu*, "to touch." Correspondingly, the verbal noun šu-dug_4-ga, which appears in similar contexts (e.g., Ur-"Namma C" line 111; "Sargon Legend" Segment B line 54), corresponds to *liptu*, "touch." See lugal šu-dug_4-ga-ni-me-en = *šar-ra-am li-pí-it qá-ti-šu ia-ti*, "me (Samsu-iluna), the king, the 'touch' of his hand (i.e., of Šamaš)" (RIME 4 374–378 Samsu-iluna 3:26 (Sumerian) = 3:34–35 (Akkadian)). Significantly, there are many other examples where various kings are described as *liptu* or *lipit qāti* of deities (CAD L 201 *liptu* meaning c). CAD op. cit. translates *liptu* in such contexts as "creation." However, it is unlikely that the construction a-ø šu ... dug_4 should be translated "to create seed (in the womb)," since a reference to engendering rather is expected. In view of the parallel construction a $šag_4$-a ... gar, "to place seed in the womb" (see "Išbi-Erra C" line 49, quoted above), I would rather think that a-ø šu ... dug_4 describes some form of the manipulation of the seed, such as perfecting it or simply touching, or perhaps even the action of implanting it in the womb.

I have no mother – you are my mother!
I have no father – you are my father!
It is you who *manipulated* my seed in the womb! It is you who formed me in the "womb"![301]

Clearly, this statement is a rhetorical compliment that was meant to dispose Gatumdug favorably to Gudea. Rather than to deny his human ancestry, Gudea simply emphasizes the fact that his *real* mother – like that of entire humanity – is Gatumdug.[302] The metaphoric nature of Gudea's words is confirmed by the concluding section of Cylinder B, where the goddess responsible for Gudea's birth is alternatively identified as Nin-sumun. Moreover, in the same passage Gudea is described as a "child" of Ningišzida, his personal god:

dingir-zu ᵈNin-giš-zi-da dumu-KA An-na-kam
dingir-ama-zu ᵈNin-sumun₂-na ama-gan numun zi-da
numun-e ki-ag₂-am₃
ab₂ zi-de₃ mi₂ ba-tud-da-me
mes zi ki-Lagaš^{ki}-[ta?] e₃-a
ᵈNin-gir₂-su-ka-me ...
[G]u₃-de₂-a [d]umu ᵈNin-giš-zi-da-ka

Your personal god indeed is Ningišzida, grandson of An;
your mother-goddess[303] indeed is Nin-sumun, the progenitrix[304] of true seed,
the one who loves seed.
You are the one who was gently formed / given birth by the faithful cow (i.e., Nin-sumun);
You are the legitimate hero who has arisen from the land/territory of Lagaš.

---

301 Cf. Gu₃-de₂-a unu₆ mah-a tud-da ᵈGa₂-tum₃-dug₃-ga-kam, "Gudea, the one formed by Gatumdug in the great 'womb'" (Cylinder A xvii 3–14); (Gudea) dumu tud-da ᵈGa₂-tum₃-dug₃-ke₄ (Gudea Statue D i 17–18). I assume that unu₆, "temple's dining hall," also "Holy of Holies," is here a poetic description of Gatumdug's womb, which is identical with the innermost part of her temple. Similar imagery is found in the "Keš Temple Hymn" lines 77–78, which describe Ninhursag/Nintu as a huge dragon residing in the temple's "heart/womb" (šag₄) and carrying on procreation: "Ninhursag is a great dragon, she sits in its midst; Nintu, the great mother, keeps on giving birth (there)" (tud-tud mu-un-ga₂-ga₂).
As I suggest in Essay 1 p. 33 n. 49, the Gudea passage in question may be a direct borrowing from the inscription of E-anatum describing his birth and rearing (which I cite below). On the other hand, it is clear that the same passage was later utilized for the purposes of the OB composition known as "Rulers of Lagaš." See Essay 1 pp. 42–43.
302 Note that these words are a continuation of Gudea's praise of Gatumdug as the one who creates life for the whole nation: "when you cast your eye upon the nation, fertility is created by itself; when you cast your eye on a faithful young man, you (immediately) extend his life" (Cylinder A iii 4–5).
303 As far as I know, the term dingir-ama, which clearly means "mother-goddess" or "birth-goddess," is attested only here.
304 ama-gan corresponds to Akkadian *ālittu* (CAD A/1 340–342).

You are the one of Ningirsu! ...
Gudea is a child of Ningišzida.
(Cylinder B xxiii 18 – xxiv 7)

For these conclusions, it is significant that the agency behind the engendering and birth of a child could be *male* deities as well. We have already seen that the creation (tud-da) of En-anatum I of Lagaš was attributed to the god Lugal-Urub.[305] Similarly, the Larsa king Kudur-mabuk identifies Nergal as the "creator of my head."[306] And, in a passage describing the creation and rearing of E-anatum, Ningirsu is credited with his engendering[307]:

[^{d}Ni]n-[gir$_2$]-su-[k]e$_4$ [a] ʼE$_2$ʼ-[an]-na-tum$_2$-[ma šag$_4$-g]a [šu b]a-ni-dug$_4$ ...(Inana) ^{d}Nin-hur-sag-ra du$_{10}$ zi-da-na mu-ni-tuš ^{d}Nin-hur-sag ubur zi-da-ni ʼmuʼ-[na-la$_2$] E$_2$-an-na-tum$_2$ a šag$_4$-ga šu dug$_4$-ga ^{d}Nin-gir$_2$-su-ka-da ^{d}Nin-gir$_2$-su mu-da-hul$_2$

"Ningirsu *manipulated* the seed of E-anatum in the womb ... (Inana) put (him) on Ninhursag's trusting knee; Ninhursag gave him her genuine breast. Ningirsu rejoiced over E-anatum, the seed *manipulated* in the womb by Ningirsu."
(RIME 1 126–140 E-anatum 1 iv 9 – v 5)

Male deities are implicated in the creation of kings also in the sources from later periods. In this way, Enlil is identified as the one who formed Šulgi in the womb and facilitated his birth:

e$_2$ dug$_3$-ga ^{d}Nanna dumu nun-ne$_2$ nig$_3$ al ba-ni-dug$_4$
en-ne$_2$ šag$_4$-tur-še$_3$ gal$_2$-la-na lu$_2$ zi mi-ni-u$_3$-tud
^{d}En-lil$_2$ sipad a$_2$ kalag-ga-ke$_4$ mes-e pa bi$_2$-e$_3$
dumu nam-lugal barag-ge$_4$ he$_2$-du$_7$ Šul-gi lugal-am$_3$

---

305 En-anatum I enjoyed a special relationship with Lugal-Urub, an avatar of Dumuzi and the chief deity of Patibira. This is shown by the fact that, according to one of En-anatum's inscriptions (RIME 1 180–181 En-anatum I 9 ii 13 – iii 4), it was Lugal-Urub who had granted the kinship (nam-lugal) of Lagaš to him.

306 ^{d}*Nergal i-lum ba-ni qá-aq-qá-di-ia* (RIME 4 267–268 Kudur-mabuk 2:44–45). The Sumerian equivalent of *bāni qaqqadi* is dingir-sag-du$_3$, "the creator of the head," which appears in Falkenstein 1949: 216 line 24 (^{d}Marduk sag-du$_3$-zu, referring to Samsu-iluna). Note further the common onomastic patterns DN-*bāni* and *Ibni*-DN, in which male deities usually are invoked. Cf. also the use of *šiknu*, "creation," in an inscription of the early OB ruler of Malgium named Ipiq-Eštar: ^{d}*I-pí-iq-Eš$_4$-tár* LUGAL *ši-ki-in* ^{d}*En-ki* ^{d}*Dam-ki-na* (RIME 4 669–670 Ipiq-Eštar 1:1–2). For further examples of similar figurative expressions describing OB kings, see Falkenstein 1949: 212–214.

307 As I suggest in Essay 1 p. 33 n. 49, this passage may have served as a model for Gudea Cylinder A iii 6–8, which I quote above. For the meaning of the construction a-ø šu ... dug$_4$, see above n. 300.

Nanna, the princely son, had made a request in the "sweet house";
(in response) the Lord (i.e., Enlil) formed the right man in the womb that was there,
Enlil caused the shepherd of strong arms, the hero, to emerge,
the child suitable for kingship (and) dais – it indeed was king Šulgi!
("Šulgi G" lines 17–20)[308]

Similarly, Šulgi's father Ur-Namma is described as a "touch" or "creation" of Nanna,[309] while Rim-Sin of Larsa is said to have been a "child formed by lord Nergal with greatness from the womb on."[310]

The idea that the creation of all human beings ultimately happens in the divine realm is common to all religions, even monotheistic ones. Thus, in an Egyptian hymn to Aten, the first monotheistic deity in recorded history, Aten is given the following characterization:

Creator of seed in women,
You who makes fluid into man,
Who soothes him with that which stills his weeping,
You nurse him in the womb.
(Pritchard 1969: 370)

A similar statement is found in the Quran, where Allah is said to be the one "who shapes your bodies in your mothers' wombs as he pleases" (Sura 3, 3rd verse). In the same way, Christians call God their "father" and "creator," without ever claiming any real filial relationship with Him.

As is made clear by this evidence, the Pre-Sargonic data in question do not even remotely indicate a divine status of kings, not even in some incipient form. They merely imply, in a highly poetic and figurative way, that these rulers enjoyed an especially close and intimate relationship with the divine realm, a fact that is fully consistent with their constituting a link between the divine and human societies. Because of this, they were imbued, as typical of royalty in general, with more "sacrality" than other humans.[311] However, there is no in-

---

308 The interpretation of this passage follows essentially Sallaberger 1997: 155 and n. 36.

309 šu-dug$_4$-ga-e ^{d}Nanna-a-me-en ("Ur-Namma C" line 111). In line 24 of the same composition, it is claimed that Ur-Namma was "fashioned" by Nintu: rdNin^1-tur-re ga$_2$-e mu-un-dim$_2$-dim$_2$-en.

310 dumu u$_3$-tu-ud-da en ^{d}Nergal-ta šag$_4$-ta nam-gal-ta (Hallo 1991: 382–386 line 14).

311 For this obvious explanation, see already Frankfort 1948: 299–301. Referring to the passage from Cylinder A, in which Gudea calls Gatumdug his real father and mother (see above p. 112), Frankfort observes that "the unrealistic projection of both parents in one divine person accentuates the figurative meaning of the expressions." He then goes on to discuss similar figurative phrases in Old Babylonian and Neo-Assyrian sources, concluding that "when it is said that the gods form the royal child in the womb of its mother 'with their own hands,' it is clear that they

dication that they ever aspired after divine status, nor that they claimed to be descended from gods. Here it must be emphasized that this kind of rhetoric was part of the ideology of kingship throughout Mesopotamian history, both in Babylonia and Assyria.[312]

These conclusions about the Pre-Sargonic kingship are corroborated by the evidence of the contemporaneous art, where there is even less indication of the "divinity" of kings. As I will show later, the Pre-Sargonic rulers actually went out of their way to avoid any suggestion of their distinctiveness from the rest of the population, to the point that, in art, even their institutional connection with the divine realm — namely, the fact they functioned as the earthly representatives of gods – finds no expression whatsoever.

The only form of deification that the Pre-Sargonic kings of southern Babylonia might have expected (or hoped for) was the posthumous one. It is theoretically possible that, as part of the cult of former rulers and high priests, which was characteristic of early southern Babylonia (see Essay 1 pp. 30–31), some of those rulers may have been deified after their death. However, we lack any certain evidence of this. To be sure, this form of deification was later afforded to Gudea (Suter 2013).[313] But this may have been an innovation, which possibly was influenced by the deification of the Sargonic kings. Because of this, Gudea's case cannot be projected back to Pre-Sargonic times.[314]

---

are distinguished from his physical parents. The Mesopotamian king was a mortal marked – and to some extent changed – by divine grace ... the numerous other texts in which Mesopotamian kings are called the 'sons' of gods do not imply that they are divine" (ibid. 300–301).

312 As shown by the following examples: *anāku Aššur-bāni-apli binût Aššur u Ninlil ... ša Aššur u Sin bēl agê ... ina libbi ummišu ibnû ana rē'ût māt Aššur*, "I am Assurbanipal, the creation of Aššur and Ninlil ... whom Aššur and Sin, the Lord of the Crown, ... created in the womb of his mother for the shepherdship of Assyria" (Streck 1916: 2 i 1–5); *ištu ibnanni bēlu Erua* (^{d}*Er-ú-a*) ^{d}*Marduk ibšimu nabnītī ina ummu*, "after the Lord (and?) Erua created me (and after) Marduk formed my features within my mother" (VAB 4 122 i 23–25; Nebuchadnezzar II).

313 With the evidence presently available, Gudea was the only Lagaš ensik that had been granted this honor.

314 As is suggested by the personal name *Sar-ru-GI-ì-lí*, "Sargon is my Personal God," which appears in "Maništušu Obelisk" Side A xii 8 (OIP 104 124), Sargon may have been venerated posthumously as a deity. This certainly was the case in Ur III times. See PDT 1 506:5–6, which records offerings, made in Nippur, for ^{d}Na-ra-am-^{d}Suen and ^{d}Sar-ru-gin$_7$^{in}. Another Sargonic king that was afforded this honor after his death is Maništušu, offerings for whom are mentioned in the Ur III sources from Umma (spelled ^{d}Ma-iš-ti$_2$-su or ^{d}Ma-an-iš-ti$_2$-su; UTI 3 1834:8; BPOA 6 1176:8, 1395:4; etc.). These sources also mention a hamlet or town called ^{d}Ma-an-iš-ti$_2$-su (RLA 7 355; UTI 5 3416:10), where a temple of Maništušu appears to have been situated. This settlement is documented already in Sargonic times: Ma-an-iš-t[i-s]u^{ki} (OIP 14 114:11). Cf. also the Umma personal name Ur-^{d}Ma(-an)-iš-ti$_2$/ti-su (UTI 3 1829:7; UTI 5 3375:1; etc.).

The final point that deserves a comment in this connection is the kingship of Late Uruk times. As I wrote in Essay 1 pp. 29–30, there are possible indications that the en of Uruk, the presumed leader of Uruk's political organization in that period, may have enjoyed the status of a demigod. If so, the character of his office would have differed quite considerably from that of Pre-Sargonic ensiks. However, neither surviving art nor texts offer any indication that this official was believed to be a deity (or that he was worshipped as such).

3 Historical Context of the Divination of Kings in Babylonia

Perhaps the biggest deficiency of many of the recent evaluations of Babylonian divine kingship is that they treat this issue in complete abstraction from its historical context. In my view, this is a serious error, since the deification of kings in Babylonia must be seen as a specific historical development, which can be comprehended only if one considers the political circumstances of the period in question. These evaluations also fail to pay proper attention to the Sumerian ideology of kingship, which too is absolutely necessary if one wants to obtain a full measure of the phenomenon of divine kings.

Therefore, I will begin with a brief description of the political and socio-economic conditions in Babylonia during Early Dynastic times. Although one could perhaps anchor this account in the Late Uruk period, our data are too scant and uncertain to allow any conclusions about the political organization at that time. The only point that appears to be certain is that, already at that early date, the South supported a system of city-states. See Essay 1 p. 26.

As I argued repeatedly in the past, central to the understanding of the dynamics of the Early Dynastic history is the realization that, during that period, southern Babylonia, which was mainly inhabited by the Sumerian population, differed very significantly from Babylonia's northern part, which was home to a Semitic ethnic group speaking the language later known as Akkadian or Babylonian. In fact, before the advent of Sargon and his dynasty, these two regions embraced radically different cultures and religions, and followed largely independent trajectories of socio-political development.

The key characteristic feature of the southern system was the institution of city-states, whose origins, as I noted earlier, probably belonged to the Late Uruk period. In its classic form, the southern city-state was a clearly demarcated territorial unit, comprising a major city, the state's capital, and the surrounding countryside, with its towns and villages. The city-states bordered contiguously on one another, along the permanent, divinely sanctioned borders. There was little, if any, neutral space between them.

According to the southern political theology, the city-state was "owned" by the extended divine family. The main god, the head of the family, was the de facto proprietor of the entire state. At the same time, he – together with his spouse and children – owned as his exclusive domain the capital city and its surroundings. Junior deities controlled smaller domains, centered upon towns and villages. In this arrangement, gods were considered to be the true owners of all the resources belonging to a given state, most importantly, of all its agricultural lands.

The divine families of all the city-states were united into one very large extended family, with Enlil, god of Nippur, occupying the position of *paterfamilias*.[315] Because of his rank, Enlil excercised lordship over the whole South. In this role, he served as an arbitrator in conflicts, especially border disputes, between individual city-states.

As such, the Pre-Sargonic South formed a well-ordered, highly balanced system in which each deity was assigned his or her specific role to play and owned a particular earthly domain. Perhaps the most extensive presentation of this view is found in the composition "Enki and the World Order." As narrated by this source, which likely is a veiled apotheosis of the "perfect" Ur III state, the god Enki carves up Babylonia among several deities, putting them in charge of various specialized tasks. As a result, he creates a perfect, frictionless system, which is free of conflict and strife, and where everybody has his own place, lives in harmony with his neighbors, and prospers accordingly.

This system was institutionalized, in that the pantheon was believed to form a single political body, at whose top stood an executive committee, which consisted of four or seven of the most important deities. As imagined by the Sumerians, all the members of the pantheon gathered at the end of the calendar year in a place called Ubšu-unkina in Nippur. This general assembly, called unkin in Sumerian and *puḫru* in Akkadian, collegially drew detailed plans for the next year, or, as the Sumerians described it, they "determined destinies" for the coming year. Such decisions, which had to be unanimous, were implemented by the two chief executive officers of the pantheon, An and Enlil. Occasionally, the divine assembly held special, ad hoc meetings, to render decisions for the cases of truly extraordinary importance. Good examples of such cases are the respective deifications of Naram-Suen and Šulgi (see below pp. 123–126) and the construction of the Eninnu, the temple of Ningirsu in Girsu (see below and Steinkeller

---

315 This role is assigned to Enlil already in an inscription of En-metena of Lagaš (RIME 1 194–199 En-metena 1), as well as in an even earlier literary text of Kišite origin (ARET 5 3 i 6–ii 2, ii 8–iii 2).

2016: 14). The annual gatherings of the pantheon were essentially concerned with the shape of the future on a cosmic scale (or with the "big picture," to put it differently), without intruding on the internal operations of city-states. The decisions in that regard were the prerogative of their respective divine owners, who "determined destinies" on the local level, so to speak.

From a political perspective, the single most important fact about this ideology is that it viewed the South as a closed system, with the assumed existence of permanent, divinely sanctioned borders between the individual city-states.[316] Obviously, this tenet rendered any form of territorial expansion in the South exceedingly difficult.[317] Even more importantly, it made the notion of a united South theoretically impossible. As we shall see later, these ideological constraints presented a major obstacle toward unificatory efforts, eventually leading to the remedy of divine kinship.

The rule over the city-state was exercised by an official called ensik.[318] Although the ensik's office was predominantly secular in nature, it included certain ritual roles as well. This form of kingship was based on the principle of divine election rather than on descent. In other words, it focused on the ensik's office, and not on his lineage. Although in practice a hereditary principle prevailed, in that the ensik's office usually was transferred from father to son, as the political theology had it, this official was elected by the divine owner of the city-state. He also needed to be divinely re-appointed each year.[319]

The most characteristic feature of the ensik's position was that its holder functioned as an earthly representative of the deity, taking care of the human and other resources of the city-state on the latter's behalf. In this relationship,

---

316 The existence of such borders is explicitly stated in various third millennium sources. Especially important here is one of En-metena's inscriptions (RIME 1 194–199 En-metena 1), an inscription of Giššag-kidug of Umma (RIME 1 372–374 Giššag-kidug 2), and the "Cadastre of Ur-Namma" (RIME 3/2 50–56 Ur-Namma 21 + Steinkeller 2011: 25–28 nos. 20–21). See further RIME 2 280–283 Utu-hegal 1–3.

317 This is best illustrated by the history of the border dispute between Lagaš and Umma (Cooper 1983b). For over five generations if not much longer, these two city-states fought repeatedly over a strip of agricultural land separating them. Neither of them, however, ever succeeded to absorb its neighbor, due mainly to the recognition of the sanctity of the divinely drawn borders.

318 For this official, see Essay 1 p. 28. Some Pre-Sargonic rulers used instead the title of lugal, "master" or "king." lugal is a purely secular designation, which emphasizes the ruler's political and military powers. For this title and the ways in which it differs from ensik, see Steinkeller 1999a: 112.

319 For the evidence illustrating the ensik's election, see below p. 125 n. 335, 135 n. 362, and Steinkeller 2016: 13–14.

the ensik acted very much like a steward managing the estate belonging to an absentee owner. For this reason, "steward" is probably the best approximation of ensik's functional meaning.[320] A closely similar concept is conveyed by the epithet "shepherd" or "vicar" (sipad, *re'û*), which is another designation of the southern ruler, and which, for all practical purposes, served as his alternative title. In fact, "shepherd" was the quintessential image of the head of the southern city-state. The power of this image was such that – unlike ensik, which was abandoned as a royal title in the beginning of the second millennium – sipad continued to serve as a favored epithet of kings, both in Babylonia and Assyria, till the very end of the cuneiform civilization.

Since the focal point of the southern kingship was the ruler's office, and not his person and lineage, the ensik, as he appears in written sources, is invariably a generic type. Although this official shares a special relationship with the gods (which was due entirely to the peculiarities of his office), in all other respects he is just like any other member of the temple community. The only characteristics that set him apart from the rest of the society are his exceptional devotion and obedience, thanks to which he obtained divine favor. When he is depicted in art, he invariably assumes the standard posture of piety, which conjures up the image of a humble servant or shepherd.[321] See **figs. 19–22**. He never wears any regalia (though he undoubtedly used them in real life), or any special attire for that matter, that would visually distinguish him from his contemporaries. In spite of his intimate connections with the divine realm, he is never portrayed in the company of gods.[322] Neither is he ever shown as officiating over ritual activities.[323] Without the inscriptions identifying him as a ruler, we would never suspect that he is a royal figure.[324]

---

320 As defined by *Online Etymology Dictionary*, "steward" was "the title of a class of high officers of the state in early England and Scotland, hence meaning 'one who manages affairs of an estate on behalf of his employer.'" For a possible etymology of ensik, see Appendix 1 pp. 103–104.

321 Cf. the epithet sipad sun$_5$-na, "humble shepherd," which was used by the kings of Isin (see, e.g., RIME 4 47–48 Lipit-Eštar 1:2).

322 Occasionally, humans are depicted as approaching enthroned deities, but the latter invariably are the representations of divine statues. See Essay 1 p. 29 no. 34.

323 As I point out in Appendix 1, the iconography of the archaic en of Uruk differs significantly in these respects, since the en is shown in Inana's company, and he routinely is involved in ritual activities.

324 Ornan 2013: 572 observes (correctly) that this visual imagery is devoid of "themes relating to the king's divine pedigree." This fact should have made her more cautious about finding such indications in texts.

Turning now to the socio-political realities that existed during the same time frame in the North,[325] the most striking fact here is that this region never developed a system of independent city-states even remotely comparable to that of the South. On the contrary, there is convincing evidence that, during the Early Dynastic period (2900–2350 BC), the North formed a single territorial state, which was governed by the city of Kiš. While Kiš remained the usual focal point of this state, it appears that, on some occasions, its center of power moved to Mari in the middle Euphrates valley and Akšak in the Diyala Region. The magnitude of the political power wielded by Kiš (especially during the ED I and ED II periods) is reflected in the fact that the title of the "king of Kiš" eventually became a generic designation for the authoritarian and hegemonic form of kingship.[326]

The reason why the North followed this particular path of development probably finds explanation in the "mobile pastoralist"[327] background of its population. As a consequence, these early Semitic dwellers of northern Babylonian, best defined as "Proto-Akkadians," had a markedly different society, which was characterized by the presence of tribal organization and the importance of lineages. As one may conjecture from the examples of other Mesopotamian peoples that shared similar ethnic and social origins (the Amorites, the Arameans, and the Arabs), the northern kingship was based on descent, and had a distinctive form of kingship, which was strong, authoritarian, and expressly secular in character. As such, it sharply contrasted with the southern notions of rulership, which, as I described earlier, assigned to the ensik much more circumscribed and politically weaker a role, and saw him as a partly religious functionary as well.

Having offered these characterizations of the southern and northern systems, I will now sketch a brief outline of the historical developments that led to the two episodes of royal deification.

As far as the events may be reconstructed, the ED I and ED II periods were marked by the political domination of Kiš, which not only controlled northern Babylonia and the Diyala Region, but also succeeded in establishing a hegemony over certain areas in the South (Nippur, Adab, Umma, and Šuruppak). This picture underwent a significant change in the ED IIIa period, when a number of southern city-states formed a coalition against Kiš. This coalition, which was led by Uruk, seems to have defeated and even sacked Kiš (Steinkeller 2014b).

---

325 For a detailed discussion of this issue, see Steinkeller 1993a; 2013a: 142–151.
326 For this title, see most recently Steinkeller 2013a: 145–146.
327 For this concept, see Frachetti 2008: 17 with further literature.

From then on, Kiš would no longer be an active player in the politics of the South.

During the final phase of the Early Dynastic period (ED III b) several Sumerian rulers attempted to achieve a limited political hegemony over the southern city-states. The first such attempt, apparently, was undertaken by E-anatum of Lagaš, who assumed the prestigious title of the "king of Kiš" (RIME 1 145–149 E-anatum 5). Two generations later, a ruler of Uruk by the name of En-šakušana, campaigned against Kiš and Akkade (RIME 1 429–430 En-šakušana 1; A. Westenholz 1975: 115). It is conceivable that En-šakušana harbored the ambitions of placing the entire South under his rule, as reflected in his adoption of the title "king of the Land," in which "Land" means southern Babylonia.[328]

The most successful among these early unificatory efforts was that by Lugal-zagesi of Uruk, who appears to have effectively brought the South under his rule. Importantly, Lugal-zagesi also conquered Kiš, thus putting an end to the Kišite domination of northern Babylonia. It is unlikely, however, that Lugal-zagesi ever succeeded in turning his possessions into a uniform centralized state. Given the existing ideological constraints, such a step would have been too radical for a southerner to contemplate. At best, Lugal-zagesi could only claim to be a *primus inter pares* among the southern ensiks.

As it happened, the person who managed to capitalize on Lugal-zagesi's achievement was, not unexpectedly, a northerner. His name was Sargon, and he hailed from the obscure town of Akkade, which was probably situated in the neighborhood of modern Baghdad.

After he had conquered northern Babylonia together with its traditional political center Kiš, Sargon then confronted Lugal-zagesi. In the ensuing war Sargon faced and overcame a formidable coalition of southern city-states led by Lugal-zagesi, after which he became the master of the South as far as the Persian Gulf. This accomplishment was followed by a phase of foreign conquests, as a result of which the first empire in history was created.

The reigns of Sargon and his two immediate successors, Rimuš and Maništušu,[329] constituted the formative stage of the empire. During that period, the empire acquired its physical shape, but little if any effort was made to turn it into a fully articulated system. These early Sargonic kings also failed to develop a comprehensive imperial policy. In this, they were largely prevented by the continuing opposition of the southern city-states, which had only reluctantly accepted the rule of Akkade, revolting against it at every opportunity.

---

328 For this title, see below p. 126 and n. 337.
329 The sequence of these two rulers remains uncertain. See Essay 1 p. 14.

The greatest of those revolts took place during the reign of Naram-Suen, Sargon's grandson. The rebellion was originally confined to Kiš, but it quickly spread to the South, eventually enveloping the whole empire. Having fought "nine battles in one year," Naram-Suen, almost miraculously, emerged victorious from this ordeal, defeating the rebels and restoring the empire to its former borders.

It was this experience, no doubt, that convinced him of the pressing need to strengthen the fabric of the empire. This goal was largely dependent on the prior settling of the "southern question." Naram-Suen's solution was to elevate himself to the divine plane. By becoming a god, he placed himself above all the Sumerian ensiks, thereby providing a justification for the universal character of his rule that was antithetical to the southern concepts of kingship.

It is characteristic that the deification of Naram-Suen was carried out strictly within the framework of the city-state ideology. Since to be a god meant the possession of an earthly domain, the divine Naram-Suen needed to have one too. And for Naram-Suen the choice of domain was obvious: he became the god of Akkade, by then the capital of the empire.

As we are told by one of his inscriptions,[330] this was accomplished by the unanimous decision of the key members of the pantheon, in response to a request made by Akkade's population. Thankful to Naram-Suen for having protected their city during the Great Rebellion, they appealed to the chief gods of Sumer and Akkad to make him god of Akkade:[331]

> On account of the fact that he had protected/strengthened the foundations of their city in difficult straits, (the people of) his city requested from Inana in Eana, from Enlil in Nippur, from Dagan in Tuttul, from Ninhursag in Keš, from Enki in Eridu, from Suen in Ur, from Šamaš in Sippar, (and) from Nergal in Kutha, that he be (made) god of their city, and (ac-

---

330 This inscription appears on the so-called "Bassetki Statue," which, in its present condition, consists of a massive round base on which a naked male figure (of which only the lower half survives) is depicted in a seated position. Between the legs of this figure there is the lower section of what assuredly was a gatepost. Porter 2013: 606–607 suggests that this is a representation of Naram-Suen, but, without any doubt, this is a la-ha-ma (Akkadian *laḥmu*), the "hairy one," who was one of Enki's attendants. A close visual parallel is provided by an Old Akkadian seal (Frankfort 1939: pl. 18 fig. k), which depicts a kneeling la-ha-ma, who holds a gatepost. In my opinion, there is a high probability that this object formed part of the furnishings of a temple of Naram-Suen (either in Akkade or in some other city).

331 The same protocol is followed in the beginning section of Gudea's Cylinder A, where, in order that Ningirsu may obtain a new house, the population of Lagaš needs first to petition Enlil, the head of the pantheon, assuring him that everything in Lagaš indeed is in a perfect condition, and that Ningirsu is fully deserving of such a reward. Only when Enlil grants his permission the project may be undertaken. See Steinkeller 2016: 14.

cordingly) they erected his temple in the midst of Akkade.
(RIME 2 113–114 Naram-Suen 10:20–56)

All that this solution accomplished, however, was to transfer the problem from the human to the divine level; in the new scheme it was now the god of Akkade who had become a contradiction, for the importance he assumed far outstripped his standing in the pantheon. Another consequence of Naram-Suen's becoming the god of Akkade was the ascent of Akkade to the position of the religious capital of Babylonia. This development unavoidably affected the position of Nippur and its chief god Enlil, putting Naram-Suen in direct conflict with the ruling circles of Nippur, which, understandably, must have felt threatened by Akkade's increased significance. The echoes of this conflict can be detected in the composition "The Curse of Akkade" (see in detail Essay 1 pp. 79–80; Liverani 2002: 156–157). The dissatisfaction with Naram-Suen's deification, which certainly existed at Nippur, and which probably was felt also among the managerial elites of other southern city-states, may have even been one of the factors (though minor at best) that contributed to the eventual demise of the Sargonic empire.

The divine status so earned by Naram-Suen was subsequently held by his son Šar-kali-šarri, the last great king of the Sargonic dynasty.[332] There is no evidence that either of Šar-kali-šarri's two successors, Dudu and Šu-Durul, ever presumed to be divine.

Following the collapse of the Sargonic empire, and a passage of roughly one hundred years, during which the South reverted to its traditional condition of political fragmentation, Babylonian rulers embarked on another unifying scheme. The impulse this time came from the South, where, at around 2100 BC, an ensik of Ur named Ur-Namma succeeded in putting both the South and the North under his rule.

In so doing Ur-Namma began what is known as the Neo-Sumerian or the Ur III period – the latter name referring to the dynasty's original seat and the fact that it was the third such entity stemming from Ur. The true greatness of the dynasty came with Šulgi, Ur-Namma's son and successor. During the second decade of Šulgi's reign, there began a phase of territorial expansion, which led to the formation of a mini-empire. These foreign conquests were accompanied at home by a massive program of political, economic, and administrative reforms, which transformed Babylonia into a highly centralized, patrimonial state.

---

332 In spite of some contrary claims (e.g., Michalowski 2008: 35; Brisch 2013: 41), Šar-kali-šarri's divine status is not in doubt. This is demonstrated most emphatically by his titulary, for which see below p. 136.

Alongside these institutional changes, there came about various ideological transformations, the most momentous of which was the deification of Šulgi. This event can approximately be dated to Šulgi's twentieth regnal year, when his name began to be provided with a semantic indicator DINGIR, "deity." How this was accomplished – at least on the divine plain – is described in considerable detail in one of the hymnal compositions glorifying Šulgi ("Šulgi P").[333] Unfortunately, the beginning lines of this composition are not preserved. When the text becomes intelligible, Nin-sumun and Lugal-banda (who, as we shall see later, were afforded the status of Šulgi's divine parents subsequent to his divination) seem to be discussing Šulgi's future. Nin-sumun then undertakes to execute An's order, which, apparently, was to find a deserving ruler for Sumer. Having examined the whole nation, she identifies Šulgi as the fitting "shepherd," elevating his head among all the people. She then brings this happy news to the Ubšu-unkina, the residence of An and the place where the most important destinies were determined, reporting the results of her search to An and recommending to him that Šulgi be made "shepherd" of the Land. After An accepts this recommendation and bestows his blessings on Šulgi, Nin-sumun installs Šulgi as king at Ur, praising him and offering additional blessings. Finally, in recognition of Nin-sumun's efforts and as her reward, the general gathering of the divine assembly proclaims Šulgi's godship, causing him to rise like Utu over the Land. The particularly relevant passages of this composition read as follows:

ud-ba nin-mu inim An-na-ke$_4$ ba-gub[334]
^{d}Nin-sumun$_2$-na-ke$_4$ dam!-a-ni kug ^{d}Lugal-banda^{da} nam ba-da-an-tar!-re!
sizkur-ra-na mu-da-an-^{r}kuš$_2$^{1}-u$_3$
An kug-ra Ub-šu-kin-na-ka si mu-na-ni-in-sa$_2$
a-a-mu An lugal dingir-re-ne-me-en$_3$
kalam nig$_2$ dagal-la igi mu-ni-il$_2$
sag-gig$_2$ u$_8$-gim lu-a-ba
Šul-gi gu$_2$ sag-ba ma-in-i[n?]-^{r}zi? sipad^1 zi-bi he$_2$-am$_3$[335]

---

333 For an edition and discussion of this composition, see Klein 1981b: 41–41.
334 I assume that inim ... gub has a similar sense as the construction inim-a ... si$_3$, "to be assigned to (lit: to be placed in) an order (of a deity)." See lu$_2$ inim-ma si$_3$-ga ^{d}Ba-u$_2$-ke$_4$ (Gudea Statue B i 14–15 and passim in Gudea's inscriptions).
335 This line echoes Gudea's Statue B iii 4–11, where the selection of Gudea by Ningirsu as the "shepherd" of Lagaš is described. As I argued elsewhere (Steinkeller 2016: 13 and n. 46), there existed a belief that, on the New Year's, the chief deity selected (or re-appointed) his earthly representative from among the entire population of the city-state that gathered (symbolically) for this occasion. As part of this procedure, personal gods would lift the heads of their charges above the crowd (sag zi-(g)), in order that the chief deity could take notice of them. It is likely

At that time Milady stood up (to execute) An's order.
Nin-sumun together with her husband Lugal-banda determined (Šulgi's) destiny;
she attended to his offerings (i.e., offerings/prayers made on Šulgi's behalf).
She (then) directed her way straight to An in the Ubšu-unkina.
(Nin-sumun addresses An:) "Oh my Father, master of all the gods!
I have scanned the Land in all its breadth
(and), from among its black-headed people who are numerous as sheep,
from among the gathering of all their heads, I have raised Šulgi. May he be their legitimate shepherd!"
(Segment A lines 7–14)

^{d}A-nun-na dingir gal-gal-[e-ne]
ki nam tar-ra-ba mu-da-˹sug$_2$˺-[sug$_2$-ge-eš]
nam-sipad Šul-gi-ra nig$_2$-ul-li$_2$-[a-še$_3$] pa ˹e$_3$˺ ma-[ni-in-ak-ke$_4$-eš]
Šul-gi si-sa$_2$ dingir-ra-[ne-ne-še$_3$]
kalam-ma ^{d}Utu-gim ma-ni-in-˹e$_3$˺-[eš]

(Nin-sumun speaks:) "The great Anunakene gods stood up together
at the place where destinies are determined,
(and), on my account, they made manifest the shepherdship of Šulgi for all time;
they caused Šulgi, the righteous one, to rise in the Land like the Sun God in order to be ˹their (i.e., of the people)˺ god."[336]
(Segment C lines 56–59)

So says the official theology. But what were the real facts behind this development? In my view, it is certain that in deifying himself Šulgi drew directly on the example of Naram-Suen. However, learning from the negative reactions that the deification of the Sargonic kings had provoked, he did it in a considerably more diplomatic and nuanced way. First of all, in his new divine form Šulgi refrained from associating himself with any particular city-state, becoming instead an abstract – and therefore less offensive — "god of his Land" (dingir kalam-ma-na).[337] Moreover, he claimed familial connections with the divine fam-

---

that a similar selective process is described here. I assume that gu$_2$ sag-ba /sag-bi-ak/ means "the gathering/totality of their heads," with gu$_2$ corresponding to *napḫaru*.

336 The divine status that Šulgi acquired in this way is also reflected in the name he was given on this occasion: šul an-ne$_2$ zu dingir-re-ne, "Youth whom An made known among the gods," i.e., the one who was recognized as a god ("Šulgi P," Segment C line 39).

337 For the specifics of this title, see below p. 152. When used it this context, kalam describes the territory of southern Babylonia, meaning "native land," thus being practically identical with Ki-en-gi = Sumer. Characteristically, it is never used in reference to "foreign" lands. The use of kalam as a term for southern Babylonia is documented first in late ED times, in the title lugal kalam-ma, which was borne by the Uruk rulers En-šakušana (RIME 1 429–430 En-šakušana 1:5) and Lugal-zagesi (RIME 1 433–437 Lugal-zagesi 1 i 5).

ilies of the most important southern cities, thereby legitimizing his claim to their individual kingships.[338] There are also indications that the Ur III kings underwent separate coronations in those cities, in an effort to placate the local elites and to recognize, at least symbolically, their earlier history as independent seats of royal power.[339]

By virtue of having become a god – and the one linked familially to the chief deities of Babylonia at that, Šulgi could now claim to be the absolute owner of the temple-estates and other economic resources nominally belonging to the gods. This move, which was *the* single most important development of his reign both politically and economically, and which had no antecedents in Sargonic times,[340] put Šulgi in control of all the holdings of arable land in Babylonia. From now on, arable land could only be held via the system of royal fiefs or benefices, which were granted by the king to his subjects (among whom counted even the members of his immediate family) in exchange for corvée labor and other services.[341] Obviously, this expanded the powers of the divine king enormously.

After the end of the Ur III period, deification of kings was briefly practiced by the Isin dynasty, which, at least from the perspective of the aspirations of its rulers, was the heir and a direct continuation of the Ur III empire. But, since the kings of Isin controlled only some portions of the South, never succeeding in imposing their rule on northern Babylonia, their deification manifested itself only

---

338 For a systematic discussion of these developments, see below pp. 141–150.

339 Based on the evidence of economic documents, Jacobsen (1953: 36 n. 2) suggested that the Ur III kings were crowned successively in Nippur, Ur, and Uruk. This is confirmed by literary sources, especially the hymns of Šulgi. The hymn "Šulgi E" lines 9–10 implies that this occurred at Eridu as well: sig₄ Eridug^{ki}-ga-ta aga zi ak-me-en / Unug^{ki}-ta suh za-gin₃ keš₂-ra₂-me-en, "I was provided with a legitimate crown in the brickwork of Eridu; in Uruk, a lapis lazuli diadem was tied (around my head)." For the "lapis lazuli diadem" as an attribute of the en of Uruk, see Steinkeller 1998: 93–95. However, I am not aware of any data that would point to the coronations at Girsu/Lagaš and Umma, which, from the economic point of view, were the largest and richest provinces in the South, and therefore also the most important ones politically.

340 Due, apparently, to the different land-tenure practices and traditions that existed in northern Babylonia, in the South Naram-Suen and Šar-kali-šarri rather privatized the temple-held arable land, turning it into royal and private individual estates (Steinkeller 1999b: 350–358).

341 See Steinkeller 2013d. Very similar policies were institutionalized by the deified Inka rulers. "By declaring that they owned everything, the Incas devised a rationale that gave people access to their traditional lands only in return for labor duty … many people did not happily digest the idea that they could use their ancestral lands only by the grace of the Inka" (D'Altroy 2002: 265).

on the symbolic level, being completely devoid of its former political dimensions.[342]

By the time when Babylonia had become united again, which happened around 1750 BC during the reign of Hammurabi of Babylon, the political, cultural, and religious distinctions that had existed earlier between the Sumerian South and the Akkadian North had disappeared, with Babylonia having become a single nation, which spoke one language and embraced the same Sumero-Babylonian culture and religion. Therefore, when Hammurabi successfully brought both halves of Babylonia under his rule, there simply was no need for him to engage in any ideological games – such as the presumption of a divine status – to justify his universal rule.[343] Characteristically, none of the later rulers of Babylonia and Assyria claimed to be divine either – or, as far as we know, made any attempts to achieve such a status. This fact makes it certain that the deification of kings was not an evolutionary development within the Babylonian politico-religious ideology per se that was, in a Hegelian sense, historically necessary. On the contrary, both the briefness of this phenomenon and the fact it was associated with very particular circumstances prove that it constituted an isolated and unique occurrence within Mesopotamian history, whose causes were situation specific and purely political.

This, in short, is my assessment of the question of divine kings in ancient Mesopotamia. As a matter of fact, most of this interpretation may be found in an article of mine published twenty-five years ago (Steinkeller 1992). However, since it appeared in a publication somewhat peripheral to Assyriology, that article tends to be overlooked, especially by younger scholars.

---

342 Following the Isin dynasty, the only Babylonian ruler who may have aspired to divinity was Rim-Sin of Larsa, as indicated by the determinative DINGIR that is occasionally attached to his name. It is possible that Rim-Sin considered himself to be the heir of Isin (which he had conquered and absorbed in the middle of his reign), thus adopting the Isin practice. As I note below pp. 153–154, similar claims were made by a number of peripheral kings, who ruled immediately or shortly after the fall of the Ur III empire.

343 To be sure, the subsequent history of Babylonia was not free of further attempts by the South to recover its political independence. The most important event of this nature was its revolt under Samsu-iluna, which was followed by the establishment of the First Sealand Dynasty. However, by that time, the cultural distinctiveness of the South (in particular, its characteristic ideology of kingship) had effectively ceased to exist.

4 Specifics of the Divination of Sargonic and Ur III Kings

I will now proceed to discuss specific data that demonstrate and illustrate the divinity of the Sargonic and Ur III kings. Such a review is necessary, since much of this evidence is either disputed, misunderstood or simply unknown to the scholarship at large.

A view that prevails in literature is that the main way in which the divinity of Mesopotamian kings was expressed and propagated among the population at large was the addition of the sign DINGIR, "god," to royal names.[344] This was the standard method of marking the members of the divine class on the level of text. The names of Naram-Suen and Šar-kali-šarri indeed show a DINGIR sign attached to them. The same was true later of Šulgi and his successors, as well of the rulers of the dynasty of Isin. But, while this scribal device is a useful hint for the modern scholar, it was of secondary importance at best for the actual manifestation of the rulers' divinity, since, as a general rule, written sources were inaccessible to the majority of the society, and thus they played an exceedingly limited role in spreading the idea of the rulers' divinity. As a matter of fact, during the reigns of Naram-Suen and Šar-kali-šarri the use of this marker was optional. This is demonstrated by the fact that, in the majority of texts composed after Naram-Suen's deification, the DINGIR sign is lacking in his name. And the same is true of the sources written under Šar-kali-šarri.

As generally agreed, another indication of the ruler's divinity, at least in the case of the Sargonic kings, is a horned crown, which, like the DINGIR sign, was an exclusive attribute of deities. In fact, Naram-Suen is depicted wearing such a crown on two objects, which I am going to discus later. However, since Babylonian artwork was usually confined to the sacred locales that were accessible to but a few individuals, this attribute too played only a marginal role in propagating the divinity of kings.

Here it needs to be emphasized that, in ancient Mesopotamia – as was the case in other ancient civilizations – the primary means of politico-religious propaganda were not texts but public ritual and monumental architecture, the latter taking the form of temples and palaces, and various public buildings of utilitarian nature, such as city walls and other types of defensive structures (Baines 1989; Trigger 1990; Steinkeller 2015c: 203–204). Indeed, public ritual, state pageantry, and monumental architecture were a glue that kept together many of the traditional kingdoms, both of ancient and more recent times, as in the case of

---

344 See, e. g., Ornan 2013: 570: "The paramount indicator of divine royal status in Mesopotamia was the addition of the cuneiform sign *dingir*."

the so-called "theater-states" of Southeast Asia (Geertz 1980).[345] It has been argued that also the Maya polities were essentially "theater-states," in which the ideology of kingship was played out in the arena of ceremonial centers, through the performance of festivals and rituals. As Arthur Demarest writes in reference to the Maya, "Classic period energies and resources were lavishly expended on this monumental display and architecture. Art, artifacts, and monuments provided the stages for the ideological spectacles directed by these holy lords" (2004: 207).

Because of these comparative analogues, one can be confident that the manner through which the divine status of the Sargonic and Ur III kings manifested itself most immediately and palpably was ritual. As I wrote earlier, we are lucky to have an ancient description of how the deification of Naram-Suen came about (see above pp. 123–124). According to that account, Naram-Suen assumed the status of the god of the city of Akkade. This is not just a poetic image or a figure of speech. To be a deity in Mesopotamia meant to have a regular divine cult. That cult focused on a temple, in which the deity's statue was housed and afforded daily veneration. The text is question tells us that there indeed was a temple of the divine Naram-Suen in Akkade. It is known that similar temples existed in other cities as well. A tablet from Girsu in southern Babylonia (ITT 5 9289), which dates to either Naram-Suen or Šar-kali-šarri, locates a temple of the god of Akkade in that city. Interestingly, this document also mentions the temples of Annunitum and Ištar, the former deity being an avatar of Ištar in her martial form, with whom, as I will show later, Naram-Suen was particularly closely associated:

		(beg. destr.)
obv.	1′)	azlag₃(GIŠ.TUG₂.PI.KAR.D[U])
	2′)	4 šu-ut e₂ An-[nu]-ni-tim
	3′)	6 šu-ut e₂ ᵈIštar(INANA)
	4′)	10 la₂ 1 [š]u-ut é Ìl(DINGIR)-A-g[a]-dèᵏⁱ
		(rest destr.)
rev.		(beg. destr.)

---

345 "The driving aim of higher politics was to construct a state by constructing a king. The more consummate the king, the more exemplary the center. The more exemplary the center, the more actual the realm" (Geertz 1980: 124). In its radical form, Geertz's analysis, which focuses on the ideology to the exclusion of the material dimensions of power, appears to be applicable only to the incipient manifestations of states, such as, e. g., Babylonia of Late Uruk times and archaic Egypt. In the case of more developed polities (such as the Sargonic and Ur III empires), the politics of kingship and the strategies of state-building undoubtedly were shaped by economic considerations as well.

1')   i₃ zi-ga
2')   mu URUxA
3')   im-ma-kam
       (space)
4')   Gir₂-su^{ki}-a
5')   nig₂-ŠID-bi ba-ak
       (rest destr.)

[x] fullers,
4 (fullers) – those of the temple of Annunitum,
6 (fullers) – those of the temple of Ištar,
9 (fullers) – those of the temple of the God of Akkade,
[...]
The expended oil
in the year of ...,
the previous year.
In Girsu
this balanced account was made.[346]

That the cult of the divine king was a countrywide phenomenon is further indicated by a group of Sargonic sources that appear to stem from the site of Umm el-Hafriyat, situated ca. 28 km east of Nippur."[347] These documents, which in all likelihood belong to the reign of Šar-kali-šarri (A. Westenholz in Milano and A. Westenholz 2015: 16), mention a number of individuals designated as the "servants of the God of Akkade" (ARAD₂ *Il-A-ga-de₃*^{ki}).[348] Included among them are two scribes and a farmer.[349] Unless this designation is simply a more flowery

---

346 A. Westenholz thinks that the temples in question were situated in Akkade (Milano and Westenholz 2015: 20). Although such a possibility cannot completely be ruled out, the fact that the transaction took place in Girsu, and that it involved low-ranking fullers, makes it quite certain that the locus of these temples indeed was Girsu. If these workers resided in Akkade, the reason why their oil provisions were recorded in a tablet from another city would otherwise be difficult to account for.

347 For the evidence, see A. Westenholz in Milano and A. Westenholz 2015: 13–15. Based on one of the tablets from this group (CUSAS 27 212 rev. 5'), Westenholz further suggests that the ancient name of Umm el-Hafriyat was Maškan-Ili-Akkade.

348 Cf. CT 50 148 ii 5 (probably from Lagaš), which lists a "man of the God of Akkade" (lu₂ Dingir-A-ga-de₂^{ki}).

349 Dug₄-ga-ni DUB.SAR DUMU DINGIR-gu₂ DINGIR-KA-me-ir ⸢2⸣ ARAD₂ *Il-A-ga-de₃*^{ki} (CUSAS 27 206:24–27); LUGAL-KA DUB.SAR ARAD₂ *Il-A-ga-de₃*^{ki} (ibid. 203:8–9, 205:12–13); Puzur₄-Lu-lu ARAD₂ *Il-A-ga-de₃*^{ki} (ibid. 202:10–11); Ur-su ENGAR šu *Il-A-ga-de₃*^{ki} (ibid. 201:16–17). In addition, CUSAS 27 148 identifies a number of persons collectively as šu-ut ARAD₂ *Il-A-ga-de₃*^{ki}. Note that this tablet also mentions two "servants of god Nergal of Cutha" (ARAD₂ ^{d}Nergal Gu₂-du₈-a^{ki}) (lines 12–14).

way of saying that they were servants of the king, it is likely that these persons worked for a local temple-household of the God of Akkade.[350]

The cult of the divine kings of Ur took manifested itself in similar ways – and here our evidence is incomparably more extensive and informative. Beginning with Šulgi, the Ur III kings were provided with temples, not only throughout Babylonia, but also in the conquered periphery. In Babylonia, such temples are known to have existed in the cities of Girsu, Umma, Urusagrig, and Ešnuna, as well as in many of the local southern towns (Sallaberger 1999: 54; Pitts 2015: 41–53).[351] In the periphery, they are documented at Susa,[352] Urbilum,[353] Neber-Šu-Suen,[354] and Duhduli.[355] The temples of divine kings were routinely provided with their statues, which served as a focal point of their worship (Brisch 2006; Pitts 2015). There is copious evidence that such statuary was often installed and venerated also in the shrines belonging to other deities.

In addition, festivals celebrating their divine status were established. Those were of such cultic importance that they even gave names to the months of the official Ur III calendar.[356]

A particularly interesting development of this period is the phenomenon of hymns composed in honor of divine kings, a privilege otherwise reserved for

---

350 In either case, these sources, as likely dating to Šar-kali-šarri's reign, provide an additional proof of this ruler's divine status.

351 At Ur, Šulgi seems to have been worshiped in a building called E_2-hur-sag. This may have been his palace originally. As suggested by "Temple Hymns" lines 119–134, where the E_2-hur-sag is identified as a temple of Šulgi, following Šulgi's death this structure was turned into his temple. It is characteristic that no temples of deified kings are documented at Nippur, where their presence probably would have been too offensive to Enlil and his cult.

352 e_2 alam ^{d}Šu-^{d}Suen kar Šušin^{ki} du$_3$-de$_3$, "(issues of oils) to erect a temple of Šu-Suen's statue at the quay of Susa" (TCTI 2 3390:1–7; ŠS 5/i).

353 32 ur$_2$ $^{giš}u_3$-suh$_5$ ... e_2 ^{d}Šu-^{d}Suen-ka Ur-bi$_2$-lum^{ki}-še$_3$, "32 beams of pine ... for the temple of Šu-Suen in Urbilum" (SAT 1 377:1–8; ŠS 7/-).

354 e_2 alam ^{d}Šu-^{d}Suen ba-ab-šeš$_4$ šag$_4$ Ne-be$_6$-er-^{d}Šu-^{d}Suen, "(x oil) was used to anoint the temple of the statue of Šu-Suen in Neber-Šu-Suen" (Nisaba 15 359:1–6; ŠS 6/1); ki-gal alam lugal šag$_4$ Ne-be$_6$-er-^{d}Šu-Suen ba-ra-ab-du$_8$, "(x bitumen) was used to caulk the pedestal of the king's statue in Neber-Šu-Suen" (Nisaba 15 368:1–7; ŠS 6/iii).

355 alam Šu-^{d}Suen-ka ^{de3}Duh-hu-li$_2$^{ki}-še$_3$ gin-na, "(expenditures of foodstuffs) when the statue of Šu-Suen was sent to Duhduli" (RTC 390:1–3; no year).

356 The "festival of Šulgi" (ezen ^{d}Šul-gi) gave the name to the seventh month of the official Ur III calendar (eighth month since year Šu-Suen 4). This month-name was also incorporated into the local calendars of Girsu/Lagaš and Umma. The "festival of Šu-Šuen" (ezen ^{d}Šu-Suen), which appears to have been created in year Šu-Suen 3, gave name to the ninth month of the official calendar. For the "festival of Šulgi," see Pitts 2015: 118–122.

gods. Although it cannot be excluded that such hymns existed already in Sargonic times, no certain examples of them survive.[357] The overwhelming majority of the Ur III compositions of this type are devoted to Šulgi (Klein 1981a; 1981b; Michalowski 2016), making it certain that the origin of this literary genre was intimately connected with the divination of kings. Here it is characteristic that nearly all of Šulgi's hymns focus entirely on his person. As such, they have commonly been classified as "praises" of Šulgi. Similar compositions were written in honor of Šu-Suen and Ibbi-Suen, but those are much less numerous. Also, they are properly hymns addressing particular deities, which merely intercede on the king's behalf. Compositions of the latter type continued to be written for the kings of Isin, and even those of Larsa. Although there also survives a group of hymns devoted to Ur-Namma (Flückiger-Hawker 1999), most of them undoubtedly were composed following Ur-Namma's death, and probably also as a retroactive reflection of Šulgi's deification.

The ritual background of the Ur III and Isin royal hymns appears to be unquestioned. It has been suggested that many of them were composed to commemorate specific political or cultic events (Frayne 1981; 1983; 1998: 24–26). If so, there is a strong possibility that these compositions formed part of staged rituals, during which they were actually recited and perhaps even theatrically enacted.

The dogma of divine kingship affected not only the king's status but also that of his wives. Since these women had become spouses of a god, their standing needed to be upgraded as well. Accordingly, they were afforded the title of lukur, which, in the Sumerian pantheon, identified the junior wife of a male deity (Steinkeller 1981: 81–82; Sharlach 2008: 178–179).[358] Importantly, this usage of lukur continued in Isin times,[359] to be abandoned subsequently.

---

357 Possible examples of such hymns are the compositions "Naram-Suen and Erra" and "Elegy on the Death of Naram-Suen," both of which survive in Old Babylonian copies (J. G. Westenholz 1997: 189–220).

358 This interpretation rests primarily on Gudea Cylinder B xi 3–12, where the seven divine lukurs of Ningirsu are identified as lukur ki-ig-ni (phonetic for ki-ag$_2$-ga$_2$-ni) ... dumu-maš imin ^{d}Ba-u$_2$-me banda$_3$^{da} en ^{d}Nin-gir$_2$-su-ka-me, "his beloved lukurs ... the septuplets of Ba'u, the junior (wives) of lord Ningirsu." One of those lukurs, Hegirnuna, is called "beloved lukur" (lukur ki-ag$_2$) of Ningirsu also in the inscriptions of Urukagina (RIME 1 269–275 Urukagina 3 v 16'–18', 280–281 Urukagina 7:26–28). In the Gudea passage, lukur ... banda$_3$^{da} obviously stands for dam banda$_3$^{da}, which is the usual designation of a junior wife. As a consequence of lukur having become a title of the king's junior wife, this term came to be used in reference to the junior wives of commoners as well (Steinkeller 1981: 81–82). Apart from lukur, junior wives of the Ur III and Isin kings sometimes are also designated as lukur kaskal-la-ka-ni. See, e.g., RIME 3/2 172–173 Šulgi 69:6 and the examples cited in the following note. I assume that, in this title, kaskal

A close reading of the Ur III economic documentation reveals that the kings and their immediate families played an exceedingly active role in the cultic life, much of which centered on their own personae.[360] As argued by Audrey Pitts 2015, this phenomenon should almost certainly be attributed to their divine status.

Yet another important aspect of the deification of kings that needs to be mentioned here is the invocation of divine rulers in personal names. Such names appeared for the first time during the reign of Naram-Suen, becoming exceedingly popular under the Ur III kings (Pitts 2015).[361] With the data presently available, 267 patterns of such names may be identified. The names of this type were borne by the members of all social strata, showing that the cult of the divine king was widely practiced, and that it affected the entire Ur III society. In many cases it may be shown that such names were adopted by their bearers late in their life, either in reflection of their particular closeness to the cult of the divine king or because of their association with royal family and the ruling circles more generally. It is likely that this practice reflected popular piety as well, with at least some people naming their children after the divine kings simply because of their authentic feelings for these individuals.

---

has a metaphoric sense, meaning "life's journey" rather than "expedition/travel" specifically. Thus kaskal-la-ka-ni is to be translated as "the one of his life's journey." Cf. German *Gefährtin*, "female companion," which etymologically means "one who rides (with him)." This designation perhaps invokes the image of the Sun God's never-ending travel. For the identification of the Ur III kings with the Sun God, see below pp. 145–150.

359 There survive two documented cases of such Isin "junior wives": ^{d}Na-na-a-ib$_2$-sa$_2$ lukur ki-ag$_2$ kaskal-la-ka-ni, "Nanaya-ibsa, his (i.e., of Bur-Sin) beloved lukur of his life's journey" (RIME 4 70–71 Bur-Sin 3:8–9); Nu-ṭù-up-tum lukur ki-ag$_2$ [kaskal-l]a-ka-ni [ama ibi]la-na-ke$_4$, "Nuṭup-tum, his (i.e., of Sin-magir) beloved lukur of life's journey, [mother] of his heir" (RIME 4 98–99 Sin-magir 2:9–11).

360 For a detailed study of this problem, see Pitts 2015.

361 There were also geographical names named after divine kings. Sargonic sources mention two such toponyms: (*a-na*) *Maš-gán*^{ki}*-ni-Ìl-A-ga-dè*^{ki} (CUSAS 27 212:5′) and *Dur*(BAD$_3$)*-Ìl-A-ga-de$_3$* (MDP 14 8:17). They became very common in Ur III times. Among the known examples, see ^{d}Šul-gi-^{d}Nanna^{ki} (UET 3 75:6), ^{d}Šul-gi-he$_2$-gal$_2$ (SumRecDreh 22:3), I-šim-^{d}Šul-gi^{ki} (CT 32 19 i 9, etc.), Ne-be$_6$-er-^{d}Šu-^{d}Suen (Nisaba 15/2 359:6, etc.), and the examples cited in Steinkeller 2013d: 357 nn. 39–41.

5 The Titulary of the Divine Kings and Their Familial Connections with the Divine Realm

The divine nature of the Sargonic and Ur III rulers is reflected also in another area, and this is their royal titles. Contrary to what some scholars of philological persuasion may be inclined to think, royal titles are not just rhetorical devices, whose functionality is confined to the level of text. These designations had a physical reality behind them, which was actualized through cultic rituals. To illustrate this point with a concrete example, it appears highly likely that the title sipad, "shepherd" or "vicar," which, as I emphasized earlier, is one of the most potent images of the Sumerian ruler, had its own particular ritual counterpart. As it can be reconstructed, that ritual, which formed part of the New Year festivities, enacted the election of the ruler, by which the divine owner of the city-state chose his earthly representative, his "shepherd," from among the entire nation.[362] In my view, it is highly likely that the titles borne by the divine Naram-Suen and Šar-kali-šarri found physical manifestation in similar cultic performances.

The first three rulers of the Sargonic dynasty (Sargon, Rimuš, and Maništu-šu) used two titles: "king of Akkade" (lugal A-ga-de$_3$^{ki}) and "king of the totality/universe" (lugal KIŠ).[363] While abandoning the title of the "king of the totality," Naram-Suen retained that of the "king of Akkade." In addition, he created three new titles, all of which were introduced by him subsequent to – and clearly in reflection of – his deification:

---

362 I base this hypothesis on the descriptions of how this happened on the divine plane. See Steinkeller 2016: 13–14, where the evidence of Gudea's inscriptions is discussed. My assumption is that there existed a corresponding rite in real life, which symbolized the selection of the "shepherd." Here note that the selection of the "shepherd of the Land" is also described in "Šulgi E" lines 1–8, where this title is bestowed on Šulgi by Enlil. Similar statements are found in "Šulgi D" line 60 and "Šulgi Q" lines 47–48. And the same phraseology is later applied to Šu-Suen as well: lugal ^{d}En-lil$_2$-le šag$_4$ kug-ge pad$_3$-da nam-sipad kalam-ma u$_3$ AN-ub-da-limmu-ba-še$_3$, "king whom Enlil chose in (his) holy heart for the shepherdship of the Land and of the four quarters of the world" (RIME 3/2 322–323 Šu-Suen 12:5–8; also ibid. 317–320 Šu-Suen 9 x 9–12). It is likely, I think, that the coronations of Šulgi and other Ur III kings at Nippur involved similar enactments. Another, and even more certain example of such a ritual actualization is the presentation of bridal gifts by Ningirsu to Bau, as described in the inscriptions of Gudea (Statues E and G). Since these sources name *real* gifts, there must have existed a ritual during which Gudea, impersonating his personal god Ningišzida, transported these gifts by boat to Bau's temple in Urukug.
363 For this title, see most recently Steinkeller 2013a: 145–146.

(1)	*il Akkade*	Naram-Suen
	il qarrādu Akkade	Šar-kali-šarri
	il māti Wari(URI)	Šar-kali-šarri
(2)	*šar kibrātim arba'im*	Naram-Suen
(3)	*dannum*	Naram-Suen, Šar-kali-šarri
(4)	*šar ba'ulāti Enlil*	Šar-kali-šarri

Since I have already discussed the title of the "god of Akkade" and its ritual implications, there is no need to dwell on it any further, except to note that, under Šar-kali-šarri, two new forms of this designation were introduced: "heroic god of Akkade,"[364] and "god of the land of Warium."[365] In the latter title, Uri/Warium is an ancient designation of northern Babylonia and the Diyala Region.[366]

Thus, I move on to the second title, the "king of the four quarters of the world," which implies universal domination. A related designation, though not as far reaching in its implications, is "king of the subjects (of the lands) of Enlil," which was introduced by Šar-kali-šarri.[367] A royal statue called "king of the four quarters of the world" is actually mentioned in Ur III tablets.[368] It is very probable, therefore, that there existed a specific ritual action associated with this title, which symbolized a rule over the entire world, and perhaps was similar to that performed as part of the coronation of the Egyptian Pharaoh, during which the new Pharaoh "shot arrows to four cardinal points to symbolize or actualize his mastery of the world, and four birds were released to the cardinal points to carry the news of the accession of the new Horus" (Lloyd 2014: 69).

As for the third title, *dannum*, "the mighty one," our first reaction is to see in it a fundamentally profane designation. This is suggested by the fact that this adjective emphasizes the ruler's physicality, and therefore, apparently, his human nature. Paradoxically, however, this title likewise pertains to the king's divinity. I will return to this problem shortly later.

First, however, I need to discuss another area in which the divinity of kings manifested itself, and that is the ruler's relationship to other deities. On the theological level, both the Sargonic and Ur III kings established strategic familial links with the pantheon. Already Naram-Suen considered himself to be the

---

364 Škš DINGIR UR.SAG A-ga-de₃,ᵏⁱ (RIME 2 201 Šar-kali-šarri 2005:1–3).

365 ᵈŠkš *da-núm* DINGIR *ma-ti* URIᵏⁱ (RIME 2 205–206 Šar-kali-šarri 2012:1–3).

366 See, most recently, Steinkeller 2013a: 137.

367 ᵈŠkš DUMU da-ti ᵈEn-lil₂ *da-núm* LUGAL A-ga-de₃ᵏⁱ *ù ba₁₁-ú-la-ti* ᵈEn-lil₂ (RIME 2 188–189 Šar-kali-šarri 2:1–8); ᵈŠkš LUGAL *ba₁₁-ú-la-ti* ᵈEn-lil₂ (RIME 2 198–199 Šar-kali-šarri 2001:1–2). Apparently, this title refers to Enlil's status as the "master of all the foreign lands" (lugal kur-kur-ra).

368 alan lugal AN-ub-da limmu-ba (UET 9 366:1–2, 5; Amar-Suen 7/iii; Nisaba 5/1 165).

spouse (*mutu*) of the goddess Ištar, in particular, of her martial avatar Annunitum, whose name means "the one of battle."[369] Apart from its mentions in Sargonic historical sources, this connection is borne out by a remarkable art object,
which was published and extensively studied by Donald P. Hansen (2002; 2003a;
2003b). See **figs. 35–37.**

This object is a fragment of a limestone mould. In all probability, the mould
was used to cast a flat roundlet, probably made of gold, which was shaped as a
disk crowned with an aureole of eight or nine radial streams or star points. It appears that each of the radial streams depicted a similar scene, which was the
submission of a foreign land to Naram-Suen[370] and his divine patron and spouse
Ištar-Annunitum. On the preserved fragment of the mould, the divine Naram-
Suen is shown seated next to the goddess, with whom he shares the nose-
ropes controlling two mountainous countries and their respective gods. As is
made certain by the divine crown he is wearing, this representation celebrates
Naram-Suen as a divine figure. This point is further underscored by the fact
that he and Ištar-Annunitum are depicted as equals. For a detailed discussion
of this representation, see Appendix 2.

Apart from sharing a spousal relationship with Ištar-Annunitum, Naram-
Suen also claimed to be the son of Enlil, the head of the Sumerian pantheon.[371]
In this he was followed by Šar-kali-šarri, who likewise called Enlil "his father"
and described himself as Enlil's "beloved son."[372] But the deity after whom
both Naram-Suen and Šar-kali-šarri had patterned their divine image most immediately was the Mesopotamian Sun God, who was known as Utu to the Sumerians, and as Šamaš to the Akkadians. Among the Mesopotamian gods, the Sun
God cut by far the most heroic figure. As the Mesopotamian and some other ancient mythologies imagined it, the nightly progress of the Sun God through the

---

369 NS *mu-ut* ᵈINANA *An-nu-ni-tim* (RIME 2 88–90 Naram-Suen 1 ii 8′–9′); *in ri-ma-ti* ᵈINANA
dar-a-mu-su₄, "through the love of Ištar who developed love for him" (RIME 2 113–114 Naram-
Sin 10:10–13). It is likely that, in adopting Ištar as his spouse, Naram-Suen drew on an earlier,
Urukean tradition, which professed that the en of Uruk was a symbolic husband of Inana.

370 The fact that the two foreign lands referenced in this representation likely are Elam and
Marhaši (see Appendix 2) makes it quite certain that the ruler depicted in it is Naram-Suen (rather than Šar-kali-šari).

371 [NS] *maḫ-ri-iš* ᵈEn-lil₂ *a-bi-su* [*u-sa-ri-ib*], "[NS] brought (the captured enemies) before Enlil"
(RIME 2 109–111 Naram-Suen 8 v 3–6).

372 ᵈSar-*ga-li*-LUGAL-ri ⌈DUMU *da*⌉-*ti-su* ... [*mah-ri-iš* ᵈEn-lil₂] *a-bi-*⌈*su*⌉ *a-na* Nibru^ki *è-la-kam al-
su i-za-az*, "Šar-kali-šarri, his beloved son, ... goes [before Enlil] in Nippur (and) stands up before
him" (RIME 2 194–195 Šar-kali-šarri 6 i 4 – ii 5); ᵈSar-*ga-li*-LUGAL-ri DUMU *da-ti* ᵈEn-lil₂ (RIME 2
188–189 Šar-kali-šarri 2:1–2).

Netherworld was unbelievably arduous and of truly heroic character.[373] Equally remarkable was the fact that this *Sol invictus* re-emerged from his daily ordeal unscathed and always in the flower of youth.[374] These feats earned him the titles of ur-sag, "hero," and šul, "youth" (Woods 2005a), or, as Piotr Michalowski has put it felicitously, "the ever-youthful one" (2016: 22). In fact, these two designations are the most common epithets of the Sun God in Sumerian literature.[375]

That the Sargonic kings thought of themselves as an earthly image of the Sun God is shown by the composition "The Curse of Akkade," in which it is said that "Naram-Suen rises like the Sun on the holy dais of Akkade":

---

373 See Alaura and Bonechi 2012: 23 n. 99: "Si può speculare quindi che 'eroe (e) primo in rango' rimandi unitariamente all'oscurità ed alla luminosità, cioè alla pericolosità del viaggio notturno del coraggioso del sole ed alla gloria del viaggio diurno dello stesso dio vittoriosamente uscito dalla notte e dagli inferni."

374 Similar characteristics belong to Helios, whose mythology almost certainly had been influenced by that of Utu/Šamaš. Like the Babylonian Sun God, Helios too traversed the sky in a horse-drawn chariot, rising from the river Okeanos in the east, and descending in the land of Hesperides (Evenings) in the west, at the "gates of Helios." From there, during the night, he was carried back to the east in a golden bowl or bed, which had been made for him by Hephaistos. As described in the proem of Parmenides' *On Nature*, on his arrival at the "gates [separating] the ways of Day and Night," the narrator (a double of Helios) is greeted by an unnamed goddess as a *kouros*, "young man." In a study of this passage, Laura D. Steele suggests a connection between this description and the Akkadian *eṭlu*, an epithet of both Šamaš and Gilgameš, concluding that this "point of similarity is too apt to be coincidental" (2002: 586). For the mythology of Helios, see the useful collection of data at the online site "Theoi Greek Mythology" (www.theoi.com). For the horse-drawn chariot of the Sun God in Babylonian and Hittite mythologies, see Alaura 2011; Alaura and Bonechi 2012.

375 Here it may be instructive to note that the mythology and cult of the Sun God were essential ingredients of the ideology of divine kingship also among the Inka (Conrad and Demarest 1984: 107–110, 181–182; D'Altroy 2002: 147). The Inka king, titled *Sapa Inka*, "the only Inka," and *Inka Qhapaq*, "mighty Inka," was considered to be a "god" (*Apu*) and the son of Inti, the Sun God. Although solar deities had been worshipped earlier in Andean religions, it was only with the rise of the Inka to power that the Sun God acquired a highly elevated status. The Inka rulers eventually turned his worship into a centerpiece of the official religion, apparently also introducing the symbol of the solar disk. Other places where divine kings were associated with solar deities are Egypt, Rome, and Japan (as well as France under Louis XIV!), to name only the most obvious examples. The popularity of this belief shows that divine kingship was commonly (if not universally) conceptualized through the use of solar analogies, probably because the sun, as all seeing, life-giving, protective, reassuring in its regular movements, and always victorious, epitomized the qualities belonging to a perfect – and so a divine – ruler. It is not by accident, therefore, that solar imagery was applied to rulers throughout Mesopotamian history, and almost as a matter of course, as, for instance, in OB times (Charpin 2013). However, such metaphors fall under the category of royal sacrality, in no way bespeaking the kings' divinity.

lugal-bi sipad ^{d}Na-ra-am-^{d}Suen-e
barag kug A-ga-de$_3$^{ki} -še$_3$ ud-de$_3$-eš$_2$ im-e$_3$.
("The Curse of Akkade" lines 40–41)

However, the best illustration of this point is provided by Sargonic art. Of particular importance here is the famous "Victory Stele" of Naram-Suen, which depicts the divine king while vanquishing his enemies in the Zagros mountains. See **figs. 38** and **39**. As far as I know, it was Claudia Fischer who first suggested that the image of Naram-Suen as depicted on the "Victory Stele" draws on the contemporary representations of the Sun God at the moment of his rising (2002: 131–132).[376] Particularly relevant here are two cylinder seals, both of which belonged to the governor of Lagaš by the name of Lugal-ušumgal. These two seals are dedicated to Naram-Suen and Šar-kali-šarri respectively.[377] See **figs. 40** and **41**.

While the images depicted on Mesopotamian cylinder seals usually are purely decorative, being completely unrelated to the owner of the seal and his occupation and social standing, there is no doubt that, in these two particular cases, the choice of the Sun God was intentional. We can be certain, I think, that Lugal-ušumgal had used the image of the Sun God as a direct reference to Naram-Suen and Šar-kali-šarri, who are explicitly named in the seals' inscriptions. In other words, the rising Sun God stands here for the divine king.

We need to return now to the "Victory Stele," in order to take a closer look at Naram-Suen's body. In her ground-breaking article of 1996, entitled "Sex, Rhetoric, and the Public Monument: The Alluring Body of Naram-Sîn of Agade," Irene Winter perceptively observed that the manner in which Naram-Suen's body is depicted on the "Victory Stele" constitutes a complete innovation in Mesopotamian art. As Winter argued, what is particularly novel about this image is the king's "perfect, alluring, 'heroic,' body ... [which] represents a conscious strategy of representation" (1996: 16). Winter then brought attention to Naram-Suen's title *dannum*, "the powerful one," offering the following explanation:

> This focus on the (male) *potestas* of the ruler as part of the formal title, I would argue, is rendered visually not only by the weapons he carried in hand, but also by the life force/vitality of his perfect and alluring (hence sexually desirable, for which, read "potent") body. (1996: 17)

---

376 For this conclusion see also Suter 2010: 341–342.
377 Amiet 1976: 115 figs. 83 (AO 24062) and 84 (AO 24065).

The divine kings's physicality is emphasized, even more assertively, on the Hansen roundlet. There, Naram-Suen's bulging musculature makes him appear almost like a body builder. What is even more interesting about this representation is the fact that the foreign gods appearing in it are similarly muscular and beefy. The message is clear: Naram-Suen's body is like that of the gods.[378]

And these are precisely the qualities expressed by the adjective *dannu*, which, apart from meaning "powerful, strong," also carries the connotations of health and youth.[379] This adjective was not used as a royal title prior to Naram-Suen's deification, *except* – and this is important, I believe – in reference to Gilgameš,[380] who, as the ancients believed, was a demigod.[381]

These facts convince me that *dannu* is a marker of Naram-Suen's divinity. Further support for this contention may be sought in the evidence of ancient Greek art. Addressing the question of the anthropomorphic representations of gods in ancient Greece – or, in other words – why did the Greeks depict their

---

378 A completely different reading of Naram-Suen's body was offered by Porter 2013: 608: "The gods are corporal but ever unseen except in their wooden/silver/stone personae, while Naram-Sin *is* knowable. He is knowable through his human visibility and he can never therefore be truly god-like no matter his adoption of the insignia of divinity, because his body is unchanged ... in rendering the body of Naram-Sin, he [i.e., the artist] rendered indeed, in its muscular beauty, its humanness and not its otherworldliness." In my view, the significance of Naram-Suen's body is just the opposite.

379 In the "Ebla Vocabulary" line 825 (MEE 4 292), *dannu* is translated as silim-ma, "healthy, sound," literally "be healthy!" It is characteristic that since very early on silim(-ma) was consistently associated with the Sun God. For the examples of this association and an extensive discussion of this problem, see Steinkeller 2015a, to which add: $^{r}e_2$^{1}-ta hul$_2$-la-ni nam-ta-e$_3$ ud agrun(E$_2$.NUN)-na-t[a?] / kalam-ma-ni ^{d}Utu-e$_3$-gim silim-ma mu-na-du (for du$_{11}$), "she (i.e., Nin-Isina) emerged joyfully from her house; her Land greets her (lit.: says "Be healthy!) like (one greets) Utu when he rises from his bed chamber" (M.E. Cohen 1975: 609 lines 5 and 7).

380 In the inscriptions on two Pre-Sargonic maceheads presented ex-voto to divine Gilgameš (George 2003: vol. 1 122 n. 127), Gilgameš bears the title of lugal kalag(-ga), "mighty king." The adjective kalag-ga is also used in reference to two Pre-Sargonic rulers, En-anatum I of Lagaš and Giššag-kidug of Umma: nita kalag-ga-mu, "my (i.e., of Ningirsu) mighty male" (RIME I 170–173 En-anatum I 2 x 4); er$_3$ kalag-ga-ni, "his (i.e., of Lugal-Urub) mighty servant" (RIME I 182 En-anatum I 10 i 2); ensi$_2$ kalag-ga ^{d}En-lil$_2$-la$_2$-ke$_4$, "the mighty ensik of Enlil" (RIME 1 372–374 Giššag-kidug 2 i 15–16). It is possible that these designations invoke Gilgameš imagery. However, because of their exceptional nature, they do not qualify to be called royal titles proper.

381 "Two-thirds of him god, one third of him humanity" ("Gilgameš" SB Version, Tablet I line 48). This calculation apparently assumes that Gilgameš's mother, goddess Nin-sumun, was responsible for two-thirds of his genetic material, with his father, the mortal Lugal-banda, contributing the remaining third.

gods as youthful and beautiful human creatures – the classicist Jean-Pierre Vernant offered the following explanation:

> Does it mean that for the Greeks the gods were conceived of and represented in the image of human beings? To me it seems the opposite – that the human body became perceptible to Greek eyes when it was in the flower of its youth, when it was like an image or a reflection of the divine. (1991: 159)

Similar conclusions, which draw on Vernant's interpretation, were reached by Louise B. Zaidman and Louise S. Pantel:

> The fact that the Greeks sculpted such statues of their gods does not imply a belief that the gods resembled men or had bodies that were in every respect human; what the Greeks did believe was that the beauty, youth or perfection of a real human body evoked qualities of the divine. (1992: 217)

The notion that a perfect human body signaled the sublime qualities of the divine existed also in ancient Egypt. One of the titles used by the Pharaoh was *nefer* (*nfr*), which, as explained by Alan B. Lloyd,

> is often translated "good" but whose connotations lie much deeper in that it evokes concepts of youth and pristine strength and power associated with the sun-god as he rises over the eastern horizon in the morning. (2014: 67)

The phenomenon of kings becoming an integral part of the pantheon assumed an even greater dimension in Ur III times. To use a figurative expression, it may be said that the Ur III kings wormed their way into the local panthea, a development that, as I noted earlier, was motivated entirely by political considerations.

In terms of their genealogical orientation, the Ur III kings traced their descent primarily to the mythical, semi-divine kings of Uruk, such as Lugalbanda and Gilgameš. Although it may have begun already under Ur-Namma,[382] it was only during the reign of Šulgi that this development acquired its full formulation.

---

382 In his original inscriptions, Ur-Namma bears the title of the en of Unug (RIME 3/2 35 Ur-Namma 12:7) and identifies Nin-sumun as "his personal deity" (dingir-ra-ni) (RIME 3/2 58–59 Ur-Namma 23:1–2). These facts attest to his connection with Uruk and its pantheon. However, the claims that Ur-Namma was a child of Nin-sumun and Lugal-banda, which are found in the literary compositions devoted to him, obviously are retroactive interpolations. See the discussion below.

The Urukean genealogy of Šulgi was an elaborate theological construct. Growing out of the traditional rhetoric that identified particular deities as the agents responsible for the creation and birth of kings, this theology eventually became a fully-fledged argument about Šulgi's divine parentage. The course of this development may be traced by the comparison of two compositions, "Šulgi D" and "Šulgi P." Although "Šulgi D" may not necessarily be the earlier of the two, it offers a more modest – and therefore probably an earlier – picture of Šulgi's connections with the divine realm, which is still couched in traditional rhetoric:

> sipad Šul-gi a-zu [šag₄ ku]g-ga ba-an-ri-a
> ama ugu₂-zu[383] ᵈNin-sum[un₂-ke₄] mu-u₃-tud-[en]
> dingir-zu kug ᵈLu[gal-banda₃ᵈᵃ] mu-u₃-dim₂-e-[en]
> ama ᵈNin-tur-re [mi₂ zid mu-u₃-dug₄-ge-en?[384]]

> Oh shepherd Šulgi! When your seed was ejaculated into the womb,
> Nin-sumun, your creatrix, formed you;
> holy Lugal-banda, your personal god, fashioned you;
> mother Nintu [caressed? you].
> ("Šulgi D" lines 40–43)

That this text reflects an earlier theological situation finds corroboration in one of Šulgi's original inscriptions, which dates to before his deification.[385] There, Nin-sumun and Lugal-banda are identified as Šulgi's "personal deity" and his "master" respectively.[386] Although, in this instance, it is not Lugal-banda but Nin-sumun who is called Šulgi's personal deity, this source demonstrates that, prior to Šulgi's deification, Nin-sumun and Lugal-banda were associated with Šulgi merely as his protective deities, without any suggestion of their being his parents.

This ideological picture changed with Šulgi's deification, when, as a consequence of having become a *bona fide* deity, Šulgi was elevated to the status of Nin-sumun's and Lugal-banda's natural son. This development is illustrated by

---

383 The terms ama ugu/ugu₂ and a-a ugu/ugu₂, whose literal meaning is "mother/father of the head/cranium," appear to derive from the Akkadian *bāni qaqqadi*, for which see above p. 114 n. 306. Note also a ugu₄(KU)-mu in Gudea Cylinder A x 1. On the basis of these terms, lexical texts erroneously equate ugu/ugu₂/ugu₄ with *banû* and *alādu* (Ea I 137–138 = MSL 14 184; CAD A/1 288).

384 This restoration, which follows Klein 1981a: 94, is uncertain.

385 This is demonstrated by the titles Šulgi is assigned there. For the history of Šulgi's titulary, see in detail below pp. 151–153.

386 ᵈNin-sumun₂ dingir-mu ᵈLugal-banda₃ᵈᵃ lugal-mu (RIME 3/2 182 Šulgi 85:10–13).

the hymn "Šulgi P," which describes the deification of Šulgi. As we have seen earlier, this momentous event occurred thanks to the initiative and efforts of Nin-sumun. Undoubtedly in reflection of Šulgi's new status, Nin-sumun and Lugal-banda are now presented as Šulgi's real parents:

> Šul-gi amar kug tud-da-mu-me-en₃
> a ʾdug₃ʾ ᵈLugal-banda₃ᵈᵃ -me-en₃
> ur₂ kug-mu-a mu-ni-ib₂-bulug₃-en₃
> ubur₂ kug-mu-a nam ma-ra-ni-tar ...
> a-a ugu₄-zu ᵈLugal-banda₃ʾᵈᵃʾ-a
> šul an-ne₂ zu dingir-re-ne mu-še₃ ʾmuʾ-ri₂-in-sa₄
>
> (Nin-sumun speaks:) "Oh Šulgi, you are my holy calf born of me,
> you are the sweet seed of Lugal-banda.
> I reared you on my holy lap,
> I determined your fate at my holy bosom ...
> Lugal-banda, your creator,
> named you 'Youth whom An made known among the gods.'"
> (Segment C lines 22–25, 38–39)

The tenet of Šulgi's being a natural son of Nin-sumun[387] and Lugal-banda in turn permitted his identification as a brother of Gilgameš (Klein 1976; Michalowski 2008: 36; Woods 2012: 79). This point is elaborated most extensively in the hymn "Šulgi 0," where Šulgi is repeatedly called the "brother and friend" of Gilgameš (Segment A lines 50, 86, 139, Segment D line 6),[388] and where he meets Gilgameš in person, praising the latter's strength (nam-kalag) and "heroism" (nam-ur-sag), as well as his manifold military feats. As demonstrated by this and other literary sources whose origins belong to Ur III times, Gilgameš was one of Šulgi's favorite role models.[389]

Once this genealogy had been firmly established, it was then retroactively assigned to Ur-Namma, clearly with an objective of bolstering Šulgi's divine status still further. From now on it was claimed that it was already Ur-Namma who

---

387 Šulgi is called son of Nin-sumun also in "Šulgi X" line 47, "Šulgi O" Segment A line 29, and "Šulgi Q" line 43.

388 See also Šul-gi ... šeš ku-li-ni en ᵈBil₃-ga-mes in "Šulgi D" line 292.

389 This is also reflected in the various stories about Gilgameš, which were composed in Ur III times. The allusions to Šulgi as a *Doppelgänger* of Gilgameš are particularly obvious in "Gilgameš and Akka" and "Gilgameš and Huwawa." In the latter composition, Version A line 20, Utu calls Gilgameš a dumu-gir₁₅, "native son," which is probably a play on Šulgi's name, "Local/native youth" (Steinkeller 2005b: 309).

descended from gods. The fullest presentation of these views is found in the composition "Ur-Namma C"[390]:

> a!-mu šag$_4$ kug-ge ba-ri-a-ta ...
> ^{d}Nin-tu tud-ʼtudʼ-a <mu->un-gub-bu!
> šag$_4$ ama-mu ^{d}Nin-sumun$_2$-ka-ta
> nam-tar-ra sag$_5$-ga ma-ta-e$_3$

> After my seed was ejaculated in the holy womb ...
> Nintu accompanied my birthing,
> from the womb of my mother Nin-sumun
> a propitious destiny came out for me.
> (lines 43–49)

> šu-dug$_4$-ga-e ^{d}Nanna-a-me-en
> šeš ^{d}Bil$_3$-ga-mes gu-la-me-en
> [dumu t]ud-da ^{d}Nin-sumun$_2$-ka-me-en numun nam-en-na-me-en

> I am a creation of Nanna,
> I am the elder brother of Gilgameš,
> I am a child born by Nin-sumun, I am the seed of en-ship.
> (lines 111–113)

In agreement with the above, in "Ur-Namma A" line 16 Nin-sumun is called ama lugal-la, "mother of the king."[391] The secondary nature of this theology is proved by the fact that, like Šulgi before his deification, in his original inscriptions Ur-Namma too refers to Nin-sumun merely as his personal deity.[392]

The Ur III kings invented yet another divine genealogy for themselves, which independently linked them with Uruk and its deities. This genealogy, an antecedent of which probably existed already in Sargonic times (see above p. 136), was derived from the fact that the Ur III kings were holders of the ancient office of the en of Uruk.[393] This made them symbolic and ritual spouses of Inana as well. Based on this connection with Inana, they could consequently claim to be the latter-day apparitions of Dumuzi, a lover/husband of Inana, and possibly one

---

390 There is no doubt that this self-laudatory hymn was composed following Ur-Namma's death, through the use of various materials pertaining to Šulgi.

391 Note also that Ur-Namma is called dumu tud-da ^{d}Nin-sumun$_2$-ka ʼemedu$_2$(AM.A.TU)ʼ ki-ag$_2$-ga$_2$-ni in "Ur-Namma Laws" 37–40 (= RIME 3/2 47). This may be a later interpolation as well.

392 ^{d}Nin-sumun$_2$ dingir-ra-ni (RIME 3/2 58–59 Ur-Nammu 23:1–2).

393 See Steinkeller 1999a: 105 and n. 4. Note also that in the hymn "Šulgi D" line 387 Enlil grants to Šulgi en-ship (nam-en nam-lugal-la ud sud-da nam-še$_3$ gu$_2$-mu-ri$_2$-ib$_2$-tar^{ar}), where the en-ship of Uruk undoubtedly is meant.

of the mythical archaic rulers of Uruk (see Essay 1 p. 29–30). The identification with Dumuzi in turn made them the brothers of Dumuzi's sister Geštinana.[394]

The figure of Dumuzi was one of the characteristic images of the divine king (Woods 2012: 88–89). The adoption of Dumuzi for these purposes must have been motivated, at least in part, by the fact that, very much like Gilgameš, Dumuzi too had a mixed, partly divine and partly human nature.[395] As such, Dumuzi constituted a perfect model for the divine king. In literature, the Ur III and Isin rulers are often compared to Dumuzi or even identified with him. This point is particularly clear in the hymn "Šulgi X" lines 1–73. When Šulgi arrives in Uruk to pay a visit to Inana, Inana joyfully receives him as the "shepherd Dumuzi" (su_4-ba du_5-mu-zi-de_3), recalling the pleasurable moments the two spent in each other's company in the past. On account of those good times, she then determines destiny for Šulgi, bestowing upon him the "legitimate shepherdship of all the foreign countries," and vouching her active support on the battlefield — this time, however addressing him as "shepherd Šulgi."[396]

It appears that Dumuzi mythology occupied an especially important place in the beliefs about the afterlife of divine kings. There is compelling evidence for the existence of a notion that, following his death, the king continued his existence by becoming an immortal star. Since Dumuzi had an astral form, that belief likely was based on Dumuzi's own history (Steinkeller 2013b: 462–463, 472–473). As speculated by this author, there may have even existed a special ritual, which symbolized the transition of the dead king from the netherworld to his astral position in the sky (Steinkeller 2013b).

However, the deity whom Šulgi and his successors adopted as their primary divine image was the Sun God. In this they clearly emulated the Sargonic rulers. Since the Sun God happened to be Inana's brother, this made the divine king a brother-in-law of the Sun God. In fact, Šulgi repeatedly claims to have been Utu's "brother and companion" (see below). This genealogical link further cemented the connection of the Ur III kings with Uruk and its pantheon.[397]

---

394 nin_9!-mu ᵈGeštin-an-na ("Šulgi E" line 21); ᵈGeštin-an-na nin_9 lugal-la-ke_4 ("Šulgi P" Segment C line 43). Interestingly, Šulgi calls himself "son" of Geštinana in an inscription dating to before his deification (RIME 3/2 163 Šulgi 62:1). As I suggested many years ago (1981: 78), this inscription may refer to Šulgi's real mother, SI.A-tum, who, as there are reasons to believe, was posthumously venerated as a deity ᵈGeštin-an-na SI.A-tum.

395 Cf. Essay 1 pp. 29–30.

396 It is clear that, at least in the Ur III and Isin periods, the royal title of sipad, "shepherd," was consistently associated with Dumuzi.

397 For the role of Utu in the Uruk pantheon and his connections with the Ur III kings, see the extensive discussion by Woods 2012. As Woods demonstrates, the mythological kings of Uruk were solar heroes in their own right. This is shown by the fact that both Mes-kiag-gašir and

Indeed, the Sun God figures very prominently in the Ur III royal hymns, especially those of Šulgi. We have already seen (above pp. 125–126) that, as part of his deification, the gods "caused Šulgi, the righteous one, to rise in the Land like the Sun God in order to be [their (i.e., of the people)] god":

> Šul-gi si-sa₂ dingir-ra-[ne-ne-še₃]
> kalam-ma ᵈUtu-gim ma-ni-in-ᵣe₃¹-[eš]
> ("Šulgi P," Segment C line 59)

Sun God imagery is applied to Šulgi also in the following passage:

> uru-mu ᵈUtu-gim ba-ta-e₃-en šag₄-ba bi₂-la₂
> E₂-temen-ni₂-guru₃ me ki us₂-sa
> gug-a nam-nun-ni mu-ni-ib₂-si-nam

> I rise over my city like Utu, I suspend myself in its midst;
> Etemen-niguru, the place established by the divine forces,
> I fill with (the radiance of) princely carnelian.
> ("Šulgi C" lines 25–27)

Elsewhere, the Sun God is described as Šulgi's "brother and companion," as well as the one who provides him with strength:

> šeš ku-li-mu šul ᵈUtu-am₃
> ki zi-šag₄-gal₂-la-ka igi mu-na-ni-du₈
> ᵈŠul-gi-me-en dalla e₃-bi-a inim mu-un-da-bala-e-en
> dingir igi sag₉ me₃-ga₂-a-kam
> šul ᵈUtu kur-ra ki-ag₂ ᵈLama ᵍⁱˢtukul-ga₂-a-kam
> inim-ma-ni-še₃ ga-mu-un-kalag-ge la ga-mu-un-ne₃?-e
> me₃ giš giš-e la₂-a-ba ᵈUtu ga₂-ar ma-an-e₃,

> My brother and companion indeed is the ever-youthful Utu;
> he gazed upon me! at the place where the life force (is created);
> I am Šulgi, I exchange words with him at his brilliant rising;
> he is the god (who casts) an auspicious eye on my battles;
> (during my campaigns) in foreign lands the ever-youthful Utu shows love for the protective

---

his son Enmerkar are called sons of Utu (ibid. 81). It appears that most of this mythology was an invention of the Ur III period. This particularly concerns Mes-kiag-gašir, whose name is an implausible mixture of Sumerian and Akkadian: "Beloved Hero, the Strong One." This artificial formation is based on the names like Erra-gašir, where *gašru*, "strong, heavy," is also a by-name of Nergal (Steinkeller 1987: 165–166; 1990: 58). However, some elements of it may have been older. Apart from the data cited by Woods 2012: 93–94, there is the fact that already the Sargonic kings cultivated a connection with the Sun God. It is possible, therefore, that this notion harkened back to an earlier time.

deity of my weapon;
by his command I become stronger; I …
when the weapons join in battle, Utu comes out for me (as helper).
("Šulgi B" lines 40–46)

The Sun God is also credited with granting the "kingship of the Land" to Šulgi:

^{d}Utu lugal nig$_2$-si-sa$_2$ a zi-de-eš$_2$ tum$_2$-ma
šen-na dalla mu-na-ni-in-e$_3$ sipad zi Šul-gi-ke$_4$
am gal an kug-ta šul ^{d}Utu izi-gar-gim ga$_2$-ga$_2$ ud kalam-ma igi-gal$_2$ …
Šul-gi-ra ^{d}Utu-u$_3$ ꞌnamꞌ-lugal kalam-ma mu-na-an-sum

Utu, the king of justice,
made Šulgi glorious on the battle field, the one who is fit be the legitimate seed, the one who is the legitimate shepherd.
The great wild bull, the ever youthful Utu, the one who like a torch sets (light) in the sky, who makes light/day visible in the Land …
Utu granted to Šulgi the kingship of the Land.
("Šulgi Q" lines 5–11)

šul ^{d}Utu sipad šag$_4$-ge bi$_2$-i$_3$-pad$_3$
Šul-gi sipad zi lugal mu he$_2$-gal$_2$-la$_2$ nam-še$_3$ tar-ra-am$_3$
sipad zi ^{d}Utu-u$_3$ nam tar-ra-ra
^{d}En-lil$_2$-le eš$_3$-e Nibru^{ki}-ta sag-e-eš$_2$ mu-ni-rig$_7$

The ever youthful Utu chose the shepherd in (his) heart.
For Šulgi, the legitimate shepherd, the king, years of abundance were destined (by Utu).
To the legitimate shepherd, the one granted destiny by Utu,
in the shrine of Nippur Enlil granted (the years of abundance).
("Šulgi Q" lines 45–48)[398]

The hymns of Šulgi are replete with references to his youth, heroism, strength, and physicality. While these descriptions primarily draw on the Sun God imagery, they also invoke the representations and characterizations of Gilgameš and Naram-Suen. Particularly common here are the references to Šulgi as "mighty" (kalag-ga) and "hero" (ur-sag). An epithet that is uniquely Šulgi's own is

---

398 The association of the divine kings with the Sun God is also reflected in the existence of personal and geographical names in which these rulers are likened to the Sun God. See ^{d}Šul-gi-Ša-am$_3$-ši (ITT 2 728 i 4; AnOr 1 248:6; Nisaba 22 158:13; etc.) / ^{d}Šul-gi-^{d}Utu-mu (BPOA 6 746:2ꞌ; TCTI 2 3999:4; etc.), ^{d}Amar-^{d}Suen-^{d}Utu-mu (L'uomo 62 iii 13ꞌ; BPOA 5 135, 138 Talon-Van-derroost 1 rev. viii 31), ^{d}Šu-^{d}Suen-^{d}Utu-mu (MVN 16 607:4), and ^{d}Šul-gi-^{d}Utu^{ki} (TCL 2 4688:4; RIME 3/2 213–214 Šulgi 2028:6). Note also Amar-Suen's title dingir zi ^{d}Utu kalam-ma-na (RIME 3/2 262–264 Amar-Suen 16:10–11).

"youth" (šul), which, apart from being Utu's designation, plays on Šulgi's own name, whose meaning is "Local/native youth."[399] Offered below is a selection of the most representative descriptions of this type:

ʾšulʾ ^{d}Utu-u$_3$ sag-ki zalag-ga-ni mu-ši-ib$_2$-zi-zi-[(x)]
ʾŠulʾ-gi sipad zi Ki-en-gi-ra-ra nam mu-ni-[ib$_2$-tar-re]
l[ugal] ka gun$_3$-gun$_3$ igi sag$_9$-sag$_9$
ur-sag kalag-ga pirig-še$_3$ tud-da
sumun$_2$ tur nam-šul-ba gub-ba
lipiš tuku ne-ni-e nu-keš$_2$-ra$_2$

The ever youthful Utu raises his bright forehead (and)
determines destiny for Šulgi, the legitimate shepherd of Sumer:
'Oh [king] of flowery mouth and beautiful face!
You indeed are a mighty hero, the one born to be a lion,
a young wild bull, the one who stands in the prime of youth.
a brave one, the one whose strength cannot be restrained.
("Šulgi X" lines 80–85)

kalag-ga-mu mu-bi a$_2$ bi$_2$-su$_3$-ud ...
^{d}Šul-gi dingir nam-guruš-a sag-kal eren$_2$-na-me-en ...
^{d}Šul-gi nir-gal$_2$ usu gal-gal-la-me-en
kalag-ga-me-en ...
anše eren$_2$-na-mu zi-bi nu-mu-e-da-šub-be$_2$
šeš ku-li-mu šul ^{d}Utu-gim
zag-še$_3$ pirig-gim sug$_2$-sug$_2$-ge-ga$_2$
anše sahar la$_2$ ug-gim sig$_4$-gi$_4$-a-ga$_2$ kuš$_7$ sag$_9$-ga-bi-me-en
dur$_3$^{ur3}-gim kas$_4$-a ne$_3$/ne-mu nu-silig-me
kas$_4$-ta e$_3$-a-me-en dug$_3$ nu-kuš$_2$-u$_3$-me-en
nam-te nu-gal$_2$-me-en išiš-a gud-gu$_4$-ud-me-en

The fame of my strength is spread far ...
I am Šulgi, the god of manliness, the leader of soldiers ...
I, Šulgi, am a prince of immense bodily power,
I am mighty ...
The spirit of the donkey team (pulling my wagon) never subsides for me.[400]
Like my brother and companion Utu I stride forward like a lion.
I am a fine coachman of the dust-raising donkeys that bray like lions.

---

399 See above n. 389.

400 This and the following two lines invoke the image of Utu as he drives in his wagon pulled by a team of donkey stallions. See ni-is-ku EREN$_2$ mu tuku EREN$_2$ ^{d}Utu ki-ag$_2$, "the famous team of steeds, the beloved team of Utu" (Gudea Cylinder A xiv 25); EREN$_2$ kug ^{d}Utu sag bala-e-dam, "(it was) as if the (donkeys of the) holy team of Utu were tossing their heads" (ibid. xix 16). For a discussion of the Gudea passages and other data bearing on the team of the Sun God, see in detail Alaura and Bonechi 2012: 14–16. Cf. also Bonechi 2010; 2011; Alaura 2011.

When I run like a stallion, my strength does not cease.
When I finish the run, my knees are not tired.
I have no fear. I dance with joy.
("Šulgi B" lines 53, 81, 119–120, 122–128)

kalag-ga nam-ur-sag-ga$_2$ tum$_2$-ma ...
nam-ur-sag-zu-u$_3$ pa he$_2$-e$_3$-e$_3$
nam-kalag-ga-zu-u$_3$ mi$_2$ dug$_3$ he$_2$-e

(Oh Šulgi) the mighty one, the one fit for heroism ...
may your heroism shine fourth,
may your might be sweetly praised!
("Šulgi D" lines 4, 16–17, 38–39, 63–64)

Šul-gi-ra nam mu-ni-ib$_2$-tar-re
lugal nam gi$_4$-ri$_2$-ib$_2$-tar^{ar} nam dug$_3$ gu$_2$-mu-ri-ib$_2$-tar^{ar} ...
nam-ur-sag nam-še$_3$ gu$_2$-mu-ri-ib$_2$-tar^{ar}

(Enlil) determines destiny for Šulgi:
'Oh king, I will determine a destiny for you! I will determine a propitious destiny for you!
I will determine heroism as your fate!
("Šulgi D" lines 383–386)

^{d}Suen-e E$_2$-kiš-nu-gal$_2$-ta
nam-ur-sag nam-kalag-ga nam-til$_3$ nig$_2$-dug$_3$ sag-e-eš rig$_7$-ga

Suen in Ekišnugal
presented (Šulgi) with heroism, might, and sweet life.
("Šulgi A" lines 96–97).

Šul-gi sipad zi Ki-en-gi-ra-ke$_4$
šeš ku-li en ^{d}Bil$_3$-ga-mes
nam-kalag-ga-na mu-ni-in-i-i
nam-ur-sag-ga$_2$ mu-ni-in-pad$_3$-pad$_3$-de$_3$

Šulgi, the legitimate shepherd of Sumer,
extols the might of his brother and companion Gilgameš,
he avows his heroism.
("Šulgi O" lines 49–52)

sipad a$_2$ kalag-ga-ke$_4$ mes-e

(Šulgi), the shepherd of strong arms, the young hero.[401]
("Šulgi G" line 19)

---

[401] For the full context, see above p. 114–115.

That the youth and strength were expected – and perhaps even required – attributes of the divine king is also reflected in the references to Šulgi as a "runner," particularly in the hymn "Šulgi A," whose central theme is the superhuman run that Šulgi performed, within one day, between Nippur and Ur and back. Although this "run" may have had a very prosaic, practical *Sitz im Leben* (Steinkeller 2010: 380–382), it cannot be excluded that it had a ritual dimension as well. Significantly, the same feat was later replicated by another divine king, Išme-Dagan of Isin.[402] Therefore, it is possible that such running performances were meant to demonstrate the king's physical prowess. Here one is reminded of the Heb Sed festival, as part of which the Egyptian Pharaoh was required, usually after thirty years of his reign, to run a race in order to prove that he was still physically fit for the office – and probably also to demonstrate his continued possession of the "divine" essence (Kees 1912; Frankfort 1948: 79–88; Uphill 1965). As defined by Frankfort, the objective of this festival was "a true renewal of kingly potency, a rejuvenation of rulership *ex opere operato*"[403] (1948: 79).

The identification of the Ur III kings with the Sun-God may be discerned also in Ur III art. On the whole, the image of the divine king is much more restrained than in the Sargonic period, no doubt to make his divinity more palatable and less "in-your-face." The king usually assumes a posture of piety, which, without any doubt, is a direct borrowing from the imagery of Gudea of Lagaš.[404] See **figs. 42, 44–46.** He no longer sports a divine crown. Instead, he wears a brimmed cap (*Breitrandkappe*) that is an attribute of Gudea as well, but which, in actuality, is a historic reference to the garb worn by the archaic rulers of Uruk.[405] It is characteristic that he is never accompanied by royal insignia or any other attributes of kingship, which makes him, like Gudea, practically indistinguishable from the rest of the human society. In at least one instance, however, the king is depicted as an unmistakable solar figure. The image in question appears on a

---

402 See RIME 4 36–38 Išme-Dagan 8. In line 5 of this text, Išme-Dagan is described as a "mighty male with the muscles and body of a lion, mighty youth who spreads fright" (guruš kalag sa su pirig šul kalag ni$_2$ gal$_2$-la).

403 "From the work done" or "through the rite performed," referring to the Catholic doctrine that says that divine grace can only be conferred by a sacrament.

404 Suter 2015: 517–522 labors to find in these representations features indicative of Gudea's divine status, discovering "allusions to a certain degree of divinity in Gudea's images" (ibid. 519). However, these findings are completely illusionary, since Gudea iconography is totally devoid of any suggestions of his divinity. On the contrary, this imagery *insists* on the point that Gudea was a human figure.

405 See Essay 1 pp. 26, 34. During the Ur III period, this type of cap appears for the first time in the representations of Gudea and Ur-Namma. See Boese 1973: 15–21.

cylinder seal that was presented by Šulgi to his daughter Geme-Ninlila. See **fig. 43**. There, Šulgi assumes a triumphal pose that matches closely that of the Sun-God on the Sargonic seals of Lugal-ušumgal I discussed earlier (see above p. 139 and **figs. 40** and **41**).

While the representations of the king as a pious worshipper predominate,[406] we know from historical texts that there existed Ur III victory steles, on which the divine kings were depicted as warriors, but no certain examples of those are extant. There survives, however, an uninscribed rock relief of this nature that can almost certainly be attributed to one of the Ur III kings, in all likelihood to Šulgi. This particular monument, which depicts a standing royal figure vanquishing enemies, is situated at the Darband-i Gawr pass, in the southeastern section of the Qara Dagh range of southern Kurdistan (Edmonds 1925; Boese 1973; Eppihimer 2009: 261–262). See **fig. 47**. Importantly, this region was one of the areas where Šulgi campaigned extensively, eventually incorporating it into the Ur III empire. The connection between this relief and the iconography of the Ur III kings is indicated particularly convincingly by the fact that the figure in question wears a brimmed cap that is the same as the headgear of Ur-Namma and his followers.[407] See **figs. 42–46**. Another suggestive clue for this attribution is the modeling of his beard, which is identical with that of Ur-Namma's, as depicted on the stela from Ur (see **fig. 42**).

A comparison of the Darband-i Gawr relief with the "Victory Stele" of Naram-Suen makes it apparent that the former is a direct reference to the Stele or, more likely, to the whole genre of Naram-Suen's rock reliefs that undoubtedly had existed, but did not survive to our times.

The conclusion that the deification of Šulgi was a strategic move meant to accomplish a specific political objective – which, as I argued earlier, was the unification of Babylonia – is borne out by the history of the Ur III royal titulary as well. While reviving the Sargonic title of *dannum*, "the mighty one,"[408] the founder of the dynasty Ur-Namma coined for himself a completely new title, which was

---

406 Cf. Frankfort's assessment (in reference to the "Ur-Namma Stele"): "the stele, like the seal designs, illustrates the same absorption in ritual which distinguishes the art of Gudea from that of the Akkadians" (1954: 102–104).

407 For this and other arguments in favor of the Ur III date of this relief, see Boese 1973: 15–21. For its attribution to Šulgi, see Boese 1973: 48; Suter 2010: 335.

408 In Sumerian sources, this title appears as nita kalag-ga, "mighty male," or lugal kalag-ga, "mighty king." The first version of this title was used by Ur-Namma, Šulgi, and Amar-Suen. The second, which appears for the first time under Amar-Suen, was subsequently used by Šu-Suen and Ibbi-Suen. The Akkadian sources employ *dannum* instead (RIME 3/2 Šulgi 23, 25, 29, 33).

"king of Sumer and Akkad."[409] The duality of this title is striking, since it shows that, in spite of Ur-Namma's having assumed unquestioned power over the two halves of Babylonia, a degree of political and cultural separateness between the South and the North had still existed at that time, and this situation needed an official acknowledgment, in titulary and probably also on the ritual level. This title continued to be used by Šulgi in the beginning of his reign. However, as soon as he assumed divinity (which, as noted earlier, happened around the twentieth year of his reign), he abandoned this title completely. Nor was this title used by his successors.[410] Instead, Šulgi re-introduced Naram-Suen's title of the "king of the four corners of the world."[411] He also created a new title, the "god of his Land."[412] Under Amar-Suen, this title acquired two further elaborations, "true god of his land"[413] and "true god, the Sun-God of his Land."[414] In these epithets, the "Land" obviously means a united Babylonia – or at least an *idea* of united Babylonia, since, as I noted earlier, the real creation of a Babylonian nation took place only three centuries later. But that goal would not have been possible without the unificatory policies of the Sargonic and Ur III kings.

---

409 lugal Ki-en-gi ki-Uri-ke₄ (RIME 3/2 35 Ur-Namma 12:9; et passim); LUGAL *ma-at Šu-mé-ri-im ù A-ka-di-im* (RIME 3/2 144–146 Šulgi 38:5–6, Akkadian version).

410 However, beginning with Šu-ilišu (RIME 4 18–19 Šu-ilišu 3:3), this title was revived by the kings of Isin.

411 lugal AN-ub-da limmu-ba (RIME 3/2 151 Šulgi 47:4; et passim); LUGAL *ki-ib-ra-tim ar-ba-im* (RIME 3/2 132 Šulgi 23:4–6; et passim). Immediately following the fall of the Sargonic empire, this title was adopted by a Gutian king named Erridu-pizir (RIME 2 221–223 Erridu-pizir 1 i 14–18, ii 16–20, iii 11–15, 223–225 Erridu-pizir 2 iii 3′–7′, iv 5–9). It was later also used by Utu-hegal of Uruk (RIME 2 281 Utu-hegal 1:5; et passim), as well as by Puzur-Inšušinak, the last ruler of the Awan dynasty and the contemporary of Ur-Namma, clearly in reflection of his own "imperial" ambitions (Steinkeller 2013c: 296). This title is also assigned to Ur-Namma in "Ur-Namma D" line 37, but this clearly is a later interpolation. Following the Ur III period, it was used by Išbi-Erra (RIME 4 10 2006:3) and Išme-Dagan (RIME 4 31–32 Išme-Dagan 5:4)

412 dingir kalam-ma-na (RIME 3/2 160–161 Šulgi 58:4, 368–369 Ibbi-Suen 1:2; et passim). Sometimes this title appears as dingir kalam-ma (e. g., RIME 3/2 384–385 Ibbi-Suen 2007:2), which probably is an abbreviation. In Akkadian texts, it is written DINGIR *ma-ti-šu* (RIME 3/2 140–141 Šulgi 33:2). This title is similar to Šar-kali-šarri's title "god of the land of Warium" (see above pp. 135–136). Therefore, it may have been patterned after it. In literary sources, Šulgi is also called ᵈLama kalam-ma, "protective deity of the Land" ("Šulgi G" line 23). Similarly, Ur-Namma says that "in me, the lands of Sumer and Akkad have a protective deity" (ma-da Ki-en-gi ꜝUriꜝ ᵈLama mu-un-da-an-tuku; "Ur-Namma C" line 50). These designations suggest a more circumscribed version of divinity, thus further confirming the markedly understated nature of Šulgi's deification. A related title, "master of his land" (lugal kalam-ma-na / *be-al ma-ti-šu*), was later used by Išbi-Erra and Šu-ilišu of Isin.

413 dingir zi kalam-ma-na (RIME 3/2 264–265 Amar-Suen 17:10).

414 dingir zi ᵈUtu kalam-ma-na (RIME 3/2 262–264 Amar-Suen 16:10–11).

And the notion of the divine ruler was an instrumental element of those strategies.

The Ur III royal titulary also includes epithets that reference the earlier-discussed familial links between the divine kings and the divine realm. Thus Amar-Suen calls Inana his "beloved wife,"[415] while Šu-Suen applies the same designation to Annunitum, the avatar of Ištar in her martial apparition.[416] A different genealogical connection with Inana is documented in two inscriptions of Šu-Suen stemming from Umma and dedicated to Šara, Umma's chief god. There, Šu-Suen calls himself "son of Šara" and identifies Šara as "Inana's beloved child."[417] These epithets reflect a local Umma theology, according to which Inana was Šara's mother. But it remains unclear how Šu-Suen's descent from Šara had been established.[418] Similar reference to a local theology is found in one of the inscriptions of Šulgi, where he describes the goddess Ningal as "his mother."[419] This genealogy probably rested on the argument that Šulgi was Inana's "husband." Since Inana was the daughter of Nanna and Ningal, this made Šulgi Ningal's son-in-law.

Following the end of the Ur III dynasty, various rulers of the lands that had been conquered and incorporated into the Ur III empire claimed divinity. Among those one may list Zardamu and Tišatal of Karahar,[420] Ipiq-Eštar and Takil-ilissu of Malgium,[421] Nidnuša of Der,[422] Iddin-Sin and Zabazuna of Šimurrum,[423] and

---

415 ᵈInana nin me₃ dam ki-ag₂-ga₂-ni (RIME 3/2 258–259 Amar-Suen 13:1–3). This inscription deals with the construction of Inana's gi₆-par₄ at Uruk, and so this epithet undoubtedly alludes to Amar-Suen's spousal relationship with Inana. Further, note that Amar-Suen is called Inana's "beloved" (ki-ag₂) on a seal of one of his officials (Zettler 1987: 60 fig. 1). While such epithets are missing in Šulgi's original inscriptions, he is linked with Inana in this manner in literary sources. See, e.g., "Šulgi A" line 82, where he calls Inana his "spouse" (nitalam-mu ki-sikil ᵈInana). The spousal relationship with Inana was later claimed by many of the kings of Isin. For the examples, see Steinkeller 1999a: 106 n. 4.
416 ᵀAnᵀ-nu-ni-tum dam-a-ni (RIME 3/2 330–331 Šu-Suen 20:1–2).
417 ᵈŠara₂ nir-gal₂ An-na dumu ki-ag₂ ᵈInana ad-da-ni (RIME 3/2 326–327 Šu-Suen 16:1–5, 327–328 Šu-Suen 17:1–5).
418 Logically, this would mean that Šu-Suen was the son of Šara and Nin-ura, but there is no independent evidence of this. This genealogy perhaps is the evidence that, as I suggested earlier, the Ur III kings systematically inserted themselves into the divine families of all the major (former) city-states.
419 ᵈNin-gal ama-ni (RIME 3/2 160–161 Šulgi 58:1–2).
420 RIME 3/2 452–453.
421 RIME 4 669–674.
422 RIME 4 676 Nidnuša 1:1. The same probably was true also of Anum-mutabbil of Der (RIME 4 677–679). Since the names beginning with An- do not take the divine determinative DINGIR, this

Yabrat/Ebarat, Kindattu, and Idattu of Šimaški.[424] Most of them also used the title of the "mighty king."[425] Zardamu of Karahar is an especially interesting case here. In his seal, Zardamu is called the "Sun God of his Land; beloved of Nergal, his (personal) god; Annunitum (is) his mother; ... mighty king, king of Karahar, king of the four quarters of the world; husband of Ištar."[426] A spousal relationship with Ištar/Inana may have also been presumed by Nidnuša, Anum-muttabbil, and Idattu, who identified themselves as "beloved of Inana/ Ištar."[427]

Since the titles and epithets borne by these kings obviously are borrowings from the Ur III royal titulary, they are informative about the latter phenomenon as well. Even more importantly, they and the fact that these individuals thought it desirable to seek divinity demonstrate how real and pervasive the nature of the Ur III divine kingship must have been, even in the periphery of Babylonia.

Similar inference can be made from the fact that some of the records left by these peripheral rulers are rock inscriptions.[428]As such, these materials implicate the existence of a significant repertoire of Ur III (and probably also Sargonic) inscriptions of this type, which, like the titulary found in them, must have served as models for the records in question.

6 Was Naram-Suen's Deification Inspired by a Foreign Example?

As we have seen earlier, the deification of Naram-Suen was a radical development, which violated the basic principles of the relationship between the human and divine societies, especially as concerns the place that the ruler was expected to occupy in this scheme. As the notion of the divine king was completely incongruous with the traditional Sumerian ideology, it must have

would not have been reflected in writing. A similar case is Anubanini of Lullubum (RIME 4 704–706 Anubanini 1:1), who may have claimed divinity as well.

423 RIME 4 708–716.

424 Steinkeller in George 2011: 21–22 no. 18:1–3'; Michalowski 2008: 39.

425 Here belong Zardamu, Takil-ilissu, Nidnuša and Anum-muttabbil of Der, Iddin-Sin and Zabazuna of Šimurrum, and Annubanini of Lullubum.

426 ᵈZa-ar-da-mu / ᵈUTU *ma-ti-šu* / *na-ra-am* / ᵈNergal / *ì-lí-šu An-nu-ni-tum* / *um-ma-šu* / ... LUGAL *da-núm* / LUGAL Kara₂-har^ki / *ù* LUGAL / *ki-ib-ra-tim* / *ar-ba-im* / DAM ᵈINANA (RIME 3/2 453 Zardamu 1:1–21).

427 *na-ra-am* ᵈINANA (Nidnuša and Anum-muttabbil), ki-ag₂ ᵈInana (Idattu).

428 The surviving records of this type belong to Iddin-Sin of Šimurrum (RIME 4 708–714 Iddin-Sin 1–4) and Anubanini of Lullubum (RIME 4 704–706 Anubanini 1).

been felt particularly offensive in the South. But even in northern Babylonia, where the kingship was stronger and more expansive in its claims, the divine king likely was perceived as an alien figure. As I argued earlier, there is every reason to think that Naram-Suen's deification was the response to a concrete political problem, and that it was invented quite suddenly. But how did Naram-Suen come up with this solution? Since, in my view, this could not have been suggested to him by any particular tenet of the existing Babylonian ideology, a possibility exists that his deification was inspired by a foreign example. Historically, divine kingship is an exceedingly rare phenomenon.[429] In the third millennium Near East and the immediately adjoining regions, one cannot find any documented cases of it *except* in one place, and that is Egypt. Given the geographical extent of the Sargonic expansion, which reached as far as northern Syria and Anatolia, we can be confident that the Sargonic kings were well informed about Egypt and its customs and culture. Such information certainly was available at Ebla, which, in the period just before Sargon, enjoyed commercial and diplomatic exchanges with Egypt.[430] This was even more true of the Levant, where Sargon may actually have campaigned,[431] and where Akkadian traders undoubtedly came into contact with their Egyptian counterparts. Needless to say, however, the proposition that Naram-Suen modeled his rulership after the Egyptian Pharaoh, while attractive and inherently possible, is not provable in any way or fashion.

Similar outside inspirations may have been at play in the Ur III period as well. As I as wrote elsewhere (Steinkeller 2013b), the Ur III ideas about the afterlife of the divine king match so closely the Egyptian ones that, also in this case, one cannot but think of the possibility of an Egyptian influence. But here too this must remain an unprovable supposition.

There is yet another area where an impact of Egypt on Babylonia may be considered, and this time perhaps even with some confidence. As we have seen earlier, the Ur III period (and, conceivably, the Sargonic period as well) saw the first examples of rock reliefs, which depict the king defeating his enemies. During the third millennium, such representations did not exist in Greater Mesopotamia prior to the Ur III kings, nor do we find examples of them in Iran and Anatolia. But rock reliefs glorifying rulers are documented in Egypt since

---

429 Possehl 1998: 264 thinks that early kings "are often deified, or allowed to flirt with notions of human deification. From the point of view of the citizenry, the deification of one's king might be thought of as the deification of oneself." Neither of these assertions is correct.
430 Biga 2012; 2014.
431 One of the places Sargon claims to have reached is Yarmuti (RIME 2 27–29 Sargon 11:23), which may fairly confidently be identified with the later Yarimuta near Byblos.

Early Dynastic times. Of particular interest here is a group of rock reliefs from Wadi Maghareh in the southwestern Sinai, which were left by the various rulers of the Third, Fourth, and Fifth Dynasties.[432] As generally agreed, these reliefs commemorate the mining expeditions those rulers sent to the Sinai in search of turquoise and copper. Some of these reliefs depict the Pharaoh as a vanquisher of enemies. See **fig. 48.** In this iconic image, which is a hallmark of Egyptian art at least since Narmer's time, the Pharaoh faces right, as does Naram-Suen on the "Victory Stele." In other respects, however, the scene differs substantially from that depicted on the Stele, as the Pharaoh smites a single enemy with his mace, while Naram-Suen stands in a pose of victory, trampling over two dead combatants. This makes it unlikely that the Wadi Maghareh reliefs could have served as *direct* models for the Stele and similar Babylonian materials. But they might have provided *a general idea* of such an image, as well as of this particular genre of display monuments.

An objection could be raised perhaps that Sinai may have been too far for the Babylonians to visit. It is possible, however, that similar early Egyptian rock reliefs existed also in Lebanon. Some of the Pharaohs who left their monuments in Wadi Maghareh (Sneferu and Khufu of the Fourth Dynasty and Djedkare of the Fifth Dynasty) are known to have sent expeditions to Lebanon to procure cedar, and so they might have left similar commemorative marks in that region as well. If such rock reliefs existed, none of them have come down to us. But we know that this form of commemoration was practiced in the Levant in later times. The classic example here is the site at the Nahr el-Kalb estuary north of Beirut, where a large group of ancient rock reliefs is situated. Those include three inscriptions of Ramses II, as well as a number of Neo-Assyrian and Neo-Babylonian ones. Clearly, Nahr el-Kalb served as an international showcase place, where kings demonstrated their mastery over the Levant and its trade routes, and where ideological messages, both written and visual, were advertised and exchanged.

7 Final Thoughts

A divine mortal is a contradiction in terms, of course. Just think of the interpretational problems that Jeshua the Nazarene has created! We will never know what the Sumerians and Akkadians really thought of the *divus* Naram-Suen. But, since

---

432 These are Sanakht, Djoser, and Sekhemkhet of the Third Dynasty, Sneferu and Khufu of the Fourth Dynasty, as well as some Fifth Dynasty kings (Mumford 1999).

people are not stupid (even those who lived in third millennium Mesopotamia), it is fair to assume that few of them ever bought the idea of his supposed god-ship. However, this is beside the point. The objective of Naram-Suen's deification was not to make people believe in it, but to create a socio-political reality in which he could lawfully be placed above everybody else, kings and commoners alike. Parallels of such developments – even in modern times – abound. One that immediately comes to mind is the North Korean theocracy. It is alleged that the Dear Leader Kim Jong Il, son of the Great Leader who had founded the modern dynasty, was born on the sacred Mount Baekdu, on the same spot as Tangun, the son of a bear woman and the founder of the first Korean kingdom in 2333 BC – and so just around the time when Naram-Suen became a living god.[433]

I close by quoting the comments about divine kingship made by someone with a personal experience of it (a North Korean refugee who fled to China in 2003):

> It's not that people really believe all this propaganda about Kim Jong-un, that he's a God, and need someone to tell them otherwise or show them another way of thinking. North Koreans are people, and they aren't stupid. In the North Korean system, you have to praise Kim and sing hymns about him and take it seriously, even if you think it's only a shit narrative. That's the block, you see? It's not that people are brainwashed and think he's God. These are things that people know, but they don't dare to challenge. (Richardson 2015)

---

433 According to official North Korean literature, the birth of Kim Jong-il "was heralded by a swallow and caused winter to change to spring, a star to illuminate the sky and rainbows to spontaneously appear" ("Mind-boggling 'Facts' about Kim Jong-il," *Herald Sun*, Melbourne, December 19, 2011). The North Korean ruler "is everywhere. Nothing passes his notice. He is a scientific genius (especially Kim Jong-il), and a stupendous general. His 'on the spot guidance' guarantees 'bumper harvests,' military glory, and the universal happiness of the Korean people" (Buruma 2015).

Appendix 2: The Roundlet of Naram-Suen

1 In 2002 article and subsequent studies, Donald P. Hansen published and extensively discussed a remarkable piece of Sargonic art (from the Jeanette and Jonathan Rosen Collection), which undoubtedly represents Naram-Suen of Akkade (2002; 2003a; 2003b).[434] See **figs. 35–37.** The object in question is the fragment of a limestone mould, which, in its present state of preservation, measures 11.0 cm in height, 13.5 cm in width, and between 2.8 and 5.1 cm in thickness.

It may be surmised that this mould was used to cast a flat roundlet, almost certainly made of gold (Hansen 2002: 103; 2003a: 197), which was shaped as a disk crowned with an auerola of eight or nine radial streams or star points (see **fig. 36**).[435] In view of Ištar's prominence in the accompanying image (see below), it is highly likely that this object was intended to represent a star or rosette, Ištar/Inana's astral symbol. Although Hansen speculated that this roundlet decorated a ceremonial shield (2003b: 206), these facts suggest that its function was rather that of a divine emblem or standard (Sumerian šu-nir, Akkadian *šurinnu*), which was mounted on a staff and probably permanently displayed in a ritual context (such as one of Ištar's temples).

It appears that each of the radial streams, of which only one is fully preserved, depicted an identical scene, which was the submission of foreign lands and their deities to Naram-Suen[436] and his divine patron and spouse, the goddess Ištar-Annunitum. It may be surmised that in each instance a different land or a group of lands was represented. As aptly described by Hansen, in its original form the roundlet amounted to a map of Naram-Suen's territorial conquests:

> Forever lost to us, the other scenes surrounding the center must have used different iconographies to indicate other parts of the empire stretching out from Agade in four directions. Each region would have been identifiable by appropriate signifiers associated with other

---

434 This piece was subsequently discussed by Woods 2005: 17–18; Asher-Greve 2006:14–15; Steinkeller 2014a: 695–696.

435 For a discussion of such astral discs, which served as symbolic representations of *both* the Sun God Utu/Šamaš and Inana/Ištar, see Steinkeller 2012: 265 and nn. 27–34.

436 That the Sargonic divine king portrayed on the roundlet is Naram-Suen (rather than his son Šar-kali-šarri, who was deified as well) is strongly indicated by the fact that this object likely depicts the lands of Elam and Marhaši (see below), both of which are known to have remained firmly in the sphere of Naram-Suen's political influence. No such information is available for Šar-kali-šarri, whose reign, as far as one can tell, saw little (if any) Babylonian presence in the periphery. For similar argumentation, see Hansen 2002: 91 and n. 7.

DOI 10.1515/9781501504778-005

chieftains and gods. Thus, the boss was essentially a world map of Naram-Sin's empire as seen from its center, Agade. (2003a: 197)

A brief description of the surviving section of the roundlet is in order at this point; for the details, see the excellent treatments by Hansen 2002; 2003a.

The focal point of the image is a stepped dais or tower, on whose top there are portrayed Naram-Suen and Ištar-Annunitum. This structure is likely the "holy dais of Akkade" (barag kug A-ga-de$_3^{ki}$), on which, according to the composition "The Curse of Akkade" lines 40–41, Naram-Suen "rose daily like the Sun God."[437] Both Naram-Suen and the goddess are seated, he on a folded chair,[438] and she on a similar chair decorated with two antithetical lionesses, the symbolic markers of her martial aspect.

Naram-Suen, who is shown in right profile, faces toward Ištar-Annunitum. He wears a horned divine crown, which identifies him as a deity. He is bearded and has long hair flowing down his back. Except for a fringed skirt, his body otherwise is naked and shoeless. As described by Hansen, "the upper part of his body is beautifully proportioned with fully modeled pectoral muscles and chest. There is an amazing degree of muscle articulation in the shoulders and arms" (2002: 92). Importantly, the same physical characteristics are shared by the two captive gods depicted on the roundlet (see below), offering further indication of Naram-Suen's divinity.

The goddess is depicted frontally. She has an array of weapons issuing from her shoulders. This feature, together with the representations of lionesses on her chair, assures that she appears here in her martial form, that of Annunitum, "the one of battle." With her left hand the goddess grasps the four nose-ropes attached to the captive group shown to the right (see below), passing them on to Naram-Suen with her right hand. The latter grasps with his left hand the loop terminating the ropes.

Both from the formal and the conceptual perspectives, the most striking feature of this group is the parity of Naram-Suen and Ištar. As portrayed here, the two are equals of one another, sharing the same holy dais, deciding matters together, and partaking in the rule over the conquered world. In all likelihood, this "conference scene" involving a human and a deity, which finds no parallels in Mesopotamian iconography, is a visual realization of Naram-Suen's epithet "the one who confers / discusses things with Ištar-Annunitum" (*mu-ta-wi*

---

437 See above p. 138.
438 For other representations of such folded chairs in Pre-Sargonic and Sargonic art, see Metzger 1985: 141, 175, 289.

ᵈINANA *An-nu-ni-tim*, where the verb is *atwû*). This particular epithet became known only recently, thanks to a new edition of a Naram-Suen inscription from the Hilprecht Sammlung in Jena.[439] It is equally striking that the same inscription also describes how Enlil placed in Naram-Suen's hands the "nose-ropes of (all) the people" (*ṣerrāt nišī qātiššu iddinu*; Wilcke 1997: 25 P rev. iii' 8'–16'). This is the earliest attestation of this image – which is so dramatically represented on the roundlet – in Mesopotamian written sources.

To the right of Naram-Suen and Ištar-Annunitum, a separate, highly complex group is depicted. The principal actors here are two manacled foreign rulers, each of whom is standing on top of an architectural structure, which is probably the façade of a palace (see **figs. 35** and **37**). They both face left. Either of them is accompanied by a separate god, also facing left, whose lower body forms a mountain, identifying him as a mountain deity. These two mountain gods, who are much larger than the kings they accompany, wear horned divine crowns. They are bearded and have bare upper bodies. These characteristics make them closely similar to Naram-Suen. Like Naram-Suen, the mountain gods also show markedly strong and muscular bodies. Each of them holds up in his hands a bowl overflowing with round objects, which appear to be precious gems. These they clearly present to Naram-Suen and Ištar-Annunitum as gifts. Each of the rulers and the gods has a rope attached to his nose. As described earlier, the ends of the four ropes are held by Ištar-Annunitum, who in turn passes them on to Naram-Suen, indicating that he controls the lands in question through the goddess's agency. Formally, the nose-ropes are the element that glues the two groups into one coherent image.

The two foreign rulers and their divine companions are surrounded by the mountains, from which issues a river (or a sea) terminating in a goddess. This river (or sea) goddess also holds a bowl in her hands, whose contents, however, are different from those offered by the two mountain gods. Since the bowl seems to have a cover, it should probably be explained as a receptacle that carries the water of the river (or the sea) in question, and that, like the gems carried by the mountain gods, is presented by the goddess to Naram-Suen and Ištar-Annunitum.[440]

---

439 See Wilcke 1997: 24 J viii 27–29 (restored by Wilcke after *mu-ta-wi Eš₄-tár ù An-nu-nu-tim* in the Old Babylonian version of the same inscription); discussed ibid. 29–30.

440 It is likely that the "river" terminated at the other end (now lost) in another goddess, holding an identical bowl. If so, the "river" actually consisted of two separate (but here connected) bodies of water, which were either the Euphrates and the Tigris or the Upper and the Lower Seas (the Mediterranean and the Persian Gulf). For similar Sargonic representations of dual river deities, see Woods 2005: 15–21. Rather than interpreting them as the depictions of two separate riv-

As I argued elsewhere (2014a: 696), the mountainous setting of this group makes it certain that the two lands in question were situated in Iran.[441] This conclusion is corroborated by a number of other visual hints. The most important of them are the shoes with upturned toes that are worn by the ruler standing to the right. This particular type of shoe is characteristic of the southeastern Iranian iconography of Pre-Sargonic and Sargonic date, more exactly, of the art broadly associated with the Marhaši cultural complex (Steinkeller 2014a: 694–696; Hansen 2002: 100–101). Another feature that allows us to identify this figure as an inhabitant of southeastern Iran is the hairdo worn by his divine companion. This hairdo, usually described as a "chignon" by the students of Sargonic art, likewise is a typical element of the Marhaši-related imagery (Steinkeller 2014a: 697 and n. 17). It appears that the same chignon is worn by the ruler himself, who, in addition, has a flat hat that also is amply documented in southeastern Iran (Hansen 2002: 100; Steinkeller 2014a: 697).

All these facts make it virtually certain that we find here symbolic depictions of Elam (the ruler and the god to the left) and Marhaši (the ruler and the god to the right), the two emblematic adversaries of the Sargonic kings in the east.[442] Such an interpretation agrees perfectly with the "geographical" logic of the scene: since Elam was more proximate to the "center" (i. e., Babylonia), it is depicted closer to Naram-Suen and Ištar-Annunitum, with the geographically more distant Marhaši being assigned a more removed position.

Final observation: Braun-Holzinger 2007: 93–94 n. 59 asserted that this object is a forgery. However, as I wrote elsewhere (2014a: 695 n. 13), its authenticity is beyond any question. To the arguments offered there, I wish to add the following considerations: (1) It is totally inconceivable that any forger could have produced a novel ideological message of this complexity and detail that agrees so well with the textual and art historical data neither generally known nor fully understood by the specialists and lay public alike. (2) Typically, forgers rely on the existing representation types and iconography, without engaging in experi-

---

ers, Woods suggests that they represent a single river, defined by its two banks. Such an interpretation is possible as well.

441 Similar conclusions were reached by Hansen 2002: 104. Although Hansen cited northeastern mountains as another possibility, he concluded that this scene points "most likely to the east and may refer to Lullubum, Gutium, Simash or even Elam and Anshan" (ibid. 104).

442 Hansen 2002: 104 n. 66 speculated that the two lands in question are to be identified specifically as Anšan and Susa. However, such a possibility is highly unlikely. See already Steinkeller 2014a: 696. Susa was not a mountainous region, and therefore it cannot be referenced here. As for Anšan, this land, though fitting the profile, is practically invisible in Sargonic historical sources. In contrast, Elam and Marhaši are routinely identified as Babylonia's two main eastern enemies in the inscriptions of Sargon, Rimuš, and Naram-Suen (consult RIME 2).

mentation. Therefore, the possibility that a forger could have created a completely new art form (such as the roundlet), inventing for this purpose new iconography, and going in addition through the trouble of putting the image in intaglio, is
practically nil.

2 In fact, there is a distinctive possibility that this mould – or more exactly, the
artifact produced by the use of this mould – is described in a contemporary historical record. The source in question forms part of an Old Babylonian *Sammel-
tafel* recording copies of two of Naram-Suen's display inscriptions (henceforth A
and B).[443] The inscription of interest to us is the first one (A), of which only the
middle section presently survives.[444] Although the name of the king is not preserved, it is certain that it was Naram-Suen. This is demonstrated by the phraseology of the text, which matches that of other Naram-Suen sources,[445] as well as
by the fact that inscription B belongs to Naram-Suen. Both inscriptions appear to
date to the later part of Naram-Suen's reign, the period subsequent to his
quenching of the Great Rebellion. The surviving portion of inscription A reads
as follows:

i		[^{d}*Na-ra-am*-^{d}*Suen*]
		[...]
	1′)	[^{d}*Ištar*(INANA)]
	2′)	ꜥ*An*ꜥ-*nu!*-[*ni-tum*][446]
	3′)	*ma-ḫi-ra*
	4′)	*la da-ad-ti-in-sum-ma* /taddin-šumma/
	5′)	*ṣalmam*(DÙL) *ḫuraṣam*(KUG.GI)
	6′)	*ša da-ab!-rí-a-ti* /tabri'āti/
	7′)	*tu-un-ni-su* /dunnišu/
	8′)	*ù*
	9′)	*tāḫazē*(KASKAL.ŠUDUN)^{e}
	10′)	*iš₁₁-a-ru-ni*
	11′)	*dam-si-il-su* /tamšilšu/
	12′)	*ib-ni-ma*

---

443 AO 5474, in the collection of the Louvre. See Gelb and Kienast 1990: 131, where a hand-copy
and a reconstruction of the text distribution on the tablet are presented.

444 Published in Gelb and Kienast 1990: 266–267 Narāmsīn C 7; RIME 2 160 Naram-Suen 1001.
For inscription B, see Gelb and Kienast 1990: 251–253 Narāmsīn C 4; RIME 2 88–90 Naram-Suen
1.

445 See ^{d}INANA *ma-ḫi-ra la id-ti-sum* (RIME 2 129–131 Naram-Suen 25:30–32). Moreover, note
that *dunnu*, "might," and *tamšilu*, "likeness," are otherwise mentioned only in Naram-Suen's inscriptions. See, respectively, Wilcke 1997: 24 J ix 5, and Kienast 1994: 307.

446 D. R. Frayne, RIME 2 160, restores this line ꜥ^{d}ꜥx [...] (based on a collation supplied by B. Foster). Therefore, read probably ꜥ*An*ꜥ-*nu!*-[*ni-tum*].

13')	[a]-ʿnaʾ [ᵈINAN]A?
14')	[An-nu-ni-tim?]
15')	[išruk(A.MU.RU]
	[Naram-Suen, etc.]
1')	[Ištar-]
2')	ʿAnnuʾ[nitum]
3'-4')	afforded him no rival.
5')	An image⁴⁴⁷ of gold,
6')	which is a wondrous sight⁴⁴⁸
7')	of his physical might
8')	and
9')	the battles,
10')	in which he had been victorious,
11')	(as) his likeness
12')	he fashioned.
13')	To Išta]r-?
14')	[Annunitum?]
15')	[he dedicated it.]

The restoration of Ištar-Annunitum's name in lines 1'–2' is assured by the use of a feminine verbal form in line 4', which indicates that a goddess is the subject of the verb. And the only female deity fitting this context is Ištar-Annunitum. As a matter of fact, Ištar-Annunitum is named also at the beginning of inscription B,⁴⁴⁹ suggesting that these two texts may originally have been related, perhaps sharing the same place of origin.

One of the striking things about this passage is that the "image" in question, which, as the use of the word *tamšilu*, "likeness," makes it certain, depicted Naram-Suen in some manner, was made of gold. This is highly unusual, since the references to the representations of rulers fashioned of this metal are otherwise exceedingly rare in third millennium sources. In fact, this is the only such example in the entire Sargonic corpus. Therefore, the gold "image" in question must have been quite special.

Even more unusual is the fact that this "image" depicted more than one of Naram-Suen's conflicts, and must therefore have been of considerable narrative complexity. Sargonic depictions of royal victories, such as the "Victory Stele" of

---

447 The Akkadian *ṣalmu* denotes any kind of representation: a sculpture in the round, a relief, a drawing, or a painting on plaster. See CAD Ṣ 78–85.

448 For *tabrītu*, "vision," in plural meaning "admiration, something to be admired, wondrous sight/vision" (Sumerian u₆-di), see CAD T 31–32, where many examples of *tabrātu* referring to buildings and artifacts are cited. For an extensive study of u₆-di, see Winter 2000b: 30–35.

449 (Naram-Suen) *mu-ut* ᵈINANA *An-nu-ni-tim* ... *i-nu* ᵈINANA ... (RIME 2 88–90 Naram-Suen 1 ii 8'–14').

Naram-Suen and the stele of Sargon, typically show only one military engagement. But our text is absolutely clear on that point, since it uses a plural noun, "battles/military expeditions." Because of this, we can be certain that the object referred to in inscription A portrayed a number of separate conflicts or victories. This fact would make it completely unique and seemingly without any parallels – except, of course, for the Naram-Suen mould, which manages to combine, in an extraordinarily inventive way, multiple depictions of royal victories within a single icon.

An equally important point is that inscription A attributes Naram-Suen's victories to Ištar-Annunitum, and that the "image" depicting those feats in all likelihood was dedicated to this goddess.

To sum up, all the characteristics of the "image" described in the inscription: the fact that it was made of gold, the unusual complexity of its imagery, the reference to Naram-Suen's physical might (*dunnu*), and its dedication to Ištar-Annunitum, make it highly probable that this object was – if not identical with – at least closely similar to the Hansen mould.

To be more precise, if there was a connection between the two, the "image" would have been the artifact that had actually been produced through the use of the mould. Since it is unlikely that a mould of this quality and workmanship would have been prepared to fashion just one roundlet, one might conjecture that a number of identical pieces had been manufactured, to be subsequently presented to a number of Ištar's sanctuaries.

As for inscription A, it must somehow have formed part of the arrangement in which the "image" was displayed. It is even possible that it was inscribed on the "image" itself or on the gold foil that conceivably decorated the stand or staff on which the "image" was mounted. In this connection, it is of interest that the usage of inscribed gold foil is actually attested during Naram-Suen's reign, as shown by an example from Adab, which was dedicated to Naram-Suen by one of his servants.[450] The foil in question undoubtedly was attached to an object of some sort, but, unfortunately, its identity is unknown.

---

450 RIME 2 170–171 Naram-Suen 2010.

Essay 3

Mythical Realities of the Early Babylonian History (or the Modern Historian and the Native Uses of History Past)

> The real is as imagined as the imaginary.
> Clifford Geertz

1 This essay reviews current approaches to the study of third millennium history, in particular, the recent debate over the appropriateness of using the so-called "historical-literary" texts and the sources of a transparently mythological character as a means of "filling in the lacunae" in the political history of early Babylonia as it can be reconstructed from the contemporary "historical" records. Having concluded that all such sources – including the records presumed to be authentically "historical" – are mythical in nature, it will be argued that, while these sources are of doubtful value for the program of an *histoire événementielle*, they will – if approached on their own terms – tell us a great deal about the social and political matrix of early Babylonia, through their vision of history as a symbolic or mythical reality.

2 Much of the current debate in historiography has been concerned with the place of narrative in historical writing. Should the history of events, which will always be marred by the original sin of subjectivity, be abandoned in favor of the history of structures? Or, since the structures so created turn out to be narratives themselves, should one assume that all historical writing is unavoidably and fatally a narrative, and try simply to develop new and better types of narratives, such as, for example, the Geertzian "thick description"?

If the preoccupation with such questions is the badge that lends one the right to call himself a historian, few of the historically-minded Assyriologists will meet this definition, since most of them toil without the benefit of having at their disposal even the most basic and rudimentary narrative histories of particular periods. However simplistic, naive, and unattainable the Rankean goal of "discovering what really happened" may seem to the modern historian, to us Assyriologists it is still a real and a fully rational objective.

My own interests focus on third millennium Babylonia, and therefore this essay is concerned with that particular phase of Mesopotamian history. In practical terms, this means only the period between 2400 and 2000 BC, since no narrative information of any real consequence is available from the earlier centuries. Here I hasten to note that the following observations derive nearly entirely from

DOI 10.1515/9781501504778-006

the study of third millennium data.[451] Because of this, in no way are they meant to serve as a characterization of all the historical sources stemming from ancient Mesopotamia, in particular those dating to the first millennium BC. I should also stress that this essay is concerned exclusively with the issues of political history. Clearly, in other areas of the historical research into early Babylonia, such as, for example, socio-economic studies, the situation is considerably different, both in terms of what is textually available and of what can be done with this evidence for the purposes of scientific analysis.

The starting point of this essay is the following question: are we in a position today to write a political history of Babylonia during the last four centuries of the third millennium BC? Or, to ask more modestly, can we at the very least reconstruct the events of particular sub-phases of that history, such as dynasties or individual reigns? In either case the answer, I am afraid, is a definite "no."

The reason of course lies in the nature of the surviving evidence. And what does this evidence consist of? Apart from economic or administrative records, which inform us, sometimes very eloquently, about economic and social structures, but which only rarely mention political events, what we have at our disposal are the so-called "royal" or "historical" texts, a comparatively small assemblage of contemporaneous dedicatory inscriptions, which record the names of rulers and other high officials, occasionally mention specific events, and in a few instances synchronize a local ruler with political figures active in other places. But, however hard one would try, these data are not sufficient to weave out of them even the most elementary historical narrative. This is particularly true of the Early Dynastic (or Pre-Sargonic) period, since there is practically nothing that we can say with certainty about its political history. Our ignorance is even greater in the case of the intermediate phase between the end of Šar-kali-šarri's reign (the last ruler of the Sargonic dynasty) and the advent of Utu-hegal of Uruk (who ruled just before Ur-Namma, the founder of the Third Dynasty of Ur). Not only the precise length of that phase remains unknown (probably ca. 80–100 years, see Steinkeller 2015a), but also not a single political event can confidently be reconstructed within it. We know a little bit more about the events of the Sargonic period, but certainly not as much as many of us would like to think. Thanks to economic records, we can grasp some sense of what was happening in Ur III times, but even this evidence is not informative enough to permit one to write a political history of the period.

We do, of course, have our personal histories of the third millennium, but one needs to be clear as to what these histories really are: more or less informed

---

451 See also Essay 1.

and imaginative subjective scenarios or, in other words, educated guesses, which necessarily resort to the use of fictional narrative as a way of fleshing out the few clues that are preserved in royal inscriptions and economic sources. And I cannot imagine that anyone today would seriously object to this characterization of our history writing. I think that most of us believe roughly the same thing, with a difference that some would perhaps be less blunt about it.

Being restricted by the availability of factual information, the modern historian reaches beyond historical inscriptions and economic tablets to other types of written sources in his search after such data. The most obvious candidates here are the so-called "historical-literary" texts, which are best characterized as poetic meditations over past historical events. While some of these texts may have been completely new creations, most of them are to varying degrees derivatives of the historical inscriptions that are contemporaneous with the events they describe. Another type of sources that have been used for the same purpose are literary texts *sensu stricto*, especially among them those containing overt historical references, such as, for example, "The Lament for Sumer and Ur," or the ones believed by some to be historical metaphors, such as the composition "Inana and Šukaletuda."

The last three decades witnessed a passionate debate over the place of such evidence in historical reconstructions. Some scholars have argued that the "historical-literary" sources, if of any factual value at all, are a potential source of information about the period in which they were written down, though certainly not about the times they purport to deal with. The adherents of this view, believing that this category of sources are negotiations of the present through the use and manipulation of the past, thus have sought to identify historical settings or even specific circumstances that had given rise to at least some of these compositions.

The most vocal representative of this approach is Mario Liverani. His articles of 1973 and 1993 did in fact initiate the whole debate. And Liverani has been defending his position ever since (2002). Among other Assyriologists who have tried to analyze "historical-literary" texts in this manner I should single out Marvin A. Powell (1991) and Steve Tinney (1995).

Other scholars have taken a less extreme position on this issue, thinking that some sort of a "middle course" is possible (e. g., Potts 2001). Their view has been that the "historical-literary" sources should not outright be dismissed as irrelevant for the historical reality they describe; rather, they should be treated as individual cases, with the eyes being kept open for a possibility that occasionally some factual information may be extracted from them after all. In taking this stance, such scholars have also argued against the attempts to match these compositions with later historical situations and events, for the simple reason that such attempts are not only exceedingly risky but also suspect methodologically, for they explain the little known by recourse to that which often is even less known.

And, in my opinion, this criticism is well founded, since there is an inherent risk to all such speculation. On the most basic level, there is always a danger that a given dating or attribution will be disproved by the appearance of new, contrary evidence. A good case in point is Marvin A. Powell's attempt to attribute the so-called "Cruciform Monument" of Maništušu to Naram-Suen (1991). The document in question is a Neo-Babylonian source concerning various benefices that were bestowed upon the temple of Ebabbar at Sippar by Maništušu. This source is a Neo-Babylonian concoction, which was fabricated, through the use of Maništušu's original inscriptions, to demonstrate the antiquity of various benefices of the priests of Šamaš of Sippar. Cf. Essay 1 p. 80. In the manuscripts that were available to Powell, the name of the ruler is not preserved, but, based on various allusions found in these sources, the earlier students of the "Cruciform Monument" had concluded that the king in question was Maništušu.

Powell's proposal was shown to be wrong, only three years after the appearance of his article, by the publication of a new manuscript of the same inscription, likewise dating to the Neo-Babylonian period, which specifically names Maništušu as its author (Al-Rawi and George 1994: 139–148).

Here I may note parenthetically that, even without the benefit of this new evidence, Powell should have known better. He had completely ignored the passage about a military campaign against Anšan and Šerihum appearing in the "Cruciform Monument" (Al-Rawi and George 1994: 142 i 34 – ii 6; Sollberger 1968: 55 lines 40–58), which is otherwise known to have been undertaken by Maništušu (RIME 2 74–77 Maništušu 1:4–8), and which in fact was the main argument for this particular attribution. Furthermore, Powell's assertion that, in the hypothetical Sargonic prototype, Maništušu could not have been described as a "son of Sargon" (1991: 22–25) is directly contradicted by an Old Babylonian reworking of one of Naram-Suen's original inscriptions, where Naram-Suen refers to Sargon as his "fore(father)."[452] The same designation may have also appeared in its Old Akkadian prototype, as plausibly restored by Claus Wilcke 1997: 25 ix 32–33.

A similar case is Liverani's proposal that the Sumerian composition "The Curse of Akkade," which is a highly poetic and metaphoric summation of the history of the Sargonic period (see in detail Essay 1 pp. 79–80), was composed during the reign of an Isin king named Išme-Dagan, who ruled ca. 1950 BC (Liv-

---

452 LUGAL-*ki-in a-bi* (J. G. Westenholz 1997: 238–245 no. 16B:16).

erani 1991: 59). However, Liverani had overlooked the fact that some of the manuscripts of this composition belong to the Ur III period (Cooper 1983a: 11), which means that its date is earlier by a century or more.

Another reason why this kind of speculation is fraught with difficulties is the fact that, almost as a rule, we do not have a complete record of the original inscriptions that may be used for comparison purposes. Accordingly, since we do not know for certain what really was and was not in the originals, it is virtually impossible reliably to identify revisions or additions in the later re-workings of the same sources.

To illustrate how risky such attempts can be, let me cite the article by Steve Tinney (1995), in which Tinney tried to identify later revisions in the Old Babylonian versions of the sources dealing with the so-called "Great Rebellion," an event which occurred during the reign of Naram-Suen, and which is described both in Sargonic originals and in later (mostly Old Babylonian) versions of those inscriptions. Among the original sources pertaining to the "Great Rebellion," the most important are RIME 2 103–108 Naram-Suen 6 and Wilcke 1997: 22–26 mss J and P. The corresponding Old Babylonian sources are J. G. Westenholz 1997: 231–257 no. 16 A (Mari Version), no. 16B (Geneva Version), and no. 17 ("Gula-AN and the Seventeen Kings against Naram-Sin").

To begin with, some of the revisions proposed by Tinney were invalidated by the subsequent re-edition of one of the originals by Claus Wilcke (1997). For example, it turns out that the passage describing how Sargon, Naram-Suen's grandfather, wrested Kiš from Lugal-zagesi's control and freed its citizenry from the obligation to provide corvée work (J. G. Westenholz 1997: 231–237 no. 16 A:5–8, 238–245 no. 16B:16–20), which Tinney believed to be an Old Babylonian "anecdote" (1995: 8), was in fact part of the Old Akkadian original (Wilcke 1997: 25 ix 32 – x 14, discussed ibid. 30).

Tinney also speculated that the Old Babylonian version of the "Great Rebellion" was inspired by the Old Babylonian tribal politics (1995: 9–10), basing this interpretation on a passage according to which Iphur-Kiš assembled the citizens of Kiš, who then raised him to kingship: "he gathered (the citizens of) Kiš, and they raised him to kingship" (J. G. Westenholz 1997: 238–245 no. 16B:26–28). Tinney proposed that this passage was added in the Old Babylonian period in reflection of the tribal customs of the time, which allegedly favored the election of leaders by public assemblies. But, as the case of the "anecdote" about Sargon teaches us, we cannot be certain that this particular passage had not been part of the original formulation.

Moreover, contrary to Tinney's interpretation, the intent of this passage is clearly negative. Rather than approving of this type of election (as thought by Tinney), it blames Iphur-Kiš for having assumed kingship in this particular

way, namely, by having been brought to power by his followers or mob. Obviously, that manner of election made Iphur-Kiš illegitimate, both from the traditional
Babylonian perspective (which favored divine election), and from the standpoint
of tribal kingship, which subscribed to the hereditary principle. That Iphur-Kiš
was believed to be an usurper is in fact implied by one of the Sargonic originals,
where his rise to power is described as follows: "in Kiš they elevated Iphur-Kiš to
kingship and in Uruk they elevated Amar-Girid to kingship" (RIME 2 103–108
Naram-Suen 6 i 1′–9′). Clearly, what the latter source says is that both Iphur-
Kiš *and* Amar-Girid were illegitimate rulers.

In this connection, it should also be noted that the form of kingship envisioned by Tinney, namely, "a kingship owed not to divine authority or heritage
but to local tribal consensus" (1995: 13), is entirely of his own making. As far it
can be ascertained from the surviving written record, such an elective system
was not practiced in any period of Mesopotamian history.

3 Apart from the formal (i. e., text-related) objections that are raised by this
kind of scholarly endeavor, there is also the more general issue of the very purpose of the alleged later re-workings. Almost without exception, the scholars
who believe to have identified such alterations take it for granted that the sources so revised or doctored were intended to serve as propaganda tools, and that
the agency behind these revisions – or sometimes the creation of entirely new
texts, as the case may be – invariably was the ruling class. In other words,
such authors assume that these compositions were directly commissioned by
kings to further their political objectives, either in response to specific political
developments or as part of their long-term propaganda offensives. However,
these scholars never bother to visualize how such written pieces could have
functioned as propaganda tools in real life. I believe that it is incumbent on
the proponents of such attributions in each case to offer a feasible scenario of
how these purported political messages were disseminated among the population at large. For example, if someone tries to persuade me that the Sumerian
composition "Gilgameš and Akka," which deals with legendary characters of
the archaic age, was commissioned by an Old Babylonian ruler to advance his
political ends, I believe that it is his duty to offer a plausible scenario of how,
once written down, this composition was then effectively used to promote the
objectives in question. And, unless he is able to offer such an explanation, his
or her theory does not deserve serious consideration – at least in my personal
judgment.

One of the scholars who at least recognizes the problem is Piotr Michalowski. Michalowski has suggested that such messages would be disseminated
through the medium of scribal schools, as a way of shaping the political orien-

tation of future administrators and members of the ruling class more generally (1987: 63). But this kind of subtle indoctrination, to which students would be subjected over the many years of their schooling, is quite different from direct political propaganda, which usually seeks and expects to obtain immediate results.

In my opinion, a more reasonable – and potentially a much more productive – approach to this question is to focus instead on the individuals who actually produced this literature, i.e., the Babylonian literati. I think it would be highly desirable to be able to know more about these individuals and their worldview, in particular, their political aspirations. Did this group have its own intellectual and political agenda that perhaps was independent of the royal ideology and its political objectives? To what extent did they use literature to propagate their ideology and to advance interests of their own "class"?

In line with these suggestions, in Essay 1 I attempted to obtain a closer understanding of this "class" and to place it in a specific socio-historical context. As I concluded there, this group of individuals, whom I broadly identify as the Managerial Class, was a highly influential and remarkably durable social group, whose existence, in one form or another, can be detected throughout Babylonian history, from the archaic age (Uruk III) down to the Seleucid period. There are many reasons to think that the Managerial Class had its own political agenda, which significantly differed from that of the kings. As part of their efforts to advance their own political causes and to secure their economic position, this social group resorted to using texts as a way of legitimizing their traditional status vis-à-vis the ruling elites. Toward that goal members of the Managerial Class created texts such as the "Antediluvian King List" and the "Story about the Seven Sages," and recopied archaic lists such as the Lu A. By invoking the testimony of these sources, they claimed to be the original source of political power in Babylonia, as well as the masters of statecraft, thereby making themselves indispensable (or at least hoping to be perceived as such) to the kings.

If this interpretation is correct, the intended audience of at least some of the texts that appear to have a didactic or propagandistic intent likely was the ruling circles, especially the king. And, as it happens, this is the situation one often encounters in ancient historical literatures – as, for example, the Arabic and Indo-Persian historical writing of medieval times, whose intended reader was the Sultan, members of the court, and "posterity" – and which, significantly, was highly didactic in character, often taking the form of *Fürstenspiegel* narratives.[453] In ref-

---

453 The classic work here is Fouchécour 1986. See also Meisami 2004; Marlow 2004; 2009; Dar-

erence to the Babylonian situation, a particularly apt parallel is provided by the role played by historians and their works at the court of the Delhi sultanate:

> As prominent leaders and holders of high office in the courts of Delhi, historians were themselves collectively engaged in the sultan's imperial project. Although there was no ti-tled position of court historian in the Delhi sultanate (and, in that limited sense, there were no "official" histories), historians held influential posts in the government and acted as ad-visors. In the capacity of court counselor, historians advised sultans on matters of state from war and diplomacy, to law and economy. They utilized their understandings of history to influence the course of the sultan's judgment and they shaped their own histories for these didactic purposes. (Auer 2012: 16)[454]

It goes without saying that there must have existed other "audiences" of texts as well. If, as it appears virtually certain, the hymns written in honor of the Ur III and Isin kings had a ritual setting, their recipients would have been the partic-ipants of the events during which these compositions were recited and perhaps theatrically performed. On the other hand, certain compositions, such as the Aratta cycle, the Sumerian tales about Gilgameš, and the so-called "Disputa-tions," may have had their origin in the theatrical productions that were per-formed at the courts of the Ur III kings (Jacobsen 1987: 277; Wilcke 2012: 7–36; Steinkeller 2014a: 704). In that case, the "audience" would have been the attend-ees of those performances. And, as I wrote earlier, the intended "readers" of the majority of the so-called "royal" or "historical" inscriptions were the deities to whom they were dedicated. No doubt, other "audiences" or "readers" of Sumer-ian literary texts remain yet to be identified.

4 While the interpretation of "historical/literary" texts as propaganda tools that were used by later rulers to shape the events of their own time is a dubious procedure, an even riskier and more suspect enterprise is to try to find political messages in overtly mythological sources. As examples of such efforts may serve Claus Wilcke's (1995) and Konrad Volk's (1995) readings of various literary com-positions as metaphoric criticisms of the Sargonic kings and their policies. This is not because Sumerian and Akkadian myths did not have such subtexts – or be-cause they were immune to being subjected to such readings – but simply be-

---

ling 2013. I owe some of these references to Dr. Justine K. Landau, my colleague at Harvard. For propaganda in medieval Islam, see Humphreys 1991: 150–152.

454 Cf. the role of the *ummânū* during the first millennium, as discussed in Essay 1 pp. 69, 78.

cause we do not know enough about the political history of Babylonia to be able to make such inferences with sufficient confidence.[455]

5   The most common argument given by the proponents of the "middle course" approach in support of the use of "historical-literary" texts and literary sources more generally in historical reconstructions is the scarcity of contemporaneous historical sources, which makes it necessary for us – and at the same time absolves us of any methodological sin – to look for any data available in order "to fill in the lacunae," as advocated by one writer (Hallo 2001: 198). As a general proposition, this is a reasonable argument, with which it is impossible to disagree. The problem, however, is that such an approach does not work very well when applied to the third millennium situation specifically. The word "lacuna" implies the presence of at least some sort of a structure, pocketed with holes perhaps, but nevertheless a structure, reassuringly solid and physically present.

Unfortunately, no such edifice – in my view at least – is in place or can realistically be constructed at this time for the third millennium history of Babylonia. Here it will be sufficient to point out that even the system of periodization we all take for granted and use in our work in dealing with the third millennium is an artificial one, since it derives from the chronological scheme of the SKL, a literary text of uncertain date and of even more uncertain authority as a historical source. Thus, for example, we refer to the dynasty of Ur-Namma as that of the Third Dynasty of Ur even though we have no corroborative evidence of any sort that the second dynasty of Ur, which is named only in the SKL, ever existed.

To be able to write a history of facts one needs facts, and those are usually provided either by the records of daily life or the descriptive sources of historiographic nature or a combination of both. In the case of third millennium Babylonia, we do have a great deal of economic and legal documentation at our disposal, but this evidence is not very informative as regards political events. Even

---

455 For a critical assessment of these interpretations, see Cooper 2001. In my view, Cooper's criticisms are right on target. But I take an exception to the following statement of his: "A strong argument against these historicizing interpretations of Sumerian literature is that the compositions exist that are explicitly about historical events, and do not hide real rulers and places in divine garb. If we have Sumerian literary texts that are explicitly about the rise and fall of Akkade or the fall of Ur, why should we assume that purely mythological texts are meant to be allegories of political events?" (ibid. 135). There is no reason why these two forms of historical messages, explicit and metaphoric, should not exist concurrently. Cases of such dual messaging abound in all literatures, ancient and modern. Moreover, as I am arguing in this essay, in the Babylonian situation there is no essential difference between "historical" sources proper and what is usually referred to as "literature." Even the texts seemingly concerned with "historical" figures and events are firmly part of the mythological discourse.

more serious is the fact that the third millennium did not bequeath to us any sources that can be classified as authentically historical. By this I mean documents of patently historiographic or chronographic nature, such as dynastic chronicles, summary descriptions of individual reigns, or records of particular events, whose primary and main objective is to preserve information about the past. Of course, many of the so-called royal or historical inscriptions mention or allude to historical events, but this fact alone is not sufficient to lend them such a designation, since the information of this kind is found in various other types of documents, such as economic records, for example. For an extensive discussion of these issues, see Essay 1.

As I wrote there, it can safely be generalized that virtually all of the early texts we classify as "royal" and "historical" served as dedicatory or votive inscriptions, whose messages were part of a communicational scheme with the divine plane, and which in no way were meant to engage in a discourse with a human audience, whether contemporary or future (see Tadmor 1997; Essay 1 p. 11). That these sources were not addressed to society at large, and that, therefore, they had no propagandistic purposes, is shown by the fact that none of them were ever subject to public display or scrutiny of any sort. In third millennium Babylonia political or ideological messages were communicated to the society not through inscriptions but through architecture and public ritual. Thus, for example, the ideas expressed in the temple hymns of Gudea were communicated to the population of Lagaš via the very process of the Eninnu's construction and the associated ritual activity, and not through the medium of texts (Steinkeller 2015c: 203–204). Although the rituals associated with the building of the Eninnu may have involved a recitation of the hymns, the written message itself never engaged in a discourse with the living audience, its sole recipients being the divine lords of the city-state of Lagaš. Since only written messages survive, we naturally, but wrongly, tend to substitute them for public ritual.

And it is not difficult to demonstrate that what the so-called "historical" sources are really about is *mythical history*, and not the history of facts. If we consider a source such as, for example, the "Stele of the Vultures," it is impossible not to realize that the events described there, both in the written message and in its visual counterpart, take place in a mythical reality. Although a particular historical event must have been behind this monument, the conflict between Lagaš and Umma as its is narrated there is bleached of its historical specificity; it is generalized to the point of becoming a mythologized paradigm of the Lagaš-Umma relationship, a cosmic struggle between good and evil on the plains of Gu'edena – as seen of course from the Lagaš perspective. As far as the surviving section of this inscription allow us to ascertain, the ruler of Umma is not even named in it.

Or, consider the Nippur inscription of Lugal-zagesi, in which an act of divine selection leads directly to the paradisiac conditions of peace, prosperity, and harmony, with not a single "real" event taking place and the only human figure named being Lugal-zagesi himself – although plenty of deities appear there. Although commonly treated as a historical source,[456] and used extensively as such for the reconstruction of the events of late Pre-Sargonic times, this inscription too is essentially about mythical history, and not the history of Ranke.

To be sure, some of the sources of this type are occasionally more historically informative, for they sometimes name political figures other than the author of the dedication and provide more factual information, or even organize facts into sequential narratives. Such a source, for example, is the inscription describing the military campaign of Utu-hegal against the Gutian king Tirigan.[457] Structured as a narrative, and offering a precise chronology and topography of Utu-hegal's progress,[458] this text is on one level the down-to-earth account of a specific historical event. More deeply, however, this is a story about a divine mission, a kind of Sumerian *jihad*. That other, truer story takes place on a mythical plane. There, the real actors and the makers of events are the gods, with Utu-hegal being merely an instrument of divine will.

But even the documents such as the one I have just described, however rich they may be in terms of factual information, do not essentially differ from the literary sources that seemingly fail to mention any historical facts at all, such as the Gudea cylinders, the "Nanše Hymn," "The Curse of Akkade," "The Death of Ur-Namma," and the Ur III and Isin hymns glorifying Šulgi and other deified kings, to offer just a few examples.

In suggesting that all the so-called historical sources deal primarily with a mythical history, and that, therefore, they properly belong together with literary texts, by no means do I intend to dump the entire history of the third millennium, as we know it, into the deconstructionist's wastebasket. As it will shortly become apparent, my intentions are much more pragmatic. However, before any practical measures may be considered, it is necessary first, I believe, to take stock of the existing situation and be honest as to where we stand. As I have already argued, we are in no position today to write a political history of the third millennium, either with or without the recourse to "historical-literary" texts or any other sources. Also, we should realize that much of what we think we

---

456 As I am arguing in Essay 1 pp. 10–11, in fact this inscription is more "historical" than many Pre-Sargonic sources of this nature.
457 See Essay 1 p. 11.
458 See Steinkeller 2001: 41–45.

know about that history is not actually there, since very little of it can be verified in accordance with standard historical criteria.

All of this does not mean that our attempts to extract facts from the so-called royal or historical inscriptions should be abandoned. Obviously, we should and will continue to do this kind work, and I see no reason why literary sources should be exempted from this type of procedure. I submit, however, that a more productive approach at this time – and this is the main thrust of this essay – would be to focus our attention on mythical history as a subject in itself.

While the sources I have just discussed are of limited value for the history of events, they present us with a coherent and fairly complete record of the native vision of history, or, as I prefer to call it, Mythical History. This form of history is broadly akin to what Jan Assmann defines as "cultural memory"[459]:

> Cultural memory, then, focuses on fixed points in the past, but again it is unable to preserve the past as it was. This tends to be condensed into symbolic figures to which memory attaches itself – for example, tales of the patriarchs, the Exodus, wandering in the desert, conquest of the Promised Land, exile – and that are celebrated in festivals and are used to explain current situations. Myths are also figures of memory, and here any distinction between myth and history is eliminated. What counts for cultural memory is not factual but remembered history. One might even say that cultural memory transforms factual into remembered history, thus turning it into myth. Myth is foundational history that is narrated in order to illuminate the present from the standpoint of its origins. The Exodus, for instance, regardless of any historical accuracy, is the myth behind the foundation of Israel; thus it is celebrated at Pesach and thus it is part of the cultural memory of the Israelites. Through memory, history becomes myth. This does not make it unreal – on the contrary, this is what makes it real, in the sense that it becomes a lasting, normative, and formative power. (2011: 37–38)

My Mythical History is also similar to the understanding of cultural history offered by John Elsner:

> What matters about any particular version of history is that it be meaningful to the collective subjectivities and self-identities of the specific group it addresses. In other words, we are not concerned with "real facts" or even a coherent methodology, but rather with the consensus of assumptions and prejudices shared by the historian ... and his audience ... It is this consensus of shared assumptions – a shared subjectivity in response to the world out there – that forms the frame within which explanations of monuments or works will compete and, it is hoped, convince. (1994: 226)

---

459 Assmann's concept of "cultural memory," which derives from the earlier ideas of Maurice Halbwachs, was subsequently adopted and applied to the Mesopotamian situation by Gerdien Jonker 1995.

I subscribe to the view that the concepts and categories of a particular culture shape the ways in which its members perceive and interpret whatever happens in their time, or to put it in a simpler and reversed form, that events are shaped or ordered by culture. A history so construed runs a course parallel to that of the history of facts, and the two remain in a dialectical relationship with one another, in that not only the categories of culture (or Mythical History) shape the events, but also because each time such categories are used to interpret the changing reality they are put at risk and they themselves become transformed. Thus, in the process of negotiating or absorbing real events, "the culture is reordered" (Sahlins 1981: 8). Because of this dialectical nexus, a study of Mythical History is not irrelevant for the history of facts. If we approach it in a sensitive manner and take time to listen to it, Mythical History will tell us a great deal about historical change itself.

The Sumerian composition usually referred to as "The Curse of Akkade" may not be concerned with any specific historical event, but its plot occupies a specific place within the symbolic or Mythical History of third millennium Babylonia.[460] In the same way, the deification of Naram-Suen was not a historical fact *sensu stricto*; the act of Naram-Suen's actually becoming a god occurred only on a mythical plane. In real life, this event materialized in the establishing of Naram-Suen's cult, as reflected in the construction of his temples, the fashioning of his statues and providing them with offerings, and the placement of a divine determinative in front of his name.[461]

In the Mythical History I am postulating, the events of "The Curse of Akkade" and the deification of Naram-Suen both constitute parts of a much larger and broader reality, which is sequentially (or chronographically) structured, and can be studied as any other historical narrative. Having suspended our disbelief, we should let that history unfold before our eyes. We need to follow its own internal logic, without constantly trying to cross-reference it with the history of events, in order, so to speak, to bring it down to the level of facts.

Here I need to point out that what I am proposing is neither new nor original, since much of what has been written about third millennium Babylonia is, in fact, an exercise in Mythical History, not too infrequently without the authors being fully aware of that fact. We grapple with Mythical History in our work all the time, but only piecemeal, and usually only as a way of discovering the objective "truth" behind individual mythologems.

---

460 See Essay 1 pp. 79–80.
461 See Essay 2 pp. 129–132.

Not too uncommonly, such scholarship is schizoidly torn between, on the one hand, the recognition that the facts of Mythical History are "just so stories," and, on the other hand, the belief that some "real" truth may be extracted out of them after all.[462] An anecdote preserved in one of the manuscripts of the SKL about an archaic ruler of Uruk named Dumuzi, who allegedly was taken prisoner by En-mebaragesi of Kiš, is of considerable interest from the perspective of Mythical History, for it belongs to that history and makes sense only as part of a larger narrative. However, this anecdote has no place in the history of events, if only because there is no way to verify its veracity. Therefore, the two approaches cannot be used simultaneously.

Commenting on this particular anecdote about Dumuzi, Jacob Klein alleged that it offers "new historical data" (2008: 79). Klein then used this information to reconstruct a significant chunk of Uruk's early history. Klein's narrative begins with the "general-king" Lugal-banda, who is succeeded by Dumuzi, a fisherman from Kuwara. Uruk is subsequently conquered by En-mebaragesi of Kiš, who removes Dumuzi from the throne, replacing him with Gilgameš and making the latter his vassal. Though admitting that this reconstruction is "highly speculative," Klein at the same time argued as follows:

> But we should not forget the numerous synchronisms between Gilgameš and the dynasty of Enmebaragesi, provided by hymnic and epic literature originating in the Ur III period, and the new synchronism between Dumuzi and Enmebaragesi, which is found in a historiographical source and *has the nature of a factual historical note*. We also should bear in mind that Dumuzi and Gilgameš lived in a relatively late period, on the verge of history, and *many of the later traditions about them agree with each other*. Therefore, we should not dismiss these traditions as merely the product of the respective authors' imagination [emphases added]. (2008: 79)

Perhaps somewhat paradoxically, Klein's analysis falls perfectly under the type of approach I am advocating, for it has nothing to do with the history of facts, being entirely about Mythical History. That the accounts about Dumuzi, En-mebaragesi, and Gilgameš Klein is referring to, and which he invokes as evidence of the historicity of the episode in question, are internally consistent is precisely what one expects, since all of them formed part of one and the same mythical narrative, which was generated by the common cultural tradition – or, if one wants to use Assmann's term, the same complex of "figures of memory."[463] In

---

462 This procedure is often described as a search after the "kernel of truth." One of its most vocal exponents was William W. Hallo. See, especially Hallo 2001: 202–203.
463 "Cultural memory has its fixed point; its horizon does not change with the passing of time. These fixed points are fateful events of the past, whose memory is maintained through cultural

fact, as I emphasize in Essay 1 p. 43, practically all the information about Pre-Sargonic history that is found in Old Babylonian and later sources is directly dependent on *one source only:* the SKL.[464]

If we treat Mythical History as a kind of historical narrative, and approach it on its own terms, we will gain a much better understanding of its individual parts or episodes, since, as I would submit, those can only be fully comprehended if seen as interrelated parts of a larger story.

6 To illustrate these suggestions with a specific example, I will consider the anecdote about Ur-Zababa of Kiš and Sargon, which is preserved in the SKL and a number of other "historical-literary" sources. Let me begin with a listing and discussion of the relevant data:

(1) Ur-^{d}Za-ba$_4$-ba$_4$ dumu Puzur$_4$-^{d}Suen-$^⌈$na$^⌉$-ke$_4$ mu 400 (var.: 6) i$_3$-ak, "Ur-Zababa, son of Puzur-Suen, ruled 400 (var.: 6) years" (preceded by his father Puzur-Suen and his grandmother Kug-Bau, the tavern-keeper) (SKL lines 247–249).

(2) Ur-^{d}Za-ba$_4$-ba$_4$-ke$_4$ mu 6 i$_3$-na, "Ur-Zababa ruled 6 years" (preceded by Puzur-Suen, and probably by Kug-Bau) (Ur III ms of SKL iii 4–5 = Steinkeller 2003: 271).

---

formation (texts, rites, monuments) and institutional communication (recitation, practice, observance). We call these 'figures of memory'" (Assmann and Czaplicka 1995: 129).

464 The notion that the mentions of ancient "historical" figures and events in literary texts contain at least some "kernel of truth" has a long history in Assyriology. Much of it can be traced to Jacobsen's edition of the SKL (1939). See, in particular, the following assertion, which is central to Jacobsen's position regarding the historicity of this source: "People cannot suddenly have begun to tell stories and anecdotes about Etana, Lugal-banda, Gilgames, Ku(g)-Baba, and Sargon when these personages had long ago been forgotten by all but a few learned scribes; these stories must first have been told when the leading characters were still familiar to the listeners and held their interest" (1939: 146). Here it is characteristic that Jacobsen takes it for granted that the mythical characters such as Etana, Gilgameš, Lugal-banda, and Kug-Bau were as real historical figures as Sargon. [Similarly, in the quotation cited earlier, Klein assumes that Dumuzi and Gilgameš were historical personages.] As I write in Essay 1 pp. 42–44, there is little evidence of a robust oral historical tradition in third millennium Babylonia, in whose existence Jacobsen so firmly believed. To be more precise, it is of course possible that such a tradition did exist in some forms (such as historical epics, which were never committed to writing, or popular stories about particular real-life figures). But, as far as one can tell, this hypothetical oral literature did not impact the written historical record in any appreciable way. It appears that the latter consists entirely of the data that had been either extracted from earlier texts or invented *de novo* by the scribes.

(3) Sar-ru-ki-in ab-ba-ni nu-^{giš}kiri$_6$ sagi Ur-^{d}Za-ba$_4$-ba$_4$, "Sargon, his father was a gardener, he (himself) was the cup-bearer of Ur-Zababa" (SKL lines 266–268).

(4) The composition known as the "Sargon Legend" (Cooper and Heimpel 1983) describes how Ur-Zababa appoints Sargon as his cup-bearer.[465] The two get embroiled in a conflict, which eventually comes to involve Lugal-zagesi as well. As indicated by its grammar and contents, this story undoubtedly was composed in Old Babylonian times, through the use (at least in part) of earlier literary motifs.[466] The derivative character of the "Sargon Legend" is especially clear in lines 6–7 of Segment A, which are a direct borrowing from "The Curse of Akkade" lines 40–41 (Cooper 1983: 27):

> lugal-bi sipad Ur-^{d}Za-ʿba$_4$-bʾ[a$_4$] e$_2$ Kiš^{ki}-a-ka ^{d}Utu-gim am$_3$-e$_3$
> Its king, the shepherd Ur-Zababa, rose like Utu over the House of Kiš.
> ("Sargon Legend" Segment A lines 6–7)

> lugal-bi sipad ^{d}Na-ra-am-^{d}Suen-e barag kug A-ga-de$_3$^{ki}-še$_3$ ud-de$_3$-eš$_2$ im-e$_3$
> Its king, the shepherd Naram-Suen, rose like the Sun on the holy dais of Akkade.
> ("The Curse of Akkade" lines 40–41)

A similar textual clue is provided by Segment A line 8, which describe how An and Enlil decided to terminate Ur-Zababa's kingship: nam-lugal-la-na bala-bi šu kur$_2$-ru-de$_3$, "to change the turn/period of his kinship." This line too is a derivation, which probably goes back to nam-lugal-la ki-tuš-bi kur$_2$-ru-de$_3$, "to change the seat of kingship," in "The Lament for Sumer and Ur" line 17. Here also note that, as I argue later in this essay, the very concept of dynasties being a subject to cyclical changes is a post-Ur III development.

(5) Ur-Zababa and Sargon are linked together also in "Weidner Chronicle" lines 46–47 (Grayson 1975: 148; Al-Rawi 1990: 5). This incompletely preserved passage seems to suggest that Ur-Zababa had instructed Sargon to exchange (or to withdraw?) the wine offerings intended for the temple Esagila. But Sargon, apparently, did not follow Ur-Zababa's orders, perhaps adding fish to those offerings instead. Like the entire Chronicle, this account undoubtedly is derived from the SKL.

---

465 The term used is MUŠ$_3$.KA.UL, which is otherwise unattested. However, as the gloss sagi in Segment B line 6 makes it certain, this term must represent an alternative word for "cup-bearer" (Cooper and Heimpel 1983: 79).

466 As characterized by Cooper and Heimpel 1983: 68, "the composition is full of grammatical and syntactic peculiarities that suggest a later Old Babylonian origin. This is also supported by the frequent quotations from and allusion to other Sumerian literary texts."

(6) A bilingual Old Babylonian school exercise mentions Sargon and Ur-Za-baba: "Sargon left the palace of Ur-Zababa; having neared the canal of the garden,[467] Sargon, having reclined by the canal of the garden" (Westenholz 1997: 52–55 Sargon Text 5:1–3). The mention of "the canal of the garden" evidently invokes Sargon's beginnings as a gardener. It may be safely assumed that, like the "Sargon Legend" and the account included in the "Weidner Chronicle," this exercise too ultimately derives from the SKL.

(7) Several Ur III economic tablets mention a settlement called Ur-Zababa, which appears to have been situated in the vicinity of Sippar (Steinkeller 2010: 369–376). One may presume that this place was named after a person bearing that name. The individual in question *may* have been the Ur-Zababa of the SKL, but this is by no means certain. Equally well, he could have been somebody else.

What conclusions may one reach regarding the historicity of these data? To begin with, the proposition that Sargon was a cup-bearer of Ur-Zababa is invalidated by the SKL's own evidence, namely, the fact that lines 250–257 of this composition name five (or six) additional kings of Kiš following Ur-Zababa.[468] This evidence precludes any possibility that Sargon could have served Ur-Zababa before his ascent to the throne of Akkade.[469]

Next, let us consider what may plausibly be inferred about the Ur-Zababa-Sargon anecdote from the contemporary historical sources. Most importantly, these offer no indication that Sargon was in any way connected with Kiš *prior* to his conflict with Lugal-zagesi. According to their testimony, Kiš had been conquered by Lugal-zagesi, to be subsequently captured by Sargon as part of his war on Lugal-zagesi. Thus, Naram-Suen reports that his grandfather Sargon freed Kiš from Lugal-zagesi's oppression.[470] That Sargon had no earlier connection with Kiš is further indicated by the fact that, as there is every reason to think, he stem-

---

467 pa₅ sar-ra-ta = *a-na pa-lag mu-ša-ri-e* (line 2). For *mušarû*, "garden, cultivation," see CAD M/2 233–234 *musarû* B, 261–262 *mušaru*.

468 The Ur III ms. of the SKL lists following Ur-Zababa five additional kings (iii 6 – iv 1′ – Steinkeller 2003: 271).

469 Jacobsen 1939: 158–161, 179 tried to overcome this dilemma by assuming that those additional kings "reigned after the hegemony of Babylonia had passed to Uruk and to Agade" (ibid. 161). However, as I note below, it appears certain that, during the Sargonic period, Kiš was governed by local governors (ensik), who were royal appointees.

470 Wilcke 1997: 25 ix 32 – x 14; J. G. Westenholz 1997: 231–237 no. 16 A:5–8, 238–245 no. 16B:16–20. For this passage, see also above pp. 171–172.

med from Akkade.[471] For this conclusion, it is important that, in his royal inscriptions, Sargon uses the title of the king of Akkade, never laying claims to the kingship of Kiš.[472] As far as one can tell, under the Sargonic kings Kiš was administered by local governors; one of them, apparently, was Iphur-Kiš, who revolted against Naram-Suen during the "Great Rebellion."

Another historical datum that speaks against the Ur-Zababa-Sargon connection is the fact that En-šakušana, who appears to have ruled over Uruk directly before Lugal-zagesi, is known to have sacked Kiš, and to have taken captive its king Enbi-Eštar (RIME 1 429–430 En-šakušana 1:8–12). This evidence contradicts directly the testimony of the SKL, according to which Ur-Zababa, the presumed contemporary of Sargon and Lugal-zagesi, was preceded on the throne of Kiš by Puzur-Suen and Kug-Bau, his father and grandmother respectively. Since En-šakušana's reign was proximate to that of Sargon, perhaps even overlapping with it (Schrakamp and Sallaberger 2015: 93), there in no way to account for this discrepancy.[473] This too unavoidably means that the SKL is wrong about the Ur-Zababa-Sargon synchronism.

Nevertheless, it is still theoretically possible that, despite the SKL's own evidence arguing to the contrary, Ur-Zababa indeed was the last independent king of Kiš before its sack by Lugal-zagesi.[474] But, even if this were to prove correct, for the reasons stated earlier it would be exceedingly difficult to envision how Sargon could have been Ur-Zababa's cup-bearer before the latter's defeat by Lugal-zagesi. However, neither this possibility can be ruled categorically, if only because anecdotal information not uncommonly reflects historical truth, and is known to be exceedingly long-lived and persistent in some cases. Here one is reminded by ditties such as "London bridge is falling down" or "Mary, Mary quite contrary."

---

471 According to the "Sargon Birth Legend," Sargon was born in the town/city of Azupiranu on the Euphrates (J. G. Westenholz 1997: 36–49 line 4). In "Sargon Legend" Segment A line 10 the name of Sargon's town is not preserved (uru-ni ur[u ...]), but the context makes it certain that it was other than Kiš.

472 Sargon's alternative title of lugal KIŠ, "king of the totality/universe," is a separate issue. See Essay 2 p. 135 and Steinkeller 2013a: 145–146.

473 Here note that Jacobsen's reconstruction of Enbi-Eštar's name in the SKL (1939: 96 and n. 159, 169) has no foundation. See Marchesi 2010: 235.

474 In fact, this is what, writing over twenty-five years ago, I considered to be possible myself (Steinkeller 1992: 726). Some Assyriologists still adhere to the view that Ur-Zababa was a historical figure, and that he was Sargon's predecessor. See, most recently, Schrakamp 2016: 1.

Personally, I am inclined to think that the anecdote about Sargon and Ur-Za-baba is a complete fabrication.[475] But the veracity of the anecdote is irrelevant here. What really matters is that Mythical History *insists* on this particular point; for one reason or another Sargon's being a cup-bearer of Ur-Zababa made sense from its own perspective. As I will try to show in the following, the advent of the Sargonic empire was such a radical departure from the earlier Babylonian experience that it caused a tremendous crisis and then a dramatic restructuring of native symbols. The contemporaneous and later reactions to the Sargonic empire were highly ambiguous, a mixture of positive and negative feelings (see in detail below pp. 188–192). This, I believe, is the context in which the story about Sargon and Ur-Zababa is to be placed. The view of Sargon in the anecdote and the Legend is not a flattering one, since by making Sargon a cup-bearer, and therefore an official in whom the highest trust is vested – in other words, an epitome of trust – they imply that Sargon was not only an upstart and an usurper, but also a person of treacherous nature. In contrast to Sargon, Ur-Zababa is presented as a positive figure, perhaps even as Sargon's antithesis.[476] As narrated in the Legend, following his elevation to the throne, Ur-Zababa makes concentrated efforts to restore Kiš to its former glory. However, for unexplained reasons,[477] An and Enlil, the heads of the pantheon, decide that Ur-Zababa's kingship be terminated. Ur-Zababa learns about this decision from a combination of his own premonition and the dream Sargon describes to him. This dream, whose meaning Sargon is unable to grasp – but which is obvious to Ur-Zababa – foretells that Ur-Zababa will be killed by Sargon. Although Ur-Zababa seeks ways to reverse his fate, these attempts inevitably fail. [478] Unfortunately,

---

475 Apart from the Ur III toponym discussed earlier, which might offer evidence of the historicity of Ur-Zababa (thought not necessarily as a king of Kiš and a contemporary of Sargon), an official of that name appears in the ED "Names and Professions List" line 91 (Archi 1981), where he is associated with the city of Adab. Since there are indications that some of the names listed in that source provided material for the SKL, it is conceivable that also the Ur-Zababa of Kiš was invented by the same process (Steinkeller 2013a: 151 n. 87).

476 Interestingly, in Segment B of "Sargon Legend" Ur-Zababa's name is consistently provided with a divine determinative DINGIR. This suggests that the author of this particular manuscript had some notion of Ur-Zababa's divine status, a fact that is not corroborated by any other data. Be that as it may, this individual must have viewed Ur-Zababa as a positive figure.

477 Most probably, it was just divine whim. Similar literary instances of such unexplained reversals of fortune involve the death of Ur-Namma and the fall of the Ur III dynasty. See Steinkeller 2016: 15–16.

478 Once the fate was determined by the general gathering of the pantheon, it could not be reversed. For a detailed discussion of this problem and the examples of such situations, see Steinkeller 2016: 12–20.

the end of the Legend is not preserved. We can be certain, however, that it described how Ur-Zababa eventually ended up as Sargon's victim.[479]

7 While this approach is of potential help in elucidating the meaning of individual mythologems, its greatest value lies in its ability to follow long-term transformations of complex symbolic structures. A perfect example of such a structure is the southern Babylonian (or Sumerian) idea of the city-state as an exclusive domain of an extended divine family (see Essay 1 pp. 28–29, Essay 2 pp. 117–120). The human members of such a domain formed an egalitarian temple community, which was headed by an official named ensik, who functioned as a steward or shepherd of the domain's divine owners. The community toiled for the gods, and, having satisfied their appetites and other needs, shared the surplus equally among themselves. To what extent these noble ideas ever found actualization in real life, it is for the socio-economic historian to judge. But they should not be dismissed as mere propaganda, since symbols like these are an expression of collective consciousness and common historical experience, and reproduce, if only in an idealized way, the matrix of the society.[480] The concept of the Sumerian temple community and of the role that its ruler played in it tells us as much about the Sumerian society as does the Declaration of Independence about the social reality of the early United States. A symbol of the society as an egalitarian temple community led by a divinely selected steward or shepherd was extremely long-lived, since it persisted, in one form of another, down to the very end of Babylonia's history.

Superficially, this situation is a perfect illustration of the adage *plus ça change, plus c'est la même chose*. However, as the anthropologist Marshall Sahlins tells us (1981), the relationship between symbols and events is a dialectical one: although the symbols of a given culture inform the way in which individual historical events are initially understood, symbols themselves are altered by historical events. In other words, cultures deal with social crises by continually re-evaluating and renegotiating the relationships among symbols or categories – without abandoning the symbols themselves. Thus, as Sahlins argues, the above adage should better be reversed: "the more things remain the same, the more they change" (1981: 7).

The event that precipitated the greatest crisis in the history of third millennium symbolic structures undoubtedly was the advent of the dynasty of Sargon

---

479 But there are also sources that present Sargon as a positive figure. I cite and discuss this evidence below.
480 Here I follow Marshall Sahlins's dictum that "symbols are symptoms, direct or mystified, of the true force of things" (1981: 7).

and the subsequent creation of a unified Babylonian state. The main innovation here was the turning of independent divine domains into a unified system ruled by a single king, which changed the relationship between gods and humans quite dramatically.

The coming of Sargon in many ways was as momentous and traumatic an event as was the landing of Captain Cook on the Hawaiian Islands in year 1779 AD. The latter occurrence was used by Sahlins as a kind of litmus test to reveal the structures of the Hawaiian culture (1981; 1985).[481] The first step of his procedure was to ascertain how this event was understood in terms of the existing native symbols: the Hawaiians perceived Captain Cook as a manifestation of their god Lono,[482] because Cook was obviously powerful, and because his arrival coincided with Lono's annual reappearance, which was celebrated by the great Makahiki festival (Sahlins 1981: 17–22; 1985: 105–120).[483]

The question Sahlins asked next was how the symbols were reordered by the events:

> When Captain Cook was killed at Kealakekua Bay, this victory became a novel source of the legitimacy of Hawaiian kings for decades afterwards. Through the appropriation of Cook's bones, the *mana* of the Hawaiian kingship itself became British. And long after the English as men had lost their godliness, the Hawaiian gods kept their Englishness. (1981: 7)

Analogously, I submit, the Sargonic episode could be used as a litmus test to obtain a deeper understanding of the Babylonian symbolic structures, in particular, of how they changed in response to the historical developments of the Sargonic period. This, in turn, might tell us something new about the historical facts themselves.

If we follow Sahlins and apply his procedure to the Babylonian situation, we first need to consider how the coming of the Sargonic dynasty was renegotiated in the light of existing symbols. As expected, in the agreement with the existing

---

481 These studies provoked a lively debate among social anthropologists, with some of the reactions being negative. Sahlins responded to his critics in a subsequent book (1995), in which he analyzed the Cook episode and its impact on the Hawaiian native structures in a much greater detail.

482 The god of agriculture, very much in the tradition of seasonal "dying" deities (such as Dumuzi, Osiris, etc.) (Sahlins 1981: 17–22; 1995: 171–172; Valeri 1985: 14 *et passim*).

483 The Hawaiian society was ruled by a small group of exceedingly powerful elites called *ali'i*. The highest-ranking *ali'i* were believed to be divine, being explicitly referred to as "god-kings" (*ali'i akua*) (Valeri 1985: 143–153; Kirch 2010: 41). It is possible, therefore, that the perception of Captain Cook as a deity by the Hawaiians was facilitated by the fact that the notion of a semi-divine human being had already existed there.

ideology, Sargon's rise to power was initially explained as an act of divine election. But this traditional explanation was hardly sufficient, since the unified state that Sargon had created was an antithesis of the southern symbolic system, in which each city-state constituted the household of a separate divine family, and which formed, therefore, an entity that was *ex definitio* completely independent politically. A partial solution to this problem was to raise the king of Akkade to the divine plane. By becoming a god, and acquiring his own earthly domain, he could then claim a special kind of kingship and special political prerogatives. In the world of symbols, the story of divine Naram-Suen was not unlike that of Captain Cook, who, upon his landing in the Hawaiian Islands, was understood by the natives as an apparition of the god Lono.

The next step is to ask how the creation of the Sargonic world empire and its subsequent demise led to the reordering of symbols. When we enter the following historical phase, that is, the period of the Third Dynasty of Ur, the concepts of the society as a temple community and of the king as a steward or shepherd of its divine owners are still alive and very much in force. But this is only on the surface, since deep inside these concepts had undergone major transformations. Kingship became profoundly Sargonized so to say, in that the Ur III kings now assume the posture of active, history- and future-shaping individuals in the mould of Naram-Suen, who are substantially different from the pious and slightly passive ensiks of Early Dynastic times. Very tellingly, however, their historical referents or intended prototypes are not the Sargonic kings, but the heroic rulers of Uruk's hoary past, such as Gilgameš and Lugal-banda. In other words, Mythical History is embellished – or possibly even a completely new episode is invented and inserted into it, in order both to legitimize a historical change and to mystify the true source of that change itself. What the Ur III kings are saying is the following: if we look and act like the Sargonic kings this is only because we directly descend from Gilgameš, who had been a ruler of this type long before Sargon appeared on the scene.

In my opinion, therefore, the Ur III period is a perfect illustration of "the more things remain the same, the more they change" principle. Cf. Sahlins's summation of the Cook episode:

> In the upshot, the more things remained the same the more they changed, since every such reproduction of the categories is not the same. Every reproduction of culture is an alteration, insofar as in action, the categories by which a present world is orchestrated pick up some novel empirical content. The Hawaiian chief for whom "King George" of England is the model of celestial *mana* is no longer the same chief, nor in the same relation to his people. (1985: 144)

8   The approach I am advocating in this essay could also be useful in assessing the question of how the Ur III period and later posterity viewed Akkade. Here the scholarly opinions differ widely, from the position that there was a strong resentment against Akkade and its legacy in the Ur III period (Wilcke 1993), to the view that "there is no reason to think that anti-Akkade feelings were strong or even present in Ur III times, nor are there grounds for believing that the Sumerian literary texts redacted in that period had 'an important function' in an 'argument against the thought and political-religious goals of the Akkad period'" (Cooper 2001: 140).

I submit that we will gain a better understanding of this issue if we look at it from a purely native perspective, that is, by weaving the relevant sources into a sequential mythical narrative, rather than by dealing with such pieces individually, with an objective of finding historical reality behind them. When one attempts something like that, one discovers that, not unexpectedly, ancient views of the Sargonic period were mixed and ambivalent. I said "not unexpectedly," since this is precisely the kind of reaction that axial events are expected to elicit; the examples of Alexander the Great and Napoleon will suffice here.

As posterity saw it, the problem with the Sargonic empire was not that it came into being, but that it failed, and so miserably at that. The economic benefits that the empire had brought were obvious, even to the elites of southern Babylonia, so that it was not too difficult to accommodate its concepts into the existing symbolic structures. It proved much more difficult to negotiate the trauma and confusion that the collapse of the empire had created in the collective mythical psyche. As already discussed, the resulting reactions were, therefore, equally confused. Even the question of the origins of Akkade was a source of conflicting feelings. The Sargonic empire was such a radical departure from the past that its appearance could not be comprehended on the logic of the existing Mythical History; it had to be attributed to unusual and extraneous causes. Since, from the perspective of Mythical History, Akkade was an anomaly, its origins had to be anomalous too. In this way, Sargon is consistently portrayed as an outsider and a *parvenu*. Both the SKL and the "Sargon Birth Legend" emphasize his extremely humble origins, identifying him as the son of a gardener or the foundling adopted by a water-drawer.[484] The latter description may even imply

---

[484] Sar-ru-ki-in ab-ba-ni nu-kiri$_6$ (SKL lines 266–267); *Aq-qí* LU$_2$-A.BALA *i-na ṭi-i[b da]-ʾli¹-[e-šú l]u ú-še-la-an-n[i] Aq-qí* LU$_2$-A.BALA *a-na ma-ru-ti-ʾšú¹ ú-rab-ba-ni-ma Aq-qí* LU$_2$-A.BALA *a-na* LU$_2$.NU.KIRI$_6$-*ti-šú lu-u iš-kun-an-ni*, "Aqqi, the water-drawer, when lowering his bucket, did lift me up; he raised me as his adopted son; he assigned me to be his gardener" (J. G. Westenholz 1997: 36–49 lines 8–11). The "Sargon Legend" Segment A line 11, identifies Sargon as the son of a certain La-i-bu-um */laʾibum/*. For this personal name, which is documented in Sargonic sources,

that he was a slave, since water-drawers, one of the lowest professional and so-cial groups in ancient Mesopotamia, commonly were enslaved (and often blind-ed) prisoners of war (Steinkeller 2013a: 144). Sargon's marginality is further un-derscored by the fact, that, according the "Sargon Birth Legend," he stemmed from an obscure (and therefore insignificant) place called Azupiranu on the Eu-phrates.[485] Also, as we have seen earlier, Mythical History paints Sargon as a treacherous character.

According to this logic, not only Sargon, but also his city, Akkade, had to be a new and abnormal creation. Thus, Mythical History makes Sargon the founder of Akkade.[486] However, this fact finds no historical corroboration of any sort. As far as one can ascertain, Akkade existed as a town or city before Sargon. This is demonstrated quite securely by a date-formula of En-šakušana of Uruk (Lugal-zagesi's predecessor), who was involved in a conflict with Akkade.[487]

While these stories may be considered critical in tone, others are more sym-pathetic to Sargon. Thus "The Curse of Akkade" offers a favorable view of his reign. In particular, it stresses the fact that Sargon ascended to the throne of Ak-kade as a result of divine election, the traditional way of becoming a king in southern Babylonia.[488] That Sargon enjoyed divine favor is also reflected in his unusually close connection with Ištar, who made Sargon her favorite and estab-lished her home in Akkade.[489] As argued by this composition, Akkade's "prob-

---

see CAD L 45. If this name indeed means "affected by the *li'bu* disease" (so CAD), we would find here yet another allusion to the marginality of Sargon's social background.

485 *a-li* ^{uru}*A-zu-pi-ra-nu*/*-a-ni šá i-na a-ḫi* ^{id2}*Buranuna šak-nu* (J. G. Westenholz 1997: 36–49 line 4). This toponym is documented only here. Cf. "Sargon Legend" Segment A line 10, where name of Sargon's town is not preserved.

486 Sar-ru-ki-in … lugal A-ga-de$_3$^{ki} lu$_2$ A-ga-de$_3$^{ki} mu-un-du$_3$-a (SKL 266–270). Figurative descrip-tions of this event are offered by the "Weidner Chronicle" and "Chronicle of Early Kings," both of which accuse Sargon of making a "replica" of Babylon (i.e., Nippur) and of establishing it in Akkade. See Essay 1 p. 80 n. 216.

487 ECTJ 81:7, 9. Schrakamp and Sallaberger 2015: 93 assert that this date-formula "can be taken as the first indirect proof for the existence of Sargon as a contemporary of Enshakushana." Cor-rectly, all that this evidence proves is the existence of Akkade at the time of En-šakušana. While it does not exclude the possibility that Sargon ruled over Akkade at that time, it in no way dem-onstrates it.

488 Sar-ru-GI lugal A-ga-de$_3$^{ki}-ra sig-ta igi-nim-še$_3$ ^{d}En-lil$_2$-le nam-en nam-lugal-la mu-un-na-an-sum-ma-ta, "when Enlil granted to Sargon, king of Akkade, the en-ship and kingship from south to north" ("The Curse of Akkade" lines 4–6).

489 ud-ba eš$_3$, A-ga-de$_3$^{ki} kug ^{d}Inana-ke$_4$ ama$_5$ mah-a-ni-še$_3$, im-ma-an-du$_3$-du$_3$ Ul-maš^{ki}-a ^{giš}gu-za ba-ni-in-gub, "at that time Holy Inana erected the shrine of Akkade as her great woman's do-main, she set up (her) throne in Ulmaš" ("The Curse of Akkade" lines 7–9). The same motive ap-pears in the "Sargon Birth Legend," where Sargon's ascent to power is likewise attributed to the

lems" began only later, with Naram-Suen's "attack" on the Ekur. That event almost certainly is a metaphoric allusion to the deification of Naram-Suen, and the rise of Akkade to the status of Babylonia's chief religious center.[490] However, in the "Weidner Chronicle" lines 47–52b (Grayson 1975: 149), these events are telescoped and attributed to Sargon, thereby portraying his reign as a mixture of positive and negative elements: while Sargon provided offerings for Marduk, he subsequently offended Marduk by building a replica of Babylon (read Nippur) in Akkade.[491]

Another favorable view of Sargon may be offered by the tradition that Sargon's mother was an *ēntu* priestess (most likely that of Nanna/Suen), and that he did not know his father.[492] This tradition may subtly intimate that Sargon was a demigod. The reasoning, apparently, was that since *ēntu* priestesses were not allowed to have children, a child born of an *ēntu* could only have been fathered by the god to whom she was dedicated. Thus, the implication is that the unknown father of Sargon was a god (evidently, Nanna/Suen).

However, by far the best evidence of positive attitudes toward the Sargonic episode in Ur III times is the fact that the kings of Akkade and their manifold achievements and feats were a source of admiration and imitation on every level, as amply documented by the imperial policies of Šulgi and his successors.[493] Here it is also significant that Sargon, Maništušu, and Naram-Suen

---

patronage of Ištar: "when I was (still) a gardener, Ištar developed an affection for me" (J. G. Westenholz 1997: 36–49 line 12). Ištar's protection and her active support of Sargon are also emphasized in "Sargon Legend," especially Segment B line 7: kug ^{d}Inana-ke$_4$ da-bi-a muš$_3$ nu-tum$_2$-me, "Holy Inana unceasingly stood by him."

490 See Essay 1 pp. 79–80.

491 A similar account is found in the "Chronicle of Early Kings" lines 18–23 (Grayson 1975: 153–154). Cf. Essay 1 p. 80 n. 216.

492 *um-mi e-ni-tum a-bi ul i-di* ... *i-ra-an-ni um-mu e-ni-tum i-na pu-uz-ri ú-lid-da-an-ni*, "my mother was an *ēntu* priestess, my father I never knew... my mother, the *ēntu* priestess, conceived me, in concealment she gave birth to me" (J. G. Westenholz 1997: 36–49 "Sargon Birth Legend" lines 2 and 5).

493 On the basis of his understanding of lines 320–326 of the hymn "Šulgi B," Liverani asserted that, in this passage, "the Akkadian stelae are quite patently criticized as manifestations of a specific ideology, which is not the same ideology as that of the Ur king, it is even its reverse. Shulgi imagines setting up a stela (*mu-sar-ra*) of his own, with a boast that is the reverse of the Akkadian boasts (with their insistence on cities destroyed and walls pulled down)" (2002: 153–154). In my view, however, the meaning and intent of this passage are quite different: "Nobody can say under oath that, as of this day, (there are included) in my inscriptions cities that I have not destroyed, city walls that I have not pulled down, foreign lands that I have made tremble like a reed hut, (and any other) praises that I have not completely verified. Why would a singer put them in songs? Veracity is the vanguard of lasting fame. What is the use of lies if there is

were worshipped as gods (though only in a marginal way) during the Ur III period,[494] a situation that would be impossible to imagine had their reigns been viewed in a totally negative way. Further proof of this is the fact that their monuments and inscriptions had been carefully preserved in the Ekur, where they must have been studied and copied by Ur III scribes, providing models for the contemporaneous display inscriptions.[495] It is characteristic that of all the third millennium dedicatory texts that had been stored in the Ekur only the Sargonic and the Ur III ones were selected to become part of the Old Babylonian scribal curriculum (Essay 1 pp. 46–47). This too must be interpreted as a sign of admiration and approval (Cooper 2001: 139).

But even the Ur III period (or, at the very least, the prelude leading to it) was not free of openly negative reactions toward the Sargonic policies and worldview more generally. Here it is sufficient to recall the universe of Gudea's inscriptions, in which everything happens in a timeless mythical dimension, and no political events ever take place, other than those of ritual activity. Is not this universe a total rejection of the Sargonic values,[496] with their stress on historical change and individual accomplishment? Is not the total self-abasement and subordination to the divine will that is displayed by the builder of the Eninnu an antithesis of the posture of Naram-Suen, as the latter rebels when he is denied the divine "yes" to rebuild the Ekur?

9 My final illustration of how Mythical History works, and how its lessons may be used to further our understanding of the history of events is the SKL. I have already referred to this composition many times, both in this and the preceding essays.[497] The completely preserved version of this fascinating text dates to the Old Babylonian period. One of the characteristic features of this version is the manner in which it deals with the history of Early Dynastic times. As described there, kingship circulated among several cities, with Kiš, Uruk, and Ur having held it more than once. Thus, Kiš is credited with four separate dynasties, Uruk with three dynasties, and Ur with two dynasties. Surprisingly, however, several cities that are known to have been very influential in Early Dynastic times are not included in it at all. Especially striking here is the omission of Lagaš,

---

no truth in them?" As a matter of fact, Šulgi's hymns are full of boasts about destroyed cities and terrorized foreign lands (including Šulgi B"!). Note also that mu-sar-ra means "inscription"; the term for "stele" is na-du$_3$-a. See also Cooper 2010: 329 and n. 20.

494 See Essay 2 p. 116 n. 314.

495 Cf. Essay 1 p. 37.

496 See Essay 1 p. 32–34.

497 See especially Essay 1 pp. 40–42, 44–45.

which was one of the leading city-states of Sumer, and which may have even achieved political supremacy at one point in time (under E-annatum).

Over the years scholars tried to establish when exactly the SKL was composed. Among the proposed datings were the reign of Utu-hegal of Uruk, the time of the Third Dynasty of Ur, and the early Old Babylonian period – more specifically, the so-called Isin period, which followed immediately after Ur III. Moreover, mainly as a corollary to the dating efforts, attempts were made to unravel the internal logic of this composition. The question one asked here, in particular, was why some Early Dynastic dynasties are included in it – some among them more than once, whereas others are not. Thus, for example, the inclusion of as many as four Uruk dynasties was thought by some scholars to be an indication that the origins of the SKL were somehow associated with Uruk. This, in turn, suggested to them that the SKL was composed either during the reign of Utu-hegal of Uruk (Jacobsen 1939) or the Third Dynasty of Ur (Wilcke 1988), whose rulers, as is well known, traced their political and genetic roots to the mythical kings of Uruk.

A different explanation of the date and purpose of the SKL was offered by Piotr Michalowski (1983), who, building on the earlier suggestions by J. J. Finkelstein (1979), interpreted it as a foundational charter of the Isin dynasty.

Other scholars believed to have discerned the presence of various internal patterns in this composition. For example, it was observed that the transfer of kingship from one place to another appears to follow a regular sequence, which runs as follows: from Kiš to Uruk, from Uruk to Ur, and then back to Kiš again. Jean-Jacques Glassner claimed to have identified an even more complicated pattern – a "sinusoidal scheme" – which, in his view, underlines the entire list (2004: 68–70).

Claus Wilcke, on the other hand, speculated that the inclusion of at least some cities in the SKL had more to do with the geographic extent of the Ur III state than with the realities of Early Dynastic history (1988). What Wilcke proposed, specifically, is that certain peripheral cities were included in it to mark the furthest extensions of the Ur III state. In other words, the SKL served as a sort of metaphorical map of the Ur III territorial possessions or conquests.[498]

Our understanding of the origins and the evolution of the SKL has been considerably enhanced by the publication of an Ur III manuscript of this composition (Steinkeller 2003). The manuscript in question almost certainly dates to the reign of Šulgi, the second ruler of the House of Ur, since it ends with the reign of

---

[498] As such, the SKL would be comparable to the roundlet of Naram-Suen (for which see Essay 2 p. 137 and Appendix 2), which is a visual realization of the same idea.

Ur-Namma, Šulgi's predecessor, and since it actually invokes Šulgi: "Šulgi, my king, may he live long days!" (Steinkeller 2003: 274). This dating is further corroborated by its script, which clearly belongs to Ur III times. Unfortunately, only the upper half of the tablet survives, so that the reconstruction of the entire text is uncertain. Based on what survives, however, it is certain that the Ur III list differed very significantly from the Old Babylonian version. It begins with one continuous listing of the rulers of Kiš, which combines the four Kiš dynasties. Then there is a short lacuna in the tablet, which may have included a few rulers of Uruk (but certainly not all of the dynasties of Uruk), immediately after which there is the Sargonic dynasty. From then on the tablet follows more or less the order of the Old Babylonian version (the exception is the dynasty of Adab, which is not mentioned in the latter source).

As far as one can tell, the most significant difference between the Ur III king list and its later version is that the former organizes the events in an unmistakably linear fashion: after the kingship descended from heaven in time immemorial, it remained for thousands and thousands of years in Kiš down to Sargon's very day. This veritable Age of Kiš was apparently followed by an Urukean interlude, with Akkade and the successive dynasties then following suit. In other words, the Ur III king list embraces a linear vision of history, which probably even reflects a chronologically correct historical sequence. Unlike in the Old Babylonian version, there is no suggestion in it that, in Early Dynastic times, kingship wandered cyclically from place to place.

So now, of course, we need to ask: when and why was the fatalistic vision of history as a chain of recurring cycles imposed on the king list? In all probability, this happened not earlier than in Isin times (ca. 2000–1850 BC), mainly as a response to the traumatic experiences that the fall of Ur had visited upon Babylonia. Here it should be realized that the demise of the House of Ur was much more complete – and probably also even more unexpected – than that of the Sargonic empire.[499] It was very likely this horrific event that called for a radical re-evaluation and re-arrangement of the existing symbols. "A linear sequencing of events did not make sense any longer: while the fall of the suspect Akkade could be comprehended, no existing explanation might have accounted for the demise of the seemingly perfect Ur. And so history had to be given a cyclical pattern, in which kingship circulates among a number of cities in a fairly regular sequence, never staying in one place for long" (Steinkeller 2003: 285–286).

---

499 According to Hallo, "the fall of Ur was thus not as cataclysmic an event as the [city] lamentations, for their own reasons, made it out to be, and certainly not a watershed event on a par with the fall of Akkad earlier or the fall of Babylon at the end of its First Dynasty" (2001: 204–205). In my opinion, the situation was just the opposite.

What happened, therefore, is that the existential perspective that had been gained from the fall of Ur was read back into the past, all the way to the beginning of history. What the Old Babylonian redactors of the SKL are telling us is the following: history moves in cycles, no political center is able to hold on to power forever. It was always like that.

And certainly the political realities of post-Ur III times, when Babylonia was subdivided among a number of warring states that no longer shared a common city-state ideology (such as existed in southern Babylonia in the Early Dynastic period) reinforced this view of history still further.

In my view, the conceptual shift from a linear to a cyclical understanding of the course of history I have proposed is best illustrated by a juxtaposition of "The Curse of Akkade" with a number of post-Ur III compositions. The "Curse," whose composition assuredly belongs to Ur III times, organizes events in a sequential fashion, attributing the rise of dynasties and kings to divine favor and election:

> sag-ki gid$_2$-da ^{d}En-lil$_2$-la$_2$-ke$_4$
> Kiš^{ki} gud-an-na-gim im-ug$_5$-ga-ta
> e$_2$ ki-Unug^{ki}-ga gud mah-gim sahar-ra mi-ni-ib-gaz-a-ta
> <<KI>> ud-ba Sar-ru-GI lugal A-ga-de$_3$^{ki}-ra
> sig-ta igi-nim-še$_3$ ^{d}En-lil$_2$-le
> nam-en nam-lugal-la mu-un-na-an-sum-ma-ta

> When Enlil's displeasure
> had slain Kiš like the Bull of Heaven,
> had slaughtered the house of Uruk land in the dust like a great ox,
> and then, to Sargon, king of Akkade,
> Enlil, from south to north,
> had granted en-ship and kingship.
> ("The Curse of Akkade" lines 1–6)

By contrast, the city laments, which offer a poetic vision of the demise of the Ur III state, operate with a concept of the royal reign (bala) that is unstable and changeable by its very nature. These changes are unrelated to the performance of rulers (as the original southern Babylonian ideology had it), being rather entirely dependent on the fickleness of deities. As such, they are totally unpredictable, devoid of logic, and, therefore, beyond human comprehension. No turn of reign will last forever. Though it may be long in some instances, it will exhaust itself in the end:

> Urim$_2$^{ki}-ma nam-lugal ha-ba-sum bala da-ri$_2$ la-ba-an-sum
> ud ul kalam ki gar-ra-ta zag un lu-a-še$_3$

bala nam-lugal-la sag-bi-še₃ e₃-a a-ba-a igi im-mi-in-du₈-a
nam-lugal bala-bi ba-gid₂-e-de₃ šag₄-kuš₂-u₃-de₃

Ur indeed was given kingship; (but) was not given an eternal reign.
From time immemorial, since the Land was founded, until the population became numerous,
who has ever seen a turn of kingship that would take precedence (for ever)?
The turn of its (i.e., of Ur) kingship had been long indeed, but it exhausted itself (in the end).
("The Lament for Sumer and Ur" lines 366–369)

bala-ba ud sud-ra₂ na-ma-ni-in-gar-re-eš-am₃

(Ningal speaks): "They (i.e., the great gods) indeed did not assign to me a reign of distant days."
("The Lament for Ur" line 114).

This fatalistic concept of the royal reign presupposes that any tenure of kingship will unavoidably end in violence and destruction:

a-a ᵈEn-lil₂ nam mu-e-tar-ra galga ba-ra-an-du₈-du₈ ...
ᵈEn-lil₂-le dumu-ni ᵈSuen-ra inim zi mu-un-na-ab-be₂
dumu-mu uru nam-he₂ giri₁₇-zal ša-ra-da-du₃-a bala-zu ba-ši-ib-tuku
uru gul bad₃ gal bad₃-si-bi si₃-ke u₃-ur₅-re bala an-ga-am₃

(Nanna speaks): "Oh Father Enlil, the destiny you determined cannot be explained!" ...
Enlil speaks true words to his son Suen:
"My son, the city that was erected for you amidst abundance and joy, you possessed it as your turn of reign –
but also destroyed cities (and) great walls with their leveled battlements are part of the reign!"
("The Lament for Sumer and Ur" lines 457–462)

As I pointed out earlier, the same notion of the royal reign appears also in the "Sargon Legend" Segment A line 8, where, in spite of Ur-Zababa's good efforts, the gods decide, suddenly and inexplicably, to terminate his tenure of kingship (nam-lugal-an-na bala-bi šu kur₂-ru-de₃).

I will conclude this assessment of the SKL by emphasizing that my findings (if correct) do not necessarily contradict the existence of deeper symbolic patterns in this composition, such as those proposed by Glassner and Wilcke. The beauty and uniqueness of the myth lies in the fact that it always has multiple sub-texts, allowing alternative, equally valid readings.

10 I hope that I have succeeded in getting across at least the basic sense of my argument. The Mythical History I am advocating simply recognizes the fact that the so-called "historical" sources do not substantially differ from literary texts, in that both of them are but symbolic negotiations of historical events. But this fact does not render all this evidence irrelevant to historical analysis. Instead of dismissing such symbols as "symptoms of false consciousness" (Karl Marx and co.), we should treat them seriously, as true reflections of the social matrix. This, I believe, will provide us with considerable rewards.[500] As I stressed earlier, such an approach by no means is entirely novel. But it has not so far been used in a really focused manner. And this, essentially, is what I am arguing for.

---

[500] For examples of such benefits, see Beckman 2005. Having analyzed a number of Hittite historical sources, Beckman demonstrated that these accounts lack historical veracity. At the same time, he pleaded as follows: "But please note that each of the elements we can now recognize as misrepresentation in itself tells us something significant about Hittite society or its ideals" (ibid. 352). Similarly, Van De Mieroop, who, in reference to the "historical-literary" sources dealing with the Sargonic period, argued that "unless we believe that there was a mindless copying of texts because of antiquarian interests, there should have been a relevance to them when they were written. This approach allows us to work with the texts in the form that is available to us. It becomes irrelevant whether they were newly composed, verbatim copies of an earlier manuscript, or reworkings of something earlier. I contend that that in all three cases the texts still had a meaning within the society for which the manuscripts were written" (1999: 329).

List of Abbreviations

1 Bibliographic Abbreviations

Abbreviations used are those of the *Assyrian Dictionary of the Oriental Institute of the University of Chicago* (Chicago, 1956–2010) and/or cdli: Cuneiform Digital Library Initiative [cdli.ucla.edu], "Abbreviations for Assyriology."

Titles of Sumerian literary compositions generally are those used by ETCSL: The Electronic Corpus of Sumerian Literature, Oriental Institute, University of Oxford [etcsl.orinst.ac.uk].

2 Other Abbreviations

AKL	"Antediluvian King List"
DN	Divine Name
ED	Early Dynastic
ms	manuscript
mss	manuscripts
OB	Old Babylonian
SB	Standard Babylonian
SKL	"Sumerian King List"
ULKS	"Uruk List of Kings and Sages"

DOI 10.1515/9781501504778-007

Bibliography

Alaura, Silvia. 2011. "The Sun-god's Quadriga in the *Prayers to the Sun-god for Appeasing an Angry Personal God (CTH 372–374)* and Its Mesopotamian Background." Pp. 32–51 in *Proceedings of the Eighth International Congress of Hittitology, Warsaw, 5–9 September 2011*, ed. by P. Taracha and M. Kapeluś. Warsaw: AGADE.

Alaura, Silvia, and Marco Bonechi. 2012. "Il carrro del dio del sole nei testi cuneiformi dell'età del Bronzo." *Studi Micenei ed Egeo Anatolici* 54: 5–115.

Al-Rawi, F. N. H. 1990. "Tablets from the Sippar Library 1. The 'Weidner Chronicle': A Supposititious Royal Letter Concerning a Vision." *Iraq* 52: 1–13.

Al-Rawi, F. N. H., and A. R. George. 1994. "Tablets from the Sippar Library III. Two Royal Counterfeits." *Iraq* 56: 135–148.

Alster, Bendt. 2005. *Wisdom of Ancient Sumer*. Bethesda MD: CDL Press.

Amiet, Pierre. 1961. *La glyptique mesopotamienne archaïque*. Paris: Éditions du Centre national de la recherché scientifique.

Amiet, Pierre. 1976. *L'art d'Agadé au Musée du Louvre*. Paris: Éditions des Musées Nationaux.

André-Leicknam, Béatrice, and Christiane Ziegler. 1982. (eds.). *Naissance de l'écriture: cuneiformes et hiéroglyphes. Galeries nationales du Grand Palais, 7 mai – 9 août, 1982*. Paris: Ministère de la Culture, Éditions de la Réunion des musées nationaux.

Archi, Alfonso. 1981. "La 'Lista di nomi e professioni' ad Ebla." *Studi Eblaiti* 4: 177–204.

Archi, Alfonso. 1987. "The 'Sign-List' from Ebla." Pp. 91–113 in *Eblaitica: Essays on the Ebla Archives and Eblaite Language*, vol. 1, ed. by C. G. Gordon, G. A. Rendsburg, and N. H. Winter. Winona Lake IN: Eisenbrauns.

Archi, Alfonso. 1996. "Chronologie relative des archives d'Ébla." Pp. 11–28 in *Mari, Ebla et les Hourrites. Dix ans de travaux*, ed. by J.-M. Durand. Amurru 1. Paris: Éditions Recherches sur les Civilisations.

Archi, Alfonso. 2001. "The King-List from Ebla." Pp. 1–13 in *Historiography in the Cuneiform World, Proceedings of the XLVe Rencontre Assyriologique Internationale*, Part 1, ed. by T. Abusch et al. Bethesda MD: CDL Press.

Archi, Alfonso. 2012. "Cult of the Ancestors and Funerary Practices at Ebla." Pp. 5–31 in *(Re-) Constructing Funerary Rituals in the Ancient Near East*, ed. by P. Pfälzner et al. Qatna Studien Supplementa 1. Wiesbaden: Harrassowitz.

Aruz, Joan. 2003. (ed.) *Art of the First Cities. The Third Millennium B.C. from the Mediterranean to the Indus*. New York: The Metropolitan Museum of Art.

Asher-Greve, Julia M. 1985. *Frauen in altsumerischer Zeit*. Bibliotheca Mesopotamica 18. Malibu: Undena.

Asher-Greve, Julia M. 2006. "The Gaze of the Goddess: On Divinity, Gender and Frontality in the Late Early Dynastic, Akkadian, and Neo-Sumerian Periods." *NIN* 4: 1–59.

Assmann, Jan. 2001. *The Search for God in Ancient Egypt*. Ithaca NY: Cornell University Press.

Assmann, Jan. 2011. *Cultural Memory and Early Civilization. Writing, Remembrance, and Political Imagination*. Cambridge: Cambridge University Press. Originally published as *Das kulturelle Gedächtnis. Schrift, Erinnerung und politische Identität in frühen Hochkulturen*. München: C. H. Beck, 1992.

Assmann, Jan, and John Czaplicka. 1995. "Collective Memory and Cultural Identity." *New German Critique* 65: 125–133.

DOI 10.1515/9781501504778-008

Auer, Blain H. 2012. *Symbols of Authority in Medieval Islam: History, Religion and Muslim Legitimacy in the Delhi Sultanate*. London: I. B. Tauris.

Averbeck, Richard E. 2002. "Sumer, the Bible and Comparative Method: Historiography and Temple Building." Pp. 88–125 in *Mesopotamia and the Bible. Comparative Explorations*, ed. by M. W. Chavalas and K. L. Younger, Jr. Grand Rapids MI: Baker Academic.

Bagley, Robert W. 2004. "Anyang Writing and the Origin of the Chinese Writing System." Pp. 190–249 in *The First Writing. Script Invention as History and Process*, ed. by S. D. Houston. Cambridge: Cambridge University Press.

Baines, John. 1988. "Literacy, Social Organization, and the Archaeological Record. The Case of Early Egypt." Pp. 192–214 in *State and Society. The Emergence and Development of Social Hierarchy and Political Centralization*, ed. by J. Gledhill, B. Bender, and M. T. Larsen. London: Unwin Hyman.

Baines, John. 1989. "Communication and Display: The Integration of Early Egyptian Art and Writing," *Antiquity* 63, 471–482.

Baines, John. 2004. "The Earliest Egyptian Writing: Development, Context, Purpose." Pp. 150–189 in *The First Writing. Script Invention as History and Process*, ed. by S. D. Houston. Cambridge: Cambridge University Press.

Beaulieu, Paul-Alain. 1992. "The Antiquarian Theology in Seleucid Uruk." *ASJ* 14: 47–75.

Beaulieu, Paul-Alain. 1994. "Antiquarianism and the Concern for the Past in the Neo-Babylonian Period," *Bulletin of the Canadian Society for Mesopotamian Studies* 28: 37–42.

Beaulieu, Paul-Alain. 2007a. "The Social and Intellectual Setting of Babylonian Wisdom Literature." Pp. 3–19 in *Wisdom Literature in Mesopotamia and Israel*, ed. by R. J. Clifford. Society of Biblical Literature Symposium Series 36. Atlanta: Society of Biblical Literature.

Beaulieu, Paul-Alain. 2007b. "Nabonidus the Mad King: A Reconsideration of His Steles from Harran and Babylon." Pp. 137–166 in *Representations of Political Power. Case Histories from Times of Change and Dissolving Order in the Ancient Near East*," ed. by M. Heinz and M. H. Feldman. Winona Lake IN: Eisenbrauns.

Beckman, Gary. 2005. "The Limits of Credulity (Presidential Address)." *JAOS* 125: 343–352.

Biga, Maria G. 2012. "Tra Egitto e Siria nel III millennio a.C." *Accademia delle Scienze di Torino, Atti di Scienze Morali* 146: 17–36.

Biga, Maria G. 2014. "Third Millennium Political and Cultural Landscape." Pp. 93–110 in *Constituent, Confederate, and Conquered Space in Upper Mesopotamia. The Emergence of the Mittani State*, ed. by E. Cancik-Kirschbaum, N. Brisch, and J. Eidem. Berlin: De Gruyter.

Biggs, Robert D. 1971. "An Archaic Sumerian Version of the Kesh Temple Hymn from Tell Abū Salābīkh." *ZA* 61: 193–207.

Biggs, Robert D. 1974. *Inscriptions from from Tell Abū Ṣalābīkh*. OIP 99. Chicago: The University of Chicago Press.

Boehmer, Rainer M. 1965. *Die Entwicklung der Glyptik während der Akkad-Zeit*. Untersuchungen zur Assyriologie und Vorderasiatischen Archäologie 4. Berlin: De Gruyter.

Boehmer, Rainer M. 2014. "Ein frühnächtliches Fest zu Ehren der Stadtgöttin von Uruk, Inanna." *Zeitschrift für Orient-Archäologie* 7: 126–135.

Boese, Johannes. 1973. "Zur stilistischen und historischen Einordnung des Felsreliefs von Darband-i-Gaur." *Studia Iranica* 2: 3–48.

Boltz, William G. 1986. "Early Chinese Writing." *World Archaeology* 17: 420–436.

Bonechi, Marco. 2001. "The Dynastic Past of the Rulers of Ebla." *UF* 33: 53–64.

Bonechi, Marco. 2010. "On BM 78614 (Bilingual Hymn to Utu)." *NABU* 2010/70.

Bonechi, Marco. 2011. "The Animals of the Sun-god's Team in the *Incantation to Utu A*." *NABU* 2011/86.

Bourguignon, Alexandra. 2012. "La liste Lú A et la hiérarchie des fonctionnaires sumériens." Pp. 249–256 in *Organization, Representation, and Symbols of Power in the Ancient Near East*, Proceedings of the 54th Rencontre Assyriologique Internationale at Würzburg 20–25 July 2008, ed. by G. Wilhelm. Winona Lake IN: Eisenbrauns.

Braun-Holzinger, Eva A. 1977. *Frühdynastische Beterstatuetten*. Berlin: Mann.

Braun-Holzinger, Eva A. 1991. *Mesopotamische Weihgaben der früdynastischen bis altbabylonischen Zeit*. Heidelberger Studien zum Alten Orient 3. Heidelberg: Heidelberger Orientverlag.

Braun-Holzinger, Eva A. 2007. *Das Herrscherbild in Mesopotamien und Elam. Spätes 4. bis frühes 2. Jt. V. Chr.* AOAT 342. Münster: Ugarit-Verlag.

Braun-Holzinger, Eva A. 2013. *Frühe Götterdarstellungen in Mesopotamien*. OBO 261. Fribourg: Academic Press Fribourg.

Brisch, Nicole. 2006. "The Priestess and the King: The Divine Kingship of Šu-Sîn of Ur." *JAOS* 126: 161–176.

Brisch, Nicole. 2008. (ed.) *Religion and Power: Divine Kingship in the Ancient World and Beyond*. Oriental Institute Seminars 4. Chicago: The Oriental Institute of the University of Chicago.

Brisch, Nicole. 2013. "Of Gods and Kings: Divine Kingship in Ancient Mesopotamia." *Religion Compass* 7: 37–46.

Buchanan, Briggs. 1981. *Early Near Eastern Seals in the Yale Babylonian Collection*. New Haven CT: Yale University Press.

Burstein, Stanley M. 1978. *The Babyloniaca of Berossus*. Sources and Monographs, Sources from the Ancient Near East, volume 1, fascicle 5. Malibu CA: Undena Publications.

Buruma, Ian. 2015. "In North Korea: Wonder & Terror." *The New York Review of Books* June 4, 2015: 46–48.

Cavigneaux, Antoine. 2014. "Une version sumérienne de la legende d'Adapa (Textes de Tell Haddad X)." *ZA* 104: 1–41.

Cervelló-Autuori, Josep. 2003. "Narmer, Menes and the Seals from Abydos." Pp. 168–175 in *Egyptology at the Dawn of the Twenty-first Century. Proceedings of the Eighth International Congress of Egyptologists, Cairo, 2000*, vol. 2, ed. by Z. Hawass. Cairo: The American Univrsity in Cairo Press.

Chang, Kwang-Chih. 1980. *Shang Civilization*. New Haven CT: Yale University Press.

Charpin, Dominique. 1980. *Archives familiales et propriété privée en Babylonie ancienne: Étude des documents de "Tell Sifr."* Genève: Librairie Droz.

Charpin, Dominique. 1986. Le clergé d'Ur au siècle d'Hammurabi (XIXᵉ–XVIIIe siècles av. J.C.). Genève: Librairie Droz.

Charpin, Dominique. 2013. "'I am the Sun of Babylon'": Solar Aspects of Royal Power in Old Babylonian Mesopotamia." Pp. 65–96 in *Experiencing Power, Generating Authority: Cosmos, Politics, and the Ideology of Kingship in Ancient Egypt and Mesopotamia*, ed. by J. A. Hill, Ph. Jones, and A. J. Morales. Philadelphia: University of Pennsylvania Museum of Archaeology and Anthropology.

Charvát, Petr. 2012. "From King to God: The NAMEŠDA Title in Archaic Ur." Pp. 265–274 in *Organization, Representation and Symbols of Power in the Ancient Near East*, Proceedings of the 54th Rencontre Assyriologique Internationale at Würzburg 20–25 July 2008, ed. by G. Wilhelm. Winona Lake IN: Eisenbrauns.

Chen, Y. S. 2013. *The Primeval Flood Catastrophe: Origins and Early Development in Mesopotamian Traditions*. Oxford: Oxford University Press.

Civil, Miguel. 1985. "Sur les 'livres d'écolier' à l'époque paléo-babylonienne." Pp. 67–78 in *Miscellanea Babylonica. Mélanges offerts à Maurice Birlot*, ed. by J.-M. Durand and J.-R. Kupper. Paris: Éditions Recherche sur les Civilisations.

Civil, Miguel. 1987. "*KBo* 26 53 and Funerary Personnel." *NABU* 1987/9.

Civil, Miguel. 2013. "Remarks on AD-GI$_4$ (A.K.A. 'Archaic Word List C' or 'Tribute')." *JCS* 65: 13–67.

Coe, Michael D., and Justin Kerr. 1998. *The Art of the Maya Scribe*. New York: Harry N. Abrams.

Cohen, Mark E. 1975. "Incantation-Hymn, Incantation or Hymn?" *JAOS* 99: 592–611.

Cohen, Yoram. 2009. *The Scribes and Scholars of the City of Emar in the Late Bronze Age*. Harvard Semitic Studies 59. Winona Lake IN: Eisenbrauns.

Collon, Dominique. 1987. *First Impressions: Cylinder Seals in the Ancient Near East*. Chicago: The University of Chicago Press.

Conrad, Geoffrey W., and Arthur A. Demarest. 1984. *Religion and Empire: The Dynamics of Aztec and Inca Expansionism*. Cambridge: Cambridge University Press.

Cooper, Jerrold S. 1983a. *The Curse of Agade*. Baltimore: Johns Hopkins University Press.

Cooper, Jerrold S. 1983b. *Reconstructing History from Ancient Inscriptions: The Lagash-Umma Border Conflict*. Sources from the Ancient Near East, volume 2, fascicle 1. Malibu CA: Undena Publications.

Cooper, Jerrold S. 2001. "Literature and History: The Historical and Political Referents of Sumerian Literary Texts." Pp. 131–147 in *Historiography in the Cuneiform World, Proceedings of the XLVe Rencontre Assyriologique Internationale*, Part 1, ed. by T. Abusch et al. Bethesda MD: CDL Press.

Cooper, Jerrold S. 2008. "Incongruent Corpora: Writing and Art in Ancient Iraq." Pp. 69–94 in *Iconography Without Texts*, ed. by P. Taylor. London: The Warburg Institute.

Cooper, Jerrold S. 2010. "'I have forgotten my burden of former days!' Forgetting the Sumerians in Ancient Iraq." *JAOS* 130: 327–335.

Cooper, Jerrold S., and Wolfgang Heimpel. 1983. "The Sumerian Sargon Legend." *JAOS* 103: 67–82.

D'Altroy, Terence N. 2002. *The Incas*. Oxford: Blackwell.

Damerow, Peter, and Robert K. Englund. 1987. "Die Zahlzeichensysteme der Archaischen Texte aus Uruk." Pp. 117–166 in M.W. Green and H. J. Nissen *Zeichenliste der archaischen Texte aus Uruk*. ATU 2. Berlin: Gebr. Mann Verlag.

Darling, Linda T. 2013. "*Mirrors for Princes* in Europe and the Middle East: A Case for Historiographical Incommensurability." Pp. 223–242 in *East Meets West in the Middle Ages and Early Modern Times: Transcultural Experiences in the Premodern World*, ed. by Albrecht Classen. Berlin: De Gruyter.

Darnell, John C. 2002. *Theban Desert Road Survey in the Egyptian Western Desert, vol. 1, Gebel Tjauti Rock Inscriptions 1–45 and Wadi el-Hôl Rock Inscriptions 1–45*. OIP 119. Chicago: The Oriental Institute of the University of Chicago.

Demarest, Arthur. 2004. *Ancient Maya: The Rise and Fall of a Rainforest Civilization.* Cambridge: Cambridge University Press.

Dijk, J. van. 1962. "Die Inschriftenfunde." *Vorläufiger Bericht über die ... Ausgrabungen in Uruk-Warka* 18: 44–52 and pl. 27.

Dreyer, Günter. 1986. "Ein Siegel der frühzeitlichen Königsnekropole von Abydos." *Mitteilungen des Deutschen Archäologischen Instituts, Abteilung Kairo* 43: 33–43.

Dreyer, Günter. 2011. "Tomb U-J: A Royal Burial of Dynasty O at Abydos." Pp. 127–136 in *Before the Pyramids: The Origins of Egyptian Civilization,* ed. by E. Teeter. Oriental Institute Museum Publications 33. Chicago: The Oriental Institute of the University of Chicago.

Dreyer, Günter, et al. 1996. "Nachuntersuchungen im frühzeitlichen Königsfriedhof. 7./8. Vorbericht." *Mitteilungen des Deutschen Archäologischen Instituts, Abteilung Kairo* 52: 11–81.

Drouot-Montaigne. 2000. *Archéologie: Vente aux enchères publiques. Le dimanche 1ᵉʳ Octobre 2000 ..., collection Jean-Alain Mariaud de Serres; le lundi 2 Octobre ... appartenant à divers amateurs.* Paris: Drouot-Montaigne.

Edmonds, C. J. 1925. "Two Ancient Monuments in Southern Kurdistan." *The Geographical Journal* 65: 63–64.

Eichmann, Ricardo. 2013. "Frühe Großarchitektur der Stadt Uruk." Pp. 117–127 in *Uruk — 5000 Jahre Megacity. Begleitband zur Ausstellung "Uruk – 5000 Jahre Megacity" im Pergamonmuseum – Staatliche Museen zu Berlin, in den Reiss-Engelhorn-Museen in Mannheim,* ed. by N. Crüsemann et al. Petersberg: Michael Imhof Verlag.

Ellis, Richard S. 1968. *Foundation Deposits in Ancient Mesopotamia.* Yale Near Eastern Researches 2. New Haven CT: Yale University Press.

Elsner, John. 1994. "From the Pyramids to Pausanias and Piglet: Monuments, Travel and Writing." Pp. 224–254 in *Art and Text in Ancient Greek Culture,* ed. by S. Goldhill and R. Osborne. Cambridge: Cambridge University Press.

Englund, Robert K. 1995. "Late Uruk Pigs and other Herded Animals." Pp. 121–133 in *Beiträge zur Kulturgeschichte Vorderasianes. Festschrift für Rainer Michael Boehmer,* ed. by U. Finkbeiner, R. Dittmann, and H. Hauptmann. Mainz: Philipp von Zabern.

Englund, Robert K. 1996. *Proto-Cuneiform Texts from Divserse Collections.* MSVO 4. Berlin: Gebr. Mann Verlag.

Englund, Robert K., and Jean-Pierre Grégoire. 1991. *The Proto-Cuneiform Texts from Jemdet-Nasr.* MSVO 1. Berlin: Gebr. Mann Verlag.

Englund, Robert K., and Hans J. Nissen. 1993. *Die lexikalischen Listen der archaischen Texte aus Uruk.* ATU 3. Berlin: Gebr. Mann Verlag.

Eppihimer, Melissa A. 2009. "The Visual Legacy of Akkadian Kingship." Unpublished PhD dissertation, Harvard University.

Evans-Pritchard, E. E. 1962. "The Divine Kingship of the Shilluk of the Nilotic Sudan," *in Social Anthropology and Other Essays.* New York: Free Press.

Falkenstein, Adam. 1949. "Ein sumerisches Kultlied auf Samsu'iluna." *Archív Orientální* 17: 212–226.

von Falkenhausen, Lothar. 2011. "The Royal Audience and Its Reflections in Western Zhou Bronze Inscriptions." Pp. 239–270 in *Writing and Literacy in Early China: Studies from the Columbia Early China Seminar,* ed. by L. Feng and D. P. Branner. Seattle: University of Washigton Press.

Fash, William. 2002. "Religion and Human Agency in Ancient Maya History: Tales from the Hieroglyphic Stairway." *Cambridge Archaeological Journal* 12: 5–19.

Finkelstein, J. J. 1979. "Early Mesopotamia, 2500–1000 B.C." Pp. 50–110 in *Propaganda and Communication in World History, vol. 1: The Symbolic Instrument in Early Times*, ed. by H. D. Lasswell, D. Lerner, and H. Speier. Honolulu: The University Press of Hawaii.

Finkelstein, J. J. 1963. "The Antediluvian Kings: A University of California Tablet," *JCS* 17: 39–51.

Fischer, Claudia. 2002. "Twilight of the Sun-God." *Iraq* 64: 125–134.

Flückiger-Hawker, Esther. 1999. *Urnamma of Ur in Sumerian Literary Tradition*. OBO 166. Fribourg: University Press Fribourg Switzerland.

Forte, Elizabeth W. 1976. *Ancient Near Eastern Seals: A Selection of Stamp and Cylinder Seals from the Collection of Mrs. William H. Moore*. New York: The Metropolitan Museum of Art.

Fouchécour, Charles-Henri de. 1986. *Moralia: Les notions morales dans la littérature persane du 3ᵉ/9ᵉ au 7ᵉ/13ᵉ siècle*. Bibliothèque Iranienne 32. Paris: Éditions Recherche sur les Civilisations.

Foxvog, Daniel A. 2007. "The Sumerian Abgal and Nanše's Carp Actor." *NABU* 2007/67.

Frachetti, Michael D. 2008. *Pastoralist Landscapes and Social Interaction in Bronze Age Eurasia*. Berkeley: University of California Press.

Frankfort, Henri. 1939. *Cylinder Seals: A Documentary Essay on the Art and Religion of the Ancient Near East*. London: Macmillan and Co.

Frankfort, Henri. 1948. *Kingship and the Gods. A Study of the Near Eastern Religion as the Integration of Society and Nature*. Chicago: The University of Chicago Press.

Frankfort, Henri. 1954. *The Art and Architecture of the Ancient Orient*. Harmondsworth: Penguin Books.

Frankfort, Henri. 1955. *Stratified Cylinder Seals from the Diyala Region*. OIP 72. Chicago: The University of Chicago Press.

Frayne, Douglas R. 1981. "The Historical Correlations of the Sumerian Royal Hymns (2400–1900)." Unpublished PhD dissertation, Yale University.

Frayne, Douglas R. 1983. "Šulgi, the Runner." *JAOS* 103: 739–748.

Frayne, Douglas R. 1998. "New Light on the Reign of Išme-Dāgan." *ZA* 88: 6–44.

Friberg, Jöran. 1997/1998. "Round and Almost Round Numbers in Proto-Literate Metro-Mathematical Field Texts." *AfO* 44/45: 1–58.

Geertz, Clifford. 1980. *Negara: The Theater State in Nineteenth-Century Bali*. Princeton NJ: Princeton University Press.

Gelb, I. J., and B. Kienast. 1990. *Die altakkadischen Königsinschriften des dritten Jahrtausends v. Chr*. FAOS 7. Stuttgart: Franz Steiner.

Gelb, I. J., P. Steinkeller, and Robert M. Whiting. 1991. *Earliest Land Tenure Systems in the Near East: Ancient Kudurrus*, 2 vols. OIP 104. Chicago: The Oriental Institute of the University of Chicago.

George, A. R. 1993. *House Most High: The Temples of Ancient Mesopotamia*. Mesopotamian Civilizations 5. Winona Lake IN: Eisenbrauns.

George, A. R. 2011. (ed.) *Cuneiform Royal Inscriptions and Related Texts in the Schøyen Collection*, ed. by A. R. George. CUSAS 17. Bethesda MD: CDL Press.

George, A. R., and Junko Taniguchi. 2010. "The Dogs of Ninkilim, Part Two: Babylonian Rituals to Counter Field Pests." *Iraq* 72: 79–146.

Giesey, Robert L. 1997. "The Two Bodies of the French King." Pp. 224–239 in *Ernst Kantorowicz: Erträge der Doppeltagung Institute for Advanced Study, Princeton, Johann Wolfgang Goethe-Universität, Frankfurt*, ed. by R. L. Benson and J. Fried. Frankfurter historische Abhandlungen 39. Stuttgart: F. Steiner.

Glassner, Jean-Jacques. 2000a. *Ecrire à Sumer: l'invention du cunéiforme*. Paris: Seuil.

Glassner, Jean-Jacques. 2000b. "Les petits Etats mésopotamiens à la fin du 4e et au cours du 3e millénaire." Pp. 35–53 in *A Comparative Study of Thirty City-State Cultures*, ed. by M. H. Hansen. Historisk-filosofiske Skrifter 21. Copenhagen: The Royal Danish Academy of Sciences and Letters.

Glassner, Jean-Jacques. 2004. *Mesopotamian Chronicles*. Atlanta: Society for Biblical Literature. Originally published as *Chroniques Mésopotamiennes*. Paris: Les Belles Lettres, 1993.

Glassner, Jean-Jacques. 2014. "L'invention de l'écriture en Mésopotamie et le renforcement du prestige des élites." Pp. 25–33 in *Le Prestige. Autour des formes de la différenciation sociale*, ed. by F. Hurlet et al., Colloques de la MAE, René-Ginouvès, 10. Paris: Éditions de Boccard.

Glassner, Jean-Jacques. 2015. "The Diviner as Historian." *Studia Mesopotamica. Jahrbuch für altorientalische Geschichte und Kultur* 2: 131–147.

Grayson, A. K. 1975. *Assyrian and Babylonian Chronicles*. TCS 5. Locust Valley NY: J. J. Augustin.

Grayson, A. K. 1980. "Assyria and Babylonia." *Or. NS* 49: 140–194.

Green, Anthony. 1983. "Neo-Assyrian Apotropaic Figures." *Iraq* 45: 87–96.

Green, Anthony. 1986. "A Note on the Assyrian 'Goat-Fish,' 'Fish-Man' and 'Fish-Woman.'" *Iraq* 48: 25–30.

Green, M. W. 1984. "Early Sumerian Tax Collectors." *JCS* 36: 93–95.

Green, M. W. 1986. "Urum and Uqair." *ASJ* 8: 77–83.

Green, M. W., and Hans J. Nissen. 1987. *Zeichenliste der archaischen Texte aus Uruk*. ATU 2. Berlin: Gebr. Mann Verlag.

Grube, Nikolai. 1995. "Transformations of Maya Society at the End of the Preclassic: Processes of Change between the Predynastic and Dynastic History." Pp. 1–5 in *The Emergence of Lowland Maya Civilization*, ed. by N. Grube. Möckmühl: Verlag Anton Saurwein.

Hallo, William W. 1963. "On the Antiquity of Sumerian Literature." *JAOS* 83: 167–176.

Hallo, William W. 1970. "Antediluvian Cities." *JCS* 23: 57–67.

Hallo, William W. 1990. "The Limits of Skepticism." *JAOS* 110: 187–199.

Hallo, William W. 1991. "The Royal Correspondence of Larsa: III. The Princess and the Plea." Pp. 377–388 in *Marchands, diplomates et empereurs: Études sur la civilisation mésopotamienne offertes à Paul Garelli*, ed. by D. Charpin and F. Joannes. Paris: Éditions Recherche sur les Civilisations.

Hallo, William W. 1998. "New Directions in Historiography (Mesopotamia and Israel)." Pp. 109–128 in *dubsar anta-men, Studien zur Orientalistik: Festschrift für Willem H. Ph. Römer*, ed. by M. Dietrich and O. Loretz, AOAT 253 Münster: Ugarit-Verlag.

Hallo, William W. 2001. "Polymnia and Cleo," Pp. 195–209 in *Historiography in the Cuneiform World, Proceedings of the XLVe Rencontre Assyriologique Internationale*, Part 1, ed. by T. Abusch et al. Bethesda MD: CDL Press.

Hallo, William W. 2006. "A Sumerian Apocryphon? The Royal Correspondence of Ur Reconsidered." Pp. 85–104 in *Approaches to Sumerian Literature. Studies in Honour of*

Stip (H. L. J. Vanstiphout), ed. by P. Michalowski and N. Veldhuis. Cuneiform Monographs 35. Leiden: Brill.

Hansen, Donald P. 1970. "Al-Hiba, 1968–1969, a Preliminary Report." *Artibus Asiae* 32: 243–258.

Hansen, Donald P. 1998. "Art of the Royal Tombs of Ur: A Brief Interpretation." Pp. 43–72 in *Treasures from the Royal Tombs of Ur*, ed. by R. L. Zettler and L. Horne. Philadelphia: University of Pennsylvania, Museum of Archaeology and Anthropology.

Hansen, Donald P. 2002. "Through the Love of Ishtar." Pp. 91–112 in *Of Pots and Plans: Papers on the Archaeology and History of Mesopotamia and Syria presented to David Oates in Honour of His 75th Birthday*, ed. by L. al-Gailani Werr et al. London: Nabu Publications.

Hansen, Donald P. 2003a. "Art of the Akkadian Dynasty." Pp. 189–198 in *Art of the First Cities. The Third Millennium B.C. from the Mediterranean to the Indus*, ed. by J. Aruz. New York: The Metropolitan Museum of Art.

Hansen, Donald P. 2003b. "Mould Fragment with a Deified Ruler and the Goddess Ishtar." Pp. 206–207 in *Art of the First Cities. The Third Millennium B.C. from the Mediterranean to the Indus*, ed. by J. Aruz. New York: The Metropolitan Museum of Art.

Hansen, Donald P. 2003c. "Art of the Early City-States." Pp. 21–37 in *Art of the First Cities. The Third Millennium B.C. from the Mediterranean to the Indus*, ed. by J. Aruz with R. Wallenfels. NewYork: The Metropolian Museum of Art.

Harper, Prudence O., et al. 1995. *Assyrian Origins: Discoveries at Ashur on the Tigris: Antiquities in the Vorderasiatisches Museum, Berlin*. New York: The Metropolitan Museum of Art.

Heinrich, Ernst. 1936. *Kleinfunde aus den archaischen Tempelschichten in Uruk*. ADFU 1. Berlin: Deutsche Forschungsgemeinschaft.

Hockmann, Daniel. 2008. "Die Warka-Vase – eine neue Interpretation." *AOF* 35: 326–336.

Houston, Stephen D. 2000. "Into the Minds of Ancients: Advances in Maya Glyph Studies." *Journal of World Prehistory* 14: 121–201.

Houston, Stephen D. 2004. "Writing in Early Mesoamerica." Pp. 274–309 in *The First Writing. Script Invention as History and Process*, ed. by S. D. Houston. Cambridge: Cambridge University Press.

Hsu, Shih-Wei. 2010. "The Palermo Stone: the Earliest Royal Inscription from Ancient Egypt." *AOF* 37: 68–89.

Humphreys, R. Stephen. 1991. *Islamic History: A Framework for Inquiry*. Revised edition. Princeton NJ: Princeton University Press.

Jacobsen, Thorkild. 1939. *The Sumerian King List*. AS 11. Chicago: The University of Chicago Press.

Jacobsen, Thorkild. 1953. "The Reign of Ibbī-Suen." *JCS* 7: 36–47.

Jacobsen, Thorkild. 1963. "Ancient Mesopotamian Religion: The Central Concerns." *PAPS* 107/6: 473–484.

Jacobsen, Thorkild. 1976. *Treasures of Darkness. A History of Mesopotamian Religion*. New Haven CT: Yale University Press.

Jacobsen, Thorkild. 1987. *The Harps that Once … Sumerian Poetry in Translation*. New Haven CT: Yale University Press.

Jonker, Gerdien. 1995. *The Topography of Remembrance: The Deed, Tradition and Collective Memory in Mesopotamia*. Studies in the History of Religions (*Numen* Book Series) 68. Leiden: Brill.

Kantorowicz, Ernst H. 1957. *The King's Two Bodies: A Study in Medieval Political Theology.* Princeton NJ: Princeton University Press.

Kaplony, Peter. 1963. *Die Inschriften der ägyptischen Frühzeit.* 3 volumes. Wiesbaden: Harrassowitz.

Kees, Hermann. 1912. *Der Opfertanz des ägyptischen Königs.* Leipzig: J. C. Hinrichs.

Kienast, B. 1994. *Glossar zu den altakkadischen Königsinschriften.* FAOS 8. Stuttgart: Franz Steiner.

Kirch, Patrick V. 2010. *How Chiefs Became Kings: Divine Kingship and the Rise of Archaic States in Ancient Hawai'i.* Berkeley: University of California Press.

Klein, Jacob. 1976. "Šulgi and Gilgameš: Two Brother-Peers (Šulgi O)." Pp. 271–297 in *Kramer Anniversary Volume. Cuneiform Studies in Honor of Samuel Noah Kramer*, ed. by B. L. Eichler et al. AOAT 25. Neukirchen-Vluyn: Verlag Butzon & Bercker Kevelaer.

Klein, Jacob. 1981a. *Three Šulgi Hymns. Sumerian Royal Hymns Glorifying King Šulgi of Ur.* Ramat-Gan: Bar-Ilan University Press.

Klein, Jacob. 1981b. *The Royal Hymns of Shulgi King of Ur: Man's Quest for Immortal Fame.* Transactions of the American Philosophical Society vol. 71, part 7. Philadelphia: The American Philosophical Society.

Klein, Jacob. 2008. "The Brokmon Collection Duplicate of the Sumerian Kinglist (BT 14)." Pp. 77–91 in *On the Third Dynasty of Ur: Studies in Honor of Marcel Sigrist*, ed. by P. Michalowski. Boston: American Schools of Oriental Research.

Klein, Jacob, and Yitschak Sefati. 2014 . "The 'Stars (of) Heaven' and Cuneiform Writing." Pp. 85–102 in *He Has Opened Nisaba's House of Learning: Studies in Honor of Åke Waldemar Sjöberg on the Occasion of His 89th Birthday on August 1st 2013*, ed. by L. Sassmannshausen. Cuneiform Monographs 46. Leiden: Brill.

Klengel-Brandt, Evelyn. 1997. (ed.) *Mit sieben Siegeln versehen: Das Siegel in Wirtschaft und Kunst des Alten Orients.* Mainz am Rhein: P. von Zabern.

Kramer, Samuel N. 1963. *The Sumerians: Their History, Culture, and Character.* Chicago: The University of Chicago Press.

Krebernik, Manfred. 1984. *Die Beschwörungen aus Fara und Ebla. Untersuchungen zur ältesten keilschriftlichen Beschwörungsliteratur.* Texte und Studien zur Orientalistik 2. Hildesheim: Georg Olms Verlag.

Lambert, W. G. 1957. "Ancestors, Authors, and Canonicity." *JCS* 11: 1–14.

Lambert, W. G. 1962. "A Catalogue of Texts and Authors." *JCS* 16: 59–77.

Lambert, W. G. 1967. "Enmeduranki and Related Matters." *JCS* 21: 126–138.

Lambert, W. G. 1969. *Atra-ḫasīs: The Babylonian Story of the Flood.* Oxford: Oxford University Press.

Lambert, W. G. 1974. "The Seed of Kingship." Pp. 427–440 in *Le Palais et la Royauté: Archéologie et Civilisation, Compte rendu de la XIXᵉ rencontre assyriologique internationale*, ed. by P. Garelli. Paris: Geuthner.

Lambert, W. G. 1981. "Studies in UD.GAL.NUN." *Oriens Antiquus* 20: 81–97.

Lambert, W. G. 1998. "The Qualifications of Babylonian Diviners." Pp. 141–158 in *Festschrift für Rykle Borger zu seinem 65. Geburstag am 24. Mai 1994*, ed. by S. M. Maul. Cuneiform Monographs 10. Groningen: STYX Publications.

Landsberger, Benno. 1931. Review of C. J. Gadd, L. Legrain, and S. Smith, Royal Inscriptions, Ur Excavation Texts 1 (London, 1928). *OLZ* 34: 115–136.

Larsen, Mogens T. 1988. "Introduction: Literacy and Social Complexity." Pp. 173–191 in *State and Society: The Emergence and Development of Social Hierarchy and Political Centralization*, ed. by J. Gledhill, B. Bender, and M. T. Larsen. London: Unwin Hyman.

Lenzen, Heinrich. 1940. "Die Grabungsergebnisse." Pp. 6–31 in *Elfter vorläufiger Bericht über die von der Deutschen Forschungsgemeinschaft in Uruk-Warka unternommenen Ausgrabungen*, ed. by A. Nöldeke and H. Lenzen. Berlin: Verlag der Akademie der Wissenschaften.

Lenzi, Alan. 2008a. "The Uruk List of Kings and Sages and Late Mesopotamian Scholarship." *JANER* 8/2: 137–169.

Lenzi, Alan. 2008b. *Secrecy and the Gods: Secret Knowledge in Ancient Mesopotamia and Biblical Israel*. State Archives of Assyria, Studies 19. Helsinki: Neo-Assyrian Text Corpus Project.

Lindemeyer, Elke, and Lutz Martin. 1993. *Uruk Kleinefunde III: Kleinfunde im Vorderasiatischen Museum zu Berlin: Steingefässe und Asphalt, Farbreste, Fritte, Glas, Holz, Knochen/Elfenbein, Muschel/Perlmutt/Schnecke*. Ausgrabungen in Uruk-Warka, Endberichte 9, Deutsches Archäologisches Institut, Abteilung Baghdad. Mainz: Philipp von Zabern.

Liverani, Mario. 1973. "Memorandum on the Approach to Historiographic Texts." *Or. NS* 42: 178–194.

Liverani, Mario. 1993. "Model and Actualization. The Kings of Akkad in the Historical Tradition." Pp. 41–67 in *Akkad: The First World Empire. Structure, Ideology, Traditions*, ed. by M. Liverani. History of the Ancient Near East, Studies 5. Padua: Sargon srl.

Liverani, Mario. 2002. "Response to Gebhard Selz." Pp. 151–159 in *Material Culture and Mental Spheres. Rezeption archäologischer Denkrichtungen in der Vorderasiatischen Altertumskunde. Internationales Symposium für Hans J. Nissen, Berlin, 23.–24. Juni 2000*, ed. by A. Hausleiter, S. Kerner, and B. Müller-Neuhof. AOAT 293. Münster: Ugarit Verlag.

Lloyd, Alan B. 2014. *Ancient Egypt: State and Society*. Oxford: Oxford University Press.

Longhena, María. 2000. *Maya Script: A Civilization and Its Writing*. New York: Abbeville Press.

MacArthur, Elise V. 2010. "The Conception and Development of the Egyptian Writing System." Pp. 115–121 in *Visible Language. Inventions of Writing in the Ancient Near East and Beyond*, ed. by Ch. Woods with E. Teeter and G. Emberling. Oriental Institute Museum Publications 32. Chicago: The Oriental Institute of the University of Chicago.

McCaffrey, Kathleen. 2013. "The Sumerian Sacred Marriage: Texts and Images." Pp. 227–245 in *The Sumerian World*, ed. by H. Crawford. London: Routlege.

Marchesi, Gianni. 2010. "The Sumerian King List and the Early History of Babylonia." Pp. 231–248 in ana turri gimilli: *Studi dedicati al Padre Werner R. Mayer, S.J. da amici e allievi*, ed. by M. G. Biga and M. Liverani. Vicino Oriente, Quaderno V. Rome: Università degli Studi di Roma "La Sapienza."

Marchesi, Gianni, and Nicolò Marchetti. 2011. *Royal Statuary of Early Dynastic Mesopotamia*. Mesopotamian Civilizations 14. Winona Lake IN: Eisenbrauns.

Marcus, Joyce. 1992. *Mesoamerican Writing Systems: Propaganda, Myth and History in Four Ancient Civilizations*. Princeton NJ: Princeton University Press.

Marlow, Louise. 2004. "*The Way of Viziers and the Lamp of Commanders (Minhāj al-wuzarāʾ wa-sirāj al-umarāʾ)* of Aḥmad al-Iṣfahbadhī and the Literary and Political Culture of Early Fourteenth-Century Iran." Pp. 169–193 in *Writers and Rulers: Perspectives on Their*

Relationship from Abbasid to Safavid Times, ed. by B. Gruendler and L. Marlow. Literaturen im Kontext: Arabisch – Persisch – Türkisch 16. Wiesbaden: Reichert Verlag.

Marlow, Louise. 2009. "Surveying Recent Literature on the Arabic and Persian Mirrors for Princes Genre." *History Compass* 7: 523–538.

Martin, Simon, and Nicolai Grube. 2008. *Chronicle of the Maya Kings and Queens: Deciphering the Dynasties of the Ancient Maya*. London: Thames and Hudson.

Matthews, Donald M. 1990. *Principles of Composition in Near Eastern Glyptic of the Later Second Millennium B.C.* Freiburg Schweiz: Universitätsverlag.

Matthews, Roger J. 1993. *Cities, Seals and Writing: Archaic Seal Impressions from Jemdet Nasr and Ur*. MSVO 2. Berlin: Gebr. Mann Verlag.

Meisami, Julie S. 2004. "Rulers and the Writing of History." Pp. 73–95 in *Writers and Rulers: Perspectives on Their Relationship from Abbasid to Safavid Times*, ed. by B. Gruendler and L. Marlow. Literaturen im Kontext: Arabisch – Persisch – Türkisch 16. Wiesbaden: Reichert Verlag.

Merhav, Rivka, et al. 1981. (ed.) *A Glimpse into the Past: The Joseph Ternbach Collection*. Jerusalem: The Israel Museum.

Metzger, Martin. 1985. *Königsthron und Gottesthron: Thronformen und Throndarstellungen in Ägypten und im Vorderen Orient im dritten und zweiten Jahrtausend vor Christus und deren Bedeutung für das Verständnis von Aussagen über den Thron im Alten Testament*. AOAT 15/1 and 15/2. Kevelaer: Verlag Butzon & Bercker.

Michalowski, Piotr. 1983. "History as a Charter: Some Observations on the Sumerian King List." *JAOS* 103: 237–248.

Michalowski, Piotr. 1987. "Charisma and Control: On Continuity and Change in Early Mesopotamian Bureaucratic Systems." Pp. 55–68 in *The Organization of Power: Aspects of Bureaucracy in the Ancient Near East*, ed. by McG. Gibson and R. D. Biggs. Studies in Ancient Oriental Civilization 46. Chicago: The Oriental Institute of the University of Chicago.

Michalowski, Piotr. 2003. "An Early Dynastic Tablet of ED Lu A from Tell Brak (Nagar)," *CDLJ* 2003/3. URL: http://cdli.ucla.edu/pubs/edij/2003/cdlj2003_003.html.

Michalowski, Piotr. 2006. "The Strange History of Tummal." Pp. 145–165 in *Approaches to Sumerian Literature. Studies in Honour of Stip (H. L. J. Vanstiphout)*, ed. by P. Michalowski and N. Veldhuis. Cuneiform Monographs 35. Leiden: Brill.

Michalowski, Piotr. 2008. "The Mortal Kings of Ur: A Short Century of the Divine Rule in Ancient Mesopotamia." Pp. 219–235 in *Religion and Power: Divine Kingship in the Ancient World and Beyond*, ed. by N. Brisch. Oriental Institute Seminars 4. Chicago: The Oriental Institute of the University of Chicago.

Michalowski, Piotr. 2011. *The Correspondence of the Kings of Ur: An Epistolary History of an Ancient Mesopotamian Kingdom*. Mesopotamian Civilizations 15. Winona Lake IN: Eisenbrauns.

Michalowski, Piotr. 2016. "The Ur III Literary Footprint and the Historian." Pp. 105–126 in *Not Only History: Proceedings of the Conference in Honor of Mario Liverani Held in Sapienza – Università di Roma, Dipartimento di Scienza dell'Antichità, 20–21 April 2009*, ed. by G. Bartoloni and M. G. Biga. Winona Lake IN: Eisenbrauns.

Milano, Lucio, and Aage Westenholz. 2015. *The "Šuilišu Archive" and Other Sargonic Texts in Akkadian*. CUSAS 27. Bethesda MD: CDL Press.

Miller, Naomi F., Philip H. Jones, and Holly Pittman. 2015. "Sign and Image: Representations of Plants on the Warka Vase of Early Mesopotamia." Posted March 16, 2016, at ScholarlyCommons, http://repository.upenn.edu/penn_museum_papers/2

Mittermayer, Catherine. 2012. "Die Uruk-Isin Dynastie – ein Konstrukt der Isn-Dynastie?" Pp. 313–326 in in *Organization, Representation and Symbols of Power in the Ancient Near East*, Proceedings of the 54th Rencontre Assyriologique Internationale at Würzburg 20–25 July 2008, ed. by G. Wilhelm. Winona Lake IN: Eisenbrauns.

Monaco, Salvatore F. 2011a. "Two Archaic Mathematical Tablets." *SEL:* 28: 1–5.

Monaco, Salvatore F. 2011b. *Early Dynastic mu-iti Cereal Texts in the Cornell University Cuneiform Collections*, CUSAS 14. Bethesda MD: CDL Press.

Monaco, Salvatore F. 2014. *Archaic Bullae and Tablets in the Cornell University Collections.* CUSAS 21. Bethesda MD: CDL Press.

Monaco, Salvatore F. 2016. *Archaic Cuneiform Tablets from Private Collections.* CUSAS 31. Bethesda MD: CDL Press.

Moortgat-Correns, Ursula. 1989. *La Mesopotamia, Storia universale dell'arte, Sezione prima, Le civiltà antiche e primitive.* Torino: UTET.

Mumford, Gregory D. 1999. "Wadi Maghara." Pp. 875–878 in *Encyclopedia of the Archaeology of Ancient Egypt*, ed. by K. Bard and S. Shubert. London: Routledge.

Muscarella, Oscar W. 1981. (ed.) *Ladders to Heaven: Art Treasures from the Lands of the Bible.* Toronto: MacClelland and Stewart Ltd.

Muscarella, Oscar W. 1988. *Bronze and Iron: Ancient Near Eastern Artifacts in The Metropolitan Museum of Art.* New York: The Metropolitan Museum of Art.

Muscarella, Oscar W. 2003. "Foundation Peg with Tablet of Enmetena." Pp. 80–81 in *Art of the First Cities. The Third Millennium B.C. from the Mediterranean to the Indus*, ed. by J. Aruz with R. Wallenfels. NewYork: The Metropolian Museum of Art.

Nissen, Hans J. 1986. "The Archaic Texts from Uruk." *World Archaeology* 17: 317–334.

Nissen, Hans J., Peter Damerow, and Robert K. Englund. 1993. *Archaic Bookkeeping: Early Writing and Techniques of Economic Administration in the Ancient Near East.* Chicago: The University of Chicago Press.

O'Connor, David. 2011. "The Narmer Palette: A New Interpretation." Pp. 145–152 in *Before the Pyramids: The Origins of Egyptian Civilization*, ed. by E. Teeter. Oriental Institute Museum Publications 33. Chicago: The Oriental Institute of the University of Chicago.

Oppenheim, A. L. 1954. "The Seafaring Merchants of Ur." *JAOS* 74: 6–17.

Ornan, Tallay. 2013. "A Silent Message: Godlike Kings in Mesopotamian *Art.*" Pp. 569– 595 *in Critical Approaches to Ancient Near Eastern Art*, ed. by B. Brown and M. H. Feldman. Berlin: De Gruyter.

Parkinson, Richard B. 1999. *Cracking Codes: The Rosetta Stone and Decipherment.* Berkeley: University of California Press.

Parrot, André. 1960. *Sumer.* L'Universe des forms 1. Paris: Gallimard.

Paulus, Susanne. 2014. *Die babylonischen Kudurru-Inschriften von der kassitischen bis zur frühneubabylonischen Zeit.* Münster: Ugarit-Verlag.

Pittman, Holy, and Joan Aruz. 1987. *Ancient Art in Miniature: Near Eastern Seals from the Collection of Martin and Sarah Cherkasky.* New York: The Metropolitan Museum of Art.

Pitts, Audrey. 2015. "The Cult of the Deified King in Ur III Mesopotamia." Unpublished PhD dissertation, Harvard University.

Pomponio, Francesco. 1987. *La prosopografia dei testi presargonici di Fara.* Studi Semitici NS 3. Rome: Univerità degli Studi "La Sapienza."

Pongratz-Leisten, Beate. 1999. *Herrschaftsformen in Mesopotamien: Formen der Kommunikation zwischen Gott und König in 2. und 1. Jahrtausend v.Chr.* State Archives of Assyria Studies 10. Helsinki: The Neo-Assyrian Text Corpus Project.

Porada, Edith. 1995. *Man and Images in the Ancient Near East*. Wakefield RI: Moyer Bell.

Porter, Anne. 2013. "When the Subject *is* the Object: Relational Ontologies, the Partible Person and the Images of Naram-Sin." Pp. 597–617 in *Critical Approaches to Ancient Near Eastern Art*, ed. by B. Brown and M. H. Feldman. Berlin: De Gruyter.

Possehl, Gregory L. 1998. "Sociocultural Complexity Without the State: The Indus Civilization." Pp. 261–291 in *Archaic States*, ed. by G. M. Feinman and J. Marcus. Santa Fe NM: School of American Research Press.

Postgate, Nicholas. 2005. "New Angles on Early Writing." *Cambridge Archaeological Journal* 15: 275–280.

Postgate, Nicholas, Tao Wang, and Toby Wilkinson. 1995. "The Evidence of Early Writing: Utilitarian or Ceremonial?" *Antiquity* 69: 459–480.

Potts, Timothy. 2001. "Reading the Sargonic 'Historical-Literary' Tradition: Is there a Middle Course?" Pp. 397–408 in *Historiography in the Cuneiform World, Proceedings of the XLVe Rencontre Assyriologique Internationale*, Part 1, ed. by T. Abusch et al. Bethesda MD: CDL Press.

Powell, Marvin A. 1991. "Narām-Sîn, Son of Sargon: Ancient History, Famous Names, and a Famous Babylonian Forgery." *ZA* 81: 20–30.

Pritchard, James B. 1969. (ed.) *Ancient Near Eastern Texts Relating to the Old Testament*. 3rd ed. with supplement. Princeton NJ: Princeton University Press.

Rashid, Subhi A. 1983. *Gründungsfiguren im Iraq*. Prähistorische Bronzefunde, Abteilung I; Bd. 2. Munich: C. H. Beck.

Reade, Julian. 2002. "Early Monuments in Gulf Stone at the British Museum, with Observations on Some Gudea Statues and the Location of Agade." *ZA* 92: 258–295.

Reiner, Erica. 1961. "The Etiological Myth of the 'Seven Sages.'" *Or. NS* 30: 1–11.

Renger, Johannes. 1969. "Untersuchungen zum Priestertum der altbabylonischen Zeit. 2. Teil." *ZA* 59: 104–230.

Richardson, Christopher. 2015. "North Korea's Kim Dynasty: The Making of a Personality Cult." *The Guardian*, February 6, 2015.

Sahlins, Marshall. 1981. *Historical Metaphors and Mythical Realities: Structure in the Early History of the Sandwich Islands Kingdom*. ASAO Special Publications 1. Ann Arbor MI: The University of Michigan Press.

Sahlins, Marshall. 1985. *Islands of History*. Chicago: The University of Chicago Press.

Sahlins, Marshall. 1995. *How "Natives" Think About Captain Cook, For Example*. Chicago: The University of Chicago Press.

Sallaberger, Walther. 1997. "Nippur als religiöses Zentrum Mesopotamiens im historischen Wandel." Pp. 147–168 in *Die orientalische Stadt: Kontinuität, Wandel, Bruch*, ed. by G. Wilhelm. Saarbrücken: Saarbrücker Druckerei und Verlag.

Sallaberger, Walther. 1999. "Ur III-Zeit." Pp. 121–390 in *Mesopotamien: Akkade-Zeit und Ur III-Zeit*, ed. by P. Attinger and M. Wäfler. OBO 160/3. Freiburg: Universitätsverlag Freiburg Schweiz.

Sallaberger, Walther. 2002. "Den Göttern nahe – und fern den Menschen? Formen der Sakralität des altmesopotamischen Herrschers." Pp. 85–98 in *Die Sakralität von Herrschaft. Herrschaftslegitimierung im Wechsel der Zeiten und Räume*, ed. by F.-R. Erkens. Berlin: Akademie Verlag.

Sallaberger, Walther. 2003. "Nachrichten an den Palast von Ebla. Eine Deutung von níĝ-mul (an)." Pp. 607–611 in *Semitic and Assyriological Studies Presented to Pelio Fronzaroli by Pupils and Colleagues*. Wiesbaden: Harrassowitz.

Schele, Linda, and Mary Miller. 1986. *The Blood of Kings: Dynasty and Ritual in Maya Art*. New York: Brazillier.

Schmandt-Besserat, Denise. 1993. "Images of Enship." Pp. 201–219 in *Between the Rivers and over the Mountains: Archaeologica anatolica et mesopotamica Alba Palmieri dedicata*, ed. by M. Frangipane et al. Rome: Dipartimento di Scienze Storiche e Antropologiche dell'Antichità, Università di Roma "La Sapienza."

Schmidt, Jürgen, et al. 1972. *Vorläufiger Bericht über die ... Ausgrabungen in Uruk-Warka 26 and 27*. Abhandlungen der deutschen Orient-Gesellschaft 16. Berlin: Gebr. Mann Verlag.

Schrakamp, Ingo. 2016. "Akkadian Empire." Pp. 1–10 in The Encyclopedia of Empire, ed. by J. M. MacKenzie. Hoboken NJ: John Wiley & Sons.

Schrakamp, Ingo, and Walther Sallaberger. 2015. "Philological Data for a Historical Chronology of Mesopotamia in the 3rd Millennium." Pp. 1–136 in in *Associated Regional Chronologies for the Ancient Near East and the Eastern Mediterranean: History and Philology*, ed. by W. Sallaberger and I. Schrakamp. ARCANE 3. Turnhout: Brepols.

Selz, Gebhard J. 1998. "Über Mesopotamische Herrschaftskonzepte. Zu den Ursprüngen mesopotamischer Herrscherideologie im 3. Jahrtausend." Pp. 281–344 in *dub-sar anta-men: Studien zur Altorientalistik. Festschrift für Willem H. Ph. Römer*, ed. by M. Dietrich and O. Loretz. AOAT 253. Münster: Ugarit-Verlag.

Selz, Gebhard J. 2008. "The Divine Prototypes." Pp. 13–31 in *Religion and Power: Divine Kingship in the Ancient World and Beyond*, ed. by N. Brisch. Oriental Institute Seminars 4. Chicago: The Oriental Institute of the University of Chicago.

Sharer, Robert J. 2012. "Time of Kings and Queens." *Expedition* 54: 26–35.

Sharer, Robert J., and Loa P. Taxler. 2006. *The Ancient Maya*. 6th ed. Stanford CA: Stanford University Press.

Sharlach, Tonia M. 2008. "Priestesses, Concubines, and the Daughters of Men: Disentangling the Meaning of the Word lukur in Ur III Times." Pp. 177–183 in *On the Third Dynasty of Ur: Studies in Honor of Marcel Sigrist*, ed. by P. Michalowski. Boston: American Schools of Oriental Research.

Shaughnessy, Edward L. 2010. "The Beginnings of Writing in China." Pp. 215–221 in *Visible Language. Inventions of Writing in the Ancient Near East and Beyond*, ed. by Ch. Woods with E. Teeter and G. Emberling. Oriental Institute Museum Publications 32. Chicago: The Oriental Institute of the University of Chicago.

Sjöberg, Åke W. 1976. "The Old Babylonian Edubba." Pp. 159–179 in *Sumerological Studies in Honor of Thorkild Jacobsen*. AS 20. Chicago: The University of Chicago Press.

Smith, Adam. 2011. "The Evidence for Scribal Training at Anyang." Pp. 173–205 in *Writing and Literacy in Early China: Studies from the Columbia Early China Seminar*, ed. by L. Feng and D. P. Branner. Seattle: University of Washington Press.

Sollberger, Edmond. 1954/1956. "Sur la chronologie des roix d'Ur et quelques problèmes connexes." *AfO* 17: 10–48.

Sollberger, Edmond. 1968. "The Cruciform Monument." *Jaarbericht Ex Oriente Lux* 20: 50–70.

Sollberger, Edmond. 1969. "The Rulers of Lagaš." *JCS* 21: 279–291.

Sotheby's. 1992. *Western Asiatic Cylinders and Antiquities from the Erlenmeyer Collection (Part 1)*. Sotheby's, London, Thursday 9th July, 1992. London: Sotheby's.

Stauder, Andréas. 2010. "The Earliest Egyptian Writing." Pp. 137–147 in *Visible Language. Inventions of Writing in the Ancient Near East and Beyond*, ed. by Ch. Woods with E. Teeter and G. Emberling. Oriental Institute Museum Publications 32. Chicago: The Oriental Institute of the University of Chicago.

Steele, Laura D. 2002. "Mesopotamian Elements in the Proem of Parmenides? Correspondences between the Sun-God Helios and Shamash." *The Classical Quarterly* 52: 583–588.

Steible, Horst. 1982. *Die altsumerischen Bau- und Weihinschriften, Teil II*. FAOS 5. Wiesbaden: Franz Steiner.

Steible, Horst. 1983. *Glossar zu den altsumerischen Bau- und Weihinschriften*. FAOS 6. Wiesbaden: Franz Steiner.

Steinkeller, Piotr. 1981. "More on the Ur III Royal Wives." *ASJ* 3: 77–92.

Steinkeller, Piotr. 1987. "The Name of Nergal." *ZA* 77: 162–168.

Steinkeller, Piotr. 1988. "Grundeigentum in Babylonien von Uruk IV bis zur frühdynastischen Periode II." *Jahrbuch für Wirtschaftswissenschaften* 1987/88: 11–27.

Steinkeller, Piotr. 1990. "More on the Name of Nergal and Related Matters." *ZA* 80: 53–59.

Steinkeller, Piotr. 1992. "Mesopotamia in the Third Millennium B.C." Pp. 724–732 in *The Anchor Bible Dictionary*, vol. 4 ed. by D. N. Freedman. New York: Doubleday.

Steinkeller, Piotr. 1993a. "Early Political Development in Mesopotamia and the Origins of the Sargonic Empire." Pp. 107–229 in *Akkad – The First World Empire: Structure, Ideology, Traditions*, ed. by M. Liverani. History of the Ancient Near East / Studies 5. Padua: Sargon srl.

Steinkeller, Piotr. 1993b. Review of A. Westenholz, Old Sumerian and Old Akkadian Texts in Philadelphia. Part Two: The 'Akkadian' Texts, The Enlilemaba Texts, and the Onion Archive (Copenhagen, 1987). *JNES* 52: 141–145.

Steinkeller, Piotr. 1995a. Review of J. Marzahn, Altsumerische Verwaltungstexte aus Girsu/Lagaš, VAT 25 (Berlin, 1991). *JAOS* 115: 540–543.

Steinkeller, Piotr. 1995b. Review of M.W. Green and H. J. Nissen, Zeichenliste der Archaischen Texte aus Uruk, ATU 2 (Berlin, 1987). *BiOr* 52: 689–713.

Steinkeller, Piotr. 1998. "Inanna's Archaic Symbol." Pp. 87–100 in *Written on Clay and Stone: Ancient Near Eastern Studies Presented to Krystyna Szarzyńska on the Occasion of Her 80th Birthday*, ed. by J. Braun, K. Łyczkowska, M. Popko, and P. Steinkeller. Warsaw: Agade.

Steinkeller, Piotr. 1999a. "On Rulers, Priests and Sacred Marriage: Tracing the Evolution of Early Sumerian Kingship." Pp. 103–137 in *Priests and Officials in the Ancient Near East: Papers of the Second Colloquium on the Ancient Near East – The City and Its Life*, ed. by K. Watanabe. Heidelberg: Universitätsverlag C. Winter.

Steinkeller, Piotr. 1999b. "Land-Tenure Conditions in Southern Babylonia under the Sargonic Dynasty." Pp. 553–571 in *Munuscula Mesopotamica: Festschrift für Johannes Renger*, ed. by B. Böck, E. Cancik-Kirschbaum, and Th. Richter. Alter Orient und Altes Testament 267. Münster: Ugarit-Verlag.

Steinkeller, Piotr. 2001. "New Light on the Hydrology and Topography of Southern Babylonia in the Third Millennium." *ZA* 91: 22–84.

Steinkeller, Piotr. 2002a. "Stars and Stripes in Ancient Mesopotamia: A Note on Two Decorative Elements of Babylonian Doors." Pp. 359–371 in *Ingenious Man, Inquisitive Soul: Essays in Iranian and Central Asian Archaeology for C. C. Lamberg-Karlovsky on the Occasion of his 65th Birthday*, ed. by D. T. Potts. Iranica Antiqua 37. Gent.

Steinkeller, Piotr. 2002b. "Archaic City Seals and the Question of Early Babylonian Unity."
Pp. 249–257 in *Riches Hidden in Secret Places: Ancient Near Eastern Studies in Memory of Thorkild Jacobsen*, ed. by T. Abusch. Winona Lake IN: Eisenbrauns.

Steinkeller, Piotr. 2002c. "More on the Archaic City Seals." *NABU* 2002/30.

Steinkeller, Piotr. 2003. "An Ur III Manuscript of the Sumerian King List." Pp. 267–292 in *Literatur, Politik und Recht in Mesopotamien: Festschrift für Claus Wilcke*, ed. by W. Sallaberger, K. Volk, and A. Zgoll. Orientalia Biblica et Christiana 14. Wiesbaden: Harrassowitz.

Steinkeller, Piotr. 2004a. "The Function of Written Documentation in the Administrative Praxis of Early Babylonia." Pp. 65–88 in *Creating Economic Order: Record-keeping, Standardization, and the Development of Accounting in the Ancient Near East*, ed. by M. Hudson and C. Wunsch. International Scholars Conference on Ancient Near Eastern Economies 4. Bethesda MD: CDL Press.

Steinkeller, Piotr. 2004b. "Studies in Third Millennium Paleography, 4: Sign KIŠ," *Zeitschrift für Assyriologie* 94: 175–85.

Steinkeller, Piotr. 2005a. "Of Stars and Men: The Conceptual and Mythological Setup of Babylonian Extispicy." Pp. 11–47 in *Biblical and Oriental Essays in Memory of William L. Moran*, ed. by A. Gianto. *Biblica et Orientalia*. Rome.

Steinkeller, Piotr. 2005b. "The Priestess *égi-zi* and Related Matters." Pp. 301–310 in *"An Experienced Scribe Who Neglects Nothing": Ancient Near Eastern Studies in Honor of Jacob Klein*, ed. by Y. Sefati et al. Bethesda MD: CDL Press.

Steinkeller, Piotr. 2010. "On the Location of the Towns of Ur-Zababa and Dimat-Enlil and on the Course of the Arahtum." Pp. 369–382 in *Festschrift für Gernot Wilhelm anläßlich seines 65. Geburtstages am 28. Januar 2010*, ed. by J. C. Fincke. Dresden: ISLET.

Steinkeller, Piotr. 2011. "Third-Millennium Royal and Votive Inscriptions." Pp. 1–28 in *Cuneiform Royal Inscriptions and Related Texts in the Schøyen Collection*, ed. by A. R. George. CUSAS 17. Bethesda MD: CDL Press.

Steinkeller, Piotr. 2012. "New Light on Marhaši and its Contacts with Makkan and Babylonia." Pp. 261–274 in *Aux marges de l'archéologie. Hommage à Serge Cleuziou*, ed. by J. Giraud & G. Gernez. Travaux de la Maison René-Ginouvès 16. Paris: Éd. De Boccard.

Steinkeller, Piotr. 2013a. "An Archaic 'Prisoner Plaque' from Kiš." Pp. 131–157 in *Mélanges Paolo Matthiae*, ed. by M. G. Biga, J.-M. Durand, and D. Charpin. *Revue d'Assyriologie* 107. Paris.

Steinkeller, Piotr. 2013b. "How Did Šulgi and Išbi-Erra Ascend to Heaven?" Pp. 459–478 in *Literature as Politics, Politics as Literature: Essays on the Ancient Near East in Honor of Peter Machinist*, ed. by D. S. Vanderhooft and A. Winitzer. Winona Lake IN: Eisenbrauns.

Steinkeller, Piotr. 2013c. "Puzur-Inšušinak at Susa: A Pivotal Episode of Early Elamite History Reconsidered." Pp. 293–317 in *Susa and Elam. Archaeological, Philological, Historical and Geographical Perspectives, Proceedings of the International Congress Held at Ghent University, December 14–17, 2009*, ed. by K. De Graef and J. Tavernier. Mémoires de la Délégation en Perse 58. Leiden: Brill.

Steinkeller, Piotr. 2013d. "Corvée Labor in Ur III times." Pp. 347–424 in *From the 21st Century B.C. to the 21st Century A.D. Proceedings of the International Conference on Sumerian Studies Held in Madrid 22–24 July 2010*, ed. by S. Garfinkle and M. Molina. Winona Lake IN: Eisenbrauns.

Steinkeller, Piotr. 2014a. "Marhaši and Beyond: The Jiroft Civilization in a Historical Perspective." Pp. 691–707 in *"My Life is Like a Summer Rose": Maurizio Tosi e l'Archaeologia Come Mode di Vivere. Papers in Honour of Maurizio Tosi for his 70th Birthday*, ed. by C. C. Lamberg-Karlovsky and B. Genito. BAR International Series 2690. Oxford: Archaeopress.

Steinkeller, Piotr. 2014b. "A Campaign of Southern City-States against Kiš as Documented in ED IIIa Sources from Šuruppak (Fara)." Unpublished paper presented at the 224th Meeting of the American Oriental Society, Phoenix, March 14–17, 2014.

Steinkeller, Piotr. 2015a. "The Gutian Period in Chronological Perspective." Pp. 281–288 in *Associated Regional Chronologies for the Ancient Near East and the Eastern Mediterranean: History and Philology*, ed. by W. Sallaberger and I. Schrakamp. ARCANE 3. Turnhout: Brepols.

Steinkeller, Piotr. 2015b. "On the Reading of the Pre-Sargonic Personal Name DI-[d]Utu and Related Matters." *JNES* 74: 39–44.

Steinkeller, Piotr. 2015c. "The Employment of Labor on National Building Projects in the Ur III Period." Pp. 137–236 in *Labor in the Ancient World*, ed. by P. Steinkeller and M. Hudson. Dresden: ISLET.

Steinkeller, Piotr. 2016. "Luck, Fortune, and Destiny in Ancient Mesopotamia — Or How the Sumerians and Babylonians Thought of Their Place in the Flow of Things." Pp. 5–24 in *Fortune and Misfortune in the Ancient Near East, Proceedings of the 60th Rencontre Assyriologique Internationale at Warsaw, 21–25 July, 2014*, ed. by O. Drewnowska and M. Sandowicz. Winona Lake IN: Eisenbrauns.

Steinkeller, Piotr. 2017. "An Estimate of the Population of the City of Umma in Ur III Times." Pp. 535–566 in *At the Dawn of History. Ancient Near Eastern Studies in Honour of J. N. Postgate*, ed by Y. Heffron, A. Stone, and M. Worthington. Winona Lake IN: Eisenbrauns.

Stewart, David. 2015. "The Ancient World's Most Massive Inscription." Maya Decipherment. Ideas on Maya Writing and Iconography Weblog, July 8, 2015. Posted on https: decipherment.wordpress.com.

Streck, Maximilian. 1916. *Assurbanipal und die letzten assyrischen Könige bis zum Untergange Niniveh's*. VB 7. Leipzig: J. C. Hinrichs.

Strommenger, Eva. 1962. *Fünf Jahrtausende Mesopotamien. Die Kunst von den Anfängen um 5000 v. Chr. bis zu Alexander dem Großen*. Munich: Hirmer Verlag.

Sun, Yan. 2003. "Bronzes, Mortuary Practice and Political Strategies of the Yan during the Early Western Zhou Period." *Antiquity* 77: 761–770.

Suter, Claudia E. 2000. *Gudea's Temple Building: The Representation of an Early Mesopotamian Ruler in Text and Image*. Cuneiform Monographs 17. Groningen: STYX Publications.

Suter, Claudia E. 2007. "Between Human and Divine: High Priestesses in Images from the Akkad to the Isin-Larsa Period." Pp. 317–361 in *Ancient Near Eastern Art in Context, Studies in Honor of Irene J. Winter by Her Students*, ed. by J. Cheng and M. H. Feldman. Leiden: Brill.

Suter, Claudia E. 2010. "Ur III Kings in Images: A Reappraisal." Pp. 319–349 in *Your Praise is Sweet. A Memorial Volume for Jeremy Black from Students, Colleagues and Friends*, ed. by H. Baker, E. Robson, and G. Zólyomi. London: British Institute for the Study of Iraq.

Suter, Claudia E. 2013. "The Divine Gudea on Ur III Seal Images." Pp. 309–324 in *Beyond Hatti: A Tribute to Gary Beckman*, ed. by B. J. Collins and P. Michalowski. Atlanta: Lockwood Press.

Suter, Claudia E. 2014. "Human, Divine or Both? The Uruk Vase and the Problem of Ambiguity in Early Mesopotamian Visual Arts." Pp. 545–568 in *Critical Approaches to Ancient Near Eastern Art*, ed. by B. Brown and M. H. Feldman. Berlin: De Gruyter.

Suter, Claudia E. 2015. "Gudea's Kingship and Divinity." Pp. 499–523 in *Marbeh Ḥokmah: Studies in the Bible and the Ancient Near East in Loving Memory of Victor Avigdor Hurowitz*. Winona Lake IN: Eisenbraus.

Szarzyńska, Krystyna. 1987. "The Sumerian Goddess Inana-KUR." Pp. 7–14 in *Papers on Asia Past and Present*, ed. by M. Mejor, M. Popko, and B. Składanek. Orientalia Varsoviensia 1. Warsaw: Wydawnictwa Uniwersytetu Warszawskiego.

Szarzyńska, Krystyna. 1993. "Offerings for the Goddess Inana in Archaic Uruk." *RA* 87: 7–26.

Szarzyńska, Krystyna. 2011. "Observations on the Temple Precinct EŠ₃ in Archaic Uruk." *JCS* 63: 1–4.

Tadmor, Hayim. 1997. "Propaganda, Literature, Historiography: Cracking the Code of the Assyrian Royal Inscriptions." Pp. 325–338 in *Assyria 1995: Proceedings of the 10ᵗʰ Anniversary Symposium of the Neo-Assyrian Text Corpus Project, Helsinki, September 7– 11, 1995*, ed. by S. Parpola and R. M. Whiting. Helsinki: The Neo-Assyrian Text Corpus Project.

Taylor, Jon. 2008. "Lexicographic Study of the Already-Ancient in Antiquity." Pp. 203–210 in *Proceedings of the 51ˢᵗ Rencontre Assyriologique Internationale Held at the Oriental Institute of The University of Chicago July 18–22, 2005*, ed. by R. D. Biggs, J. Myers, and M. T. Roth. SAOC 62. Chicago: The University of Chicago Press.

Tinney, Steve. 1995. "A New Look at Naram-Sin and the 'Great Rebellion.'" *JCS* 47: 1–14.

Tiradritti, Francesco. 1999. *Egyptian Treasures from the Egyptian Museum in Cairo*. New York: H. N. Abrams.

Trigger, Bruce G. 1990. "Monumental Architecture: A Thermodynamic Explanation of Symbolic Behaviour." *World Archaeology* 22: 117–130.

Tsukimoto, Akio. 1999. "'By the Hand of Madi-Dagan, the Scribe and *Apkallu*-Priest' – A Medical Text from the Middle Euphrates Region." Pp. 187–200 in *Priests and Officials in the Ancient Near East: Papers of the Second Colloquium on the Ancient Near East – The City and Its Life*, ed. by K. Watanabe. Heidelberg: Universitätsverlag C. Winter.

Uphill, Eric. 1965. "The Egyptian Sed-Festival Rites." *JNES* 24: 365–383.

Valeri, Valerio. 1985. *Kingship and Sacrifice: Ritual and Society in Ancient Hawaii*. Chicago: The University of Chicago Press.

Van De Mieroop, Marc. 1999. "Literature and Political Discourse in Ancient Mesopotamia: Sargon II of Assyria and Sargon of Agade." Pp. 327–339 in *Munuscula Mesopotamica: Festschrift für Johannes Renger*, ed. by B. Böck et al. AOAT 267. Münster: Ugarit-Verlag.

Van Driel, Govert. 1973a. "On 'Standard'' and 'Triumphal' Inscriptions." Pp. 99–106 in *Symbolae biblicae et Mesopotamicae Francisco Mario Theodor de Liagre Böhl dedicate*, ed. by M. A. Beek et al. Leiden: Brill.

Van Driel, Govert. 1973b. Review of R. J. Ellis, Foundation Deposits in Ancient Mesopotamia. *JAOS* 93: 67–74.

Veldhuis, Niek. 2014. *History of the Cuneiform Lexical Tradition*. Guides to the Mesopotamian Textual Record 6. Münster: Ugarit-Verlag.

Vernant, Jean-Pierre. 1991. *Mortals and Immortals: Collected Essays*. Princeton NJ: Princeton University Press.

Vogel, Helga. 2013. "Der 'Große Mann von Uruk': Das Bild der Herrschaft im späten 4. und frühen 3. vorchristlichen Jahrtausend." Pp. 139–145 in *Uruk —5000 Jahre Megacity*.

Begleitband zur Ausstellung "Uruk – 5000 Jahre Megacity" im Pergamonmuseum – Staatliche Museen zu Berlin, in den Reiss-Engelhorn-Museen in Mannheim, ed. by N. Crüsemann et al. Petersberg: Michael Imhof Verlag.

Volk, Konrad. 1992. "Puzur-Mama und die Reise des Königs." ZA 82: 22–29.

Volk, Konrad. 1995. *Inanna und Šukaletuda. Zur historisch-politischen Deutung eines sumerischen Literaturwerkes*. SANTAG 3. Wiesbaden: Harrassowitz.

von der Osten, Hans H. 1934. *Ancient Oriental Seals in the Collection of Mr. Edward T. Newell*. OIP 22. Chicago: The University of Chicago Press.

Wagensonner, Klaus. 2010. "Early Lexical Lists Revisited: Structures and Classification as a Mnemonic Device." Pp. 285–310 in *Language in the Ancient Near East. Proceedings of the 53ᵉ Rencontre Assyriologique Internationale Vol. 1*, ed. by L. Kogan, N. Koslova, S. Loesov, and S. Tishchenko. Babel und Bibel 4/1. Winona Lake IN: Eisenbrauns.

Walker, Christopher, and Michael B. Dick. 1999. "The Induction of the Cult Image in Ancient Mesopotamia." Pp. 55–121 in *Born in Heaven, Made on Earth: The Making of the Cult Image in the Ancient Near East*, ed. by M. B. Dick. Winona Lake IN: Eisenbrauns.

Walker, Christopher, and Michael B. Dick. 2001. *The Induction of the Cult Image in Ancient Mesopotamia: The Mesopotamian Mīs pî Ritual*. State Archives of Assyria Literary Texts 1. Helsinki: The Neo-Assyrian Text Corpus Project.

Wang, Haicheng. 2014. *Writing and the Ancient State. Early China in Comparative Perspective*. Cambridge: Cambridge University Press.

Weber, Max. 1978. *Economy and Society. An Outline of Interpretive Sociology*. Edited by G. Roth and C. Wittich. Berkeley CA: University of California Press.

Wengrow, David. 2006. *The Archaeology of Early Egypt. Social Transformations in North-East Africa, 10,000 to 2650 BC*. Cambridge: Cambridge University Press.

Westenholz, Aage. 1975. *Literary and Lexical Texts and the Earliest Administrative Documents from Nippur*. Old Sumerian and Old Akkadian Texts in Philadelphia chiefly from Nippur, Part One. Bibliotheca Mesopotamica 1. Malibu CA: Undena Publications.

Westenholz, Aage. 1987. *Old Sumerian and Old Akkadian Texts in Philadelphia. Part Two: The 'Akkadian' Texts, The Enlilemaba Texts, and the Onion Archive*. Copenhagen: University of Copenhagen, Museum Tusculanum Press.

Westenholz, Joan G. 1997. *Legends of the Kings of Akkade*. Mesopotamian Civilizations 7. Winona Lake IN: Eisenbrauns.

Westenholz, Joan G. 2012. "EN-Priestess: Pawn or Power Mogul?" Pp. 291–312 in *Organization, Representation and Symbols of Power in the Ancient Near East*, Proceedings of the 54ᵗʰ Rencontre Assyriologique Internationale at Würzburg 20–25 July 2008, ed. by G. Wilhelm. Winona Lake IN: Eisenbrauns.

Wiggermann, F. A. M. 1992. *Mesopotamian Protective Spirits: The Ritual Texts*. Cuneifrom Monographs 1. Groningen: STYX & PP.

Wiggermann, F. A. M. 2010. "The Image of Dumuzi: A Diachronic Analysis." Pp. 327–350 in *Gazing on the Deep: Ancient Near Eastern and Other Studies in Honor of Tzvi Abusch*, ed. by J. Stackert, B. N. Porter, and D. P. Wright. Winona Lake IN: Eisenbrauns.

Wilcke, Claus. 1989. "Genealogical and Geographical Thought in the Sumerian King List." Pp. 557–571 in *DUMU-E₂-DUB-BA-A: Studies in Honor of Åke W. Sjöberg*, ed. by H. Behrens, D. Loding, and M. T. Roth. Occasional Publications of the Samuel Noah Fund 11. Philadelphia: The University Museum of the University of Pennsylvania.

Wilcke, Claus. 1993. "Politik im Spiegel der Literatur, Literatur als Mittel der Politik im älteren Babylonien." Pp. 29–75 in *Anfänge politischen Denkens in der Antike*, ed. by K. Raaflaub. Schriften des Historischen Kollegs. Kolloquien 24. Munich: Oldenbourg.

Wilcke, Claus. 1997. "Amar-Girids Revolte gegen Narãm-Su'en." *ZA* 87: 11–32.

Wilcke, Claus. 2005. "ED LÚ A und die Sprache(n) der archaischen Texte." Pp. 430–445 in *Ethnicity in Ancient Mesopotamia*, ed. by Wilfred H. van Soldt, R. Kalvelagen, and D. Katz. PIHANS 102. Leiden: Nederlands Instituut voor het Nabije Oosten.

Wilcke, Claus. 2011. "Eine Weihinschrift Gudeas von Lagaš mit altbabylonischer Übersetzung." Pp. 29–47 in *Cuneiform Royal Inscriptions and Related Texts in the Schøyen Collection*, ed. by A. R. George. CUSAS 17. Bethesda MD: CDL Press.

Wilcke, Claus. 2012. *The Sumerian Poem Enmerkar and En-suḫkeš-ana: Epic, Play, or? Stage Craft at the Turn from the Third to the Second Millennium B.C.* American Oriental Society, Essay 12. New Haven CT: American Oriental Society.

Wilhelm, Gernot. 2001. "Der 'Mann im Netzrock' und kultische Nacktheit." Pp. 478–483 in *Beiträge zur Vorderasiatischen Archäologie Winfried Orthmann gewidmet*, ed. by J.-W. Meyer, M. Novák, and A. Pruss. Frankfurt am Main: Johann Wolfgang Goethe-Universität, Archäologisches Institut.

Wilkinson, Toby A. H. 2000. *Royal Annals of Ancient Egypt: The Palermo Stone and Its Associated Fragments*. London: Kegan Paul.

Winter, Irene J. 1983. "The Warka Vase: Structure of Art and Structure of the Society in the Uruk Period." Paper Presented at the Annual Meeting of the American Oriental Society, Baltimore, Maryland.

Winter, Irene J. 1985. "After the Battle Is Over: The 'Stele of the Vultures' and the Beginning of Historical Narrative in the Art of the Ancient Near East." Pp. 11–32 in *Pictorial Narrative in Antiquity and the Middle Ages*, ed. by H. J. Kessler and M. S. Simpson. Studies in the History of Art vol. 16, Symposium Papers 4. Washington DC: National Gallery of Art.

Winter, Irene J. 1996. "Sex, Rhetoric, and the Public Monument: The Alluring Body of Naram-Sîn of Agade." Pp. 11–16 in *Sexuality in Ancient Art: Near East, Egypt, Greece, and Italy*, ed. by N. B. Kampen. Cambridge: Cambridge University Press.

Winter, Irene J. 2000a. "Opening the Eyes and Opening the Mouth: The Utility of Comparing Images in Worship in India and the Ancient Near East." Pp. 129–162 in *Ethnography & Personhood: Notes from the Field*, ed. by Michael W. Meister. Jaipur: Rawat Publications.

Winter, Irene J. 2000b. "The Eyes Have It: Votive Statuary, Gilgamesh's Axe, and Cathected Viewing in the Ancient Near East." Pp. 22–44 in *Visuality Before and Beyond the Renaissance*, ed. by R. Nelson. Cambridge: Cambridge University Press.

Winter, Irene J. 2007. "Representing Abundance: A Visual Dimension of the Agrarian State." Pp. 117–138 in *Settlement and Society: Essays Dedicated to Robert McC. Adams*, ed. by E. C. Stone. Los Angeles: Cotsen Institute of Archaeology, University of California, Los Angeles.

Winter, Irene J. 2008. "Touched by the Gods: Visual Evidence for the Divine Status of Rulers in the Ancient Near East." Pp. 75–101 in *Religion and Power: Divine Kingship in the Ancient World and Beyond*, ed. by N. Brisch. Oriental Institute Seminars 4. Chicago: The Oriental Institute of the University of Chicago.

Woods, Christopher E. 2004. "The Sun-God Tablet of Nabû-apla-iddina Revisited." *JCS* 56: 23–103.

Woods, Christopher E. 2005a. "On the Euphrates." *ZA* 95: 7–45.

Woods, Christopher E. 2005b. "A Unique Writing for Sippar at Abū Ṣalābiḫ – ᵈUD.KIBᵏⁱ (Addendum to ZA 95 [2005]: 7–45)." *NABU* 2005/67.

Woods, Christopher E. 2010. "The Earliest Mesopotamian Writing." Pp. 33–50 in *Visible Language. Inventions of Writing in the Ancient Near East and Beyond*, ed. by Ch. Woods with E. Teeter and G. Emberling. Oriental Institute Museum Publications 32. Chicago: The Oriental Institute of the University of Chicago.

Woods, Christopher E. 2012. "Sons of the Sun: The Mythological Foundations of the First Dynasty of Uruk." *Journal of Ancient Near Eastern Religions* 12: 78–96.

Woods, Christopher E. 2015. "Contingency Tables and Economic Forecasting in the Earliest Texts from Mesopotamia." Pp. 121–142 in *Texts and Contexts. The Circulation and Transmission of Cuneiform Texts in Social Space*, ed. by P. Delnero and J. Lauinger, SANER 9. Berlin: De Gruyter.

Woods, Christopher E. 2017. "The Abacus in Mesopotamia: Considerations from a Comparative Perspective." Pp. 416–473 in *The First Ninety Years: A Sumerian Celebration in Honor of Miguel Civil*, ed. by L. Feliu, F. Karahashi, and G. Rubio, SANER 12, Berlin: De Gruyter.

Woods, Christopher, Emily Teeter, and Geoff Emberling. 2010 (eds.) *Visible Language. Inventions of Writing in the Ancient Near East and Beyond*. Oriental Institute Museum Publications 32. Chicago: The Oriental Institute of the University of Chicago.

Woolley, Leonard C. 1926. "The Excavations at Ur, 1925–26." *The Antiquaries Journal* 6: 366–401.

Zaidman, Louise B., and Louise S. Pantel. 1992. *Religion in the Ancient Greek City*. Cambridge: Cambridge University Press.

Zettler, Richard. 1987. Review of B. Buchanan, Early Near Eastern Seals in the Yale Babylonian Collection. *JNES* 46: 59–62.

Index

List and Sources of Illustrations

1. Uruk III city-seal. After R. J. Matthews 1993: 37.
2. Statue of the Priest-King. After Strommenger 1962: pl. 33.
3. Seal depicting the Priest-King while he presents food offerings to Inana. After Vogel 2013: 143 fig. 20.5.
4. Seal depicting the Priest-King while he feeds Inana's herds. After Klengel-Brandt 1997: 63 fig. 47.
5. Seal depicting the Priest-King as a warrior. After Amiet 1961: pl. 46 fig. 659.
6. Relief depicting the Priest-King as a hunter. After Strommenger 1962: fig. 18.
7. The Warka Vase. After Lindemeyer and Martin 1993: pl. 25 fig. l.
8. The Warka Vase, detail. After Strommenger 1962: fig. 21a.
9. The Warka Vase, detail. After Strommenger 1962: fig. 21b.
10. The EN sign on an Uruk III tablet. After André-Leicknam and Ziegler 1982: no. 7.
11. Seal depicting the Priest-King and Inana. After Heinrich 1936: pl. 17 fig. d.
12. Seal depicting the Priest-King and Inana. After Heinrich 1936: pl. 18 fig. a.
13. Seal depicting the Priest-King and Inana. After Heinrich 1936: pl. 18 fig. b.
14. Seal depicting the Priest-King and Inana. After Heinrich 1936: pl. 18 fig. c.
15. Seal depicting the Priest-King and Inana. W 14772c 2. After Heinrich 1936: pl. 18 fig. d.
16. The Warka female head. After Strommenger 1962: fig. 31.
17. Jemdet Nasr seal depicting the face of a goddess and the facade of a temple. After Frankfort 1955: pl. 2 fig. q + pl. 84 fig. 880.
18. Uruk III seal depicting Inana's festival. After Boehmer 2014: 128 fig. 1.
19. Plaque of Ur-Nanše of Lagaš. Photograph by Philipp Bernard. Courtesy of the Louvre Museum.
20. Plaque Ur-Nanše of Lagaš. After Aruz 2003: 71 fig. 30.
21. Plaque of En-anatum I of Lagaš. After Strommenger 1962: fig. 71.
22. Macehead of En-anatum I of Lagaš. After Aruz 2003: 76 fig. 35.
23. Statue M of Gudea. After Aruz 2003: 430 fig. 306a.
24. Stele of Gudea of Lagaš, fragment. After Parrot 1960: 230 fig. 284.
25. Seal of Gudea of Lagaš. After Suter 2000: 54 fig. 9.
26. Pre-Sargonic plaque from Ur depicting Nanna's priestesses. After Aruz 2003: 74 fig. 33.
27. Archaic Plaque from Kiš, front. After Steinkeller 2013a: 152 = [cdli.ucla.edu/P453401].
28. Archaic Plaque from Kiš, back. After Steinkeller 2013a: 152 = [cdli.ucla.edu/P453401].
29. Alabaster foundation peg of Ur-Nanše of Lagaš, front and back views. HSM 913.2.178, Harvard Semitic Museum, Harvard University.
30. Copper foundation peg of En-anatum I of Lagaš from Al-Hiba, front and back views. After Hansen 1970: figs. 10 and 11.
31. Copper foundation peg of En-metena of Lagaš, front, back, and side views. After Braun-Holzinger 2013: pl. 4 fig. c.
32. Copper ED IIIb foundation peg, front, side, and back views. Unprovenanced but assuredly stemming from Lagaš or Girsu; given its stylistic features, probably of En-metena. After Merhav et al. 1981: 45 no. 22.
33. Copper ED IIIb foundation peg, with traces of an inscription, front views. Unprovenanced but assuredly stemming from Lagaš or Girsu. After Drouot-Montaigne 2000: 2 no. 676; The Morgan Library and Museum, New York, "Founding Figures: Copper Sculpture from

DOI 10.1515/9781501504778-009

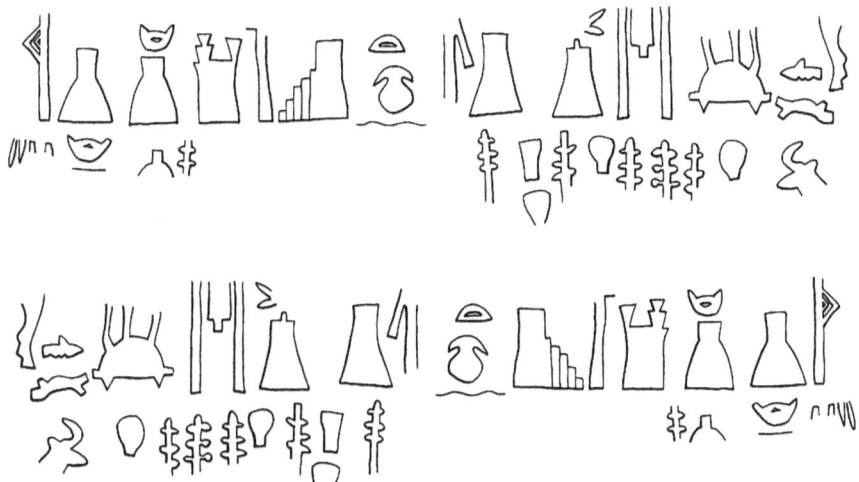

1 Uruk III city-seal. After R. J. Matthews 1993: 37.

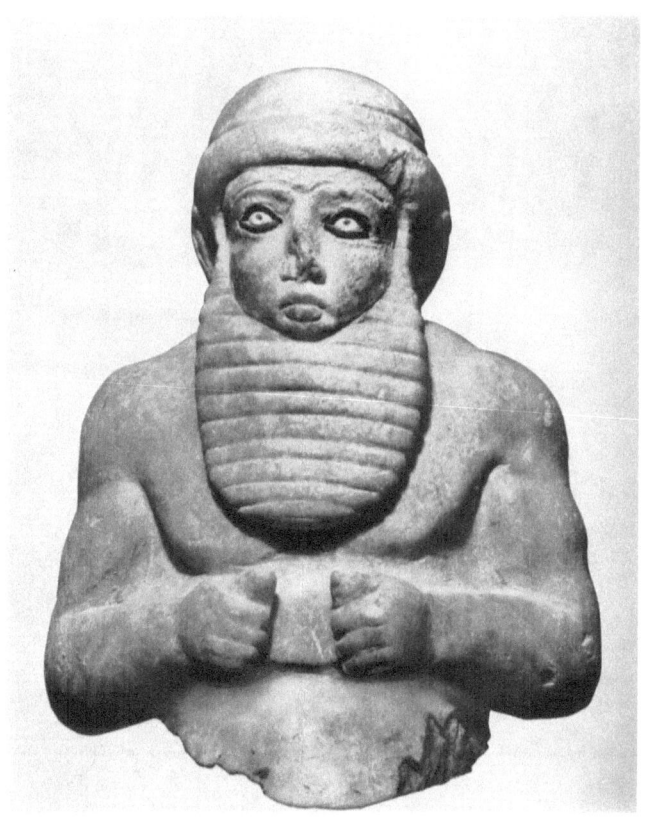

2 Statue of the Priest-King. After Strommenger 1962: pl. 33.

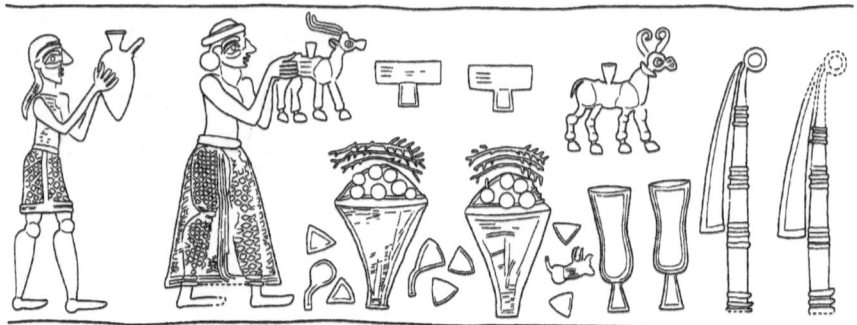

3 Seal depicting the Priest-King while he presents food offerings to Inana. After Vogel 2013: 143 fig. 20.5.

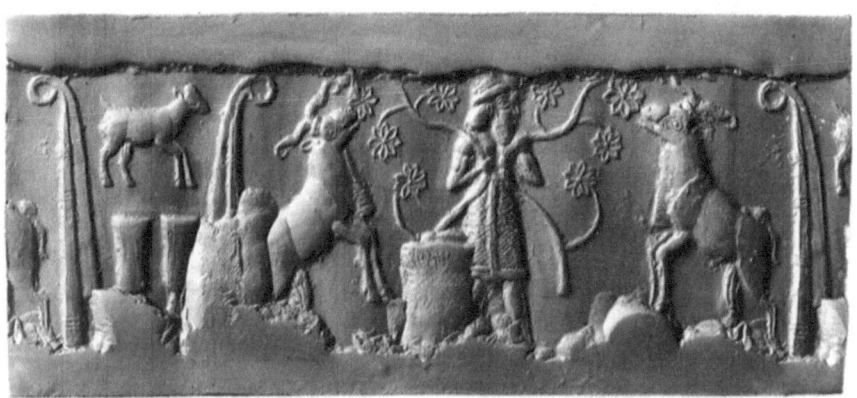

4 Seal depicting the Priest-King while he feeds Inana's herds. After Klengel-Brandt 1997: 63 fig. 47.

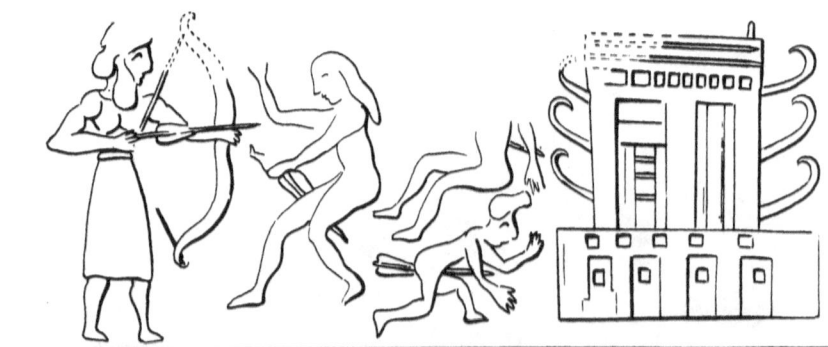

5 Seal depicting the Priest-King as a warrior. After Amiet 1961: pl. 46 fig. 659.

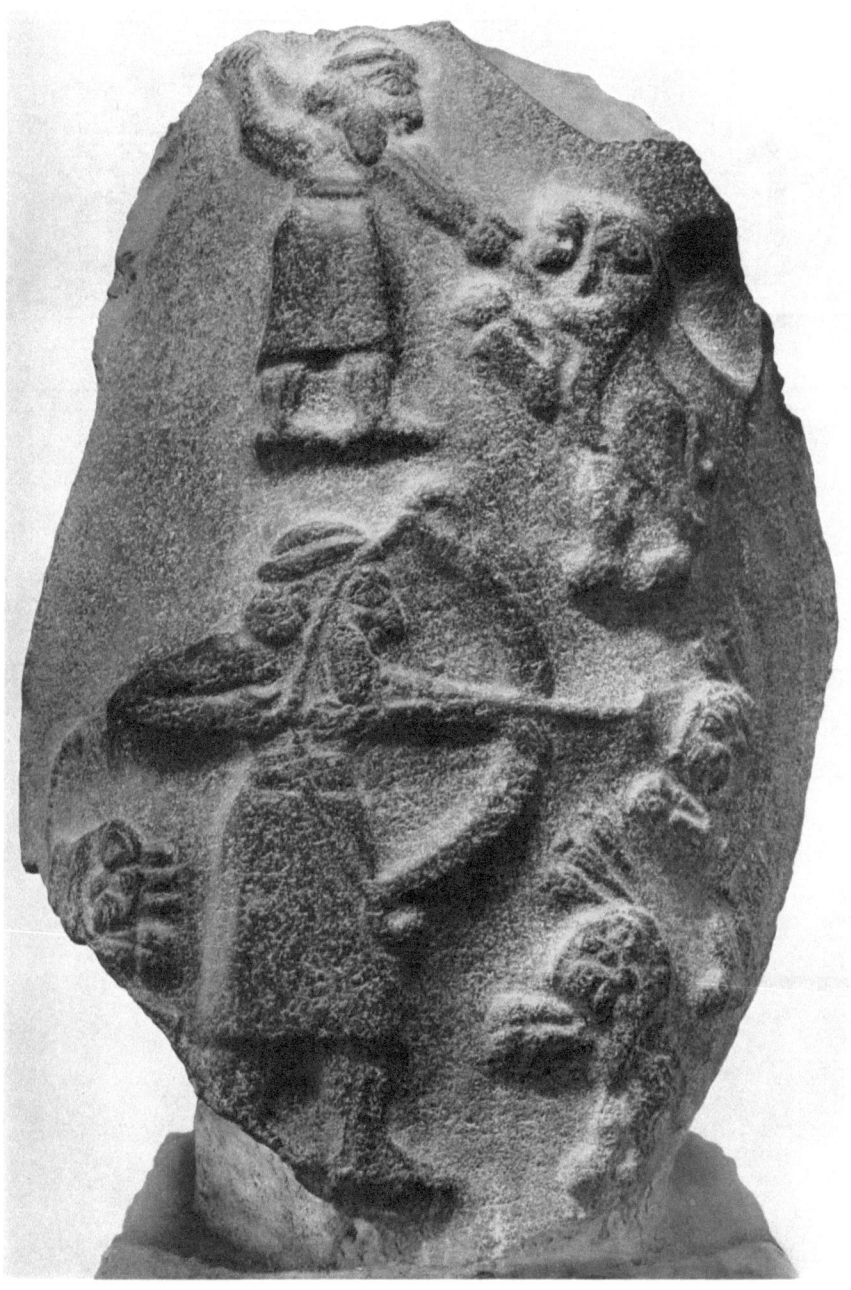

6 Relief depicting the Priest-King as a hunter. After Strommenger 1962: fig. 18.

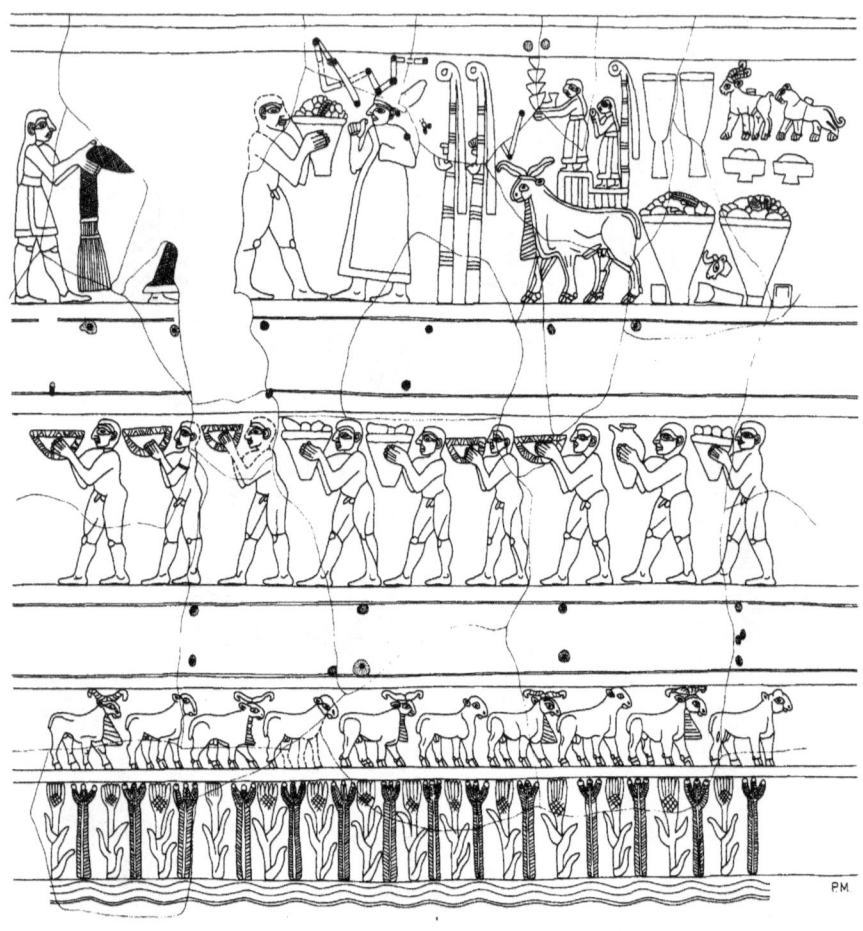

7 The Warka Vase. After Lindemeyer and Martin 1993: pl. 25 fig. l.

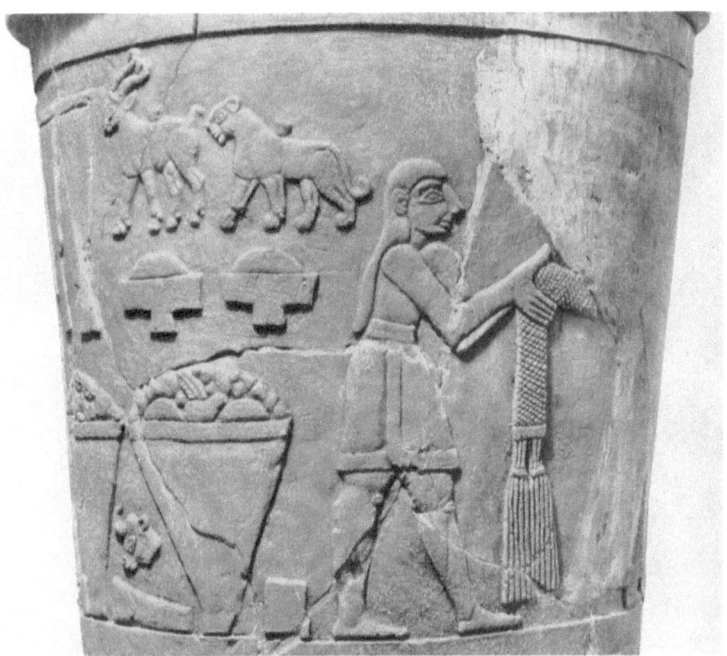

8 The Warka Vase, detail. After Strommenger 1962: fig. 21a.

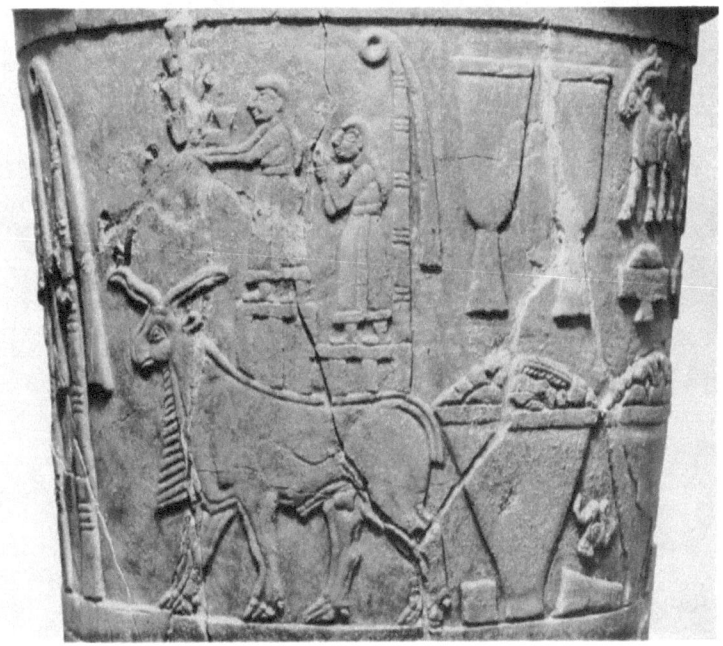

9 The Warka Vase, detail. After Strommenger 1962: fig. 21b.

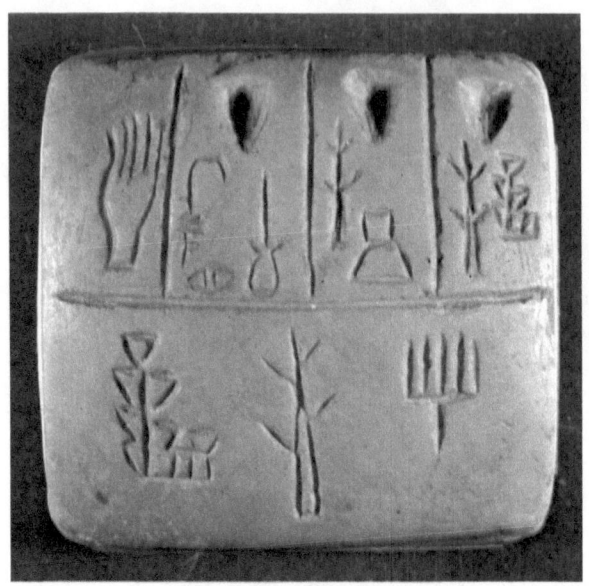

10 The EN sign on an Uruk III tablet. After André-Leicknam and Ziegler 1982: no. 7.

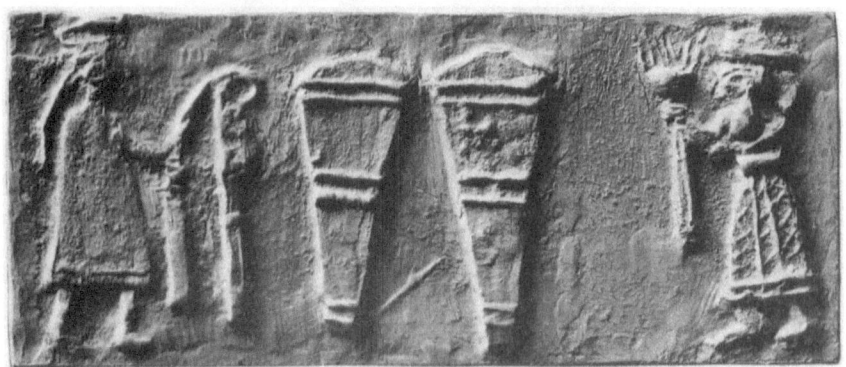

11 Seal depicting the Priest-King and Inana. After Heinrich 1936: pl. 17 fig. d.

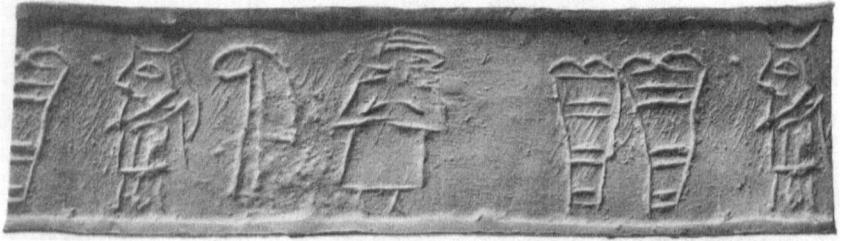

12 Seal depicting the Priest-King and Inana. After Heinrich 1936: pl. 18 fig. a.

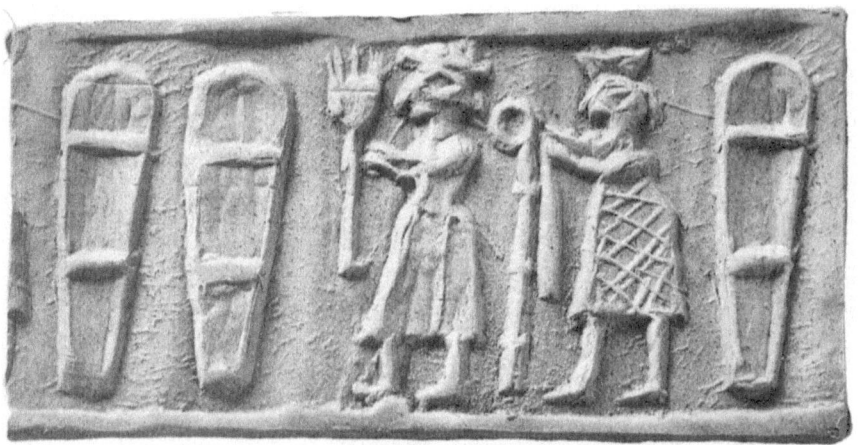

13 Seal depicting the Priest-King and Inana. After Heinrich 1936: pl. 18 fig. b.

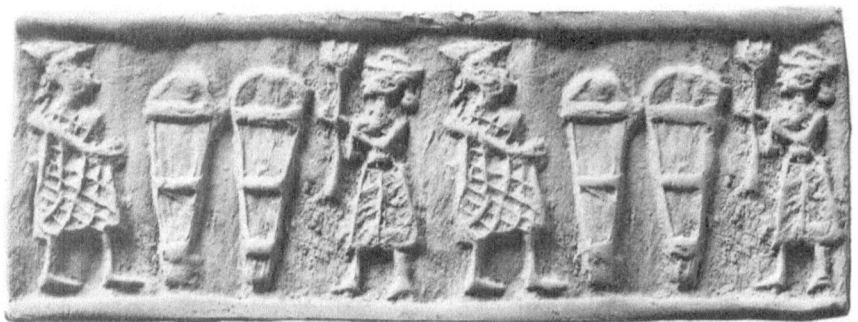

14 Seal depicting the Priest-King and Inana. After Heinrich 1936: pl. 18 fig. c.

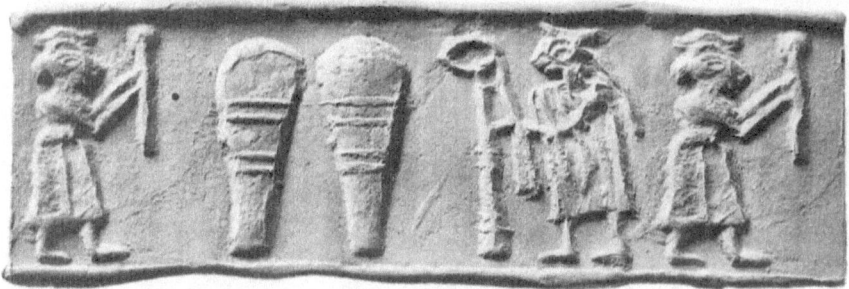

15 Seal depicting the Priest-King and Inana. W 14772c 2. After Heinrich 1936: pl. 18 fig. d.

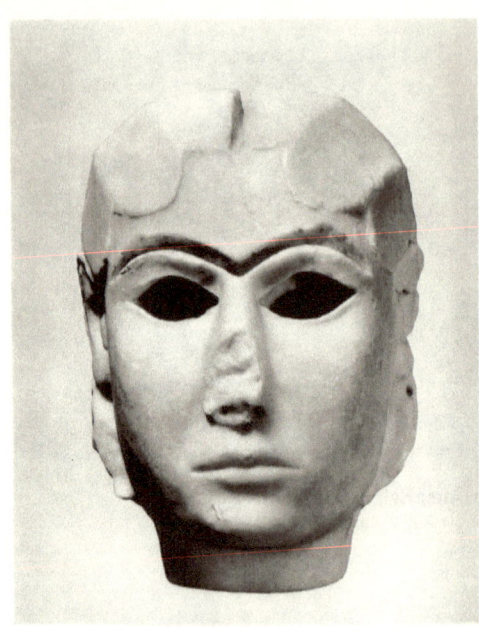

16 The Warka female head. After Strommenger 1962: fig. 31.

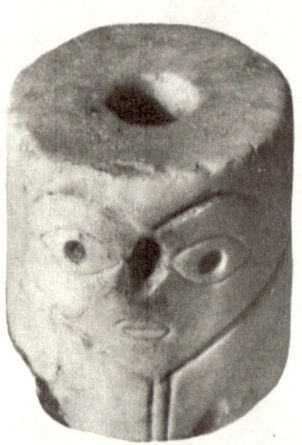

17 Jemdet Nasr seal depicting the face of a goddess and the facade of a temple. After Frankfort 1955: pl. 2 fig. q + pl. 84 fig. 880.

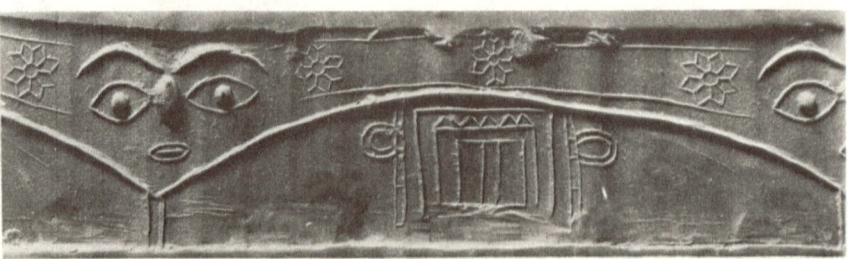

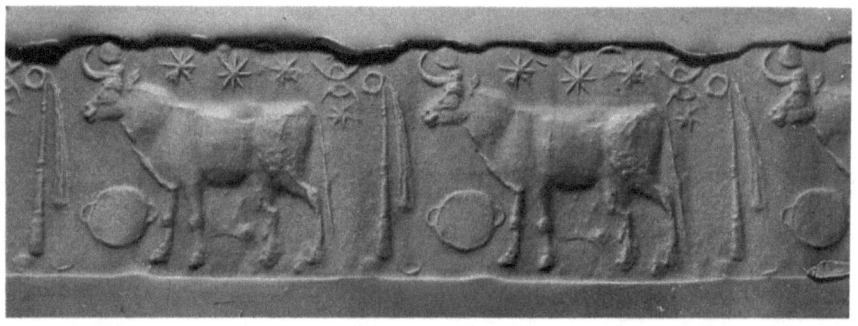

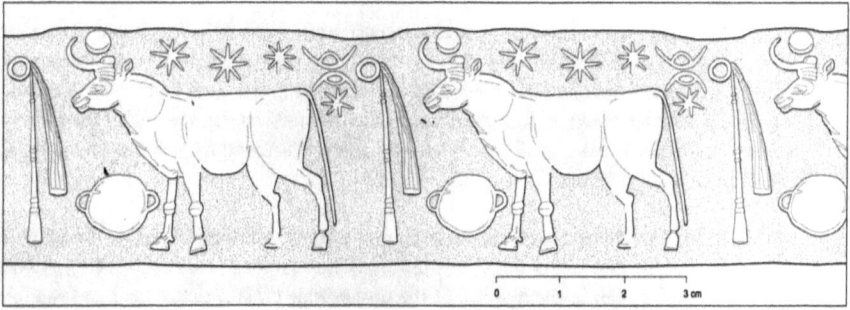

18 Uruk III seal depicting Inana's festival. After Boehmer 2014: 128 fig. 1.

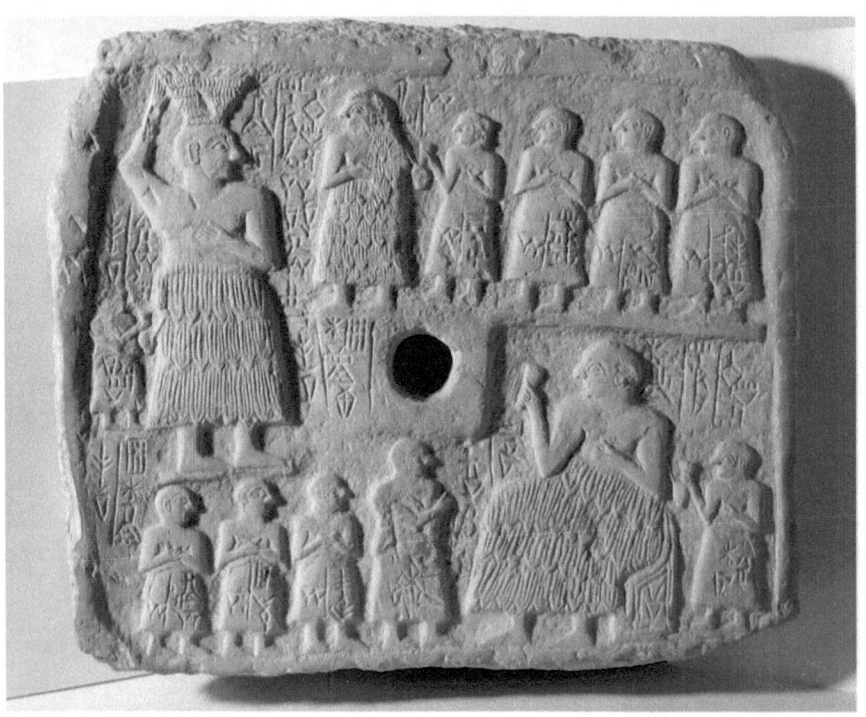

19 Plaque of Ur-Nanše of Lagaš. Photograph by Philipp Bernard. Courtesy of the Louvre Museum.

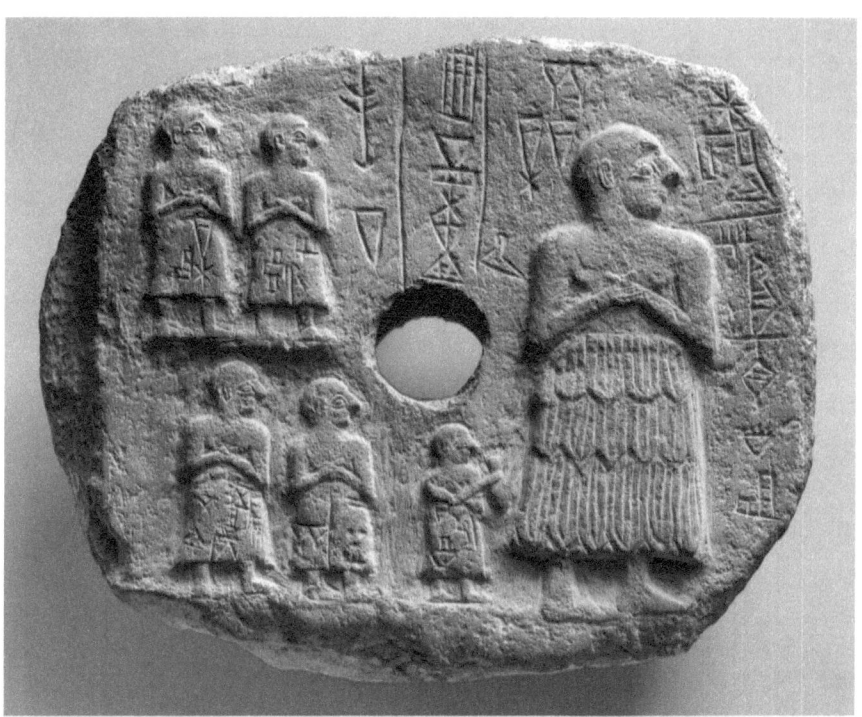

20 Plaque Ur-Nanše of Lagaš. After Aruz 2003: 71 fig. 30.

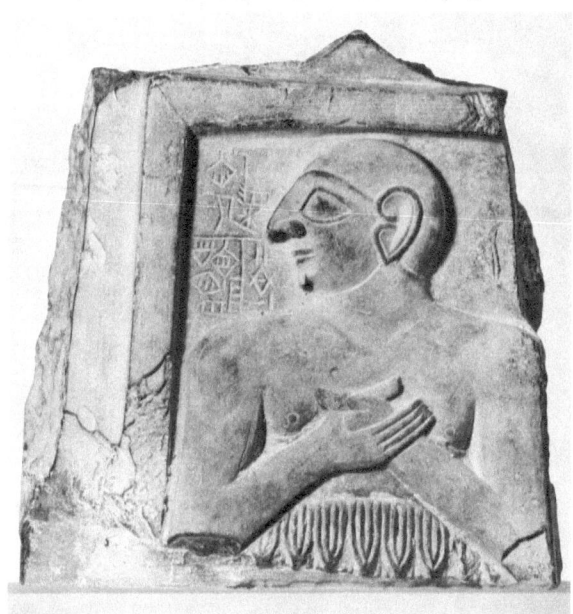

21
Plaque of En-anatum I of
Lagaš. After Strommenger
1962: fig. 71.

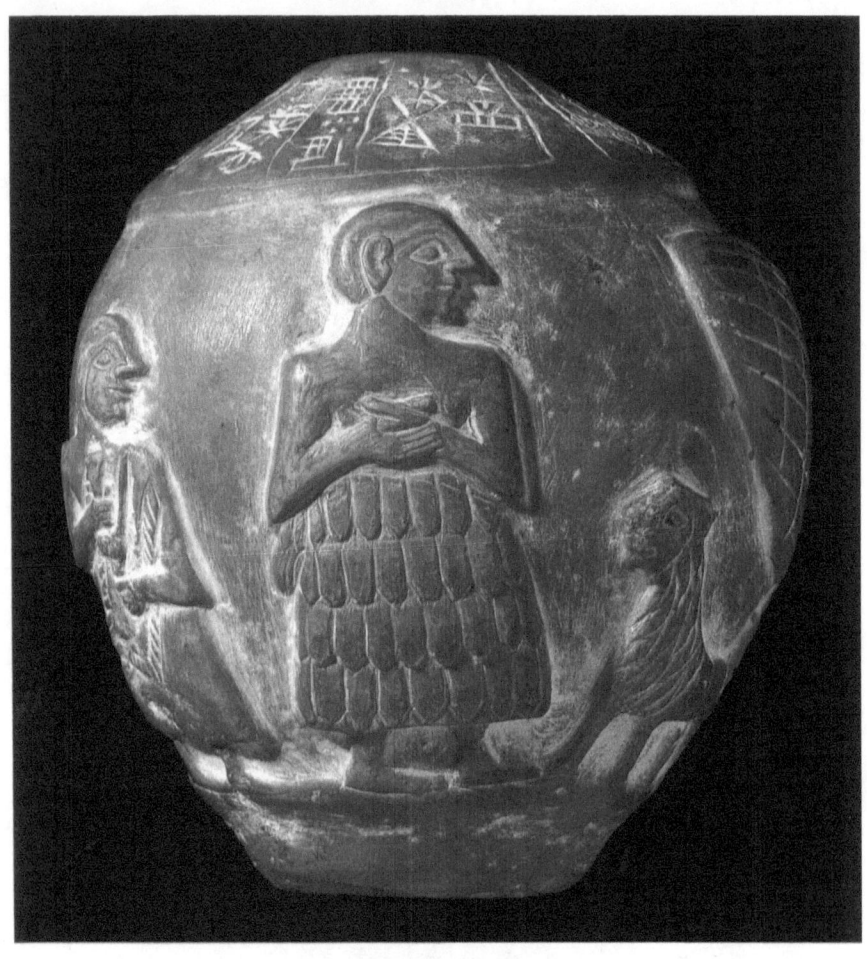

22 Macehead of En-anatum I of Lagaš. After Aruz 2003: 76 fig. 35.

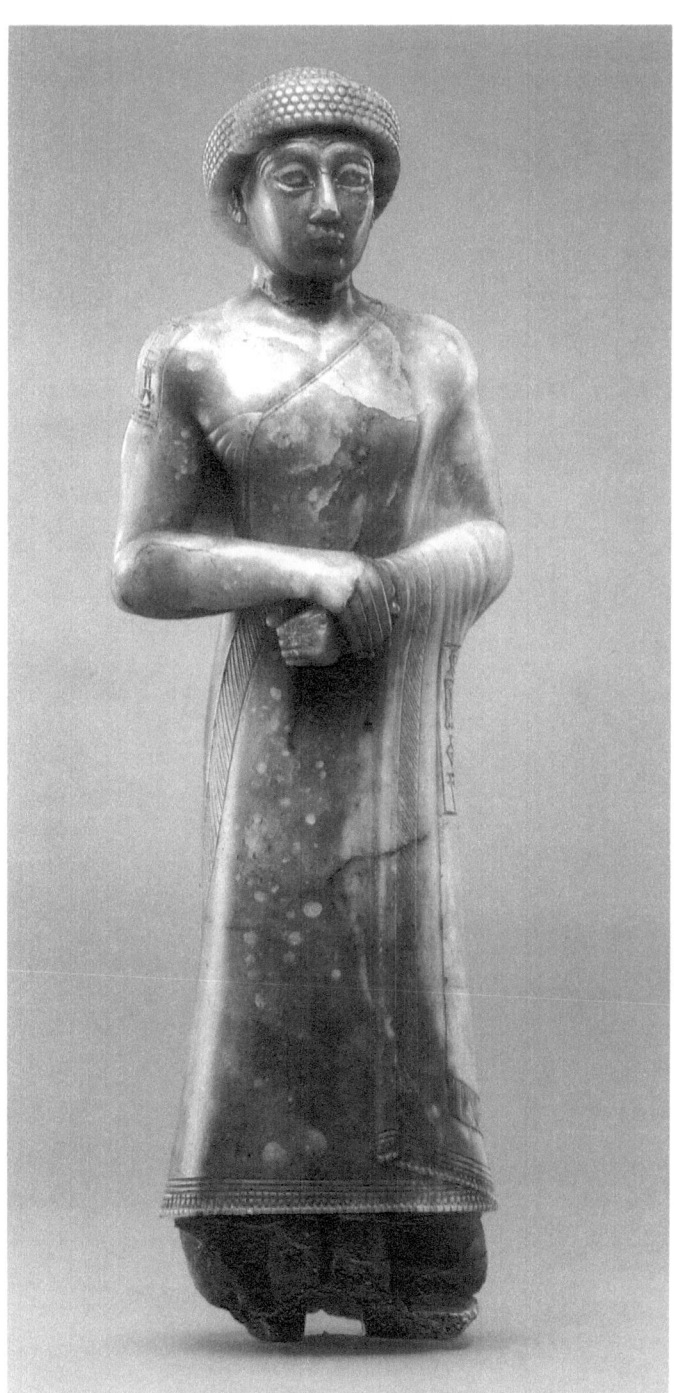

23
Statue M of Gudea.
After Aruz 2003:
430 fig. 306a.

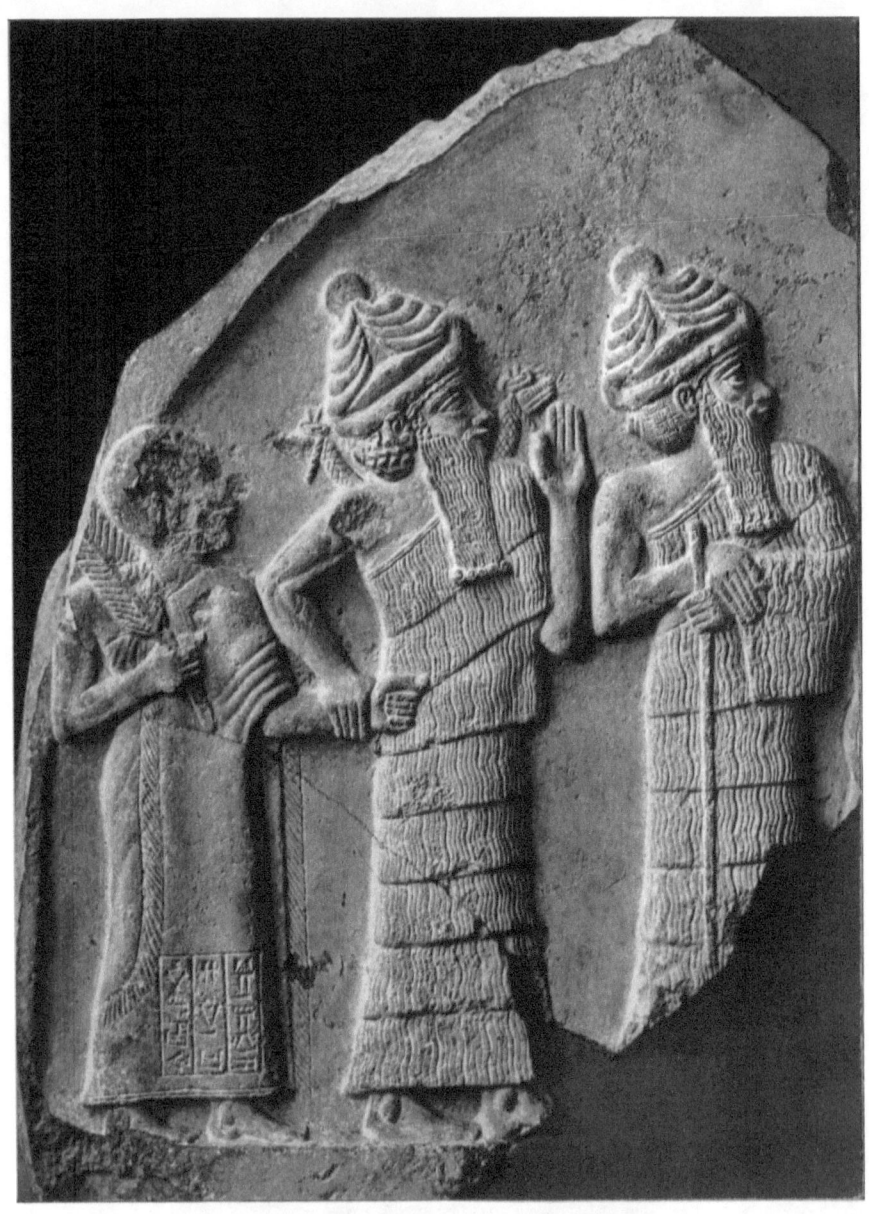

24 Stele of Gudea of Lagaš, fragment. After Parrot 1960: 230 fig. 284.

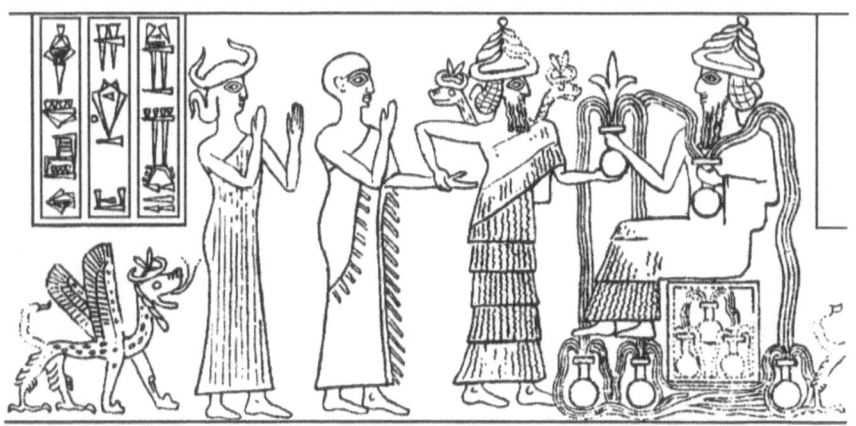

25 Seal of Gudea of Lagaš. After Suter 2000: 54 fig. 9.

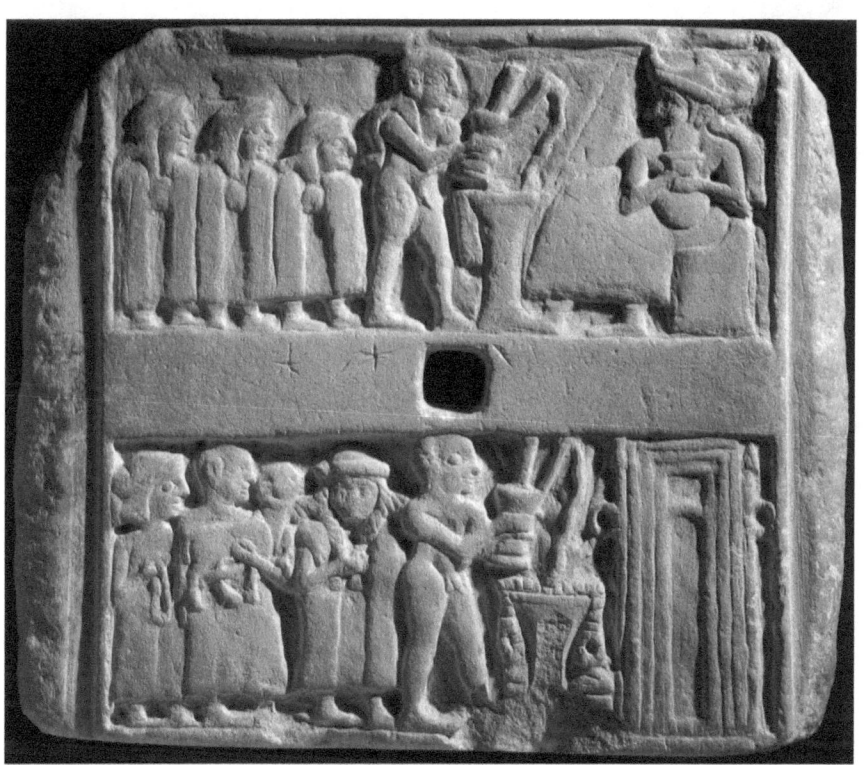

26 Pre-Sargonic plaque from Ur depicting Nanna's priestesses. After Aruz 2003: 74 fig. 33.

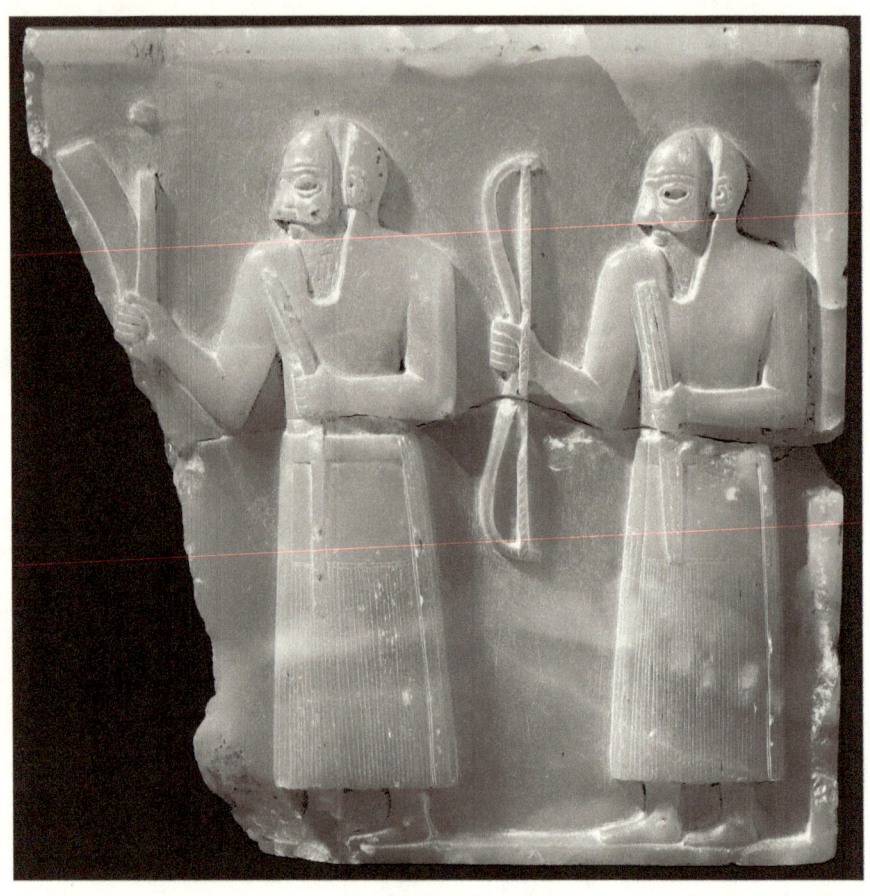

27 Archaic Plaque from Kiš, front. After Steinkeller 2013a: 152 = [cdli.ucla.edu/P453401].

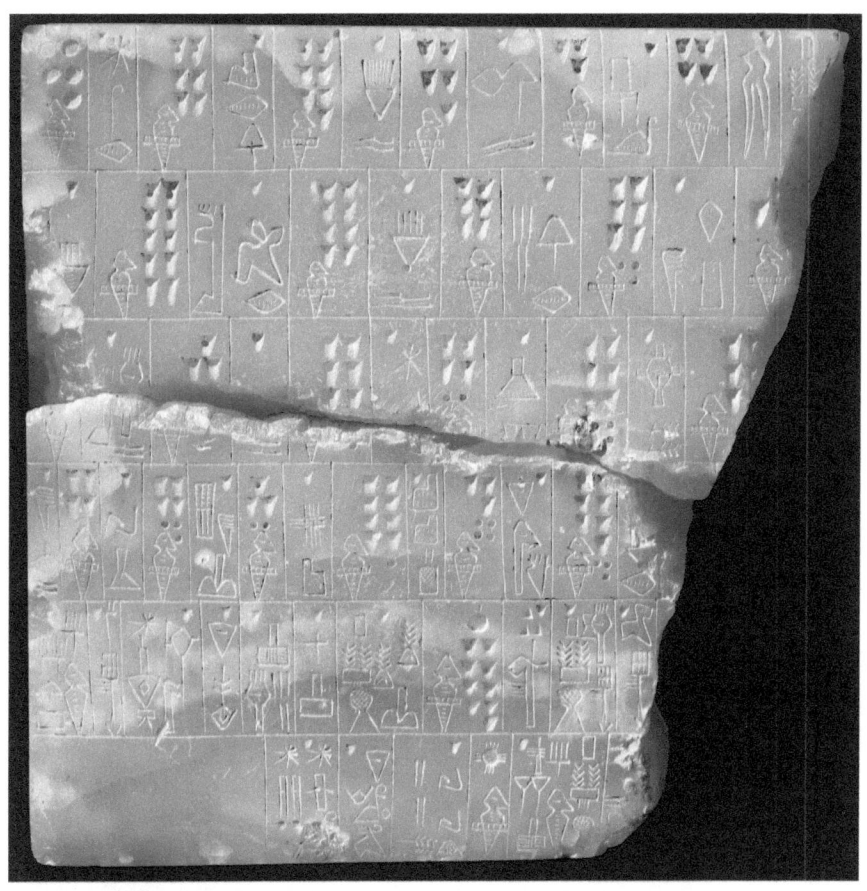

28 Archaic Plaque from Kiš, back. After Steinkeller 2013a: 152 = [cdli.ucla.edu/P453401].

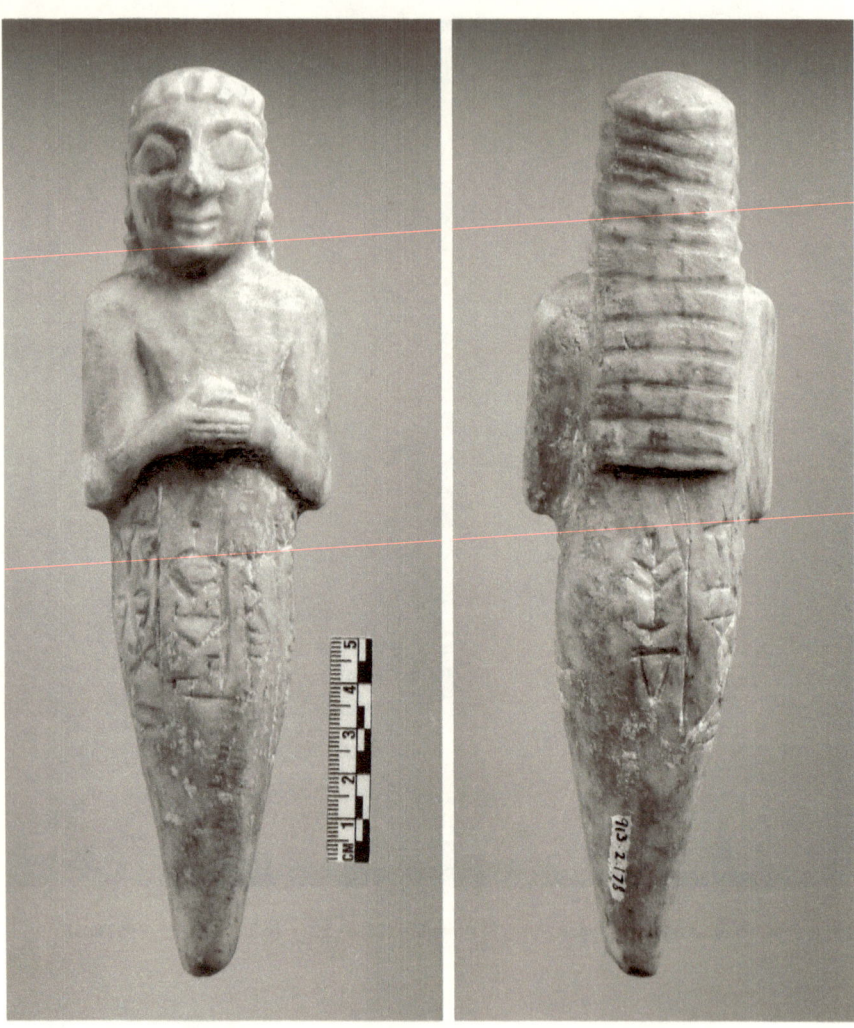

29 Alabaster foundation peg of Ur-Nanše of Lagaš, front and back views. HSM 913.2.178, Harvard Semitic Museum, Harvard University.

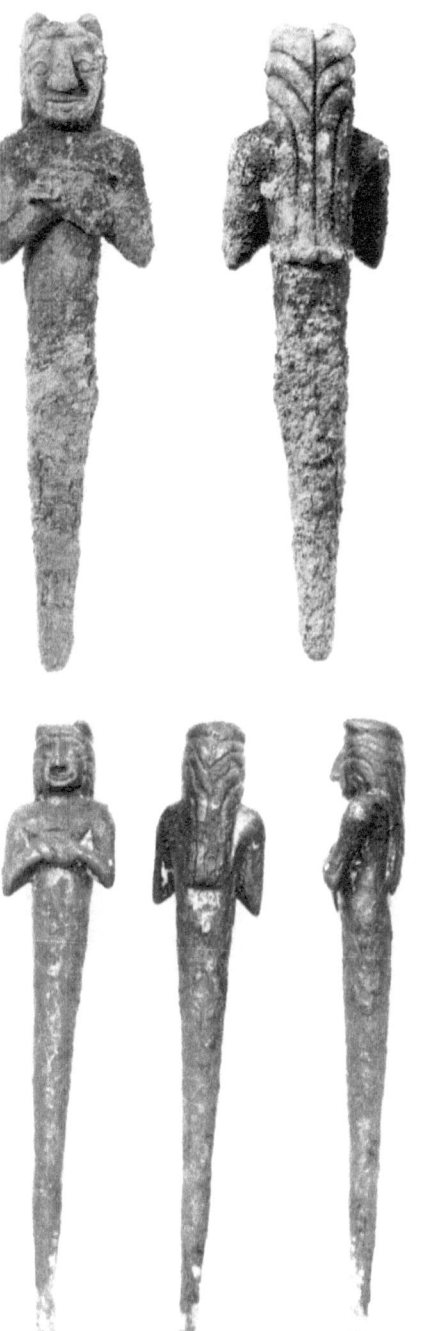

30 Copper foundation peg of En-anatum
I of Lagaš from Al-Hiba, front and
back views. After Hansen 1970:
figs. 10 and 11.

31 Copper foundation peg of En-metena of
Lagaš, front, back, and side views.
After Braun-Holzinger 2013: pl. 4 fig. c.

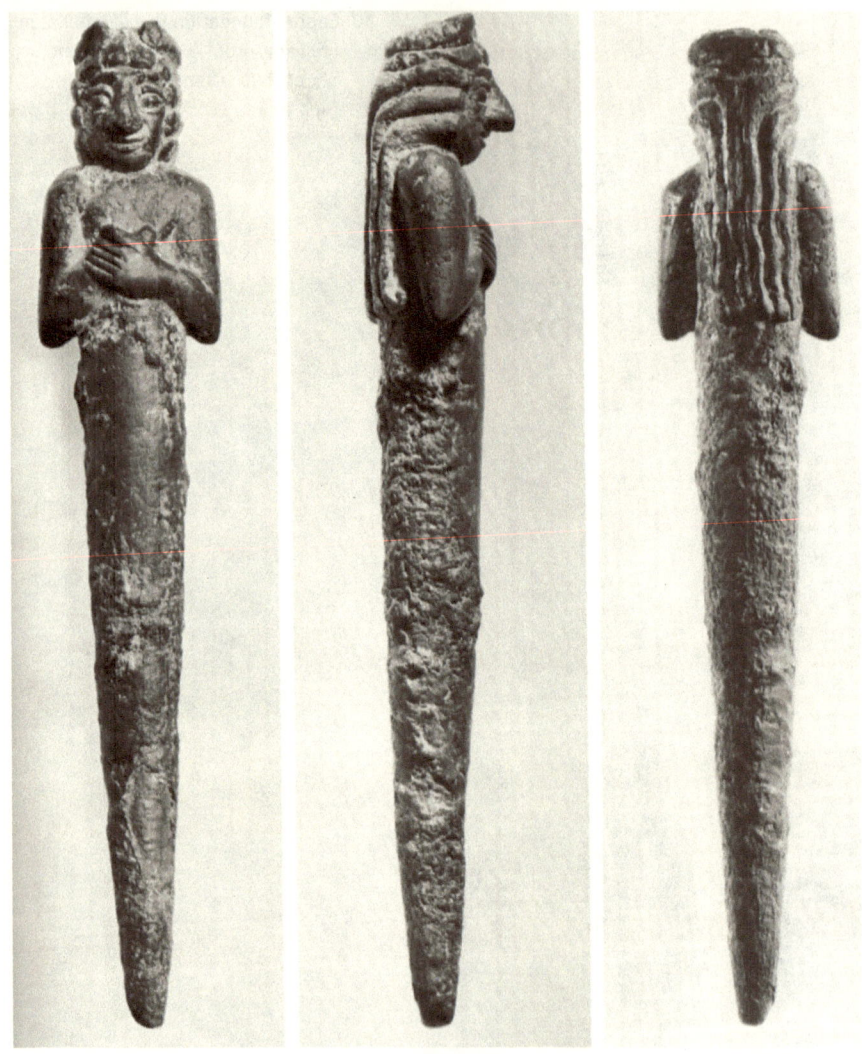

32 Copper ED IIIb foundation peg, front, side, and back views. Unprovenanced but assuredly stemming from Lagaš or Girsu; given its stylistic features, probably of En-metena. After Merhav et al. 1981: 45 no. 22.

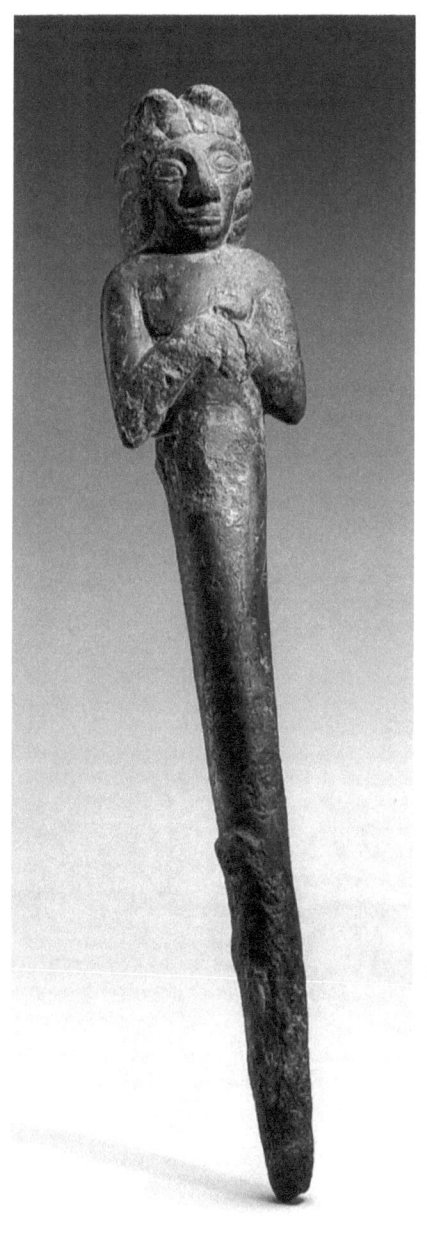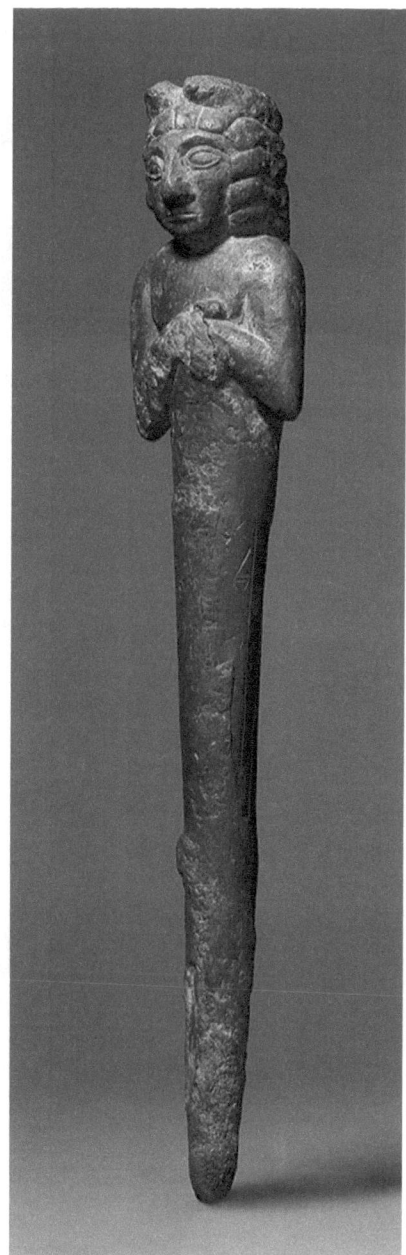

33 Copper ED IIIb foundation peg, with traces of an inscription, front views. Unprovenanced but assuredly stemming from Lagaš or Girsu. After Drouot-Montaigne 2000: 2 no. 676; The Morgan Library and Museum, New York, "Founding Figures: Copper Sculpture from Ancient Mesopotamia, ca. 3300-2000 B.C.," May 3 - August 21, 2016 [www.themorgan.org].

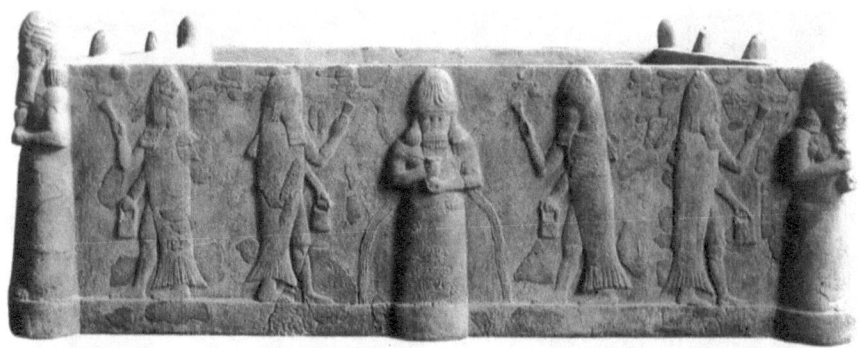

34 Neo-Assyrian water basin depicting god Enki/Ea flanked by the abgals/apkallū.
After Klengel-Brandt 1997: 132 fig. 141.

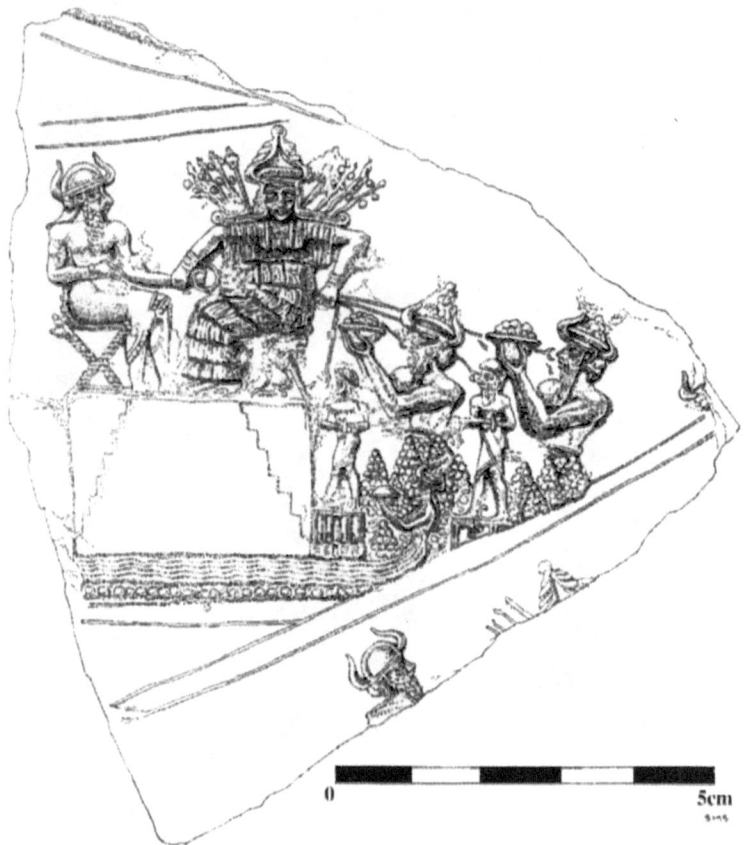

35 Naram-Suen's roundlet. After Hansen 2002: 93 fig. 3.

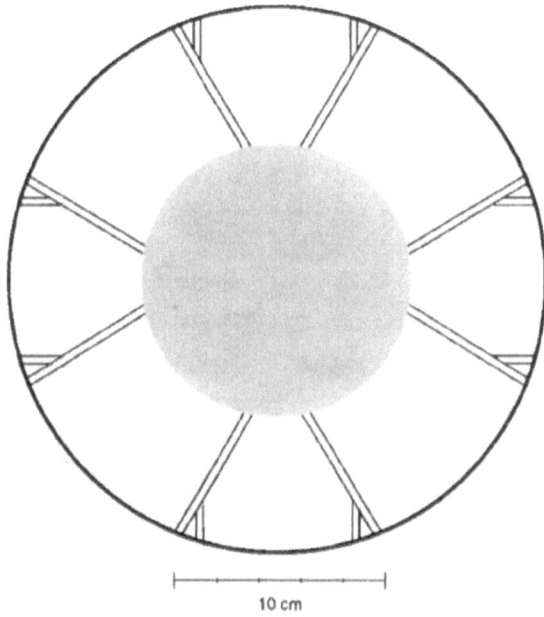

36 Naram-Suen's roundlet, reconstruction. After Hansen 2002: 103 fig. 9.

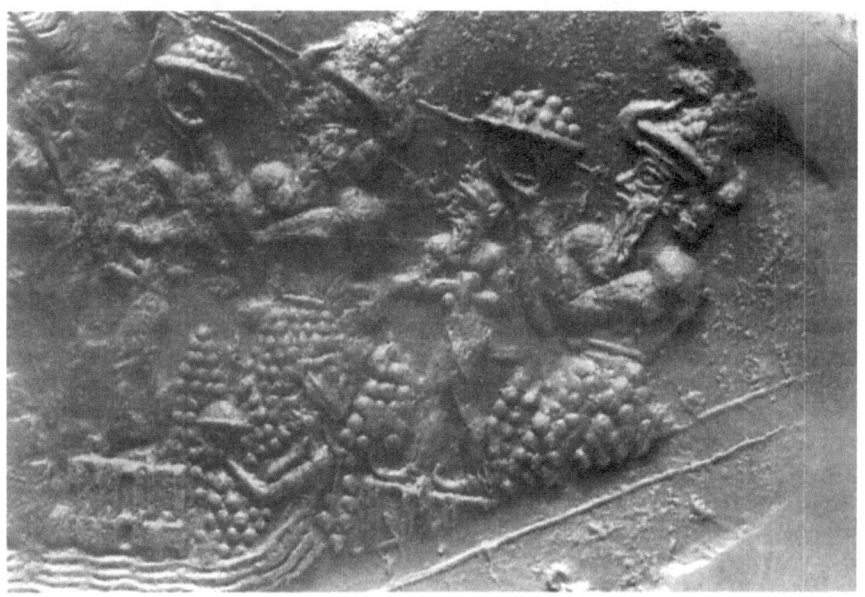

37 Naram-Suen's roundlet, detail. After Hansen 2002: 95 fig. 7.

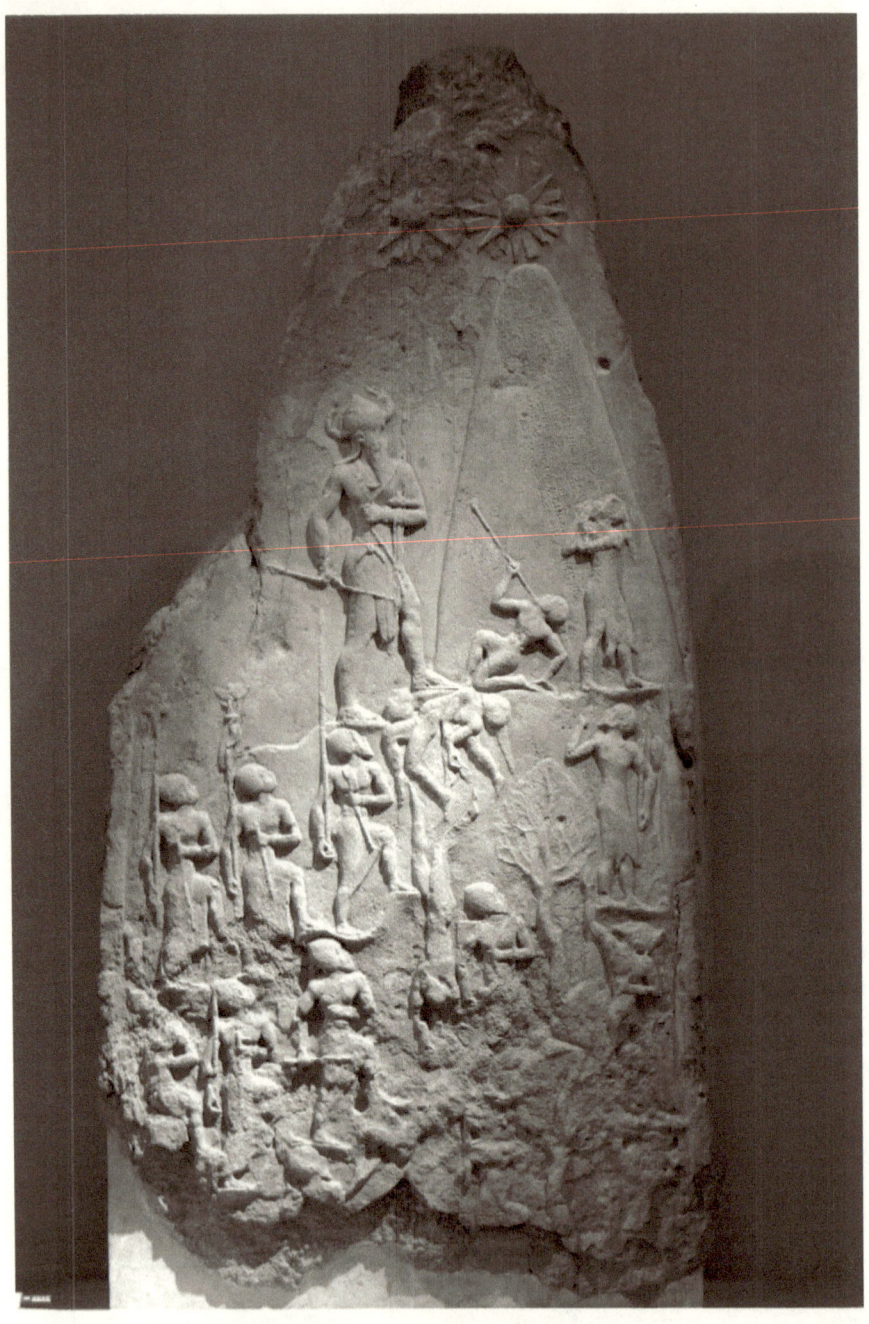

38 Victory Stele of Naram-Suen. After Aruz 2003: 196 fig. 59.

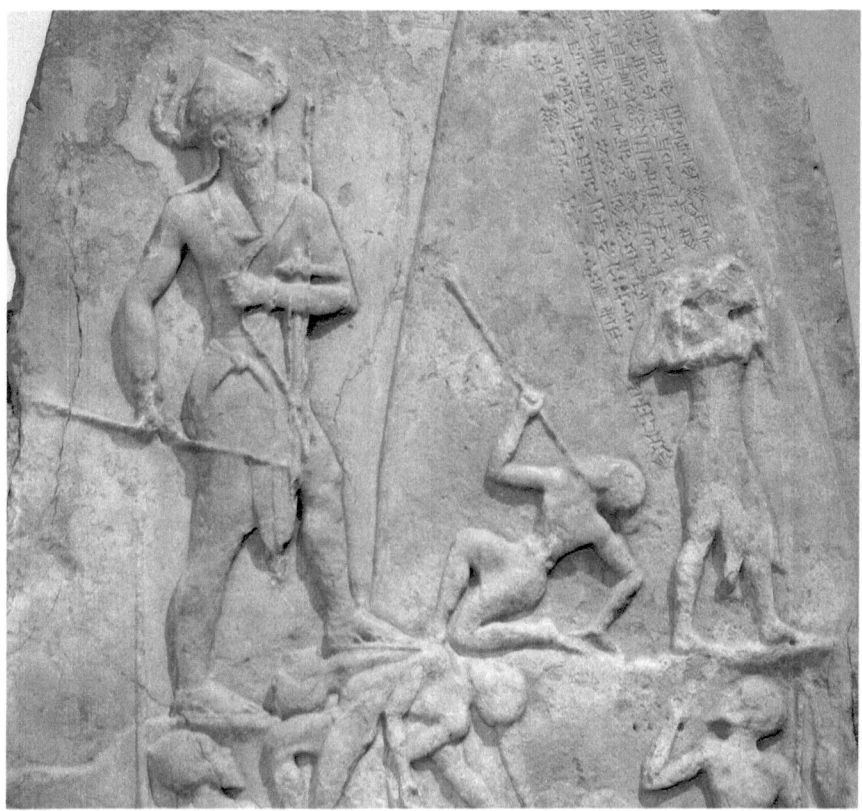

39 Victory Stele of Naram-Suen, detail. After Wikimedia Commons, [commons.wikimedia.com].

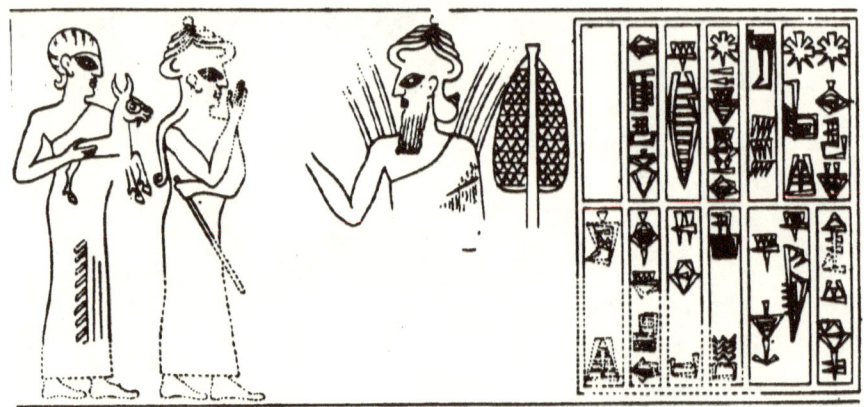

40 Seal of Lugal-ušumgal, Naram-Suen's governor of Lagaš. After Amiet 1976: 84 fig. 83.

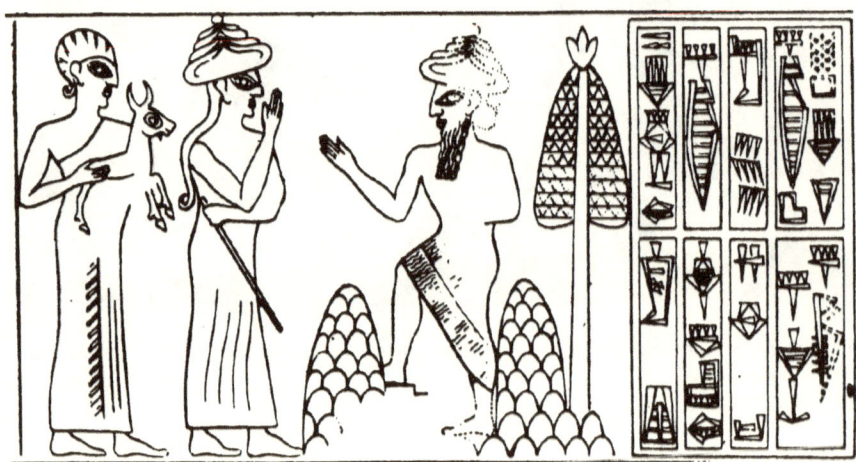

41 Seal of Lugal-ušumgal, Šar-kali-šarri's governor of Lagaš. After Amiet 1976: 84 fig. 84.

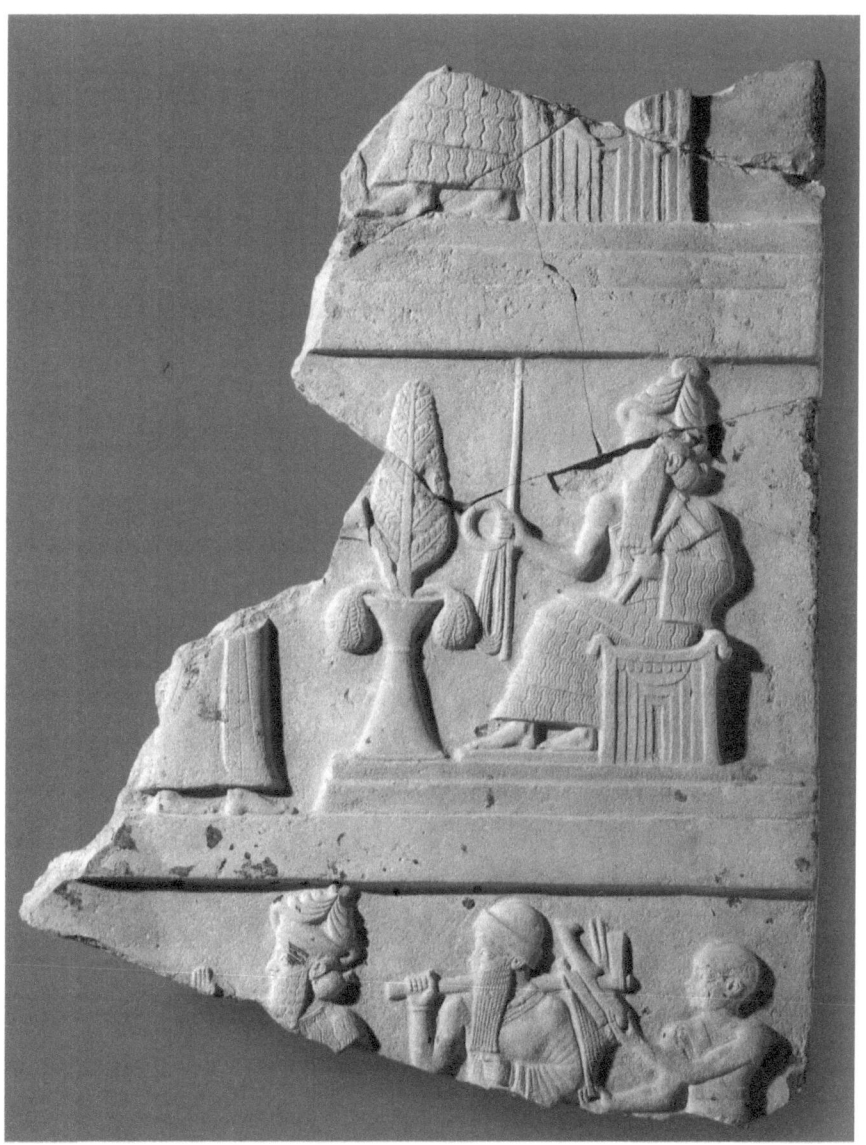

42 Stele of Ur-Namma, fragment. After Aruz 2003: 444 fig. 317.

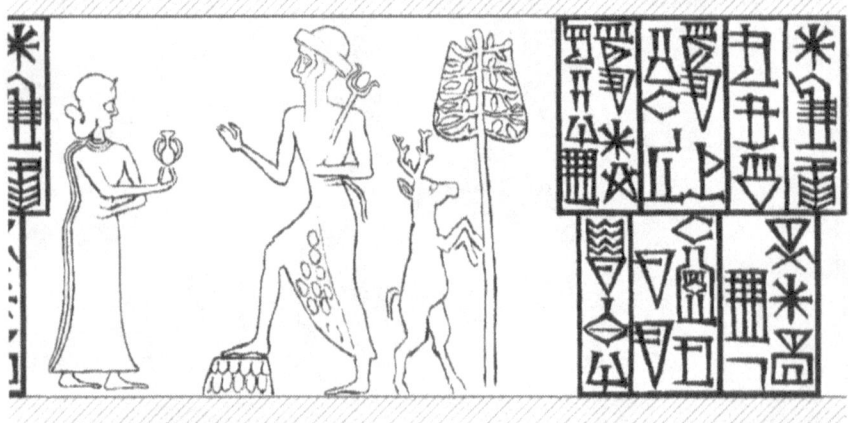

43 Seal of Geme-Ninlila, Šulgi's daughter, presented to her by Šulgi. After Suter 2010: 342 fig. 20.

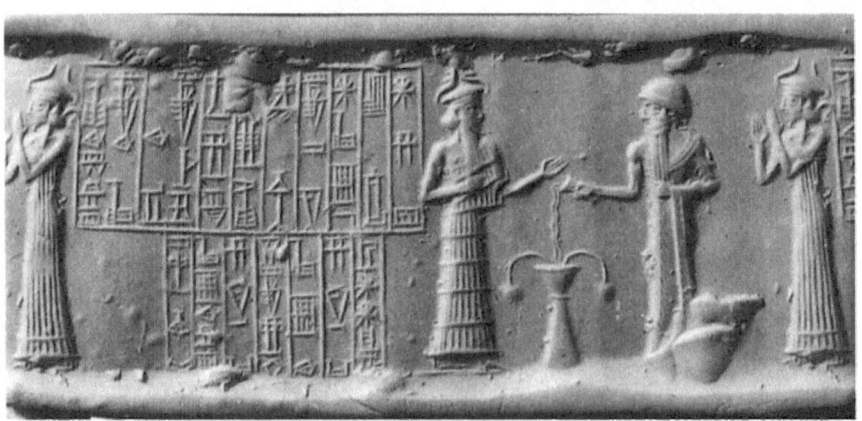

44 Seal of Ur-Nanibgal, governor of Nippur, dedicated to god Nuska for the life of Šulgi. After BDTNS no. 171488.

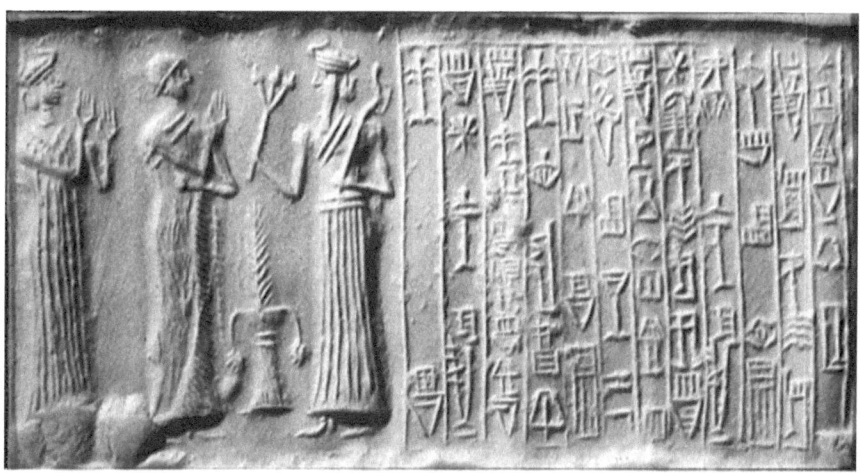

45 Seal of Kilula, a chair carrier, dedicated to Meslamtaea for the life of Šulgi. After Collon 1987: 133 fig. 567.

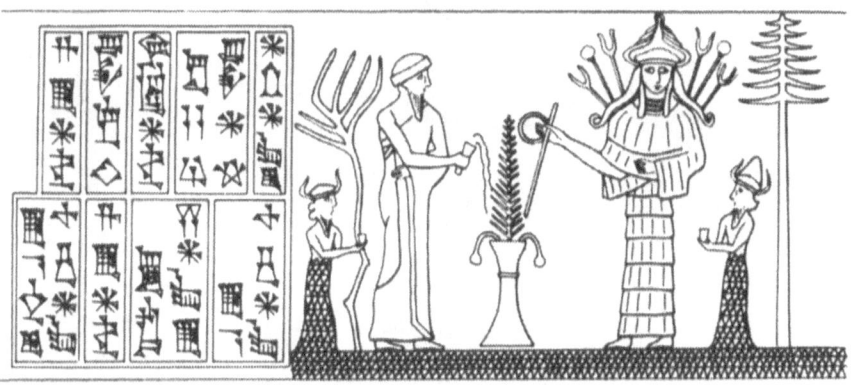

46 Seal of Lugal-engardug dedicated to Amar-Suen. After Zettler 1987: 60 fig. 1.

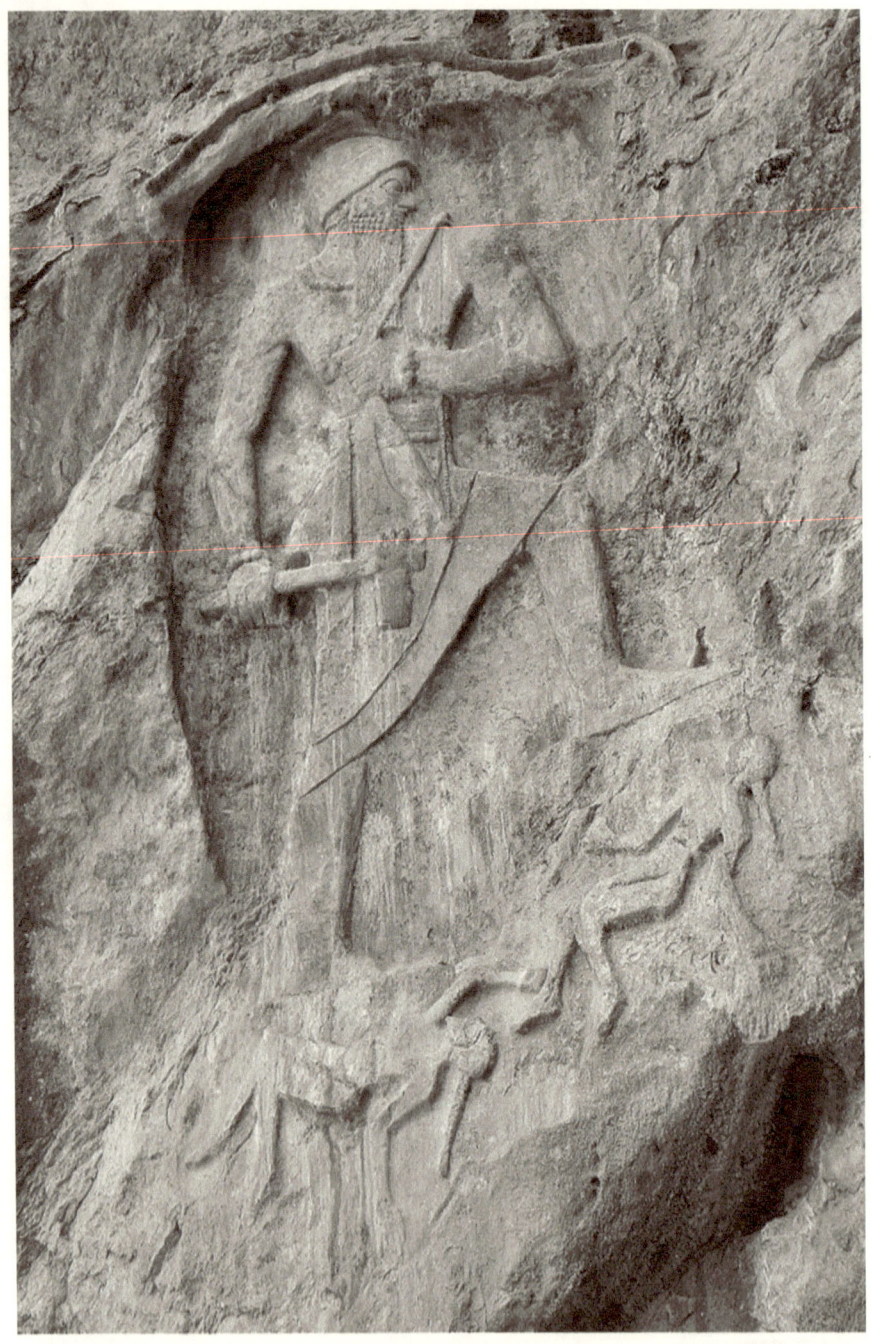

47 Rock relief of Šulgi(?) at Darband-i Gawr. After Osama S. M. Amin, "Finding the hidden Naram-Sin rock relief in Iraq," [etc.ancient.eu/travel/naram-sin-relief.iraq].

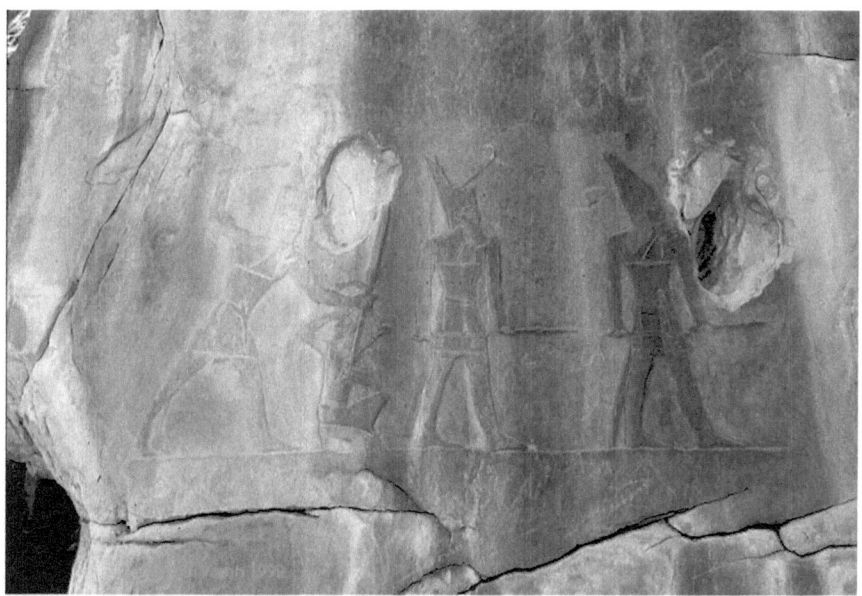

48 Rock relief of Sekhmkhet at Wadi Maghareh, Sinai. After [chromyellow.blogspot.com], 2010, a photograph taken by Uzi Varon in 1999.

www.ingramcontent.com/pod-product-compliance
Lightning Source LLC
Chambersburg PA
CBHW021403170526
45164CB00002B/488